THE SINNER *and* THE SAINT

ALSO BY KEVIN BIRMINGHAM

The Most Dangerous Book:
The Battle for James Joyce's Ulysses

THE SINNER

and

THE SAINT

Dostoevsky and the Gentleman Murderer
Who Inspired a Masterpiece

———— • ————

Kevin Birmingham

PENGUIN PRESS
NEW YORK
2021

PENGUIN PRESS
An imprint of Penguin Random House LLC
penguinrandomhouse.com

Page 399 constitutes an extension of this copyright page.

LIBRARY OF CONGRESS CATALOGING-IN-PUBLICATION DATA
Names: Birmingham, Kevin, author.
Title: The Sinner and the Saint : Dostoevsky and the
Gentleman Murderer Who Inspired a Masterpiece /
Kevin Birmingham.
Description: New York : Penguin Press, 2021. | Includes
bibliographical references and index.
Identifiers: LCCN 2021015314 (print) | LCCN 2021015315
(ebook) | ISBN 9781594206306 (hardcover) |
ISBN 9780698182882 (ebook)
Subjects: LCSH: Dostoyevsky, Fyodor, 1821–1881. Prestuplenie
i nakazanie. | Dostoyevsky, Fyodor, 1821–1881—Sources. |
LCGFT: Literary criticism.
Classification: LCC PG3325.P73 B53 2021 (print) |
LCC PG3325.P73 (ebook) | DDC 891.73/3—dc23
LC record available at https://lccn.loc.gov/2021015314
LC ebook record available at https://lccn.loc.gov/2021015315

Printed in the United States of America
1   3   5   7   9   10   8   6   4   2

Designed by Amanda Dewey

For Julia and the future

CONTENTS

———•·•———

THE SINNER *and* THE SAINT

A Bloody Enigma

—————•·•—————

There's an evil spirit here." The voice broke through every now and then, among various notes and ideas for the story. A young man, looking back upon his crimes, concludes that an evil spirit compels him. "How otherwise could I have overcome all those difficulties?"

Fyodor Mikhailovich Dostoevsky was writing in a hardcover notebook. His candle had burned down to a nub, and the hotel staff refused to give him another one until there was nothing left. They had been instructed to ignore him, to stop cleaning his clothes, to stop serving him dinner. Dostoevsky would wander around Wiesbaden in the early evening, pretending to have someplace to eat, and return at night to fill his notebook pages with bits of dialogue and plot overviews and reminders. "Very Important." *"Don't forget."*

There were fully imagined passages and pages of budding ideas. He underlined key words and phrases. He squeezed additions in the margins or between lines. He crossed out entire paragraphs that seemed blunt or excessive. He drew sketches on the pages, as if he couldn't put his pen down even when he wasn't writing. Drawings of churches and foliage. The faces of his characters appear, shouting and smiling and blending into crosshatched shadows with lines of text edging around them. Sometimes the murderer's voice would burst out. "Is it really going to continue eternally, eternally!" the voice shouts. "Oh, how I hate them all! How I would like to take them all and slaughter them all to the last one." He crossed it out.

Dostoevsky was determined to tell a murder story from the murderer's perspective, and his character couldn't be a monster. He would have flashes of anger, and he would be bitter and proud, but he would be sensitive, compassionate, and bookish. He would want to put ideas into action. He would believe that one bold, extraordinary act could change everything. He would not fantasize about slaughtering people. No. The murderer would be chilling because he wants so desperately to be good. "When I become noble," the murderer says, "the benefactor of all, a citizen, I will repent."

Readers would have to be disturbed but not repulsed so that they could get close to a murderer's mind—closer than they had ever been before—and yet continue reading. There is an evil spirit here, it's true, but a spirit that settles into something insidious and mundane, a slithering way of thinking. "It turns out that I acted logically," Dostoevsky had the murderer conclude. But that wasn't quite right either, and the strange alchemy of reason and bitterness, idealism and darkness—the quixotic and the wicked—became more difficult to handle as time went on.

It was September 1865. For more than a month, Dostoevsky had been staying at the Hotel Victoria in Wiesbaden, Germany, where he had lost all his money at the roulette tables. He wrote to Ivan Turgenev, thinking that a fellow novelist, a fellow gambler, would send money. "I am disgusted and ashamed to trouble you. But except for you I have absolutely no one at the present moment to whom I could turn." He was suffering from a fever that left him shivering at night, and the hotel's proprietor—surely familiar with cases like this—had begun threatening to summon the police. Dostoevsky was trapped in a hotel beside Wiesbaden's railway station, broke, ill, and humiliated. His murder story was his only way out.

Dostoevsky's career until 1865 could not have been more turbulent. In just four years, he had gone from being a literary sensation to a convict in chains exiled to Siberia. He was only twenty-three years old when he was celebrated throughout St. Petersburg as Russia's next great writer while his first work of fiction, a novella called *Poor Folk*, had not even been published yet—it was circulating as a manuscript. A swift downfall followed: rushed stories, negative reviews, rejection from the very people who had lionized him. His involvement in political circles led to his arrest and exile in 1849. He spent four years in a hard-labor prison camp and five years in a Siberian army battalion, and he would remain under surveillance until shortly before his death.

He knew better than anyone the high stakes of being a writer in tsarist Russia. Writers were suspect. All reading material, including newspapers, required prepublication approval from censors. Books were frequently banned, and private presses were forbidden. The path Dostoevsky had chosen was particularly treacherous at mid-century, when Russia found itself caught between the liberalism sweeping Europe and the empire's entrenched authoritarian rule. By the 1860s, disputes about the empire's direction were acrimonious. Russia, Dostoevsky declared in 1861, was becoming a nation divided into "two hostile camps."

Dostoevsky returned to Petersburg in 1859, after a decade in exile, and published his account of Siberian prison life, *Notes from a Dead House*, to great acclaim. He felt resurrected. He used his newfound clout to be his own editor in his own magazine. In less than five years, he and his brother Mikhail founded two journals and watched each of them collapse. One was crushed by debt, the other by order of the tsar.

Now, alone in his hotel room, he was forty-three years old. His wife and his beloved Mikhail had both died the previous year, three months apart. He was fifteen thousand rubles—several years' income—in debt, none of his great novels had yet been written, and he was suffering from powerful epileptic seizures. Each one left him depressed and lost in a mental fog for days or weeks. It was increasingly difficult to write.

"Why has my life ended?" the murderer finally asks himself. The question, Dostoevsky wrote in his notebook, is crucial.

Dostoevsky came to Wiesbaden thinking he could win enough money at roulette to pay off his debts and resume his literary career. It had been four years since his previous novel (*The Insulted and Injured*), and more than a decade since he needed someone else's magazine to serialize his fiction. He had frayed so many ties that he was forced to send the proposal for his new story to Mikhail Katkov, the editor of *The Russian Herald*, a man whom Dostoevsky had accused, in print, of being a mediocre businessman vulgarizing Russian literature. He pitched his story as "the psychological account of a crime." A young man succumbs to "strange, 'unfinished' ideas floating in the air" and decides to murder an old pawnbroker, take her money, and make up for his crime with altruistic acts. He was writing it "with ardor," he told Katkov. It would be around ninety pages long, and he could finish it in two weeks.

He asked for an advance and a quick decision. "In my straitened situation, every moment is valuable."

Given the circumstances, Dostoevsky was surprisingly optimistic. "The story that I'm working on now," he wrote to a friend, "may be the best thing I've written." Somehow he knew. What he could not have known, stuck in his hotel, feverish and hungry, was that he was entering the greatest phase of his career. Dostoevsky would write three crucial novels over the next seven years, including *The Idiot* and *Demons*. Then he would embark upon his magnum opus, *The Brothers Karamazov*. Two decades of hardship, contemplation, and experimentation brought the novelist to a spectacular period of creativity in which he wrote four of the greatest novels in Russian literature—in all literature. Together they depict consciousness as the atmosphere surrounding the world of objects and events rather than an interiority embedded within it, and they would become both a resource and a technology for generations of novelists laboring in his reconfigured universe. It began with *Crime and Punishment*, this story of a young man who succumbs to strange, floating ideas and decides to kill a pawnbroker. The murderer didn't have a name yet, but it was coming—Raskolnikov.

Decades later, it seemed clear that Dostoevsky started a revolution in "the *artistic thinking* of humankind"—that's how the literary critic Mikhail Bakhtin put it. He argued that Dostoevsky's novels provide "a new artistic model of the world." His novels are gatherings of autonomous voices interacting with one another beyond the control of an overriding authorial voice. His great subject was self-consciousness, and each consciousness in his novels inhabits its own world. Bakhtin called this innovation the *polyphonic* novel, a form that transcends the simplicity of centuries of monologic art. Humanity, Bakhtin argued, was still incapable of navigating Dostoevsky's complex terrain.

Even this grand assessment may not capture the fullness of *Crime and Punishment*, because Dostoevsky's murder story bridges the complexity of consciousness with a stenographic record of empirical facts in the external world. We can see that precarious connection between unfinished consciousness and established facts in the novel's central plot: a narrative where notions and theories, dreams and hallucinations seep into a criminal investigation, a quest for material evidence of a crime. The joining of the two worlds characterizes the novel's locale as well, St. Petersburg, the way fog and dust sweep over the cobblestones of the planned city and the way rows of orderly neoclassical buildings contain interiors divided up into warrens of disorienting spaces, dark corridors, windows facing walls, rooms within rooms, doors leading to doors. And the nexus of unfinished consciousness and finished material is evident in the novel's central event: a young man's vague ideas about goodness lead the reader into the middle of a room where blood is pooling around the dead bodies of two women—two autonomous voices turned into appalling empirical facts.

Crime and Punishment is a novel about the trouble with ideas. It is not a novel *of* ideas. It does not showcase or allegorize philosophical positions for readers to consider. It is not primarily the drama of a young man wrestling with ideologies. Nor is it the story of redemption from misguided thoughts and actions—the notion that Raskolnikov repents and finds God is one of the things that nearly everyone gets wrong about *Crime and Punishment*. The trouble with ideas is the way they interact with everything else that's human about us, things that have nothing to do with reason or evidence or theory. Dostoevsky's novel is about how ideas inspire and deceive, how they coil themselves around sadness and feed on bitter fruit. It is about how easily ideas spread and mutate, how they vanish, only to reappear in unlikely places, how they serve many masters, how they can be hammered into new shapes or harden into stone, how they are aroused by love and washed by great rains and flowing rivers. It is about how ideas change us and how they make us more of who we already are. It is about how ideas can do many of these things at once, or different things to different people, or the same thing to everyone around you.

Near the end of *Crime and Punishment*, Raskolnikov has a fever dream that he considers prophetic: a plague "from the depths of Asia" would one day sweep over the entire planet. The first symptoms of infection with the "microscopic creatures" are a form of madness: "Never, never had people considered themselves so intelligent and unshakeable in the truth as did these infected ones. Never had they thought their judgments, their scientific conclusions, their moral convictions and beliefs more unshakeable." The plague spreads throughout cities and countries, causing anxiety, weeping, the beating of breasts. No one can agree on what is good or evil. No one understands anyone else—"each man thought that he and he alone possessed the truth." Violence breaks out. Meaningless, spiteful murders. Armies arrayed against foreign enemies start destroying themselves on their way to battle: "The ranks would break up, the soldiers would fall upon one another, stabbing and cutting, biting and eating one another." Every collective venture disintegrates. Trades and agriculture cease. The economy halts. Alarms ring out constantly in the cities, summoning people nowhere, to nothing. Raskolnikov sees the world ravaged by fire and famine and disease, and he can't stop thinking about it. But the plague of dead certainties—the ideas "floating in the air"—were not from Asia. They were from Europe.

When people invoke nightmares of morbid individualism destroying civilization, they are usually defending broad cultural resources—a tradition, perhaps, or a regime, a language, a religion. But Raskolnikov fears for the most elemental human capacities: the ability to work together, to establish shared values, to agree upon basic facts—the things we need just to inhabit the same world and to take care of one another. All of that is vulnerable to an infectious idea. The infection goes so deep, in fact, that even the plague's end still carries the germ of individualism. "Only a few people in the whole world could be saved," Raskolnikov dreams, "they were pure and chosen," people destined "to renew and purify the earth." Raskolnikov wants to explore the limits of ideas, but their boundaries are often further off in the distance than we will ever see. To protest, to be altruistic, to seek change is to pursue an idea to an unknown continent. It may also return you to your point of origin irrevocably changed, perhaps ruined, perhaps renewed.

When Dostoevsky's novel was taking shape in Wiesbaden, he began thinking about how he could begin the story much earlier, before the crime takes place instead of months or years later, as he had originally planned. He kept circling closer, until Raskolnikov's crimes were no longer an awful memory or an offstage event but something the reader experiences directly, a brutal act unfolding in an excruciatingly detailed scene. We watch Raskolnikov hide the ax inside his coat. We follow him up the dark stairwell. We see the old woman's arm clutching the door handle as he jerks her door open. Dostoevsky wanted the reader to see her hair, her skinny legs, her yellow wallpaper. He wanted the reader to experience Raskolnikov's second thoughts, his mistakes and confusion, the way his plan tips sideways, how one victim becomes two, the frustration of bloodstains, and the sudden pounding on the door while he is still inside with the warm corpses.

Dostoevsky must have told himself that there is virtue in imagining something so awful so vividly, like standing on the edge of a cliff and picturing what it would be like to leap into the abyss. The French call the compulsion *l'appel du vide*—the call of the void. It's the desire to experience the awful magnitude of such a small step, to glimpse another world of consequences just for a moment, perhaps to ensure that you will never actually do it.

Dostoevsky had long thought about what it would be like to take that step into the void. The first stirrings of the evil spirit in *Crime and Punishment* happened years before his feverish nights, trapped in his hotel. It began with an irresistible curiosity. He sought out the stories of fellow convicts in Siberia and listened to the way they killed people. Fictional murders, from that point on, seemed cartoonish. He hunted for accounts of murders in newspapers. Russian periodicals often covered homicides in Europe, partly because reporting on domestic crime was difficult and partly because such stories were easy to find in the European press—especially in France, where broadsheets featuring violent crime circulated by the hundreds of thousands, usually untouched by government censors. Macabre stories soon spread to other formats, including daily newspapers, monthly serials, and volumes of collected stories. Dostoevsky got hold of one such collection around the beginning of 1861, when he and his brother were looking for material for their first magazine. He began reading Armand Fouquier's *Causes célèbres de tous les peuples*, which chronicles the stories and trials of dozens of infamous criminals. That's how Dostoevsky first learned about the 1835 trial of the infamous poet-murderer Pierre-François Lacenaire, an extraordinary and horrifying incarnation of evil.

Lacenaire was slender, almost delicate. He was born into a wealthy merchant family that lost its entire fortune just as he was coming of age, and the catastrophe untethered him. He deserted from the army twice, traveled to Italy and Switzerland, and settled eight disputes with dueling pistols, or so he claimed. He claimed to be thirty-three when the double murder happened, but official records indicate he was only thirty. What was clear was that Lacenaire quoted Horace and Sophocles, that he wrote poetry and songs, and that straitened circumstances did not diminish his sense of style. He wore a blue frock coat with a velvet collar and maintained a carefully trimmed mustache. He did not think of himself as handsome so much as a man with "remarkable features": gray eyes, high forehead, cleft chin, strong nose. Prison registers noted a scar on his right forehead. His hair was fine, though already starting to gray, which he attributed to incessant study and reflection. Lacenaire had vast plans. He felt possessed by a fever, a "fixed idea to *resist*," as he described it, and a compulsion to commit swift, powerful acts.

Lacenaire's plans involved killing a man named Jean-François Chardon, whom he knew from prison. Everyone called him "Aunt Madeleine"—"aunt" was a common term for men like him, men of "infamous habits," men who consorted with other men. Chardon had been convicted of theft and indecent assault and had recently been getting into blackmail and scams. He wore religious garments, posed as "a brother of the Charity of St. Camille," and pocketed the donations. Lacenaire heard that there was a large amount of money hidden in his apartment. Gold coins, silverware, and ten thousand francs in cash. Chardon lived with his mother, a sixty-six-year-old widow, so both of them would have to be killed. "Who were Chardon and his mother?" Lacenaire asked. They were nothing, useless. He would use a three-edged file—good for sharpening saws, for getting between the teeth. Lacenaire bought one, sharpened it, and fitted it with cork on one end for a better grip.

He recruited a partner named Victor Avril, another former prison mate. In the early afternoon of December 14, 1834, the two ex-convicts turned down a dark alleyway, the passage du Cheval Rouge, and walked up a muddy stairwell. The handrail was a greasy rope. Lacenaire pounded on the door, but there was no answer. When they walked back out into the alley, they saw Chardon standing there in some state of undress and holding a brush.

"We just came from your place."

"In that case, come on up with me," Chardon told his visitors.

Some words were exchanged when they entered the two-room apartment, and suddenly Avril began strangling him with his bare hands. Lacenaire pulled out his file and stabbed him repeatedly from behind, then from the front. Chardon collapsed and kicked open a cabinet filled with dishes. It is so difficult to choke someone to death—Chardon was still moving when Avril grabbed an ax hanging on the door. He swung for his skull and finished him off.

Lacenaire rushed into the bedroom and found the widow sick in bed. He stabbed her face, her eyes repeatedly. He struck her so forcefully that the opposite end of his sharpened file split through the cork and sliced his finger. He piled pillows and sheets on top of her and then went for the large armoire where the money was. He heard a nearby clock strike one as he forced the lock open, and the only things inside were some silverware and five hundred francs. There was supposed to be ten thousand.

Lacenaire started grabbing clothes—a large brown coat with a black fur collar for himself and a black silk hat for Avril. They wrapped the silverware and some more clothing in a pink vest they found. On their way out, they spotted an ivory statuette of the Virgin Mary, which also seemed worth taking. Just as they were leaving, two men appeared on the landing to see Chardon. Lacenaire tried to pull the door closed, but it was stuck on the mat. Chardon's body was visible through the doorway as he calmly informed the visitors that Chardon was unfortunately not at home.

As soon as they left, Lacenaire and Avril went to the Turkish baths a few streets away on rue du Temple, where couples could stroll in a verdant garden and where the two murderers could wash the blood off their hands and scrub the stains from their clothes and shoes. They were sporting their newly acquired apparel when they proceeded, later that night, to a basement café frequented by criminals. Lacenaire waited while Avril sold the loot. He got two hundred francs for the silverware and twenty for the coat. The merchant offered only three francs for the Virgin, so they threw it into the Seine. Then they ate dinner and went to the Théâtre des Variétés to watch a comedy show. Afterward, at around 11:00 p.m., Avril went to a brothel, and Lacenaire went home. "That was a great day for me," he said later, thinking back. "I breathed again."

The press tended to treat criminals as a biologically inferior class degraded by ignorance and poverty. But Lacenaire was different. He was handsome, stylish, and polite. He intended to study law. He wrote poetry and published an article about the criminal justice system that even Alexis de

Tocqueville cited. The collapse of his family's fortunes ended Lacenaire's studies prematurely, and he turned to forgery and petty theft. The Chardon murders were intended to net enough money to bankroll a bigger, more profitable scheme: to rob banks by luring collecting clerks into dark apartments, rented and furnished for the purpose. He would stab them and take the money and banknotes in their satchels.

The public's fascination with Lacenaire began with his trial. Press accounts noted his cheerful demeanor whenever he entered the courtroom. He described the murders with calm precision, and at one point he stood up to pantomime his stabbing technique for the jury. But more often he seemed indifferent to the proceedings. During the ninety-minute reading of the thirty indictments, he rested his head on his hand or on the bar of the dock. Reporters always remarked upon his appearance—his beautiful features, his tufted sideburns, the way his blue frock coat flattered his slender figure, the way the arteries in his neck beat visibly. The "Don Juan of Murder" was one press epithet. The "Swan of the Scaffold" was another.

Women filled the benches after obtaining many of the tickets reserved for the public. "Beautiful ladies!" one periodical exclaimed in alarm. They listened to hours of gruesome testimony while wearing silk dresses and pink hats, "shamelessly imperturbable." Their captivation was an ominous sign. Surely a nation is in peril, a writer for *La France* argued, when "women, whom the law of Christianity has elevated to the role of pure and consoling angels, prostitute themselves with such passion to applaud the dramas of cynicism and blood."

The publication of Lacenaire's memoirs, written in the weeks before his beheading, made him even more appealing to some. "I come to preach the religion of fear to the rich," he wrote, "for the religion of love has no power over their hearts." He insisted his crimes were an attack upon the foundations of an unjust society, a campaign of vengeance against the wealthy on behalf of the downtrodden citizens of France.

Crowds lined the procession route through Paris one Saturday morning when a rumor spread that Lacenaire was about to be executed. A week later, he was guillotined in front of several hundred people. A wax likeness of his head drew crowds when it was displayed in the Museum of the Academy of Medicine—the murderer's own hair and whiskers were attached. People

wanted to get as close as possible, to probe the wound, and Dostoevsky was
no exception.

Lacenaire's celebrity suggested that the vainglorious murderer was an
eruption of something deep within bourgeois society rather than some extrinsic
menace. Dostoevsky considered the story important enough that he helped
translate Fouquier's account into Russian and devoted fifty pages to it in the
second issue of his magazine *Vremya* in February 1861. Fouquier noted Lacenaire's "incomplete and superficial" education and emphasized that something
about his nature was "essentially incomplete." This, according to Fouquier, is
why things went wrong. A toxic mixture of "ferocious materialism," bitterness,
and base cravings induced a feverish delirium that led this man to murder. And
yet the most disturbing fact was that instead of recoiling at his depravity, many
Parisians were somehow enchanted. *L'affaire Lacenaire* swept Paris decades
earlier, but it remained, Fouquier wrote, "a bloody enigma."

Dostoevsky intended to solve it. He wrote in *Vremya* that Lacenaire "is a
remarkable personality, enigmatic, frightening, and gripping." Though decades in the grave, he merited the present tense. There was something perpetually disturbing about the way his vanity fused with certain base instincts,
though Dostoevsky would not elaborate. Stories like this, he told his subscribers, are "more exciting than all possible novels because they light up the dark
sides of the human soul that art does not like to approach." But why not approach it?

The following spring, in 1862, Dostoevsky was devouring Victor Hugo's
Les Misérables. The novel had just been published, and he was reading two
volumes a week. He had always loved Hugo, and *Les Misérables* would become
one of his favorite novels. It was during Dostoevsky's reading of the third
volume that Lacenaire burst forth like a shade from hell. A chapter depicts
society as an ever-changing surface resting upon a network of subterranean
mines—a "venous system of progress." An economic mine, a religious mine,
a philosophical mine, and so on. Civilization depends upon all of them, the
narrator says. Each one is filled with centuries of laborers—Rousseau, Diog-
enes, Calvin—perpetually toiling beneath the surface, altering the civilization above. But beneath the deepest mines lies a dark chasm counteracting
that progress. It is a pit where monsters reside, where creatures harbor a

"terrifying blankness," and where "the eyeless self howls, hunts, gropes, and gnaws." Whatever is left of humanity here is slowly transforming into Satan. "From this cavern," the narrator announces, "comes Lacenaire."

By the time the poet-murderer emerged briefly in *Les Misérables*, he had been lurking around French literature for years. Lacenaire's memoirs had imprinted his image indelibly into the culture. He inspired characters in novels by Stendhal and Balzac. Baudelaire admired him. Flaubert marveled at his "strange, deep, bitter philosophy," the way he dragged morality through the mud. "I love to see men like that, like Nero, like the Marquis de Sade."

How had society produced such a person? Some blamed simple greed. "Poverty is hell; wealth is paradise," Lacenaire declared in prison. But money was never a sufficient explanation. He did not have to kill in order to steal, after all, and killing was always part of his plan. Nor did greed explain Lacenaire's joy, his willingness to do it all over again. "Killing without remorse is the greatest happiness," he said.

The problem was larger than greed. A writer for *La France* argued that Lacenaire's violent crimes were less harmful than "the doctrines and instructions he has left to people of his kind," and they were everywhere. "How many unpunished Lacenaires are now occupying, let's say frankly, the top ranks of today's society?" His doctrines were pervasive. Several newspapers described Lacenaire's poetry as a versified defense of "egoism and materialism," twin philosophies that liken people to machines programmed only to seek gratification. A lead article in *Le Temps* claimed that to observe Lacenaire at trial was to see a man putting "systemic egoism" into practice, which would compel people to abandon principles for passing tastes, to weaken laws with whimsical interpretation, and to clamor for individual rights at the expense of community. An article in *La France* was more direct: Lacenaire's godless materialism signaled the ascendancy of a new "revolutionary philosophy."

The term "revolutionary" was not used loosely in 1830s France. The French Revolution did not end in the 1790s. Instead, it set in motion decades of upheavals that spread across Europe. Europeans were living in an age of revolutions. The unrest spread easily because the French Revolution was about more than regime change. It was about changing ideas—ideas about what it means to be a nation, what it means to have rights, to be free, to be sovereign. Ideas about democracy, republics, and constitutions that had been disputed by eighteenth-century philosophers suddenly became pressing issues in the streets. King Louis-Philippe came to power in his own three-day revolution in 1830, but the July Monarchy, as it was called, switched out one royal house for another and established a reign of political stasis, bourgeois economic appeasement, and, at best, incremental change. It had no place for revolutionaries.

There was good reason to think of Lacenaire as a political threat. He composed republican songs and aspired to write for a republican journal, *Le Bon Sens*, that openly opposed the king. But one of the most chilling details was that while Lacenaire waited to murder one of his victims, he was calmly reading Rousseau's *Social Contract*. "Man is born free; and everywhere he is in chains." The opening sentence alone would have drawn him in. Many French readers thought of Rousseau as the Jacobins' philosopher, the favorite of Robespierre, who hailed him as "divine." Rousseau's rejection of absolute monarchy, his secularism, his conviction that the people are sovereign, and his arguments for a government that serves the general will seemed partly responsible for the Reign of Terror, when the revolution devolved into an emergency government that arrested people en masse and guillotined seventeen thousand people in order to start French history all over again, to reset the calendar to Year One.

Rousseau was no firebrand. He believed that individuals are free only when they submit to a community's welfare, and that the general will expresses what's best for the whole, not the sum of selfish interests. But by the 1830s, all this was obscured by overzealous readers and isolated passages from the book that Lacenaire could not stop reading. "The State, set on fire by civil wars, is born again, so to speak, from its ashes, and takes on anew, fresh from the jaws of death, the vigour of youth."

Newspapers seized upon Lacenaire's interest in *The Social Contract* when it was revealed during his trial. It was "the symbol of his life," one declared. The underlying fear of the age of revolutions was that it might encourage righteous violence and principled murder. If one can rightfully take up arms against an unjust government, then surely one could take up arms against an unjust society. If one could kill a king for one's country, then why not kill a banker? Lacenaire's crime spree was captivating because it seemed to be the revolution's next rational step.

The Don Juan of Murder collapsed the distinctions between political and nonpolitical violence. He fused the evil of the murderer with the romance of the assassin. "The social structure must be attacked," Lacenaire wrote, not from the top—not by attacking the king—but at its foundations, "its morals." His principles, he insisted, will "cultivate the seeds of discontent" already sown throughout France. His principles "will arm those who suffer against the fortunate of this century who indulge." And the sight of his beheading would activate those principles among a select few people in the crowd. He was adamant. Once, when a skeptical visitor was ushered out of his prison cell by the guard, Lacenaire rushed to the cell door and shouted, "Ah, sir! you believe that Lacenaire's death will not make apostles! . . . You will see! you will see!"

People sometimes think of Dostoevsky as writing novels from the top down, beginning with an ideology he wished to explore and then looking for ways to dramatize it. But he almost always worked from the bottom up, starting with intriguing personalities, a voice, a handful of clear details, memorable scenes or circumstances. The story of Lacenaire—that "enigmatic, frightening, and gripping" personality, that voice and image—was impossible for Dostoevsky to forget, and his Frenchness was particularly useful. France epitomized the age of revolutions, the confidence and rationalism of the Enlightenment, and much of what emerged from it—materialism, industrialization, bourgeois comfort and self-regard. If this was the type of criminal such a society produced, what would happen if Russia followed?

Crime and Punishment was a sensation from its first installment in the January 1866 issue of *The Russian Herald*, and it captivated a country in crisis. Europe's age of revolutions arrived belatedly in Russia in the 1860s. An era of reforms (the abolition of serfdom and the liberalization of the economy, the justice system, and education) met a wave of radicalism that crashed on April 4, 1866, when a man walked up to Tsar Alexander II with a loaded pistol and tried to assassinate him. Russia's liberal trajectory suddenly reversed as the ensuing surge of nationalism renewed suspicion of all foreign influence, including westernizing reforms, and the tsar began reasserting authoritarian control.

Russia's 1860s crisis was about its future, and so it was ultimately about ideas—which ideas to dismiss or overthrow and which to keep or revive. The nation was divided between those who wanted Russia to be more western oriented and those who wanted its future to be a stronger version of its past. Everyone insisted that they alone possessed the truth.

Mid-century philosophies widened Russia's divisions. The "egoism" that 1830s Parisians saw in Lacenaire referred to the single-minded pursuit of self-ish needs. By the 1860s, egoism had become an extreme version of enlighten-ment individualism. It was a radical skepticism in which one's self is the only thing that undeniably exists and therefore the only thing that undeniably mat-ters. A philosopher named Max Stirner, well known to Dostoevsky, took up the banner of egoism in the 1840s, and his message was clear: whatever you are and whatever you want is good. "We are perfect altogether," Stirner wrote, "and on the whole earth there is not one man who is a sinner!" Everything impinging upon the self—morals and laws, gods and states—was a pernicious fantasy that must be destroyed. Stirner weaponized egoism. Violence, revolu-tion, and crime became virtues. Crime, in fact, was *better* than revolution. "A revolution never returns," Stirner wrote, "but a mighty, reckless, shameless, conscienceless, proud *crime*—does it not rumble in distant thunders?" Read-ing Stirner was like reading an evangelist spreading the good word of Lace-naire's life years after his execution.

And his crimes did rumble in distant thunders. By the twentieth century, Lacenaire came to represent the radical artist undermining bourgeois society. André Breton thought of him as a surrealist. Albert Camus called him "the first of the gentleman criminals." Michel Foucault claimed he was a Jacobin born too late and that he had a permanent place in "the paradise of the aes-thetes of crime."

In the hands of revolutionaries, skepticism and aesthetics can become great tools of destruction and recreation. The Russian radicals of the 1860s were just beginning to use skepticism to clear away large swaths of received wisdom, traditions, and beliefs. An enlightened individual need not simply *believe* in anything. But something was changing. That skepticism was beginning to tilt slightly, as if someone had placed a small weight on the far scale. "*Believe* in nothing" became "Believe in *nothing*." This became known in Russia—and then beyond—as nihilism. Nihilists want to sever all ties, Dostoevsky wrote to Katkov in 1866, to "immediately construct paradise on a tabula rasa." A blank slate. Nothing. All modern revolutions, Dostoevsky believed, wanted, at their core, to reset the calendar to Year One.

It seemed as radical as one could get. But what if there were one further step? Something else to wipe away? *Crime and Punishment* is disturbing—particularly for a nation in crisis—because it is a book that travels the dark road between violence and uncertainty. Many novels are violent, of course, and all novels rely upon uncertainty, but in Dostoevsky's novel the violence and uncertainty were more disturbing and elemental than readers had normally encountered. The murder scene's gruesome detail is intrusive—the most certain of things. But then the story shifts to a criminal investigation conducted by an investigator who seems strangely dismissive of the cornerstone of his entire enterprise. "Evidence, my dear, is mostly double-edged," he tells Raskolnikov. Every clue cuts in opposite directions and leads to contradictory conclusions. His skepticism doesn't subtract. It multiplies. Double-edged evidence provides a key insight into Raskolnikov's case, into the swerves a life can take and the way a desire to be altruistic can lead to an ax and nothingness. And does the investigator even have any evidence? The uncertainty began with Dostoevsky's early drafts—his revisions to the murderer's voice, nature, and motives, to the plot and the narrative mode. It seeps into the final version of the novel and persists even in the story's ending, which gestures to a way out for Raskolnikov without ever making it there. The novel doesn't resolve. It halts.

Crime and Punishment is a murder mystery, though the mystery is not who killed the pawnbroker and her sister. The mystery is why. The answer seems easy at first, but as the story progresses it starts slipping away, almost imperceptibly, until it becomes clear that Raskolnikov is a mystery even to himself.

That is the further step. A downtrodden person is most apt to rely upon himself to determine the truth, to grab an ax, and to change the world when everything appears false, when constraints and values seem vaporous, when skepticism shrinks the knowable world down to oneself and the radius of one's own perceptions. Yet Dostoevsky's novel reminds us that no perception is too small to lose its double edge. Who we are is not a thing to rely upon. We investigate ourselves and find that we are irrational, contradictory, and opaque. We do not want what we want. We are our own doubles. We are divided within ourselves. Raskolnikov's name (*raskol* in Russian) means a schism, a split. Coming to terms with that split—that doubling and doubt—is a remedy to the plague of dead certainties not because it abolishes the truth but because it is the premise of its discovery.

S everal scholars have discussed Lacenaire's influence upon the creation of Raskolnikov, including Dostoevsky's biographers Joseph Frank and Leonid Grossman. Grossman noted that Dostoevsky's image of a murderer had been developing since his time in Siberia, but it acquired new dimensions after the novelist studied Lacenaire. The character forming in his mind became more than just a fearless and amoral Siberian convict. He was now bourgeois, elite, mysterious—a "romantic titan," according to Grossman, though "exaggerated and monstrously distorted."

And yet he was much more than a monstrous distortion. To understand Dostoevsky is to inhabit a world of angels and demons, to take the soul and evil spirits as seriously as the mind and the ego. More than a century of Dostoevsky scholarship is devoted to these matters, but no book provides sustained attention to what Lacenaire meant to Dostoevsky, to how his years-long consideration of the French murderer shaped his understanding of both the nature of evil and the way it was evolving amid the century's new ideas and tribulations. Nor does any book capture how the lives of these two men—the poet-murderer and the convict-novelist—faintly resemble each other. Even a slight recognition was enough to keep the novelist circling back.

Dostoevsky was planning to write an article "about instincts and Lacenaire" in August 1864, a year before he began working on *Crime and Punishment*. He was apparently still thinking about the base instincts he mentioned in his commentary on Lacenaire's trial. Something about those instincts— perhaps more than Lacenaire's grievances and boundless vanity—now seemed central to the story and complicated enough to merit sustained discussion. Dostoevsky never wrote that article (his magazine didn't last long), so his thoughts about Lacenaire kept forming until they began to materialize in his Wiesbaden hotel room the following year.

Dostoevsky routinely borrowed ideas from real life, though he never simply transposed them onto his fiction. Raskolnikov is not Lacenaire in Russian clothes. Dostoevsky did not pluck Lacenaire out of 1830s Paris and set him down in 1860s St. Petersburg. Lacenaire was raw material for Dostoevsky's craftsmanship and genius. And so if we want to understand *Crime and Punishment* fully, then we must understand Lacenaire, a man who despised cruelty and unfairness throughout his life and who saw nothing but a cruel and unfair world, a man who, on the eve of his execution, remained wholeheartedly committed to "the doctrine of nothingness." Lacenaire showed the novelist how a man of certain instincts and circumstances could fashion himself into an ideological murderer in France so that Dostoevsky could imagine how a similar murderer could come to life in Russia. Clear differences between the French model and the Russian novel emerged: Raskolnikov's flashes of remorse, certain details of his philosophy, and the type of person he targets—not an ex-convict or a bank collector but a pawnbroker, a woman. The most important difference would be another woman, Sonya Marmeladova, who urges Raskolnikov to confess and rejoin society.

This book stages the drama of a great creative act decades in the making. It focuses on the most crucial elements of *Crime and Punishment* rather than surveying all of its narrative strands. The staging juxtaposes real lives with Dostoevsky's fictional characters, historical events with Raskolnikov's dramatic scenes, so that we can more clearly see how the novel came to be what it is and how Dostoevsky's fictional world called out to his turbulent times.

The story behind *Crime and Punishment* is instructive in ways that an argument about the novel could never be. It is crucial to imagine and experience what went into the novel's creation—the people, events, and travails that influenced it, the painstaking drafts and revisions that produced it—in order to grasp the finished work of art. This will not surprise anyone who knows Dostoevsky, for he believed that to comprehend something is to *feel* it, to have the idea enter one's flesh and blood, be it a plague or a life-giving force. In fact, the hope of conveying something more thorough than any analysis and more compelling than the most impassioned argument is why Dostoevsky chose his treacherous path in the first place. And when we follow the journey toward the completion of this monumental novel, we learn not just about the nature of Dostoevsky's creativity but about creativity in general—its slumbers and pains, its necessities, compulsions, and sudden fits.

Dostoevsky hammered at the idea of Lacenaire over and over again, reshaping, revising, altering his image. Raskolnikov commits suicide in some drafts. In others he redeems himself by heroically saving people from a great fire. Hélène Cixous, the feminist writer and scholar, marveled at this arduous process of creation. "What I love best are Dostoevsky's notebooks," she wrote, "the crazy and tumultuous forge, where Love and Hate embrace, rolling around on the ground in convulsions which thwart all calculation and all hope: no one knows who will be born of this possessed belly, who will win, who will survive."

This is the story of who survives. It is about the characters who finally emerge in Dostoevsky's novel, and the people who helped inspire them. The heat of Dostoevsky's forge came from his own tumultuous life, and the first of his great novels borrowed more from his experiences and thoughts than perhaps any of his novels before it. As Raskolnikov was taking shape, he was becoming a bit more like Dostoevsky. And so we cannot fully understand the meaning and the making of *Crime and Punishment* until we understand Dostoevsky's life, his own vanity and anxiety, his sense of guilt and evil, his ideas and ambitions, his great anger, and his great moral drive. We must see how Dostoevsky himself became a criminal, how he tried to enact his own revolutionary philosophy, how he was pursued by investigators, and how he stood on a platform waiting to die, as Lacenaire did, clutching at his life's final moments one winter morning. He, too, felt like the victim of misfortune. He was battered by a long Siberian exile, chronic illness, debt, the deaths of the people closest to him, and he still had no family of his own.

Yet he could not complete *Crime and Punishment* in time without help. A stenographer named Anna Grigorievna Snitkina would finish the novel with him, guiding him by listening, by being his first reader and his first critic. He needed her. They would work together on every novel he would ever write, and he would never be alone again.

The weight of all these years made Raskolnikov's story more urgent for Dostoevsky. Writing it was a way to survive and to return home to Russia, but it was also a path out of loneliness, a way to make sense of himself and what was happening in Russia. Writing *Crime and Punishment* made Dostoevsky the writer he always knew he could be.

PART I

———•·•———

I'll tell you of myself that I have been a child of the age, a child of disbelief and doubt up until now and will be even (I know this) to the grave. What horrible torments this thirst to believe has cost me and continues to cost me, a thirst that is all the stronger in my soul the more negative arguments there are in me.

—*Fyodor Dostoevsky*

One

The Dead Leaves

The boy's peculiarities bewildered the officers and the other engineering cadets. They noticed his awkwardness during drills and his refusal to join in on pranks. His gray eyes were deep set and penetrating. At night, the noisy cadets would scramble back to their quarters while a drummer would make his rounds and beat the cadence for lights-out, and Dostoevsky would be off somewhere else, bending over his notebook at a desk by a cold window embrasure in one of the castle's quieter corner chambers. The drum taps would echo off the imitation marble walls. The original statuary was gone. The carpets were gone. The old rosewood and mahogany floors had been pulled up and replaced with parquet after the imperial family fled.

The Engineers' Castle was originally intended to be a refuge. In 1797, Tsar Paul I, inspired by premonitions, ordered five thousand men to construct a safe residence for himself and his family, only to be strangled by his former Guards officers in his bedroom forty days after moving in. The walls were still wet. The tsar's suite was sealed up, the moats filled in, and the maps of secret vaults burned by the architect. The castle decayed for twenty years before it was renovated to house St. Petersburg's Academy of Engineers. What remained was an architectural jumble—Renaissance, Corinthian, Baroque—on jasper brick foundation stones. Ionic columns and arched windows, obelisks and niches, a dormant throne room, and ghost stories after lights-out. Sometimes, after pretending to go to sleep, Fyodor Mikhailovich would sneak back to the embrasure in his undergarments, a blanket over his shoulders, and write stories by a small, warm lamp.

Dostoevsky's mother had died of tuberculosis when he was fifteen. Her health deteriorated until she no longer had the strength to comb her hair. After she died, his father began drinking and carrying on full conversations with his wife's ghost—"my little dove," he called her. *Moy golubchik*. She had been affectionate. "The greatest pleasure in my life is when you're with me," she once wrote to her husband. She must've been the only one to call him an angel.

Fyodor had spent childhood summers with his mother in Darovoe, the family's small estate south of Moscow. He loved the wild berries, the birds and hedgehogs, and the smell of dead leaves. He spent so much time in one forest area that they called it "Fedya's Grove." Those summers with his mother were a refuge from his tempestuous father. Fyodor wrote her a letter when he was thirteen: "When you left, dear Mama, I started to miss you terribly, and when I think of you now, dear Mama, I am overcome by such sadness that it's impossible to drive it away, if you only knew how much I would like to see you and I can hardly wait for that joyous moment."

Dostoevsky arrived at the Engineers' Castle about a year after his mother's death. "I can't say anything good about my comrades," he wrote to his father. Three years later he wrote to Mikhail, his older brother, with his opinion unchanged. "I've grown very sad being all alone, my dear brother. There's no one to talk to." He despised the hierarchies and hazing rituals. The senior students poured buckets of water down the newbies' collars. They'd force mama's boys to shout obscenities and mock their embarrassment. They'd pour ink on someone's paper and force him to lick it up. They replicated the commanders' corporal punishment in after-hours punches, kicks, and whippings. If you went to the infirmary, you were told to say you fell from a ladder.

The academy's cruelty seemed exacerbated by careerism. Dostoevsky was irritated that boys of fourteen were plotting out their entire lives—scheming about how to ascend the ranks and make the most money. He, meanwhile, was indifferent to rank, squeamish about violence, outraged by bullying, pensive and sensitive and shy. He was the least soldierly cadet in the company. He executed drills awkwardly and disliked standing at attention. His shako—a tall, cylindrical military hat—did not impress. His dress coat with epaulets

and high collar was ill fitting. His rifle and knapsack, according to one company member, seemed to weigh him down like fetters. After all the drills,
lectures, and exams, he had hardly any time for himself, hardly any time to
read and write. "They're squeezing the life out of us," he told Mikhail.

Dostoevsky had little aptitude for the subjects that mattered most, like
geometry, trigonometry, and algebra ("I can't stand mathematics") or artillery
theory (he borrowed someone else's notes) or fortifications ("such nonsense").
Ten rooms in the castle displayed meticulous clay and wood models of for-
tresses from Riga to Siberia that sat next to local soil samples and their corresponding bricks. This was meant to inspire. Dostoevsky spent countless hours
drawing plans for bastions and guard towers, and yet, he confessed to his
father, "I don't draw well."

He excelled at the subjects that mattered least, the "intellectual subjects,"
he called them: history and catechism, Russian literature, French and German. He read Goethe's *Faust* and everything by E.T.A. Hoffmann. The few
friendships he had were built around discussions of literature. One cadet remembered Dostoevsky pursuing his best friend down a hallway and shouting
out one final point about Schiller. The academy's French instructor introduced
him to Racine, Corneille, and Pascal as well as contemporary French literature. He read French novelists whenever he could. He tore through most of
Victor Hugo and everything from Balzac that he could find. He wrote to his
father that it was *"absolutely essential"* that he subscribe to a French reading
library, ostensibly to read the great French "military geniuses." "I'm passionately fond of military science," he assured his father.

Finding ways to please his father became second nature. Dr. Dostoevsky
was self-righteous, demanding, and quick to condemn his children's inade-
quacies. He had recently acquired hereditary nobility for his service as a medical doctor, and he groomed his two oldest sons to be military engineers, despite
their wishes, because state service provided the best opportunity for upward
social mobility. The plan quickly faltered. Mikhail Mikhailovich was rejected
from the Academy of Engineers for health reasons, and five months after
Fyodor declared his great fondness for military science, he informed his father
that he had failed to be promoted. He listed his examination scores but ne-
glected to mention his dreadful performance in formation drill. He had to

repeat his first year at the academy—all those lonely days counted for nothing. He confessed to Mikhail the shame he felt as well as his anger. "I'd like to crush the entire world at a single stroke."

Mikhail was all Dostoevsky had. Fyodor was only twelve when Dr. Dostoevsky sent his two oldest sons away to an exclusive Moscow boarding school. Mikhail was one year older and had dark blue eyes and hair covering his ears. He was reserved, like his brother, but he was calmer, more optimistic, and almost never angry. He adjusted more easily to life away from home—the other boarders used to mock Fyodor for lagging behind Mikhail academically. The brothers were inseparable until Mikhail, following his rejection, was sent to another academy in Revel (now Tallinn, Estonia). Fyodor suffered the academy alone. "Dear Brother," Fyodor wrote after explaining his lack of promotion, "it's sad to live without hope . . . I look ahead, and the future horrifies me."

Both brothers dreamed of being writers. They discussed literature and philosophy. Mikhail sent Fyodor poems, often about their childhood—"The Walk," "Vision of Mother," "The Rose." Fyodor sent voluble, neatly written letters featuring rapturous flights and painful despairs. When he ran out of space on the page, he wrote lines vertically in the margins. The brothers cataloged their after-hours reading. Fyodor shared his thoughts about Byron and Pushkin, Shakespeare and Homer. He admired Homer's "unshakable certainty in his calling." Sometimes there were long silences between his letters, but Fyodor reassured his brother, "I was never indifferent to you; I loved you for your poems, for the poetry of your life."

Dostoevsky needed someone to hear his midnight-embrasure ideas. "It seems to me that our world is a purgatory of heavenly spirits bedimmed by sinful thought," he wrote to Mikhail. To be human is to be trapped somewhere between heaven and earth and to struggle to merge the two. "But to see only the cruel covering under which the universe languishes, to know that a single explosion of will is enough to smash it and merge with eternity, to know and to be like the last creature . . . is awful!"

In June 1839, Dostoevsky received the news that his father had been murdered by his own serfs. It happened near their Darovoe estate, and the details were murky. Rumors circulated that one of the peasants lured him into the neighboring serf village by pretending to be sick, at which point twelve to fifteen men finished him off. His body had been dumped in a roadside field. The motive was also unclear, but it was easy to imagine. The previous year's harvest had been so bad that the peasants used their own straw roofs to feed their livestock, and conditions deteriorated from there. A severe winter had given way to a drought, and Dr. Dostoevsky was so frequently drunk that he was barely capable of managing himself, let alone an estate. It's unlikely he stored enough grain for an emergency, and his distrustful, irascible nature probably frayed tensions. Tales of peasants revolting against their masters circulated widely throughout Russia, and memories of full-scale rebellions were vivid. The image of murderous serfs always hovered on the edge of the Russian landowning consciousness.

The two doctors who examined the body claimed that Dr. Dostoevsky had died of apoplexy, but rumors of murder spread from the neighbors to Dostoevsky's grandmother and then to the rest of the family. While the details were kept from the younger children, the oldest boys knew. Fyodor found out first, and he broke the news to Mikhail in a letter. The local officials who investigated, however, found no evidence of murder. The family saw this as a cover-up. It didn't take much to pay off the right people. The official cause of death might have encouraged the suspicions because "apoplexy" could refer to a heart attack, a stroke, or a cerebral hemorrhage as well as to traumatic apoplexy—the effusion of blood when something cracks your skull—or *apoplexia suffocata*, when you are hanged, drowned, or strangled. And if there *were* a murder, a cover-up would have been better for everyone. A murder like this—a crime against serfdom—would have meant that any serf involved, even tangentially, would have been exiled to Siberia, diminishing the estate's value for the seven Dostoevsky children, who were now without parents.

Whatever happened in Darovoe, it made Dostoevsky an orphan at seventeen. He hadn't seen his father since the doctor had consigned him to the academy two years earlier. His letters home revolved around urgent monetary requests: for new boots, for a new shako (everyone had their own shako, but his was academy issued), for brushes and paint, for pens and ink, for more books ("How will I spend time without books?"), for a trunk (everyone had his own trunk). He was in debt to various people. He borrowed money to mail his father a letter requesting more money. "Send me something right away.

You'll extract me from hell. Oh, it's awful to be in extremity!" At one point he itemized his expenses in a postscript: his necessities cost thirty-six to forty rubles. He insisted that he needed twenty-five by June 1. That was his last letter to his father.

If there were some mercy to the family's tragedy, it is that it liberated Dostoevsky from the academy's nettling smallnesses. Two months after their father's death, Fyodor wrote to Mikhail that he was studying human nature in earnest. "Humanity is a mystery. It needs to be unraveled, and if you spend your whole life unraveling it, don't say that you've wasted time." Death spurred the young man to reckon with larger things. "I'm studying that mystery," he wrote, "because I want to be a human being."

D ostoevsky graduated from the Academy of Engineers in August 1843 and entered active service as a second lieutenant in the Drafting Room of the St. Petersburg Engineering Corps. A year later, he announced that he was retiring, citing "family reasons." He sent a formal notification to his family regarding his late father's estate: *I renounce my entire allotment . . . for 1000 silver rubles*." Dostoevsky wanted half of the money immediately and half in monthly installments. He threatened legal recourse if it came to that.

The fact that he was demanding a somewhat modest sum—not much more than the average bureaucrat's annual salary—might have emboldened him. He renounced his estate in a letter to his brother-in-law, Peter Karepin, who had begun managing the family's affairs. Dostoevsky considered him mercenary, vain, and "stupid as an ox." He informed Karepin that he needed the money to pay off mounting debts—the interest payments alone were oner-ous. The twelve hundred rubles he claimed he owed in August 1844 climbed to fifteen hundred in September. But retiring from the Engineering Corps to pay off debt made no sense to Karepin. State servitors were protected from creditors during their service, so retiring would only empower his lenders. Dostoevsky was adamant: "Although the two ideas don't square, that's the way it is."

He told only Mikhail his real reason for leaving the Engineering Corps. "I'm finishing a novel," he wrote, and it is "rather original." His job had be-come meaningless. Sometimes he hired clerks to do his work, ensconced himself in his room, and wrote for hours, smoking his pipe. He developed a cough and a hoarse voice. He stopped responding to his flatmate's questions. It didn't seem healthy. His desk was covered in scraps of writing and full manuscript pages. "Letters spilled from his pen like gems, precisely rendered," his flatmate recalled. Dostoevsky called his novel *Poor Folk*. Telling Mikhail about it made it real. "I'm extraordinarily pleased with my novel," Dostoevsky wrote. "I can't get over it. I'll surely get money from it."

He had reasons to be optimistic. The success of Nikolai Gogol's *Dead Souls* made it clear that Russians wanted stories about the lives of those around them, and Gogol's characters were so delightfully disturbing. "It will be a long time before we will be able to cope with them," Dostoevsky wrote years later. Surely his own novels could make money as well. But getting started as a writer proved difficult. He tried writing a few plays, none of which survive. To earn money, he devised various translation schemes to serve Russia's interest in western fiction. Mikhail translated German texts, and Fyodor translated French. He believed translations were a sure path to fortune. "Why is Strugovshchikov already famous?" he asked Mikhail. All of his calculations had optimistic bottom lines—sometimes several thousand rubles. "Just wait and see, they'll come flying at us in swarms when they see the translations in our hands. There will be plenty of offers from booksellers and publishers. They're dogs."

Dostoevsky thought that a door was opening for him, briefly, and that he had to make a run for it. That meant grasping for opportunities, but it also meant abdicating responsibility for his younger brothers and sisters. "You alone will save them," he told Mikhail after their father's death. "My own goal is to be on my own." He had fantasized for years about being a "free, solitary, independent person" and pursuing a calling like Homer. Renouncing his father's estate was a way to detach himself.

Perhaps melodrama would persuade Karepin to grant him his independence. "I need *to eat*," Dostoevsky reminded him, "because *not eating* is unhealthy." He became more histrionic over time. "I am alone, without hope, without help, handed over to all the calamities, all the trials and tribulations of my horrible situation—destitution, nakedness, humiliation, shame." Dostoevsky was playing a common cultural role (Russians have five words for an aristocratic spendthrift), and he was indeed living beyond his means. He attended plays, ballets, and the opera, paying as much as twenty-five rubles per ticket. He gambled at cards with friends. He patronized prostitutes. He took advances on his salary to reimburse moneylenders—they were everywhere in Petersburg. He paid back money that he borrowed from his brother Andrei with money he borrowed from Mikhail. Paying off past expenses meant incurring immediate privation. "For Heaven's sake," he wrote to Andrei while asking for a few rubles, "I haven't had any firewood for three days now."

Karepin ignored Dostoevsky's pleas for three years. By 1844, Fyodor had already taken more than his share of the modest estate. Bit by bit, he had been receiving money for expenses and interest payments on his debts. At this point, Karepin told him, he was stealing from his six siblings and disrespecting his father's memory. Fyodor knew quite well that his father wanted his sons to be engineers—his younger brother Andrei had not yet finished his own engineering studies—and that he had sacrificed to launch them on respectable careers. And now, after his parents' unfortunate demise, Fyodor Mikhailovich wanted to betray those sacrifices to *tell stories*, to indulge in "*the pathetic daydreams and fantasies of errant youth*." That was unconscionable.

Dostoevsky expected objections like this from such a pedestrian man. "Karepin drinks, fucks, shits, drinks vodka, has a rank, believes in God," he wrote to Mikhail. He knew nothing about literature. "He says that Shakespeare and a soap bubble are the same thing." His brother-in-law had no business speaking for his own father and withholding what belonged to him. So when Karepin said it was impossible to give him any more money, Dostoevsky told him to borrow it. If he didn't get the money one way or the other, he would take on further debt at ever-higher interest rates, and the estate would be liable. "What the consequence will be, you can judge for yourself: trouble for everyone." So finally, after years of badgering, Karepin relented and sent Dostoevsky five hundred silver rubles.

Dostoevsky sensed that he was severing family connections, but he convinced himself it was his only choice. "I even consider this risk noble," he wrote to Mikhail, "this imprudent risk of changing my situation, risking my whole life for a shaky hope. Perhaps I am mistaken," he admitted. "But if I am not?"

Two

The Devil's Streetlamps

Dostoevsky described the capital of the Russian Empire in various ways. St. Petersburg is a gambler waking up with empty pockets, shivering in the damp cold, ready to pick a fight with a stranger so he can run away from this Indo-Germanic swamp forever. St. Petersburg is a society woman irritated by something that happened at last night's ball. St. Petersburg is a spendthrift son of an old-fashioned father—an arrogant, freethinking egoist, eager to instruct his elders and always in a hurry. St. Petersburg is a tubercular girl who's suddenly strong and laughing; her "eyes gleam with such fire," but only for a moment. Years later, Dostoevsky would settle on another description: "the most abstract and premeditated city on earth."

Petersburg's wide streets are called prospects. They radiate out in straight lines across canals and a flat terrain that makes it easy to survey the city's palaces and monuments, the arches and columns, and all the buildings topped by statues of warriors, angels, and personifications. Petersburg is built on an archipelago at the mouth of the Neva River. It is a horrible place for a city. Pontoon bridges and rowboats linked the municipal islands. When the river's branches froze—and they were frozen for nearly half the year—the bridges were removed. Petersburgers marked pathways across the ice with lanterns and scattered hay, and they covered the thinner spots with planks. In springtime, snowmelt turned the streets to mud. In summer and fall the city was so waterlogged that puddled side streets harbored swamp grass, ducks, and algae.

Petersburg was indeed built on an "Indo-Germanic swamp," as Dostoevsky called it, and the swamp was poised to take it all back.

The Neva flooded almost annually. During the flood of 1824, the river rose thirteen feet in a matter of hours, sending furniture, coffins, and carriages through the squares. Navy cutters swept through the streets to rescue survivors clinging to trees and roof beams. Waterborne diseases like cholera, typhoid, and malaria were endemic. The entire region's soil was too poor to grow food, so staples had to be imported. The land couldn't even support the city's buildings. The tsar's men unloaded barges carrying sixteen-foot oak beams and drove the timber vertically into the spongy ground to create foundations solid enough for construction. The whole city sits on top of an underground forest.

It was common to think of St. Petersburg as unreal, "abstract and premeditated," an idea made manifest on the reluctant earth. The idea was Peter the Great's. He wanted to make Russia a European empire not just by reforming the country but by moving the capital from landlocked Moscow to a west-facing coastal city that could be both a command center for an imperial navy and a seaport for global trade. Russia did not have such a city, so he decided to make one. When Peter first surveyed the archipelago (the Isle of Stones, the Isle of Goats, the Isle of Brushwood), he saw a future of palaces, barracks, and cathedrals for his empire. He ordered more than a hundred thousand serfs, criminals, and prisoners of war to drain marshes, drive foundations, and pave roads. Tens of thousands died from disease, exposure, and inadequate provisions to make Peter's abstract city a reality.

The best place to see westernizing Russia as it wanted to be seen was on Nevsky Prospect, Petersburg's widest thoroughfare. One could admire stately palaces lining the canals, the Imperial Public Library beside a two-story merchants' arcade, confectionery shops nestled between large churches. Compact Petersburg had more street life than sprawling Moscow. Women paraded down the wide granite sidewalks in Parisian dresses and plaited hair, and men held forth in musk-lined overcoats with beaver collars. Some people mixed Russian and western styles—silk caftans gathered at the waist, nankeen trousers tucked into high calfskin boots. Goods were advertised on trilingual signs (Russian, French, and German), and shopkeepers painted images for unlettered patrons: gentlemen's gloves or bonnets on faceless women or passably rendered fruits promoting watermelons, Crimean apples, and wineberries.

The streets were filled with officers in epaulets and plumes, singing basket vendors, and grimacing clowns. Organ grinders cranked unwieldy boxes festooned with bells, cymbals, and golden tassels. Every now and then someone would open a window and toss out a coin wadded in paper. Puppeteers had a set routine: A tiny Napoleon (blue coat, bicorne hat) would dance with sparkly ladies. Squeaky-voiced Petrushka would get himself into trouble before outfoxing his enemies. Two "Arabs" would burst onto the scene, and then Petrushka would be snatched and carried off by the devil.

Nothing about St. Petersburg's trimmings and grandeur could undo the fact that it was an idea built on a swamp. No matter how high the domes and spires climbed, people knew that for all but a few hours on the longest summer days the shadows are bigger than the monuments. Petersburg will always be a city of distant sunlight and encroaching darknesses—heavy fogs, mists, and twilights. At night the streets were lit by feeble oil lamps creating little more than a flickering, fear-conjuring chiaroscuro. Carriages would shoot out from the darkness and vanish just as quickly.

Petersburg was a false and uncalled-for capital. It was filled with counterfeit architecture and stocked with plants and animals that belonged elsewhere. The land itself was a fabrication. "Everything is deception," Gogol wrote in his short story "Nevsky Prospect," "everything is a dream, everything is not what it seems to be!" The story's final image could have been inspired by the puppeteers' routine: "The devil himself lights the streetlamps."

The deception became clearer in places like the Haymarket. Seedy taverns and brothels surrounded a square filled with canvas stalls and the smell of soups and dead animals. Petty vendors hawking kvass or salted pierogi or old clothing would mingle with beggars, pickpockets, and scammers. Women would sell boiled potatoes wrapped in layers of rags. Game salesmen would walk around with a string of goose heads slung over their shoulders. Butchers would split carcasses apart like wood and sell them to errand-running serfs.

Thousands of people crammed into the Haymarket's tenements and flophouses. Indigent families rented corners of rooms by the month. Vagrants and drunkards could have a space for the price of a few goose heads a night. The landlords resold vodka, lent money on interest, and bought sundry merchandise, no questions asked. The police rarely went into the Haymarket. There was no border crossing, no canal or wall or railway tracks unofficially marking a separate neighborhood, but here, just a short walk from Nevsky Prospect, was the uncalled-for city.

Petersburg had nearly half a million people in the 1840s. It was growing faster than London and Paris, and about 40 percent of the population was enserfed. Seven out of ten Petersburgers were men. They were building the city, staffing the empire's bureaucracy, and filling the military's ranks and academies. Russia had become increasingly martial after the Napoleonic Wars. The empire maintained a standing army of 850,000 soldiers—more than three times the size of the French army. Tsar Nicholas I took particular pleasure in military parades. Palace Square was wide enough that he could review fifty battalions—100,000 men—simultaneously as they marched past the Winter Palace balcony. For Nicholas, the spectacle was more than propaganda. It was a model of the way civilization should be. The exacting symmetry, the shining gear, and polished boots transformed strength into virtuous beauty. Nicholas redesigned his military's uniforms and obsessed over cuffs, chevrons, linings, and galloons. The heavy infantry guards' uniforms had been modified more than fifty times by 1848. The lower ranks' greatcoats were to have *nine* buttons, not ten. "Here"—in the army—"there is order," Nicholas said, "there is a strict, unconditional legality, no impertinent claims to know all the answers, no contradiction, all things flow logically one from the other; no one commands before he has himself learned to obey . . . everybody serves."

Nicholas began remaking Russian society shortly after coming to power in 1825. Bureaucratic organization increasingly resembled the workings of an army. Military academies proliferated. Military courts expanded their jurisdiction. Foreigners were struck by the uniforms. Professors wore uniforms. Female courtiers wore uniforms. Librarians, art instructors, and accountants all wore uniforms mandated by the state. Civil servants wore long green frock coats and dark caps with cockades. University students wore black sword belts in the winter months and white suede ones in the summer. They wore tasseled tricornered hats in public and *furazhkas* at home under pain of punishment. Detail is discipline.

Schools instilled the virtues of Orthodoxy, autocracy, and nationalism. Teachers endured strict oversight. One school was so unnerved by a visit from

Nicholas himself that the staff installed a system of bells and wires along the halls to alert everyone to the tsar's approaching carriage. University inspectors monitored students during meals, in their dormitories, in classrooms and courtyards. Disobedient students could be expelled or surveilled or sent to their university's student prison.

The government was redesigned to be more subservient to the Emperor and Autocrat of All the Russias. Legislative, judicial, and administrative bodies—including the Senate and State Council—all withered, and their functions were transferred to His Majesty's Own Chancery. Nicholas distrusted all institutions beyond himself—even his Chancery was suspect—and he appointed secret committees to help him govern outside the bureaucratic apparatus. He despised bureaucracy for the most common reason: it is abstract. Tsarism rests upon the belief that power is personal, something embodied in the autocrat himself. Bureaucracy's power is diffuse, difficult to supervise, and impossible to admire from the palace balcony.

The tsar's problem was that subordination only made the bureaucracy bigger and more diffuse. Strict oversight required documentation, and paperwork became a measure of obedience. Ministry reports prominently featured the tally of documents produced each year. The Ministry of Internal Affairs, for example, processed more than twenty-two million documents in 1841. Each report, application, and decree had to be registered and signed—sometimes by several people—with copies produced by hand. Officials produced documents about how to destroy documents. Routine transactions became laborious. There were five times as many civil servants (known as *chinovniks*) in 1850 as there were at the beginning of the century, and the growth rate was increasing. Directives to streamline departments elicited requests for *more* staff, and the increased staff created still more paperwork to keep track of the personnel keeping track of the paperwork.

Nearly all bureaucrats served the state their entire working lives, and few did it for the money. Lower-level bureaucrats barely made ends meet. They did not do it for love of country, either. The ethos of obedience inhibited the development of professional identity, and officials had no clear sense of ministerial purpose. They did it to improve their status in Russia's Table of Ranks, Peter the Great's strict social hierarchy. The table included fourteen positions in the military matched with corresponding civil service positions. If a bureaucrat made it onto the Table of Ranks as a collegiate registrar (the fourteenth rank), he (and it was always a he) became a noble. If he climbed to the eighth rank, his status would be hereditary: all of his descendants would be nobles, too. Each rank had a specific form of address—"Your High Honor," if you held the eighth rank, "Your Excellency," if you held the third. Everyone knew exactly where they stood, and promotions were regulated. Ascending from the fourteenth to the fifth rank without an elite education required thirty years of service. The perk was being addressed as "Your High Ancestry."

The Table of Ranks was the perfect tool for Nicholas. It roped civilians into military rankings. It tabulated a social order on state-generated categories. All things flowed logically, and everybody served. And instead of offering wealth as an incentive, the tsar could offer status. Another medal or braid. Another form of address. The Table was also a devilish tool, an elusive streetlamp specter promising more mobility than there actually was. An elite education could slash thirteen years off a bureaucrat's promotion schedule, but highly educated officials were likely to be hereditary nobles already. It was possible to earn hereditary nobility through civil service, but few people actually did.

D ostoevsky was twenty-three years old, unemployed and aimless in a city dominated by the military, the bureaucracy, and rank. Becoming a writer meant resisting the city's rational order. This was particularly difficult to do because another key to Nicholas's control of Russia was his control over literature and the circulation of ideas. Nicholas's regime considered virtually all secular literature hostile to orderly society. Nicholas expanded the dragnet for dangerous words almost immediately after his coronation. More than a dozen censorship offices in different ministries inspected virtually all printed material, and the list of banned books was updated monthly. The "Black Office" reviewed foreign periodicals arriving by mail. International tourists had to forfeit their books and wait, sometimes for days, for the Foreign Censorship Committee to clear them. Censors worried about secret codes hidden in musical scores, and phrases like "forces of nature" and "intellectual ferment" were unacceptably inflammatory. Nicholas shut down a newspaper for publishing an unfavorable review of a play he quite liked. He outlawed German philosophy altogether.

Domestic journalism was hamstrung. Every new periodical required state approval, which could take years. Censors pored over each issue before it could be printed, which made timely issues difficult and newspapers almost impossible. Editors were sometimes incarcerated for violations, as were overly permissive censors. Warier censors anticipated how an irate superior or a skittish high-ranking noble might react to any particular article or phrase. Enterprising censors rewrote questionable passages themselves.

Russian literature had been largely a state- and church-sponsored enterprise for decades. The government founded or supported dozens of journals that operated as state organs. Officials co-opted influential writers and editors by paying them. Newspapers couldn't be sold on the street or in railway stations, and commercial advertisements were banned, which kept prices high. Publications struggled to reach more than a few thousand subscribers with scattershot news items, meandering letters from Russians abroad, and reports on occasional crimes (usually foreign).

Russian censorship had long created eerie silences. There was not a single reference to Petersburg's flood of 1824 in any Russian newspaper. Hundreds of thousands of people lived through a disaster that consumed the capital, and it was as if it had never happened. Under Nicholas's reign, the silences rippled outward. While the annual number of books published in Russia had tripled in the first third of the nineteenth century, by 1837 the growth had ceased. It would remain stagnant for the next fifteen years.

Dostoevsky's decision to renounce his estate to become a writer was, by any reasonable estimate, absurd. It was nearly unheard of to make a living from literary fiction. Pulp adventure tales and illustrated chapbooks were profitable. Literature wasn't. Almost all Russian writers of note were either landed gentry deriving income from estates with hundreds of serfs or else high-ranking state or military officials. Lermontov, Pushkin, Turgenev, Goncharov, Tolstoy— none of them renounced anything in order to write fiction because no one turned to writing to pay their bills. Russian literature developed as a social grace for elites, and their disdain for professional writing helped them retain control. Genuine literature, they insisted, was unsullied by commerce. Money destroys an author's principles, keen thinking, and good taste. Dostoevsky's plan was not just an "imprudent risk." For an upwardly striving family, it was crass.

Even without its social taboos and government hostility, Russia would have been a difficult place for a writer. The mid-nineteenth-century literacy rate was low—15 percent is probably a generous estimate—while Germany, France, Britain, and the United States all had majority-literate populations. Russia's small readership forced publishers to rely on high prices. A copy of Gogol's *Dead Souls* cost ten rubles, and many novels cost twenty-five to thirty—nearly half of the average bureaucrat's monthly salary. High prices kept the book market small. There were only about a thousand titles published in Russia every year, and nearly half of them were foreign.

The best solution to the adverse market was to aggregate as many readers as possible in subscription lists for wide-ranging monthly journals. Purchasing a book was a commitment, but subscribing to a journal was a stroll through the arcade. Novels appeared in installments. If you didn't like one narrative's development, there was another one in the same issue. If you didn't like novels at all, you could read summaries of world events, or about Constantinople in the fourth century, or about recent discoveries in physiology, or "A Popular Essay on How the New Planet Neptune Was Discovered." Some contributions were specialized. "The Causes and Fluctuations of Grain Prices," for example, or "On the Possibility of Definitive Measures of Confidence in the Result of the Sciences of Observation and Particularly Statistics." Literature was bundled with everything.

They became known as "thick" journals—each issue was hundreds of pages. *The Library for Reading*, one of the first thick journals, boasted fifty-seven contributors. Its content was generally light and apolitical, but it published translations of Victor Hugo and Balzac, Dickens and James Fenimore Cooper. Seven thousand subscribers paid fifty rubles per year—the price of a few books—to be cultured and informed. More than two hundred journals came and went during Nicholas's reign. The turnover was a sign of precarity, but it was also a sign that people found the risks worth taking. By the 1840s, there was a small ecosystem of durable journals, and they paid their writers well. Book publishing still lagged behind Europe, but Russia's biggest journals had circulations about as high as their British and French counterparts. And the reach was wider than the subscription list.

For ambitious young writers like Dostoevsky, however, the thick journals' domination seemed like a trap. Russia's embryonic market allowed a handful of opportunistic publishers to band together and squeeze out competitors. It was a club sustained by bribes, threats, favors, blacklists, and mutual promotion. "It's an oligarchy," Dostoevsky complained to his brother in 1845. Submitting your work to a journal meant yoking yourself to editors and their sycophants, "to the main *maître d'hôtel*," he complained, and "to all the sluts and kitchen boys who nestle in the nests from which enlightenment is disseminated." Everyone thought the business was crass.

Nicolaevan Russia was an unlikely place for a world literature to develop, but beneath the surface there was just enough wealth and education, enough curiosity and self-scrutiny, enough daring and insecurity and pride to create a new literary capital on an old continent. Petersburg was becoming the center of Russian literature in the 1840s, and the city's readers were shaping its content. Roughly half of Russia's readers were civil servants or military officials engaged in meaningless work for a state they earnestly wanted to value. It was as if there were a surplus of meaning floating downstream looking for somewhere to land. That experience needed articulation.

The most influential person shaping Russian literature at the time was a tempestuous critic named Vissarion Belinsky. He was the first Russian writer to devote his entire career to literary criticism, and he dominated public opinion in a way no other critic ever had. Belinsky started and ended writers' careers. His reviews determined booksellers' orders. His annual roundups of the literary scene covered significant translations and trends, all the major journals, and virtually every notable Russian publication across all genres. He reviewed contemporary authors and interpreted decades-old publications. If Belinsky didn't write about you, you didn't matter.

Belinsky identified four types of literature in Russia: kopeck literature, trade literature—distinguishable only by the profit margins—"graybeard literature" (just what it sounds like), and genuine literature. He claimed there were only a dozen genuine Russian writers. Belinsky thought good critics created a literate society, which meant drawing clear lines. "Scribblers in frieze coats," he wrote, "with unshaven chins, write miserable little books at the order of petty booksellers." They "ruin the public taste, deface literature, and the calling of the literary man." Belinsky hated the kitchen boys, too. He was twenty-eight years old and already the most well-known critic in Russia when he moved from Moscow to Petersburg in 1839 to join a newly revived journal called *Notes of the Fatherland*. Its goal was to take down the oligarchs, the scribblers, the graybeards, and the status quo.

"I feel sorrow and pity for those who do not share my opinion," Belinsky said. His pity was sincere. Disagreements with him opened up into Manichaean divides between those seeking truth and those who wallowed in ignorance. Ideas *mattered*. His voice quavered and his cheeks trembled when he attacked the ignorant during disputes. His outbursts earned him the nickname Furious Vissarion.

Belinsky's ideas were routed through his emotions. "Thinking and feeling, understanding and suffering," he wrote to a friend in 1841, "are one and the same thing." He paced through his rooms while reading, agitated or thrilled. He would lock himself in his study, stand at his writing desk, fill a sheet of paper, and then throw himself into a book until the sheet's ink dried. Then he'd continue on a clean page. He'd shuttle back and forth, reading and writing, until he was too weak to go further. His finished essays featured sharp insights and succinct judgments rather than extended lines of reasoning. They were earnest, lyrical, and meandering—one of the oligarchs believed he wrote only while drunk. What readers loved about Belinsky was his fervor. He had a prophet's zeal, and it was that sense of calling, a temple-cleansing mission, that made him so persuasive.

Belinsky was the son of a provincial military doctor; he had a "plebeian origin," as Ivan Turgenev called it. He was expelled from Moscow University for his "limited capacities" (he didn't pass a single exam in three years), and the expulsion denied him both the status of the degree and the finer points of a higher education. He knew that people noticed the gaps in his knowledge (he spoke no foreign languages, not even French), and he was convinced he was too ugly to be a suitable companion.

Temperamental though he was, Belinsky thought of literature as a form of empiricism. He referred to "the mysterious laboratory of nature" and to creativity's laws. "Reality—that is the motto and the last word of the contemporary world." While this sounds like being a partisan for everything, Belinsky was rebuffing the vestiges of romanticism that seemed blind to everyday life. He preferred a nonfiction genre that the French called *physiologies*, detailed and precise descriptions of people or places. When Belinsky referred to one physiological sketch as "living statistics," it was high praise. The genre was built upon the notion that a careful delineation of a specimen can lead to general insights about the increasingly complicated world—the same way you could learn about all kidneys by dissecting one of them. The genre was an outcropping of realism, and as such it often focused on unseemly urban details. One physiology about Petersburg's tenements described the leftovers of insects smeared on the walls.

Gritty realism had its detractors. One of the Russian oligarchs objected to the tendency to rummage "in the dark corners and alleys of life." Blood-smeared walls and flies circling unconscious drunks were not, in themselves, beautiful, so how could describing it ad nauseam be art? For people like Belinsky, beholding the truth, however unsavory, was invaluable. Literature was the news when the news wasn't legal.

What Belinsky really wanted was a rendering of what it meant to be Russian. That's what drew him to Gogol. Belinsky was the first critic to praise his talent. Gogol, Belinsky wrote, gives us Russian life "in all its nudity, in all its frightening formlessness." He captured the mania and pettiness of life in a ranked society. *"Here is the Russian spirit, this smells Russian!"* Belinsky exclaimed about *Dead Souls*. Russia was fragmented by rank, but literature, he believed, could turn fragmentation into a deeper organic unity.

A sense of organic wholeness was crucial because some Russians had begun to question their nation's unity. Alongside post-Napoleonic optimism was a persistent unease about Russia—just a feeling, usually, or a budding thought, something you would repeatedly uproot. But one day it became clear that someone had allowed it to grow like a poisonous flower, and the thought was cultivated in a long letter addressed to a lady who never ultimately received it. Instead, the letter circulated for years in handmade copies passed among friends until a journal in Moscow somehow published it uncensored in 1836 under the heading "First Philosophical Letter."

What the letter announced, with alarming force and clarity, was that Russian culture, Russian history, Russian thought and literature, and even the Russian people did not exist at all. There was nothing to unify. "We belong to none of the great families of mankind," the letter stated, "we are neither of the West nor of the East, and we possess the traditions of neither." Russia had no foundation: "There are no rules, there is no home life, there is nothing to which we could be attached . . . nothing durable, nothing lasting; everything flows, everything passes, leaving no traces either outside or within us."

The letter was unsigned, though people knew it was written by Peter Chaadaev, a former officer in the Napoleonic Wars who had resigned at the height of his career and become a recluse. Chaadaev was an iconoclastic traditionalist, and for him the absence of a national tradition was Russia's defining quality, the only thing that affected all aspects of Russian life. "What is habit, instinct, among other peoples we must get into our heads by hammerstrokes. Our memories go no further back than yesterday; we are, as it were, strangers to ourselves." To read the letter was to hear someone happily demolishing Russia's overweening nationalism with his own relentless hammerstrokes. "Isolated in the world, we have given nothing to the world, we have taken nothing from the world; we have not added a single idea to the mass of human ideas; we have contributed nothing to the progress of the human spirit. And we have disfigured everything we touched of that progress."

None of these statements were even remotely acceptable—in public or in private. The censor who approved it claimed that the journal's editor had read selected passages to him while he was playing cards. It was, in any case, the embarrassing task of the head of the Chief Directorate of Censorship to inform Tsar Nicholas that an article appearing in *The Telescope* constituted a "direct attack on the past, present and future of the motherland." Nicholas swiftly denounced the "First Philosophical Letter" as a "jumble of insolent absurdities worthy of a madman." He declared Chaadaev insane and placed him under medical and police supervision. The censor lost his rank and his pension, and the editor of *The Telescope* was exiled to the edge of European Russia. The journal was banned, of course, as was any article that even mentioned it.

Chaadaev subtracted everything. The dominant theory of Russian autocracy was that tradition shaped and justified the tsar's authority, and Russian identity, in turn, flowed out from the tsar. Chaadaev's insistence that Russia did not have a tradition essentially turned the tsar into a tyrant. And so without a tradition or a legitimate ruler, Russians would have to find another way to be a people. Dostoevsky read Chaadaev's letter just as he was hoping to become a writer of national significance, and his original pursuit—studying the mystery of being human—became intertwined with another more immediate question: What does it mean to be Russian?

Ideas about national character always derive from insecurity. *Who are we?* is never far from *Why are we important?* Part of what made Chaadaev's depiction of Russia so jarring was that in the 1840s people began reading it within the context of a larger philosophy of history that highlighted global status. It was the philosophy of G.W.F. Hegel. Hegel argued that what seems like a tumble of human events in history is in fact a pageant moving inexorably toward the realization of the idea of freedom. Some nations, some events, and some people contribute to the world-historical procession, and some simply do not. History is driven by Reason, not chance or force. "Reason governs the world," Hegel wrote. It is the *"substance* and *infinite power"* of all reality. Hegel's vision of a historical elite bearing out freedom through Reason forced Russians to view their nation's historical role through the era's two contrasting lenses: in the decades after the Napoleonic Wars, Russians were apt to see their empire as a bulwark against tyranny, and yet as Nicholas's reign progressed, many Russians began questioning the empire's place in the procession toward freedom. In other words, Hegel managed to stoke Russian pride and insecurity simultaneously. By the 1840s, his philosophy had captivated Russian intellectual circles as no other western philosophy before it.

And so when Chaadaev declared that Russia was isolated from "the general progress of the human spirit," Russian intellectuals defended the nation's world-historical status. Belinsky claimed that Peter the Great led Russia into the world-historical ranks, and that was crucial because Hegel's philosophy makes participating in history akin to participating in eternity. Historical time was an illusion because, for Hegel, history is the elaboration of an idea that is already fully formed. History does not *end up* at its idea. It is the manifestation of an eternal principle that Hegel called Spirit.

What was challenging about Hegel's philosophy was also what made it thrilling. All scales of phenomena become part of a Spirit-generating cycle of causality. A lowly civil servant participates in the manifestation of Spirit as both a beneficiary and an infinitesimal cause. Spirit reveals itself through nations and centuries only because it is embedded in individual people and events. And yet some of those individuals and events play an outsize role. There are world-historical individuals—great leaders, great artists—who make Spirit manifest to extraordinary degrees, and nevertheless they derive their power from the preexisting nationhood and Spirit that make their individuality possible. The reason why anyone is self-conscious, reasoning, and free is that individuals can draw upon a national spirit that world-historical leaders, artists, and writers embody and articulate. Great individuals create great nations, which create great individuals.

But there was something disturbing about world-historical people. They are powerful, Hegel wrote, because "they respect none of the limitations which law and morality would impose upon them." A powerful will drives the world-historical individual—"everything else is sacrificed to this aim." The consequences of such willpower are severe: "So mighty a figure must trample down many an innocent flower, crush to pieces many things in its path." Manifesting Spirit requires ruthless destruction. Hegel considered Napoleon a prime example of a world-historical ruler, and for Russians that added to the ethical puzzles of Hegel's philosophy: When is destruction a virtue? If Reason is the only reality and if Spirit emerges inevitably, how should an individual act? If even wrongs lead us to Reason, then accepting the status quo would seem to be moral wisdom. You can simply pull in the oars, ride out the rapids, and float down to freedom effortlessly.

For a while, Belinsky argued exactly that—that freedom and morality are the "unconditional submission to tsarist authority." Soon, however, the idea of Spirit trampling innocents became an unacceptable expression of Reason's "*infinite power.*" In 1841, he wrote to a friend, "What good is it to me to know that reason will ultimately be victorious and that the future will be beautiful, if I am forced by fate to witness the triumph of chance, irrationality, and brute force?" What good was Napoleon's power? What good was the tsar's power? Belinsky's politics shifted from conservative fatalism to liberal activism, from reconciling with the status quo to negating it. He decided that the small things mattered most—the trampled flowers, the crushed insects, the unconscious drunks. Any truly artistic rendering of reality would move us toward the better world.

And yet there was a nettlesome problem. How could Russia be a world-historical nation if it still hadn't developed a literature sufficient to cultivate its nationhood? The French certainly had their world-historical writers. Where were Russia's? It was one of Chaadaev's deepest cuts. "Where are our wise men, where are our thinkers?" Chaadaev asked. "Who has ever thought for us? Who thinks for us now?"

Three

Sharp Claws

arly one morning in May 1845, a writer named Nikolai Nekrasov
rushed into Belinsky's apartment with a manuscript and proclaimed,
"A new Gogol has appeared!"

"You find Gogols springing up like mushrooms," Belinsky responded.

This wasn't exactly true—generous enthusiasm was uncharacteristic of
Nekrasov—but it was natural for Belinsky to gird himself against disappointment, even after an endorsement from an important young talent. Belinsky
nevertheless wasted no time reading the manuscript. When Nekrasov returned that evening, he could see the urgency in Belinsky's face. "Bring him
here," he told Nekrasov, "bring him as soon as you can!"

After Dostoevsky left the Engineering Corps, he spent "devilishly busy"
months revising his novel yet again. His former flatmate, Dmitri Grigorovich,
grew curious as he watched Dostoevsky work on *Poor Folk*, so he asked to
read it. After more than a year of solitary toil, a single reader feels like an
inspection under harsh lighting, less a reading than a determination, a judgment that seems final because it is first. Dostoevsky had fleeting moments of
confidence. He had written it with passion, after all—"Can it be that all this
is a lie, a mirage, counterfeit emotion?"—but those moments would vanish.
He wrote to his brother Mikhail, "I often stay awake the whole night through
because of tormenting thoughts." Grigorovich was living with Nekrasov, and
Dostoevsky knew they were in Belinsky's orbit. He had been reading Belinsky
for years and found him terrifying, naturally, but this was his chance. So

Dostoevsky arrived at Grigorovich's apartment, handed his manuscript over, sheepishly shook hands with Nekrasov, and departed.

Grigorovich and Nekrasov were skeptical—"we'll be able to tell from the first ten pages"—but they ended up going late into the night, taking turns reading it aloud, stopping to marvel at certain moments. In one scene, a ragged man attends the funeral of his son, a quiet tutor who dies of tuberculosis. The father fills his pockets with his son's books, salvaging them from creditors, and when the tiny memorial service ends, he trots alongside the hearse while onlookers remove their hats and point to the books falling out of his pockets and into the mud, the only things left. The main narrative chronicles the doomed love of a chinovnik (a civil servant) for a younger woman; they can see each other from their apartment windows. It's a sentimental novel narrated entirely through their letters. In the end, the woman departs for the steppes with a wealthier, younger fiancé. In his last letter, the chinovnik swears that floods will halt her departure, or that her carriage will break down, that she will write back, but none of these things happen.

It was four in the morning when Grigorovich and Nekrasov finished reading. They nevertheless decided to head straight to Dostoevsky's—"this matters more than sleep!" Dostoevsky was sitting by an open window when they walked in and embraced him. Nekrasov gripped Dostoevsky's shoulders and announced that he was going to take his novel to Belinsky immediately, and he shouldn't worry, because he'll love it. "You'll see; what a man he is, after all, what a man! You'll meet him and you'll see: what a splendid soul he is!"

Furious Vissarion was not how Dostoevsky had imagined him. Belinsky was small and pale. He had animated eyes, a sweep of thick hair, and a busy forehead topping his gaunt face. All furrows and nerves. He greeted Dostoevsky solemnly, with careful restraint, sizing him up in the dark parlor of Belinsky's ground-floor apartment. When he had visitors, he paced around in a padded gray frock coat reaching his knees. Eventually, Belinsky looked the young writer squarely in the eyes and said, "Do you, you yourself, realize what it is you have written?" He asked it repeatedly, as if the question loosened him. His weak, husky voice rose each time. "Have you comprehended all the terrible truth that you have shown us?"

Epistolary novels were old-fashioned, and yet *Poor Folk* felt new. Gogol's novels were skillfully directed by a conspicuous narrator, but here was a novel where history's innocent flowers are in control and speak in unmediated voices. The letters document an inevitable decline. Belinsky was struck by the chinovnik's humility, his love-will-conquer-all fantasy, his gratitude for such small things. "It's not a matter of compassion for the poor fellow," he told Dostoevsky, "it's horror, real horror!" Gogol described the effect of his own work as tears emerging through laughter. *Poor Folk*, by contrast, offered horror through expressions of love. The greater the chinovnik's swell of emotion, the stronger the undertow of doom. Dostoevsky remembered Belinsky's words for the rest of his life. "To you, an artist, the truth has been revealed and proclaimed; it has come to you as a gift. So cherish your gift, remain faithful to it, and be a great writer."

Dostoevsky was dazzled. He stood outside Belinsky's apartment, looked up at the sky, and knew that everything would be different, that this was his life's great turning point, Vissarion Belinsky calling him an artist. "Belinsky was the most intense person I have ever met," Dostoevsky wrote decades later, and his intensity could make others feel like diluted versions of themselves. Dostoevsky nevertheless vowed to live up to the great critic's idea of him. Fortunately, the critic was full of advice—about fighting injustice, about writing and publishing, about editors and payments, and, remarkably, about refraining from outbursts (a sure sign of "depravity of talent"). He began spreading the word about Dostoevsky. Turgenev remembered the fatherly tenderness Belinsky had for him. "Yes, my dear fellow," he proudly told Turgenev, "let me tell you it may be a tiny bird," his infant Dostoevsky, "but it's got sharp claws!"

Dostoevsky might have reminded Belinsky of himself: ambitious and idealistic and yet always out of place. A military doctor's son, Belinsky lived on a combination of loans and gifts, as well as the fees he earned from churning out pages, improvising his way through paragraphs. He wasn't drunk when he wrote. He was hungry. His editor at *Notes of the Fatherland*, Andrei Kraevsky, constantly pressed him for more articles. Kraevsky was a "bloodsucker," the critic concluded. "I sincerely wish him the worst of everything."

Belinsky was dying of tuberculosis. The disease had been ravaging his lungs for years. In the middle of an argument, he'd begin coughing blood into his handkerchief. The leather couch in his parlor doubled as his sickbed when he was too ill to write, and he began wearing a respirator whenever he walked outside. He'd nevertheless carry on lengthy conversations, despite his weakened breath and racing pulse, despite the doctor's orders. Turgenev remembered being exhausted by the consumptive critic. "We haven't yet decided the question of the existence of God," Belinsky told him, "and you want to eat!"

B elinsky began cultivating Dostoevsky. He fed his tiny bird utopian socialist ideas from writers like Pierre Leroux, Louis Blanc, and Pierre-Joseph Proudhon. What is slavery? Proudhon asked. "*It is murder!*" What is property? "*It is theft!*" Belinsky advocated for the end of property and marriage, the end of nations and religions:

> There will come a time—I fervently believe it—when no one will
> be burnt, no one will be decapitated . . . there will be no husbands
> and wives, but lovers and mistresses . . . Woman will not be the slave
> of society and man, but, like man, will fully follow her inclinations
> without losing her good name, that monstrosity of conventional ideas.
> There will be neither rich nor poor, neither kings nor subjects, there
> will be brethren.

He introduced Dostoevsky to atheist ideas—that the Gospels are merely Judaic myths built around a charismatic leader, or that God is merely a projection of human ideals, or perhaps a projection of fear, a way for people to surrender the terrifying freedom that comes with being human.

Dostoevsky was rattled by the vast consequences of eliminating God from the universe, and yet he was captivated by how easily and systematically a thoughtful mind could sweep everything away. Each new idea seemed more radical than the last. Belinsky's atheism derived largely from a group of German intellectuals calling themselves *Die Freien* (the Free Ones), who gathered in a Berlin wine bar in the early 1840s. Their meetings were raucous—even the women played billiards and smoked. Karl Marx and Friedrich Engels sometimes attended, and one night, Engels drew a sketch of the disorder:

Someone tramples pages of writing during an argument. Someone else pounds his fist on a table cluttered with bottles while a soldier next to a toppled chair slumps over his wineglass. And in the background, a slender, well-dressed man calmly smokes a cigar and watches the chaos through steel-rimmed glasses.

That man's name was Max Stirner, and he, perhaps more than anyone, embodied what it meant to sweep everything away. Though somewhat obscure today, his ideas would have vast consequences throughout Dostoevsky's lifetime. He was, for Dostoevsky, a philosopher who took hold of a great truth but clutched it too tightly. Few people knew much about him—not even his real name ("Max Stirner" was a nickname honoring his large forehead [*Stirn*]). He taught history and literature at a school for young women. He smiled thinly during Die Freien's discussions, occasionally whispering to the person next to him, and in 1844 he published a book that shocked everyone who managed to get ahold of it. Stirner argued that Die Freien's atheists were really priests in secular clothing. They simply replaced one sacred abstraction with another: humanity. "God was the Lord, now Man is the Lord; God was the Mediator, now Man is; God was the Spirit, now Man is." The secular switch was not an improvement. "If God has given us pain," Stirner wrote, "'Man' is capable of pinching us still more torturingly."

Stirner showed everyone how far skepticism could go. He insisted that all abstractions are unreal—nothing but spooks inside our heads that frighten and control us. So many things people assumed were real—nations, emperors, popes, God—were actually ghosts, "fever-phantasies." Even atheists and socialists revered ghosts. Freedom is a shimmering ghost, Stirner argued, an abstract ideal you will never reach. Property is a ghost, yes, but so is theft. Laws and rights are ghosts. Justice is a ghost. So are nations and peoples, traditions and history. "Farewell," he bade the ghost of history, "thou who hast tyrannized over thy children for a thousand years!" Stirner was like a more ruthless Chaadaev subtracting everything, not just for Russians but for everyone.

What's left after all the ghosts are slain? "I alone am corporeal," Stirner declared. And what should an individual do when everything is a phantom? *Take.* "Now I take the world as what it is to me, as *mine*, as my property; I refer all to myself." His property included other people. Stirner addressed his readers, "To me you are only what you are for me,—to wit, my object; and, because *my* object, therefore my property." Stirner offered a conqueror's philosophy in the wake of Napoleon, a philosophy in which no one needs to be a world-historical person to trample innocent flowers—world-historical people are, after all, part of the swarm of Hegelian ghosts, along with Spirit and Reason. The truth was that anyone could be a Napoleon. "I am entitled by myself to murder," Stirner wrote. Evil is a ghost.

Stirner called his philosophy egoism. His book *The Ego and Its Own* elicited anger and dismay among the Free Ones and beyond. Marx wrote a 400-page screed against Stirner. German officials impounded 250 copies of *The Ego and Its Own* but released them after determining that it was too absurd to be dangerous. Egoism made its way to Russia, to Belinsky and his circle, and to Dostoevsky. Belinsky advocated a milder egoism. He told a friend that because egoism "governs the whole living world," we must bend it toward altruism by convincing people that helping others is the greatest pleasure.

But once it seems clear that selfishness governs the world, it is difficult for an atheist to bar the path down to Stirner's depths. For if there is no God, no heaven and hell, then only persuasion will stop people inclined to rob and murder. And persuasion is such a feeble ghost, whereas Stirner's incantatory voice, once you heard it, would always be there to offer the simplest philosophy possible. "My concern is neither the divine nor the human, not the true, good, just, free, etc., but solely what is *mine* . . . Nothing is more to me than myself!"

When Petersburg's elites returned to the city from their provincial estates in the fall of 1845, Dostoevsky found himself among princes and counts in the capital's salons. One of Petersburg's most fashionable women noted how his eyes darted around the room as people tried to engage him in conversation, often unsuccessfully. When he did speak, people listened. They repeated his words. Strangers were eager to meet him. "Who is this Dostoevsky? Where can I *get Dostoevsky*?" demanded Kraevsky, Belinsky's editor.

"Half of Petersburg is already talking about *Poor Folk*," Dostoevsky wrote to Mikhail, and it wasn't even published yet. His anxiety transformed into preening satisfaction. "They're all in love with me," he boasted to Mikhail, "every last one"—even Turgenev. Dostoevsky described him as "a talent, an aristocrat, a handsome fellow, wealthy, bright, educated." Turgenev hosted an evening reading of *Poor Folk* that produced frenzied excitement in Belinsky's circle. Nekrasov offered 250 silver rubles to publish it, and that was just the beginning. Dostoevsky wrote a short story in one night, for which Nekrasov gave him another 125 rubles. He was writing a longer story called *The Double*, which "is turning out superbly." He wrote to Mikhail that he didn't have enough paper to recount all of his triumphs.

Dostoevsky was just turning twenty-four years old. No one could recall the last time a writer had burst onto the scene so spectacularly. One writer declared him "a talent that will trample them all into the dirt." The word throughout Petersburg was that Belinsky had found what everyone was looking for, "a newly born little genius who in time will kill all past and present literature with his works." The only trouble was that Dostoevsky began leading what he called a "disorderly life," despite scoldings from Belinsky and Turgenev. When he had no money, he borrowed five hundred rubles from Kraevsky. "I am now almost drunk with my own glory," he confessed to Mikhail.

His arrogance did not wear well. Turgenev started goading him into arguments, drawing him toward absurd positions. Belinsky tried to discourage the provocations ("he does not understand what he is saying," he told Turgenev), but Turgenev had a malicious streak, and he wouldn't stop. At one gathering, he started telling a thinly veiled story about a silly man from the provinces who imagined himself to be a genius. Dostoevsky turned pale, trembled, and bolted from the room.

When the reviews of *Poor Folk* appeared, they were shockingly, inexplicably bad. *The Illustration* said it had no form. *The Northern Bee* called it a failure. Several critics dismissed it as derivative of Gogol, and Gogol's own estimation would have devastated Dostoevsky if he could have heard it: "a lot of wordiness and little focus." He had read only a few pages before he started skimming. One review, Dostoevsky told Mikhail, was nothing but "swearing, not criticism." Another seemed cruel: "Dostoevsky is not an artist and will never be one." He tried comforting himself by remembering that they had mistreated Gogol and Pushkin, too. "The fools are building my fame."

But fame made him more vulnerable. When Dostoevsky was introduced to a slender, refined young lady at Count Vielgorsky's ball, he looked at her elegant clothes and luxuriant blond curls, and he fainted. He left as soon as he was revived in a back room, but the embarrassment pursued him. Turgenev and Nekrasov described the scene in a poem and referred to the unnamed young writer as a "new pimple" on the nose of Russian literature. They circulated the verses themselves. Grigorovich helped make copies. Soon Belinsky joined in on the gossip, contributing savory anecdotes about his own infant genius.

The fact that Turgenev led the mutiny confirmed Dostoevsky's sense that he never truly belonged. Turgenev's airs grated on him (he would move to kiss you and then offer his cheek), as did his Berlin education and his large inheritance—thousands of serfs across multiple estates. Dostoevsky, meanwhile, would always be the boy who grew up in cramped quarters on the grounds of a hospital for the poor, who slept with Mikhail in a windowless room, who was the second son of a man who craved gentry status, only to be murdered, reportedly, by the few serfs he managed to acquire. Dostoevsky held the lowest rank of heritable nobility, a rank that, by a recent imperial decree, no longer conferred hereditary nobility at all. He was grandfathered into his liminal status.

Literary Petersburg was teaching him a lesson. "I have a terrible defect," Dostoevsky confessed to Mikhail, "an immeasurable egoism and vanity." He nevertheless kept counting mentions of himself in the press, good or bad. There were thirty-five in two months. It was as if he were a bystander helplessly witnessing his own misdeeds. "I have such an awful, repulsive character . . . I am ridiculous and disgusting."

In February 1846, shortly after Count Vielgorsky's ball, *Notes of the Fatherland* published *The Double*. It's the story of a meek chinovnik who encounters on the street one night someone who could be his twin—the same appearance, the same unlikely name (Yakov Petrovich Golyadkin), and, it turns out, the same occupation. But his double is better at everything. Golyadkin's colleagues and superiors, women and strangers, all prefer the double. He's more fun and intelligent. They pass for each other so easily that his double begins usurping Golyadkin's life, edging out the genuine Golyadkin, erasing him, making the humble, moral, original chinovnik nothing but an impostor forced to witness and covet the now-real version of himself until he is taken away to a mental hospital.

Belinsky's review was mixed. *The Double* was more thoughtful and creative than *Poor Folk*, he wrote, and remarkably rich—"every single passage in this novel is beyond perfection." Yet its richness was excessive. The tale was too surreal. "The fantastic can have a place only in madhouses," he declared. It had no place in literature. With that, the general opinion of Dostoevsky seemed to sour: "Everyone is angry at me."

Dostoevsky blamed it on having to rush his work. Kraevsky had paid him six hundred rubles for *The Double*, but over the past five months he had spent more than three thousand, and he kept spending. He moved into a larger flat and bought elegant clothes—new vests and frock coats, a Dutch linen jacket, and a beautifully stitched top hat from Zimmerman's. His expenses seemed sustainable because Kraevsky kept giving him advances for stories he hadn't yet written. By the fall of 1846, he was sixteen hundred rubles in debt. He let his fine clothes deteriorate and began living in an expense-sharing collective. He borrowed more money while writing his way out of previous debts. This was, he said, "the system of my slavery and literary dependence."

Dostoevsky fell into the same trap that Kraevsky had laid for Belinsky. Furious Vissarion almost single-handedly built *Notes of the Fatherland*—the subscription list more than tripled in six years—and he wasn't getting enough credit or profit. So Belinsky and a couple members of his circle, including Nekrasov, took over Pushkin's old journal, *The Contemporary*, and in one year, its circulation jumped from 223 to 2,000. The following year, 1848, it increased to more than 3,000.

They wanted Dostoevsky to join them. When he arrived at Nekrasov's new editorial office, Nekrasov asked him to declare publicly that he no longer "belonged" to *Notes of the Fatherland*. But Dostoevsky was too indentured to leave, so Nekrasov demanded that he return an advance for a story he still hadn't written, which infuriated Dostoevsky. While storming out, he couldn't get into his overcoat as the footman held it for him, so he yanked it from the servant's hands and flew down the stairs. "Dostoevsky's simply lost his mind!" Nekrasov told onlookers. Kraevsky paid Dostoevsky's debt.

He was writing constantly, producing a litany of stories—"Mr. Prokharchin," "The Landlady," "White Nights," and more. He wrote nonfiction pieces. He struggled with a novel about a girl, a gifted musician named Netochka Nezvanova, "Nameless Nobody." Some stories delved deeper into the madhouse. There were gothic tales featuring dark powers, obsessions, and premonitions. Belinsky wrote scathing reviews. Why did "Mr. Prokharchin" "have to be so affected, mannered, incomprehensible"? "The Landlady" features a sorcerer who collapses in an epileptic seizure. "What terrible rubbish!" Belinsky told a friend. One could scarcely distinguish between reality and delirium. "Everything is farfetched, exaggerated, stilted, spurious and false," he wrote. Privately, Belinsky regretted calling the young writer a genius. "I, the leading critic, behaved like an ass to the nth degree."

Dostoevsky had no time to absorb what was happening ("it's as though I'm in a daze"), and nothing was working. He sank into a depression. Then he fell ill. For months he had swollen glands and abscesses on his neck. He was pallid. He was weak and losing weight. His doctor told him he had scrofula and that his blood was in a "vicious" condition. He underwent two bloodlettings with leeches. He tried various decoctions, drops, and powders, but the illness lingered. Whatever it was, he wrote to Mikhail, it disrupted his entire nervous system, and it was headed right for his heart.

Doctors told him to lead a more tranquil life and to avoid high stimulation. Stop smoking. Eat healthy food. Get more sleep. He worried about fainting, about apoplexy, about "nervous fever." He had a rapid, irregular heartbeat. He started hallucinating—he kept hearing someone snoring next to him in bed. He felt that he was close to dying, though this was not new. When he was a child, he was terrified of being buried alive. He feared his parents would mistake a deep sleep for his untimely demise, so he left little notes asking them to wait five days before holding his funeral. You can never be too careful.

Now he spent sleepless nights reading about nervous illnesses, diseases of the brain, and phrenology. He borrowed medical books from a doctor he befriended and became engrossed in the anatomical drawings. He asked detailed questions about every cranial indentation, bump, and groove. What did they all mean? The doctor assured him that he had enviable eye socket margins and an occipital bone as smooth as Socrates's. Dostoevsky's habit of inspecting his body for small signs of morbidity carried over into everything. He magnified meaningless events and distorted innocent facts, which made his prescribed tranquility impossible. An ambiguous question in a social setting was enough to enrage him (*was it a trap?*), and his instinct was to flee before saying something he'd regret. Sometimes he fled preemptively. Early one morning, he went to see Kraevsky, and a servant led him into the drawing room to wait. When Kraevsky finally presented himself, Dostoevsky had disappeared.

B y the summer of 1847, Belinsky was too weak to walk without a cane. He had buried his infant son a couple of months earlier. "I am not living," he wrote to Turgenev, "but dying a slow death." Once, after a long and painful bout of coughing, he turned to a friend and asked, "What have I accomplished?"

Belinsky's faith in literature was rattled that year by the Russian writer he most admired—Nikolai Gogol. The novelist who had given Belinsky hope for a world-historical Russian literature published a selection of his supercilious, moralizing letters, and it surprised everyone who considered the author of *Dead Souls* to be a critic of Russian autocracy. Gogol called the Russian Orthodox Church an institution "sent directly from Heaven for the Russian people." He claimed that a Russian's salvation depends upon his or her patriotism. And the critics who praised *Dead Souls* had gotten it all wrong. Gogol fully supported serfdom. God made them serfs, he insisted. "They who were born under a power must submit to that power."

Belinsky considered the book an affront to himself and to all of literature. He spent three days writing a letter to Gogol. When he read it to friends, they were at turns electrified and alarmed. "One cannot keep silent," Belinsky wrote, "when lies and immorality are preached as truth and virtue." Russia's novelist of mordant laughter had become a champion of ignorance and tyranny. It was a betrayal. "I loved you," Belinsky told Gogol. Belinsky's letter became an invective against serfdom, religion, and tyranny. "What [Russia] needs is not sermons (she has heard enough of them!) or prayers (she has repeated them too often!), but the awakening in the people of a sense of their human dignity lost for so many centuries amid dirt and refuse."

It was Belinsky's own "First Philosophical Letter," a jeremiad to be circulated among friends. He wrote without fear and for a Russia that would carry on without him. It was his great accomplishment.

Several months later, Furious Vissarion, eyes huge and glittering, was impossibly thin and addressing, he imagined, the whole of the Russian people for hours. Later that day, Dostoevsky went to the apartment of his doctor friend. "Something really terrible has happened," Dostoevsky announced. "Belinsky is dead!" Dostoevsky spent the night. At three in the morning the doctor was woken up by the sounds of Dostoevsky in the midst of violent convulsions.

Four

Némésis

Maybe it all started with the gambling. Pierre-François Lacenaire went to Paris with a thousand francs, began playing *rouge et noir*, and nearly doubled his money at the tables. His luck continued in England and Scotland, but it wouldn't last. He sat down to play with fifteen hundred francs the evening he returned to Paris, and by eleven o'clock he had nothing. His older brother sent only advice, so he approached his aunt, who lent him three hundred francs. That vanished in an hour. She gave him another three hundred, and he managed to lose it in only two hands, forcing him to return home to Lyons a failure once again.

Lacenaire, by his own account, had gotten expelled from every school he attended. His father was an imperious man and a defender of authority—"more Catholic than the Pope," Lacenaire recalled, and "more Royalist than the King." The man had no patience for his wayward second son and treated him with a mixture of neglect and reproof. One day, after being caught forging a letter from his school principal, Lacenaire walked with his father through Lyons's Place des Terreaux. It was an execution day. "Look," his father said, pointing with his cane to the guillotine. "That is how you will end up unless you change." It was as if a spell had been cast. From that moment, Lacenaire recalled, he felt a bond between himself and the "ghastly engine." He sometimes called it his fiancée. There was something voluptuous about such a death.

He had tried, nevertheless, to earn money through honest labor. His father had sent him to work for an attorney when he finished his schooling. He spent about a-year sleeping in a room adjacent to the lawyer's apartment and taking his meals with the other clerks. He worked at a notary's office (six months). He worked at a bank (two years). He worked as a traveling salesman for a wine and spirits company. He hated every job, hated his coworkers, hated the fact that he had given up reading; he had been used to devouring poetry and novels ever since his days of skipping school. His daily tasks were turning him into "a complete automaton," he said. "Is he stupid?" one of the lawyer's partners asked, with some justification. His mind was always elsewhere.

He was twenty-one when he decided to move to Paris in 1824 to try his hand at literature. He wrote political songs, submitted unpaid articles to journals, and helped write a vaudeville. The show was produced and even enjoyed some success, but not as much as he had hoped, and it paid almost nothing. Lacenaire admitted to one great defect: "being haphazard and untidy in my accounts, and dreading an empty pocket."

After his gambling failures, he started forging bills of exchange. They totaled about ten thousand francs. He forged them in Paris, exchanged them for gold in Lyons, and told his older brother where he could find two bills bearing his own name, hoping he would buy them himself for the sake of the family's reputation.

His untidy accounts remained a problem. He owed six hundred francs to a friend who was being called up to the military. Because the loan left his friend unable to afford a substitute, Lacenaire enlisted in his place. He joined an infantry regiment as a rifleman, deployed to Greece, quarreled with his commanding officers, and served time in solitary confinement. He had enlisted and deserted from the army once before, and he deserted again soon after his battalion returned to France. Later, when asked why he didn't commit to a military career, Lacenaire responded, "Because I do not know how to obey."

Dissolution and gambling, throwaway jobs and army stints, seemed like a good way to bide time until he received his inheritance, at which point he could devote himself to "my beloved literature." His father had amassed a fortune of nearly half a million francs in the Lyons iron industry before Lacenaire was born. It was therefore a rather rude shock when he discovered that his father had gone bankrupt after ventures into the silk industry. His father had kept his declining fortunes a secret for years until an economic crisis in the late 1820s devastated the luxury goods industry and finally ruined him and his family. Lacenaire belatedly realized why his father had sent him to work for an attorney: he couldn't afford the tuition for law school.

Lacenaire found out about the bankruptcy after his second army desertion. The home was empty when he returned to Lyons. He had to seek out an aunt to discover that his family had moved to Belgium. His first thought was to go to America, but the five hundred francs his mother sent him wouldn't be enough, so he looked for a job in Paris. He tried journalism once again, but when he asked to be a paid contributor, editors refused. He was alone, his pockets were empty, and he was going hungry. Lacenaire took away one lesson from his reversal of fortune: "Beware: when you have nothing left, Society will reject you on every side."

It was around this time that he killed someone—almost by accident, you could say, another turn of fortune. Lacenaire fell into a dispute with the nephew of Benjamin Constant, a prominent politician and political philosopher who championed individual liberty and a limited but robust parliament. The details of the nephew's quarrel with Lacenaire are murky, but they decided to settle it with a duel in one of the ditches in the Champ de Mars. Lacenaire's opponent fired first, and for a split second, he assumed it was all over. Then he fired his own pistol, and the young Constant fell. "The sight of his agony caused me no emotion."

Lacenaire had tried to avoid the duel, but once it was over, the victory at his fortunes' nadir seemed like an auspicious sign. "Here, properly speaking, began my duel with Society," he later wrote. Lacenaire decided to become an outlaw, though he was less interested in committing crimes than in the allure of being a criminal, "a thief and an assassin," as he put it, "the scourge of Society."

He formulated a plan after reading Eugène-François Vidocq's recently published *Memoirs*. Vidocq had been a criminal turned police informant and, eventually, the founder and chief of the Sûreté Nationale, France's criminal investigation unit. His memoir details how he learned about his fellow inmates' exploits, and it was an immediate bestseller—an alarming exposé for a nation in the middle of ambitious penal reforms. France was enhancing its bureaucracies, establishing new prisons, and adopting a "scientific" approach to punishment that emphasized strict daily routine, moral instruction, and, most important, paid labor in prison workshops. The theory was that black-smithing, cutting marble, and producing domestic goods—umbrellas or cor-sets or rosary beads—would rehabilitate France's "dangerous classes" and eliminate crime. But the reformed prisons would remain full. Lacenaire read Vidocq's memoirs as a portrait of a community bunkered at society's core. There was, he realized, a fellowship of outlaws waiting for him, and prison was where he could find a partner for a murder, which was what he really wanted. It's difficult to be a scourge all by oneself.

Getting himself imprisoned would be the beginning of a new life. "I could establish thus a line of eternal separation between me and the world," he later wrote. "I should cross the Rubicon." So one morning in June 1829, Lacenaire told the keeper at a livery stable that he wanted to hire a cabriolet for the day. As they rode out, he directed the young driver to a building and asked him to take a letter up to his friend on the third floor. While he was delivering it, Lacenaire jumped into the driver's seat and sent the horse galloping off to a man he'd met the evening before, a man who could find someone willing to pay three hundred francs for a nice black carriage with a suspicious registra-tion.

A few days later, a notice appeared in a newspaper, *Le Constitutionnel*: a man, twenty-eight to thirty years old, wearing a brown frock coat, had stolen a carriage and bay horse in broad daylight. "M. Arthemise urges the public to be good enough to give him all the information that may facilitate the re-covery of property necessary for his livelihood and that of his family." It was a small taste of fame. Lacenaire was arrested days later, after aiding his own capture. He led the driver to his aunt's building, signed an invoice to add condemnatory evidence, hung around the same café for days, and openly iden-tified himself as the thief to M. Arthemise.

Once detained at the depot prison, Lacenaire pretended to be a hardened criminal, to be inured to the stench, indifferent to cabbage soup, familiar with the gangs and subcultures. Seasoned criminals enjoyed small tributes and spe-cial protection while first-time offenders were harassed and isolated. The social hierarchy was inverted. Outside, felons were nothing. In here they were esteemed. Even the guards granted privileges to serious felons and ignored petty criminals' complaints. Lacenaire spoke so casually about his crime that he seemed to be hiding more serious offenses and concealing his real identity, which, in a way, was true. Ex-convicts said they recognized him from prior prison stints, and he would half-heartedly deny it. He spoke as little as possible to everyone except the jail's "eminences," partly to garner respect and partly because he simply didn't know how to talk. "A thief who doesn't know the slang is nobody," Lacenaire said. He got through the first few days on a handful of words he remembered from Vidocq's *Memoirs*.

Thus began Lacenaire's education in what he called "the science of crime." He studied the manner of smugglers and pickpockets, the methods of forgers, the code of conduct that killers shared. "In four days' time," he said, "I knew not only the slang but nearly all the ways of stealing." It was a great accomplishment. The correctional tribunal sentenced him to a year in prison, which brought him through an array of penal institutions: from the depot prison to La Force, from La Force to Bicêtre, and from Bicêtre to Poissy.

He soon realized his mistake. Prison, he said, "utterly disgusted me and every moment was torture." He was surrounded by scum. How could he find a partner here? He wanted an accomplice who was not yet brutalized by prison, a man who admired him so much that he would happily be his "docile instrument." The petty criminals indulged impractical fantasies, and the serious offenders were effectively serving death sentences, beaten down by incarceration, their wits and senses dulled. He found a handful of trustworthy people, but it would be many years before they could join another criminal enterprise.

His craving for books reemerged as his criminal ambitions faded. Unfortunately, there were no books in prison—they distracted from work— so Lacenaire abandoned himself to poetry. He often destroyed what he wrote, but small portions of his earlier work survive. One poem, "La sylphide," is a song for an unattainable love whom he has dreamed about since his youth. Each stanza ends in a forlorn refrain: "Vierge immortelle, attends-moi dans les cieux." ("Immortal virgin, wait for me in heaven.") Writing nevertheless made him happy—"happier perhaps than I had ever been in this world," he recalled. Poetry mysteriously lifted him up, out of prison, above humanity. He became so absorbed in writing that he stopped working. This had happened to him before. He was locked in a cell in his high school for getting into a fistfight with one of the school's priests. During his two weeks of detention, he wrote two thousand lines of verse.

When one of the officials at La Force suggested he send his poetry to a certain philanthropist, Lacenaire took the opportunity. The man responded by sending money and asking to see Lacenaire when he was released; he wanted to help. No one had been so kind to him. The gesture made him consider rejoining society, but only briefly: "I hoped that the ill I had come here to seek out had not been altogether wasted."

Prison release brought Lacenaire no joy. Writing poetry instead of toiling in the workshops meant that he had earned virtually no money. He was discharged with five francs and some clothes his aunt had sent, but when he went to visit her, she was gone. Everyone else he visited refused to see him. The philanthropist's servant relayed the message—repeatedly—that his master was not receiving visitors. So the ex-convict traded his clothes for an inferior set and some money. He went days without food and walked all night with no place to sleep.

Lacenaire spent the next few years swerving in and out of the criminal world. He adopted several aliases. He claimed to be Swiss. He got deeper into forgeries and petty scams, usually with former prison mates. He blackmailed homosexuals—"a curious kind of business," he confessed, something Chardon himself might have done. Lacenaire and a partner would pose as police officers in the Champs-Élysées and arrest "men with shameful vices" whom they caught in flagrante delicto. Sometimes they paid a young man to coax their targets into the act.

He kept returning to legitimate employment. He found work as a public letter writer drawing up petitions after the July Revolution. People were asking for recompense or decorations or jobs for the valiant role they played in toppling Charles X's regime and ushering in King Louis-Philippe. "I conspired against the fallen government!" "I killed so many Royal Guards!" The petitions gave him a firsthand glimpse into humanity's knavery and selfishness, and he could never have dreamed up so many lies and betrayals. It was the only job he ever enjoyed.

When it ended, he began a six-month spree of skeleton key thefts and gambling stints that never paid off. This taught him a valuable lesson about his great resilience: "I am gifted with such power over my imagination that when a misfortune is irreparable I immediately forget it."

Lacenaire was impervious enough to misfortune to try breaking into the literary world again. He wrote poetry for a magazine called *Némésis*, a satirical weekly that regularly attacked King Louis-Philippe. The satisfaction of getting paid was diminished by the fact that he was ghostwriting for the magazine's editor, Auguste-Marseille Barthélemy, who couldn't keep up with his issues. Lacenaire spent two years as a legal copyist at the Palais de Justice before becoming an "itinerant scribe," finding work wherever he could get it, though he never sacrificed his literary standards. When two playwrights commissioned him to make a fair copy of their play, he returned it the following day, refusing to work on it. "It's too stupid," he told them.

Lacenaire turned to violence on the night of Mi-Carême, the mid-Lenten carnival, in 1833. Parisians in costumes were drinking and celebrating at masked balls and along the *Boeuf Gras* procession. Revelers led a large ox through the streets followed by a child in a blue scarf and several fantastically dressed butchers. It was easy to be overlooked. Lacenaire and a former Poissy prison mate were waiting outside a Palais Royal gambling house with sharpened files.

They were watching a gambler with a consistent schedule, a regular route home, and a reliably large amount of cash in his pockets. They followed him through a glass-covered arcade with shops, ventriloquists, and magicians. He strolled with a friend a bit before continuing, alone, toward Place Ventadour. It was deserted, the stalls shuttered and quiet as the city's attention concentrated on the larger boulevards' revelry. The gambler decided to take a piss. Suddenly, Lacenaire's partner bolted toward their target, spun him around, and stabbed him. "Murder!" the gambler screamed repeatedly. A nearby window flew open, and the criminals ran. This was all wrong. They were supposed to sneak up, stab him from behind, and strip him of his money—likely thousands of francs. Now they had nothing but blood and witnesses.

Failure never diminished Lacenaire's ambition. After the botched robbery, he was developing detailed plans for a heist at Versailles involving 300,000 francs. So it must have been humiliating that when Lacenaire was arrested again, it was for stealing pieces of silverware from a restaurant. The typical trick was to stick utensils to the bottom of a table with wax and return for them later, when the search was off. But the trick failed.

When he was booked in La Force, he gave his name as Henri Vialet, born in Geneva, both parents dead. He claimed to be a bookkeeper by trade and homeless in Paris. The authorities recorded his ensemble: a yellow vest with a black cravat, a brown frock coat, and blue pants. In July 1833, he was sentenced to thirteen months in prison.

The persistent rumble of discontent with the July Monarchy made political prisoners fairly common. Lacenaire was serving time in La Force with a man named Vigouroux, the manager of a liberal magazine called *Le Bon Sens.* Vigouroux had sentenced to four months for offending public morals and supporting regicide. Both charges stemmed from his decision to publish an article seemingly sympathetic to a man recently guillotined for attempting to kill the king. The article was called "Encore une tête!" The jurors deliberated for ten minutes.

Vigouroux took an interest in Lacenaire, his manner, his speech, and, eventually, his writing—Lacenaire was composing song lyrics at the time, and they were quite good. Vigouroux gave Lacenaire his address and asked him to send any songs he happened to write. "When you get out," he added, "come and see me." He was sure he could help a poet like Lacenaire earn an honest living.

"What about my record?"

"Rest easy," he said. The men he worked with were "above prejudice—real philanthropists." In fact, Vigouroux had already spread the word about him.

He was about to embark upon a literary career—"it was my whole dream of happiness come true." Lacenaire wrote assiduously. He sold his bread so he could buy paper. Two months later, after Vigouroux was released, Lacenaire sent him more than a dozen songs—enough for a small volume. There were songs about financiers and members of the court brought low by fate. "Ce qui vient au son de la flûte / S'en retourne au bruit du tambour." ("What comes with the sound of the flute / Goes away with the beat of the drum.") One song, "A Thief's Petition to His Majesty," implied that there was no difference between a thief in the galleys ("J'ai le cœur dur et l'âme vile"—"I have a hard heart and a vile soul") and the police and the king's ministers and even the king himself—exactly the sort of message that men above prejudice would appreciate. Vigouroux responded a few weeks later:

> Monsieur,
>   I have received the manuscript of songs which you have sent to me. I am actively setting about making use of it, and I expect, in a few days, to inform you of a result _beyond your desires_.

After ten days of silence, Lacenaire wrote to Vigouroux, postage due. Perhaps a letter had gotten lost? Was the collection being published? Was payment forthcoming? His letter was returned unopened. Some time later, Vigouroux wrote with good news: he found a printer, and he needed a preface. Lacenaire quickly sent one. A three-month silence followed, despite Lacenaire's pleas. "Be persuaded, sir, that I will strive to deserve the benevolence that you show me." An incarcerated man will keep himself on the hook for a good while. Vigouroux eventually urged the poet to have courage: "My friends and I will do whatever we can to raise you up in your own eyes and bring you back to society."

When Lacenaire was released from Poissy in August 1834, the first person he went to see was Vigouroux. Lacenaire's former prison mate rounded up thirty francs and respectable clothes, said nothing about the song collection, and suggested that Lacenaire could write articles for _Le Bon Sens_. They'd pay him twenty-five francs per article. But he shouldn't come around to the office, he said. He should come only to his home, and he should come only at night. When Lacenaire asked about full employment with _Le Bon Sens_, Vigouroux offered him the chance to deliver the magazine. ("Me! Deliver the magazine!")

He did write one article for them, though. It was about what it's like for a young man to walk into a prison for the first time, to be alone, engulfed by a loathsome mass of criminals—"incorrigible rogues, wasps of the community, a gangrened people"—until closer inspection reveals all the society's various ranks and its narrow path to respect. A newly arriving prisoner isn't a hardened criminal yet, Lacenaire wrote, "but you may be sure that the first step is taken." The editors were pleased to publish it. When Lacenaire went to collect his payment, however, Vigouroux had to relay the editorial board's unfortunate decision. "Because you are a beginner," the manager told him, "they can only pay you five francs an article."

Lacenaire discovered the final insult much later: Vigouroux had already published a few of his songs and had been handing them around to friends looking for material. "A Thief's Petition to His Majesty" wound up in a collection of songs called *Les Républicaines*. It was published without attribution, without pay, and in an altered form. It was a disaster. But then the collection was banned, and the publisher was fined and imprisoned for six months for offending the person of the king. If only he had known sooner that the disaster would become such a triumph.

After receiving his five francs, Lacenaire, when asked who he was, began responding, "I am a thief by profession."

Five

The Petrashevsky Circle

In February 1848, the political order that ruled most of Europe began to fall apart on the streets of Paris. The French had been expressing their discontent with King Louis-Philippe's government with increasingly forceful words at increasingly public gatherings organized as banquets because political assemblies were illegal. Food, wine, and singing accompanied speeches cheered by hundreds of boisterous reformers. When the government banned a banquet in February, political frustration turned into street protests, hurled stones, skirmishes with soldiers, and then a death, an old woman knocked down by municipal guards.

By nightfall, Parisians were building thousands of barricades throughout central and eastern Paris. Planks and beams and iron railings were ballasted down by casks filled with paving stones and padded out with whatever people had—furniture, toppled carts, doors, mattresses. Men with old or looted weapons fired shots into the air, and in the heat of battle women stood atop the barricades waving flags. Troop movement was largely cut off. Revolutionaries seized police headquarters and replaced the corps with barricade fighters and political prisoners. Mobs stormed the Tuileries and ransacked the king's palace while demanding a republic. In just two days, Louis-Philippe abdicated the throne and fled to England.

Violence quickly spread across multiple cities—Munich, Vienna, Berlin, Krakow, Venice, Prague. Dozens of outbreaks across Europe featured similar demands: a constitution, civil liberties, voting rights, meaningful legislative assemblies. In Budapest, twenty thousand people stormed Buda Castle, liberated political prisoners, and chanted a nationalist poem's refrain. "We vow, we vow that we will be slaves no longer!" Riots and barricade fighting led to assaults upon tax collectors, nobles, employers, and creditors. Debtors seized promissory notes and burned them in the streets. Serf uprisings shook central and eastern Europe. Some peasants refused to pay their obligations. Others plundered estates and destroyed the charters certifying their bondage. Smiths and grinders wrecked factories. Porters sabotaged railroad tracks. Boatmen in Rhine River villages would open fire on steamships. Forest riots and land occupations spread deep into the countryside. Officials investigating a land occupation in an Italian province encountered several hundred women blocking the roadway under the Italian tricolor flag. They were demanding land and bread. "Long live the constitution," they shouted, "long live Italy!"

Hunger instigated the revolutions; 1846 was the worst grain crop in three decades. Years of poor harvests led to hundreds of food riots, and malnourishment exacerbated a cholera pandemic. The spike in food prices punctured demand for all other goods, which led to a financial panic and mass unemployment. Industrialization worsened the crisis. The process pauperized the workers it required by abandoning them to the whims of erratic business cycles and two decades of falling wages.

Everything seems broken when you're hungry. Governments were overthrown and republics declared seemingly every month. Slovaks, Czechs, Croats, Serbs, and Romanians demanded their own nation-states. Assemblies across the Austrian Empire declared the end of serfdom. Pope Pius IX fled Rome. Bavaria's king, Ludwig, abdicated after crowds stormed his residence. Prince Bibescu fled Bucharest for Transylvania. Prince Metternich, the chancellor of the Austrian Empire—and perhaps the most powerful symbol of the old order—resigned just minutes before the deadline that revolutionaries gave him.

Though elections were held across Europe, full democracy was elusive. Property restrictions often remained, and women were denied voting rights despite all their sacrifices storming palaces and castles, smuggling ammunition and intelligence in hollowed-out bread loaves, and dying on the barricades they helped build. One Parisian feminist leader, Jeanne Deroin, ran for France's

National Assembly as a socialist until the government declared her candidacy unconstitutional. She received fifteen votes anyway.

Elections were often unsatisfactory. France elected a moderate assembly that infuriated French liberals, and soon Parisians were rebelling against the republic they had just created. But this time the National Guard fought back in earnest, shelling the barricades (now ten to fifteen feet high) and storming through the breaches. Three days of combat in June 1848 left thousands dead. After months of turmoil, everything was in flux—the control of property, the distribution of power, the organization of industry, the scope of civil liberties, the flow of goods and food.

I t took nearly two weeks for news of the initial Paris revolt to reach St. Petersburg. Tsar Nicholas burst into his son's palace ballroom in the middle of Shrovetide celebrations, shouting excitedly. Reports rippled through the city within hours. One writer recalled the word spreading during an opera performance: "Suddenly, like an electric spark, the news penetrated the whole audience." In cafés, people fought over newspapers or stood on chairs while reading articles aloud to others who gathered to listen to the machinery of history turn.

To Dostoevsky, the 1848 revolutions seemed senseless. "The age-old order of things is cracking and shattering," he wrote. "At every moment the most fundamental principles of society threaten to collapse, sweeping the whole nation with them as they fall." France was beginning to enact the theories that its great *philosophes* had developed for so long. "Every day," Dostoevsky wrote, "thirty-six million people risk all their future, their property, their own existence and that of their children, gambling on it all as if they were at a card game!"

Tsar Nicholas intended to keep order. He issued a manifesto to his people: "After invoking the help of God Almighty, we are ready to meet our enemies, wherever they may appear, and, without sparing ourselves, we shall, in indissoluble union with our Holy Russia, defend the honor of the Russian name and the inviolability of our borders." "God is with us!" he concluded. He read it with tears in his eyes.

More than the hunger, the violence, and the instability, the most alarming development of 1848 was the spread of political consciousness. New forms of association—political clubs, secret societies, trade unions—engaged in sophisticated political activities, from petitions to demonstrations. Problems once considered inevitable, such as poverty and famine, now seemed to be the consequence of state mismanagement, and greater state power led to demands for greater accountability. Few things are more threatening to an authoritarian regime than a phalanx of hungry women on the roadways demanding bread and a constitution simultaneously.

Ideas did this. Newspapers made Europeans more aware of the wider world, and books detailed the possibilities for that world. The very circulation of ideas created another idea: the idea of a public, the sense that you are a part of a social singularity, and the act of reading, of being addressed by a writer, assumes and strengthens that singularity. Being part of a public encouraged readers to connect personal problems and national problems, the immediate and the abstract, food and a bill of rights. This is what the tsar intended to stop.

Russian officials drastically cut university enrollments, which had more than doubled since 1836. Philosophy was banned from the curriculum. So was constitutional law. Universities were lucky to remain open at all. Non-noble students were unwelcome, and books were only occasionally welcome. The state publication listing banned books required constant updates because roughly six hundred new titles were added every month—a separate publication singled out forbidden French books. Shops and libraries were searched throughout the empire. Editors were summoned to ministry offices and upbraided for the "general unsoundness" of their journals' content. Kraevsky responded to the new pressures by vowing to make *Notes of the Fatherland* an "organ of the government."

The tsar's ideal society would surveil itself. In the spring of 1848, Nicholas addressed a gathering of Petersburg nobles: "Gentlemen! I have no police, I do not like them. You are my police." He implored the nobles to report transgressors to him directly, "and then we shall be invincible."

Everyone knew perfectly well that the tsar had his police, and everyone knew exactly where to find them: in the rear section of an unremarkable building on the Fontanka canal, a place with interrogation rooms and holding cells, a place rumored to have trapdoors and subterranean torture chambers. This was the headquarters of what was known as the Third Section—the tsar's secret police.

This is where accusations began flowing in. Denunciation was a powerful counterpublic force, a way to turn Russians' loyalty to the tsar into isolating secrecy, paranoia, and recrimination. "People lived as if they were in hiding," one writer lamented, which made revolutions rather unlikely.

Nicholas created the Third Section shortly after his coronation, and he charged it with supplying exhaustive political intelligence gathered from statistics, covert surveillance, and broad investigations. It ordered postmasters to open mail and copy any suspicious contents. It reported on young people's immoral behavior, an early sign of disloyalty. It investigated thousands of denunciations a year. Investigations were carried out by the Corps of Gendarmes— sixty units of soldiers doubling as civil law enforcers. The corps was designed to be "feared and respected." Nicholas's political police were not to be compared with Ivan the Terrible's political enforcers, who rode through towns in black robes and bearing severed dogs' heads dangling from their saddles. Gendarmes wore distinctive blue uniforms. They were selected in part for their appearance and recruited from only the most respected families.

Part of the Third Section's job was to control ideas. It was the Third Section that had Chaadaev declared insane, his censor dismissed, and his editor exiled. It bribed editors and writers. It threatened them or "interviewed" them. After Belinsky was denounced (falsely, by a rival editor), authorities carefully monitored his waning health, and strange people were present at his small funeral. The Third Section had its own methods, enforced its own unwritten standards, and overruled censors in order to eliminate atheism and disloyalty.

Nicholas had good reasons to fear revolution. Russia was experiencing its own destabilizing cycle of hunger and disease. Its harsh climate generated lower grain yields than Europe, and the 1848 harvests were creating famine conditions. Russians were migrating in search of food. The cholera pandemic was also worse in Russia. It would ultimately kill 700,000 Russians, and there was no telling if riots would break out the way they did during the 1831 outbreak.

Even in the absence of such threats, Nicholas had authoritarian instincts— as a child he reportedly axed his toys to pieces and beat his playmates with a stick—and Russia had long favored autocrats. A strong ruler was, in fact, a part of Russia's national mythology, and many Russians considered it central to their identity and their world-historical purpose. The myth of Russian autocracy goes back to the thirteenth century, when Russia was a collection of

Slavic princedoms conquered by the Mongolian Empire's Golden Horde. For more than two centuries, the princedoms of the Rus' were the vassal states of nomadic invaders that they vastly outnumbered. The Golden Horde's khans demanded obeisance from the princes and tribute from their people. Mongol horsemen raided and destroyed their cities, including Kiev and Moscow, until the Mongol Empire receded in the fifteenth century.

It seemed, in retrospect, that the princedoms endured because the princes quashed their political infighting by submitting to a single ruler unconditionally. It seemed as if a unified Russia under a strong tsar saved European civilization from a Muslim empire. Russians found their purpose in Muscovy's formative era: they were the bulwark against invading Mongol hordes.

It hardly mattered that this wasn't true (the Mongols were defeated by their own internal divisions, Muscovy's rise happened after the Golden Horde's decline, and the Mongols invaded Europe quite successfully). Empires need a myth, and the Russian myth was about the power of obedience to save Christian civilization. For centuries, members of the Muscovite court referred to themselves as "slaves of the tsar." They bowed deeply in greeting, in petition, or in gratitude, sometimes touching the ground with their fingertips, sometimes striking their heads in abasement. Nicholas's uniforms and military parades were displays of the power of obedience updated for the nineteenth century. And now that widespread violence and protests for voting rights and constitutions were shattering "the age-old order of things," as Dostoevsky put it, Russia considered itself Europe's bulwark of stability once again. Though instead of being a bulwark against invading hordes, it would be a bulwark against invasive ideas, against the rise of a political consciousness.

Dostoevsky's own political consciousness had been forming under pressure from various influences, including the left-leaning ideas of Belinsky's circle and his increasing isolation from it. Those influences shifted one day in the spring of 1846, when a man named Mikhail Petrashevsky ran after Dostoevsky as he was leaving a café. "What is your idea for your next story, if I may take the liberty of asking?" Petrashevsky's introduction seemed innocuous, but it would lead Dostoevsky down a path to illegal political activity—revolutionary activity—and change his life forever.

Petrashevsky was both courteous and contemptuous, evasive and forceful. He wore a beard and long hair (both against regulations). He was eccentric— "original," Dostoevsky called him—but he had the sort of depth and intelligence that Dostoevsky found intriguing. He was educated at the Alexander Lyceum, Russia's most exclusive secondary school, where officials labeled him "an extremely obstinate character with a liberal mode of thought." He graduated with the lowest possible rank, a distinction that might have pleased him.

Petrashevsky stalked the streets of Petersburg in a long black cape and a bandit's hat, as one friend described it, and Dostoevsky always found him in the midst of some urgent, unspecified errand. He was the type of person who accumulated rumors. He supposedly owned several pistols and conducted target practice inside his apartment by shooting out a candle at various distances. He celebrated Jesus's death as if it were the resurrection—rum punch, Easter cake, and all. A circle of people gathered at his house weekly for clandestine discussions. He once walked into Kazan Cathedral dressed as a woman and sat among the female worshippers until a police officer approached. "Madam," the officer reputedly said, "it seems to me that you are a man"—the beard betrayed him.

Some things were certain. Petrashevsky owned two Petersburg properties and an estate with several hundred serfs. He was rejected for a teaching job at the lyceum on the grounds that he intended to "spread liberal ideas." He was steeped in French utopian socialism, in writers who began with the Hegelian idea that history culminates in freedom and who explored what that freedom could be. Representative democracy, perhaps. Or universal human rights. Or progressive taxation. Or the end of property and marriage.

When teaching didn't pan out, Petrashevsky spread liberal ideas by disguising them as harmless entries in *A Pocket Dictionary of Foreign Words Introduced into the Russian Language*, which he wrote and compiled with several people—all anonymous. Tucked in between anodyne foreign words ("labyrinth," "critic," "oasis") were definitions of subversive ideas: "materialism," "anarchy," "commune," "constitution." "Normal state" was defined, in part, as a government that "provides each of its members with means for the satisfaction of their needs in proportion to their demands." This was not how the tsar defined it. Almost any word could inspire seditious lexicography. "Bastille," "guillotine," and "barricade" valorized the French Revolution. "Negro" and "Negrophile" indirectly deplored the evils of serfdom. The first volume of the *Pocket Dictionary* (*A–Mar*) escaped official notice when it appeared in 1845, but the Chief Directorate of Censorship caught on when the second volume (*Mar–Ord*) was published the following year. Officials summarily banned *A Pocket Dictionary of Foreign Words*, and every copy they could seize was burned.

By then Petrashevsky had become a prophet of utopian socialism and representative democracy. He advocated reform to friends and acquaintances, to strangers in taverns and clubs, at balls and masquerades. He joined the Tradesmen's Dance Society so he could chat about political economy between mazurkas. He helped set up a law firm to take cases from impoverished Russians pro bono.

Then he went further. In February 1848, the month the Paris uprisings began, Petrashevsky distributed a petition to St. Petersburg's Nobles' Assembly. It was ostensibly a proposal to make land available to non-noble buyers, but buried in his nine-point plan was a stipulation that those buyers would have to convert the serfs on their new land into free tenant farmers. It incentivized emancipation. The influx of new buyers would raise land values, so the gentry would grow wealthy, merchants could be landowners, and at least some serfs would be freed—it was a win-win-win. But when the assembly leader sent Petrashevsky's proposal to the tsar, Nicholas banned all discussion of it—public or private. He saw it for what it was: a brazen attempt to upend Russia's class structure. If the tsar didn't know about Mikhail Petrashevsky before, he knew about him now. He was placed under surveillance.

There was one rumor about Petrashevsky that Dostoevsky knew was true: he really did hold meetings at his apartment on Sadovaya Street. The small gatherings, always on Friday nights, grew to ten or fifteen people by 1848. It was known as the Petrashevsky Circle. Dostoevsky had begun attending in the spring of 1847, and he brought his brother Mikhail after he moved to Petersburg that fall. The Dostoevsky brothers encountered a heterogeneous crowd: chinovniks and junior military officers, teachers and university students, petty merchants, writers, tradesmen, and several nobles, mostly impoverished.

One, however, was quite wealthy. Nikolai Speshnev was a friend of Petrashevsky's from the lyceum, likely a partner in mischief, for while Petrashevsky graduated with the lowest rank, Speshnev managed to get himself expelled. This did not diminish his erudition or worldliness. Speshnev spent several years traveling in Europe, and stories circulated about his alleged exploits abroad (that he associated with radicals and secret societies, that he had fought in a war). He, too, was the type who accumulated rumors. Speshnev was keenly intelligent, impeccably dressed, and enviably handsome. He had a neatly trimmed beard and long, dark hair flowing in waves down to his shoulders. One person thought he looked like Jesus. He was charismatic and almost preternaturally calm. He rarely spoke at Petrashevsky's meetings, which was enough to make him stand out.

The first freedom of the Petrashevsky Circle was the freedom to think ambitiously, to share big ideas and debate. Someone would stand up to speak about Adam Smith or athiesm or legislative assemblies. Informal discussion would follow. Supper would be served around nine, followed by glasses of wine, rum, and cognac, which would lead to talk of the news, or rumors of news, about the revolutions, or about socialism and atheism. People argued zealously, for its own sake, as if they had briefly escaped the tsarist world. Finally, at three or four in the morning, the Petrashevists would disperse, taking cabs back to various quarters of the city.

Many nights centered on Charles Fourier's utopian socialism, which offered an enticingly easy solution to pervasive social problems. The key to a harmonious society, Fourier argued, is gratifying human desires instead of restraining them. Fourierism rested on three premises: that human nature is unchanging, scientifically discoverable, and essentially good. Crime exists because society warps human nature, leading to warring nations, unhappily monogamous marriages, and inefficient labor. In its place, Fourier imagined self-sufficient, self-governing communes. One thousand six hundred twenty carefully selected people would live in one massive structure—a phalanstery—with enclosed, climate-controlled streets and underground tunnels. A dining hall, library, and worship spaces would occupy the center of the building. One wing would house workshops, another would have shopping, yet another would have ballrooms and meeting spaces. Phalansteries would be so clean that caterpillars and other insects would disappear. Economies of scale would generate unprecedented wealth. Instead of three hundred kitchens, there would be three. Gratifying, voluntary work would replace "*monastic-industrial* discipline." Property would remain—you could buy shares in the commune—but stealing would be unnecessary because everyone would be wealthy. Even children ("so essentially robbers of fruit") would leave apple trees unmolested.

Fourierism was systematized romanticism, Rousseau in the hands of a bureaucrat, but for the Petrashevists it was a way to supplant tsarism without barricades. Phalansteries would render the state superfluous. Even discussing Fourierism felt freeing. It was a fantasy, a game of political economy with messianic promise.

Dostoevsky enjoyed the discussions, but he was particularly drawn to Petrashevsky's collective library. Subscribers contributed about twenty silver rubles—a substantial sum—for borrowing privileges, and Petrashevsky bought books from a French bookseller with connections in Paris. In a few years it became the largest multilingual library of philosophy and economics in Russia. "Expensive editions were piled on the floor, the tables and the window sills," one person recalled. Many of the books were illegal, and the bulk of the collection was French. More than a hundred books were about socialism, and nearly half of those were about Fourierism. The shelves contained several volumes authored by members of the Free Ones—Feuerbach, Bruno Bauer, Max Stirner. Dostoevsky withdrew books by or about various socialists, from Fourier and Henri de Saint-Simon to Étienne Cabet and Louis Blanc. He read several books by Proudhon, and he explored atheism in David Friedrich Strauss's *Life of Jesus, Critically Examined*.

Dostoevsky started coming to Petrashevsky's gatherings more regularly in the fall of 1848, when the revolutions expanded the circle. There were strange faces nearly every week, and people were increasingly outspoken. A few Petrashevists tried including women (two clever women are worth five hundred men, one Petrashevist argued), but they ultimately decided that mixed company was too radical. The only acceptable lady was a figure of liberty carved into the handle of a bell that an elected chairman rang to keep order. Speshnev suggested the bell after discussions became difficult to control. Petrashevsky established a speaking schedule. They arranged chairs in a semi-circle or set up a small stage and rows of seating. Pencils and paper were available for people to write objections.

One night in November, a Siberian gold prospector with a wooden leg showed up to share tales of his exploits on battlefields and in peasant revolts.

Siberians were not under the tsar's thumb, he claimed, unlike Petersburgers. "Our trouble, gentlemen, Russians' trouble is that we have gotten quite used to the stick—we think nothing of it."

"It's a stick with two ends," Speshnev responded.

Dostoevsky thought the man was too much of a type to be authentic. "The devil knows," Dostoevsky later told Speshnev, "this man speaks Russian exactly as Gogol writes it." Then he leaned in closer to Speshnev and said the man must be a spy.

After the prospector's appearance, it was as if a seal had been broken. Some Petrashevists proposed studying socialist and utopian ideas systematically. One person declared his willingness to die for revolution in Russia. Someone else delivered a blasphemous speech arguing that the origin of all religion is irrational fear. A university student named Pavel Filippov referred to "our system of propaganda" without fully explaining what he meant. A lieutenant in the Life Guards, Nikolai Mombelli, declared that 1848 had split Europe in two: France was forging a path toward liberty, and Russia maintained the path of despotism and evil. "Emperor Nikolai is not a man but a monster," Mombelli insisted, "a wild beast, he is that Antichrist of whom it is spoken in the Apocalypse." Another Petrashevist went further: the tsars, their armies, their laws, their temples, and the entire state should all perish.

The meetings became less about revolutionary theory and more about revolutionary methods—whether to attack the tsar directly, for example, or to foment revolution from below. There was a growing sense that they were responsible for cultivating Russia's revolutionary strategies. The Petrashevists were part of a network of people in similar circles who believed they could solve national problems by studying them carefully, that genuine reform could happen with some combination of bravery, philosophical insight, and bureaucratic skill. Petrashevists were enthralled when a teacher named Jastrzembsky advanced socialist principles through a series of talks about statistics. And because even listening had consequences, every speech bound the members more tightly—the Third Section could storm in at any moment. The risks they took to discuss national affairs forged a sense of identity, as if these assorted people were forming a distinct class of purpose-driven Russians, a class that would eventually be expressed in a new word with Russian origins: "intelligentsia."

Petrashevsky found himself in the unlikely role of taming immoderate discussions and reminding people that revolutionaries would be hanged. He had to convince the Siberian gold prospector that, no, his gatherings were not a cover for a secret society. Before long, Mombelli presented Petrashevsky and Speshnev with a plan to create exactly what the prospector had in mind—an organization with secret cells, a central committee, an oath of allegiance, and written biographies to increase the society's leverage over each member.

Petrashevsky rejected the idea out of hand. He believed in gradual reform through persuasion. He believed that spreading truth would liberalize society. He believed in charm offensives, radical libraries, and subversive dictionaries rather than armed insurrection. When a University of Petersburg student named Peter Antonelli asked Petrashevsky, "Wouldn't it be a good thing to throw a few pamphlets into the army?" Petrashevsky told him it was a horrible idea. He advised Antonelli to spread republican ideas in the Caucasus or perhaps infiltrate an educational institution. He helped Antonelli compose a pro-republican tract and offered him books on "the true teaching method."

Petrashevsky's emphasis on public instruction sparked an argument with Dostoevsky—apparently the only open argument Dostoevsky ever had in the Petrashevsky Circle. The host advised the circle's authors to write more plainly, and he singled out Dostoevsky as someone who should hone his socialist message. Someone else piled on after supper, claiming litterateurs were proud, trivial men frittering away their time. Dostoevsky rarely spoke at Petrashevsky's, but, with Mikhail by his side, he fired back: literature doesn't need to be so programmatic because art inevitably moves beyond the aesthetic. "The author only has to worry about the artistic aspect," Dostoevsky replied, "and the idea will come out by itself."

But Dostoevsky did not join the Petrashevsky Circle to defend literature. He joined it to end serfdom. Russian socialism had little to do with overthrowing the bourgeoisie—Russia hardly had a bourgeoisie to overthrow. Rather, it meant overthrowing feudalism. Russia was an agricultural empire dependent upon millions of serfs bound forever to plots of land they could never own and paying their landlords in stints of labor or portions of crops or wages. They were the landowners' permanent capital assets. The values of enserfed people were set by law—a calf was worth more than a one-year-old child—and enserfed women were forced into marriages their landlords arranged,

sometimes by picking names from a list. God apparently sanctioned the institution. When a serf ran away, there was a patron saint to whom a serf holder
could pray to speed the serf's capture.

The Petrashevists opposed serfdom, but Dostoevsky was especially vehe-
ment. Serfs were legally allowed to be beaten so long as the punishment wasn't
"unreasonable," and Dostoevsky recoiled at the thought of peasants being
whipped like animals. It was no wonder that violent uprisings flared and that
serfs burned down estates or murdered their landlords, ambushing them in
large groups, perhaps, and dumping their bodies in roadside fields. Serf holders were corrupted by their power, whether they were petty tyrants or sympathetic reformers or demanding loved ones. Dostoevsky always remembered
his first trip to St. Petersburg with his father. He saw a drunken government
courier emerge from a way station, leap into his coach, and start punching his
coachman in the back of his neck relentlessly—not in anger, really, just by habit.
The coachman began lashing his lead horse just as ruthlessly as the coach tore
off down the road at top speed. Violence circulates until it touches everyone.
Dostoevsky wanted that to end.

Whatever one's reasons, opposing serfdom in 1849 was a clear threat to the
throne. The tsar required a strong and faithful elite to maintain power, and
the Russian elite needed serfs, which constituted a large portion of landowners'
wealth as well as the collateral for their loans. As time went on, more and
more serfs were held by fewer noble families, who were increasingly indebted,
so the most powerful elites—the ones closest to the tsar—needed serfdom the
most. The entire empire depended upon serfdom. As Europe industrialized,
it increasingly relied upon Russian agriculture (it was nearly 90 percent of
Russia's exports by 1860). It was the serfs who harvested Russia's crops. It was
the serfs who generated the empire's wealth. It was the serfs who paid the
empire's taxes (nobles weren't taxed at all), and it was the serfs who manned
all the battalions of the tsar's army. Russia was a feudal empire.

In April 1849, a weeks-long argument about serf emancipation unspooled
among the Petrashevists. One night, Petrashevsky insisted that they focus on
judicial reforms, which would benefit all of Russia, and then they could free
the serfs simply by beseeching the government because the tsar would see the
justice in it. When Petrashevsky finished, a young lawyer Dostoevsky invited
leaped from his chair, "No! The most crying injustice is the slavery of sixty

million peasants!" Someone shot back: it was only twenty million! "It doesn't make any difference!" he said. The entire institution was shameful, and there was no way the tsar would grant emancipation willingly. Maybe if the government purchased the serfs' freedom. But where would it find the money? And what if the nobles refused? Someone stated it bluntly: "What if emancipating the serfs turned out to be impossible by any other means than revolt?" Dostoevsky shouted back, "Then let there be a revolt!"

Dostoevsky always thought Petrashevsky was more interested in intrigue than in action, and Speshnev felt the same way. Speshnev didn't witness the argument, because he had stopped attending Petrashevsky's evenings months earlier. Around that same time—the end of 1848—Dostoevsky had begun visiting Speshnev at his home. Unlike the other Petrashevists, Speshnev was uninterested in persuading anyone. He possessed stores of confidence that seemed to make him indifferent to approval. He had little patience for debate, and his opinions, if he shared them, were ready-made declarations. Either people would see the truth or they wouldn't. Petrashevsky didn't see it. But perhaps Dostoevsky would.

Speshnev was keenly aware of people's needs. When Dostoevsky and Mikhail complained about the censors, he offered to have their works published abroad through his European connections. It was Mikhail who refused. Speshnev understood that Dostoevsky's debt to Kraevsky weighed heavily on him, that it forced him to attach his signature to hasty writing, that he experienced each substandard submission as a moral failure, and, most important, that he couldn't stop. In February 1849, Dostoevsky asked Kraevsky for one hundred rubles "*immediately*." In March, he asked for ten more to pay his landlady. Two weeks later, he requested more. "I need fifteen now, just fifteen. . . . Have mercy on me." At some point, Speshnev began lending him money, and Mikhail could not stop him.

Dostoevsky must have been wary of Speshnev even as he was drawn to him. There were rumors that Speshnev had poisoned his mistress—his neighbor's wife—after beginning an affair with a baroness. He became consumed with revolutionary ideas, including writings by the Free Ones and the Fourierists. He called himself an "inveterate atheist and materialist," someone who "believes in nothing at all." Everything he knew rested on observable facts and logical deduction because he had exorcised all the hectoring ghosts—God and morality, authority and abstraction. The apex of Speshnev's studies was Max Stirner's *The Ego and Its Own*. Speshnev enjoyed Stirner's wrecking ball mind. Everything it encountered was an obstacle, and every obstacle was subjected to the same battering method, over and over again. "Every State is a *despotism*," Stirner declared. "*Everything sacred is a tie, a fetter.*"

The tough-minded tone concealed egoism's soothing affirmations. "We are perfect altogether, and on the whole earth there is not one man who is a sinner!" God and religion have made us "terrified at *ourselves* in our nakedness and naturalness . . . we deem ourselves depraved by nature, born devils." But there are no criminals, unless everyone is a criminal. Who we are is an "unbridled ego," and the unbridled ego "is the never-ceasing criminal in the State." Society does not corrupt human nature. It simply declares human nature corrupt. For someone like Speshnev, steeped in Rousseau and Fourier and the philosophers of revolution, egoism was a liberation upon a liberation. You don't have to be nostalgic for a lost state of nature or build a phalanstery or wait for the manifestation of Spirit. You don't have to be anything other than what you already are.

Dostoevsky delivered a speech to the Petrashevists about "*individuality* and *egoism*," as he later described it, but no account of his talk survives. Whatever Dostoevsky and Speshnev spoke about during his visits also remains unknown, but around the beginning of 1849 Dostoevsky invited Speshnev to another circle at Sergei Durov's apartment, where Dostoevsky was more confident that there were no spies. He and Durov had discussed creating a circle devoted to art and literature, where writers could read their poems and short stories and where they could play music after supper.

Yet several attendees seemed more interested in forming a radical alternative to the Petrashevsky Circle. After a few weeks, Filippov, whom Dostoevsky invited, suggested that the members write and share articles analyzing Russia's problems. "Speak out boldly and openly," he said, "strip bare all the injustice of our laws, all the corruption and shortcomings of our administration." Each person would focus on a particular area—economics, legal reform, the military, and so on. The idea sounded propitious. Dostoevsky would explain socialism. It was exciting—something deeper than debate. Some people said they'd like to have copies of what everyone read, which led to complaints about the tedium of handwritten duplication, which led Filippov to suggest that they assemble their own printing press. And suddenly everyone was silent, as if a bell had rung. The night ended early.

Filippov's idea was blatantly criminal. All printing presses, no matter how small, needed to be approved and registered by the government. Even plotting to build an unregistered press was grounds for imprisonment. Dostoevsky tried to smooth things over in a conciliatory speech the following week, but nerves and trust were too frayed. Durov sent out letters canceling the next meeting, and he left his apartment that night to make his resolve clear.

In April 1849, Dostoevsky arrived at Petrashevsky's apartment clutching a notebook that a friend sent to him via Durov. It contained a handwritten copy of Belinsky's scathing letter to Gogol, which had been circulating since Belinsky's death. Certain people in Moscow and Petersburg were aware of its basic outlines, or they had heard memorable passages recited, or they had listened to other describe it, the roaring coda to Furious Vissarion's life. But it was more rumored than read. As soon as Petrashevsky discovered that Dostoevsky had a copy, he asked him to read it to the Petrashevists.

So Dostoevsky took the floor at the Petrashevsky Circle, conjured Belinsky's ghost, and let the man who launched his career be the voice of outrage against the backwardness of Russia.

"What she needs," Dostoevsky intoned, quoting Belinsky, "is not sermons (she has heard enough of them!) or prayers (she has repeated them too often!), but the awakening in the people of a sense of their human dignity lost for so many centuries amid dirt and refuse."

The audience was ecstatic. Russia was a lawless country, the letter went on, a place "where there is nothing but vast corporations of official thieves and robbers of various descriptions." And the greatest national injustices were serfdom and corporal punishment. Russia, the letter went on, "presents the dire spectacle of a country where men traffic in men, without even having the excuse so insidiously exploited by the American plantation owners who claim that the Negro is not a man."

"That's it! That's it!" Jastrzembsky shouted out as Dostoevsky read.

The government knew how the serfs were abused. It knew how many landowners were murdered each year, and it responded with symbolic measures, like forcing landowners to whip their serfs with the cat-o'-three-tails instead of the knout. "Proponent of the knout," Dostoevsky read, declaiming to the absent Gogol, "apostle of ignorance, champion of obscurantism and Stygian darkness, panegyrist of Tatar morals—what are you about! Look beneath your feet—you are standing on the brink of an abyss!"

Gogol's tsarism was a betrayal because Russians had begun to think of writers as more than writers. "You do not properly understand the Russian public," Dostoevsky read to the assembled Petrashevists. Only literature gives the people hope for progress amid autocratic oppression. "The title of poet and writer has long since eclipsed the tinsel of epaulets and gaudy uniforms." Russia now "looks upon Russian writers as its only leaders, defenders, and saviors against Russian autocracy, orthodoxy, and nationality."

Few moments in the circle's history were as rousing as this one. "The whole company was as if electrified," Antonelli noticed. They wanted to circulate copies of the letter immediately.

The first thing Dostoevsky heard, days later, climbing up through dreams toward the woken world, was the sound of a saber clanking lightly against something in his room. It was before sunrise. He had come home an hour earlier after visiting one of Speshnev's friends and had quickly fallen asleep. His eyes were not yet fully open when he felt the presence of strangers in his room, figures coming into focus against the predawn light. A police officer with full sideburns was standing next to his bed. Beside him, in a blue uniform with silver buttons, white epaulets, and braided cords draped from the shoulder, stood a lieutenant colonel of the Third Section. He looked down at Dostoevsky and said in a gentle, almost soothing voice, "Get up!"

"What's the matter?" Dostoevsky asked. An armed guard was standing in the doorway. "By imperial order . . ." the officer began, relaying the arrest orders issued only hours before and designated "Secret." They indicated that Fyodor Mikhailovich Dostoevsky, "the retired engineer-lieutenant and litterateur," shall be arrested in his room at four in the morning and transported to the Third Section headquarters. All of his books and papers are to be sealed up and delivered to the Third Section. If he has too many books to transport, the entire apartment must be sealed off. If he claims that anything in his possession belongs to someone else, ignore him.

Dostoevsky began getting out of bed. "May I . . ."

"It's all right," the lieutenant colonel said, "please get dressed. We shall be pleased to wait."

They began rummaging through his belongings, binding up all the books and papers. The police officer was using Dostoevsky's long-stemmed smoking pipe to sift through the ashes of the small apartment's furnace just in case Dostoevsky had attempted to burn incriminating evidence. The guard stood on a chair to search on top of it but lost his grip on the ledge and crashed onto the floor, which concluded that portion of the investigation. Then the officer noticed a fifteen-kopeck coin on the table—the double-headed eagle beneath a crown, a scepter and an orb in its talons. It was worn and slightly bent. At length the officer nodded to the lieutenant colonel.

"It's not counterfeit, is it?" Dostoevsky asked.

"Hmm," the officer considered. "That, in fact, must be investigated." The coin was taken into evidence.

The prisoner was escorted down the stairs, past his frightened landlady and her servant, and placed in a carriage that took a circuitous route along the Fontanka canal before crossing the chain bridge by the Summer Garden. It came to a halt in front of helmeted guards stationed outside an unexceptional neoclassical building. The Third Section headquarters. They took Dostoevsky up to the white hall. Several familiar faces were already there, mostly quiet, in shock, but the hall was soon filled as carriage after carriage arrived. More than two hundred people were arrested in connection with the Petrashevsky Circle, and this morning's arrests were the most important—Petrashevsky, of course, Speshnev, Mombelli, Filippov, Durov, and so on. As the morning wore on, nonappearances became increasingly conspicuous. A high-ranking civilian had been checking the arriving prisoners' names against a list, and as the prisoners clustered around him to snatch glimpses, Dostoevsky could see the words "agent for the given case." Next to the words was the name: Peter Dmitrievich Antonelli.

So Antonelli was the spy. Should they have suspected? Antonelli injected little provocations. ("Wouldn't it be a good thing to throw a few pamphlets into

the army?") He solicited advice about how to start a secret society, and Petrashevsky gave it to him, just as he gave him the list of books he was ordering
from his French bookseller—more than two hundred titles, nearly all of them
illegal. The authorities had accumulated plenty of evidence. Antonelli had in-
filtrated the Petrashevsky Circle months earlier, and he was present when
Dostoevsky read Belinsky's letter. Others would verify the fact, and that would
be enough.

Dostoevsky was probably looking for his brother's name on the list. He
expected Mikhail to be escorted in at any moment, but instead he saw the
guards bring in his younger brother Andrei, bewildered, standing there alone
in his overcoat, an engineering student who knew no one. Dostoevsky rushed
up to him, "Brother, why are you here?" But it quickly became obvious: they
arrested the wrong brother. Dostoevsky implored him to keep quiet, to hold
tight in prison for a week or two so that Mikhail could get his affairs in order—
his wife had just given birth to their third child. Just as Dostoevsky's words
were sinking in, two guards hauled the brothers into different rooms where
they would await their transfer to the fortress prison.

Six

The Execution

What is your name, patronymic and surname, how many
years old are you, of what denomination are you and
have you duly observed prescribed religious rites?

*Fyodor Mikhailovich Dostoevsky, twenty-seven years old, of Orthodox,
Greek-Russian denomination. I have duly observed prescribed religious
rites.*

Identify your parents and state their whereabouts, if
they are alive.

*My father was a staff-medic, the collegiate counsellor, Dostoevsky. My
mother was from the merchant class. Both are dead.*

Dostoevsky was locked up in cell No. 9 in the prison inside the Peter
and Paul Fortress, a citadel surrounded by stone walls sixty feet
thick on a small island at St. Petersburg's dead center. Thirteen
Petrashevists were held in the Alexeievsky Ravelin, a secret prison in a separate
building designated for the highest state criminals. It could have been a set
piece for a gothic tale. A cot with a straw mattress. A blanket made from old
army coats. Cold, dank air and a vaulted ceiling. There was a small stool, a
table, and a chamber pot in the corner. Sludgy oil fueled a dim, sputtering
lamp, and iron bars barricaded the window, which was smeared with paste
to obscure incoming light, as if there were anything to see.

This prison was not a panopticon. It was a visionless place, a place of sounds rising like a river to flood the mind's lowest neighborhoods. Solitary confinement made every noise disturbing. The key turning the cell door's iron lock, soldiers' footsteps echoing away down the dark corridors, a guttural moan somewhere breaching wall after wall. Petrashevsky couldn't sleep because he kept hearing tappings and whispers. He said they were torturing him. Dostoevsky's brother Andrei would never forget the sounds of rats entering his cell through hidden crevices: a tiny rustle, then another, nervier, then several rats making a run of the place. And just when the night would settle again, when you thought you might sleep, another man's cry would break the stagnant air.

The Petrashevists were imprisoned here for months while the tsar's Commission of Inquiry interrogated them repeatedly. The investigation had been going on long before the arrests. A shopkeeper next to Petrashevsky's apartment had been surveilling the activity. Then authorities set up a cabstand in the church square across the street so that Petrashevsky's guests would find cabs at all hours of the night willing to go anywhere. The drivers reported who showed up, when they left, and where they went. Meetings would last until three or four in the morning, and yet after ten months of surveillance authorities could only confirm that the group "did not play cards, but instead read, spoke, and disputed; but what exactly they spoke about was impossible to determine because of the caution and secrecy with which Petrashevsky surrounded himself."

So they recruited three spies to infiltrate the circle. One of them, Peter Antonelli, was Petrashevsky's colleague at the Ministry of Internal Affairs. As a young former student at the University of Petersburg, he fit the Petrashevist profile. Antonelli befriended Petrashevsky and began writing detailed reports. "The known individual often visits the public library," Antonelli observed on February 6. The known individual wants "to redo our government in the manner of États-Unis." He wants to go further, in fact—he wants *women* to have the right to vote. He concocted a scheme to tax women in order to give them leverage for their demands. "All his intentions," Antonelli reported, "bear the imprint of pure fanaticism." And yet he noticed that when Petrashevsky spoke with passion, his face revealed a mind fully at work, and he became "really beautiful . . . I could not help admiring him," Antonelli confessed.

He kept meticulous accounts of every meeting: who was present, who knew whom, what they said, what they did, where they socialized. He informed his superiors that Petrashevsky probably had about eight hundred acquaintances. Several members of the circle could handle three men if confronted. They might have concealed weapons, he warned, and "in the heat of the moment, God knows what they are not ready to do." Antonelli made mistakes—he kept referring to "Pyotr" Dostoevsky and claimed Mikhail was trained as an architect—but his account of the night Dostoevsky held the floor was both accurate and damning. Dostoevsky, he reported, "read Belinsky's letter in answer to Gogol at the session. This letter contains the most impertinent and criminal expressions." The spy was astounded by the reading, the Petrashevists' reactions, and the seditious discussions that followed. He pronounced the entire April 15 meeting "très orageuse." They were all arrested the following week. For all of his efforts, the Third Section paid Antonelli what they paid all informers: thirty rubles, just like Judas.

The Commission of Inquiry pursued every seditious utterance, inside the meetings and out, any discussion of republicanism and equality and the French Revolution. The searches unearthed disloyal essays and speeches, illegal translations, seditious tracts and notes and letters, and thousands of criminal books—the raid on Petrashevsky's bookseller alone yielded 2,581. The commission was taken aback by Petrashevsky's library. "One can say without exaggeration that he possesses all the most impious and revolutionary books that have been published abroad."

After weeks of isolation, Dostoevsky was escorted into a large, harshly lit interrogation room. Five men—generals and princes—sat behind a long cloth-covered table and watched the "retired engineer-litterateur," as his file referred to him, take his seat. The head of the commission (and the commandant of the fortress) was General Nabokov, the great-great-uncle of the novelist. The interrogation was led by Prince Gagarin, an aging, portly general with ponderous eyelids and a gray beard bushing out over his collar. An auditor at the end of the table recorded the proceedings and read out to Dostoevsky what he read to all the Petrashevists: "His Majesty the Emperor orders to try the exposed malefactors according to the field code"—they were being tried under military law. The commission then informed Dostoevsky that they knew he participated in the Petrashevsky Circle, that he read Belinsky's infamous letter, and that he had spoken "*like a freethinker*." These were serious problems.

The malefactors were not tortured. Some of them were threatened or pressured to sign statements of guilt, but more often they were cajoled and manipulated. Nabokov was kind to his new prisoners, and General Dubelt—handsome, with blue eyes and an elegant mustache—repeatedly tried to hearten them. Prince Gagarin, however, was bureaucratic down to his mannerisms. He consulted a red-collared official sitting at a desk behind him, but his rigid formalism gave the proceedings an air of methodical incompetence. Young Andrei Dostoevsky seemed exasperatingly unhelpful until it dawned upon one of the interrogators, "Do you have *another* brother?" Andrei had to wait in the hallway while the commission resolved to arrest the intended brother, Mikhail.

Dostoevsky spoke publicly of his interrogation only once, decades later, and what he recalled was General Rostovtsev trying to nudge him out of his cagey evasiveness. "I cannot believe that the man who wrote *Poor Folk* can be in sympathy with these vicious people," Rostovtsev declared. He had carefully coiffed jet-black hair and a gray mustache. "It is impossible. You are only slightly involved," he told Dostoevsky, maintaining a smile, "and I am fully empowered by the Tsar to pardon you if you agree to tell about the whole business."

Dostoevsky remained silent. General Dubelt seemed satisfied. He was the Third Section's second-in-command and his blue uniform made him look trim. Dubelt turned to Rostovtsev and said, "I told you so," but Rostovtsev wouldn't relent. He jumped up from his chair and began yelling, "I can no longer bear to look at Dostoevsky." He then stormed out of the room, Dostoevsky recalled, locking the door behind him, leaving the other interrogators with the astonished author of *Poor Folk*. Just as Prince Gagarin was about to proceed with the questioning, Rostovtsev shouted from the other side of the door. "Has Dostoevsky left yet? Tell me when he goes—I can't bear the sight of him!"

Months after the initial interrogations, the commission told the Petrashevists to put their answers in writing. They inquired about the minutiae of Petrashevsky's meetings and about possible propaganda or recruiting campaigns. They probed for hints that they were organizing, and the bell the Petrashevists rang to call order seemed particularly concerning. The interrogators hunted for contradictions. Any discrepancy resulted in more interrogations, which often led to more contradictions, follow-up questions, and new lines of inquiry. Why hadn't Dostoevsky mentioned this person? Why hadn't he confessed that conversation? They interrogated him about incriminating items they found in his apartment: forbidden French books, a letter from a friend that insulted the tsar, a brief but warm note of invitation from Belinsky, years old—just what kind of meeting did they have? They asked him about people he'd never met, about Fourierism and socialism, about whether Petrashevsky was dangerous and, if so, *how* dangerous. Dostoevsky was interrogated several times in April and May—both in person and in writing—and then four more times in June. A mirror in the interrogation room reflected the prisoners' deteriorating bodies.

Dostoevsky wrote out his answers in small, careful handwriting with insertions in the margins, letting his effusiveness cloud his evasions. He defended his innocence in nearly a dozen ways. Yes, he had attended Petrashevsky's meetings, but he didn't know anything about his Fourierist advocacy. Either way, Fourierism was harmless, "dilettantish," he said, "a utopia of the most unrealistic sort . . . rather more comic than terrifying." He assumed Petrashevsky's activism was one of his jokes, but then he barely knew the man. "All that I know about Petrashevsky I know incompletely, imperfectly, by guesses," Dostoevsky wrote. He had begun to avoid talking to him altogether because he was sick of arguing with him. The Petrashevists in general were more reckless than revolutionary—Filippov was a good example. During the cholera outbreak, Dostoevsky noted, Filippov drank milk and ate fruits and vegetables like a maniac.

Yes, Dostoevsky admitted, he had read Belinsky's letter to the Petrashevists, but he read the entire exchange between Belinsky and Gogol without comment. Could anyone say whose side he was on? Besides, Belinsky's letter was "too strange" and blistering to evoke sympathy. And yes, he had studied socialism, but he was by no means a "freethinker"—and what is a freethinker, anyway?

"I will say in all sincerity that there has been nothing harder for me in all the world than defining the word." Dostoevsky insisted that his interest in socialism was purely academic. He regarded it as a primitive science ("alchemy rather than chemistry, astrology rather than astronomy") and believed implementing socialism anywhere—even in France—would bring "inescapable ruin." He knew perfectly well that "the strengthening of the autocracy" had saved Russia from the Mongols, and he went further: "All that has been good in Russia has invariably originated from above, from the throne." He was unambiguously opposed to violent revolution, and in any case he was *too busy* to be a revolutionary. He spent half his time writing and the other half sick with "hypochondriacal attacks." All he wanted, he testified, was "the right to be a citizen" and to concern himself with the welfare of his nation. "Yes, if *seeking the better* is liberalism, *freethinking*, then, in this sense, perhaps, I am a freethinker."

But surely a manner of thinking was not illegal, which highlighted, as Dostoevsky explained, the epistemological problem of the entire inquiry. He hadn't actually *done* anything criminal, so the commission was left to evaluate his motives. How could they do that? "Who has seen the inside of my soul?" Dostoevsky asked the commission. "Who has determined the degree of the perfidy, damage, and rebellion that I am charged with? On what scale was this determination made?" And even if the commission could find a scale to weigh Russian souls, he argued, "who would not be found guilty if each were to be judged on the basis of his most secret thoughts?" Everyone is a criminal. The only thing that was clear about his alleged crime was its obscurity. "To this very moment," Dostoevsky lamented after months in prison, "I still do not know what the charges against me are."

The only "freethinking" idea that Dostoevsky confessed was his resentment of Russia's censorship. Banning books and journals destroyed art, he argued, and cultivated a pervasive fear that cast the world "in a joyless, forbidding light." He was, of course, genuinely opposed to Russian censorship, but his bold objections under interrogation also helped to screen his more dangerous views on serfdom. Throughout the months of questioning—through all of his excuses, explanations, and misdirections—Dostoevsky managed to conceal his hatred for the institution, even though it was exactly that hatred that had gotten him arrested in the first place. He knew what to keep hidden. Censorship was important, but serfdom was foundational.

The authorities judged Dostoevsky and the other Petrashevists against the backdrop of revolution abroad and growing unrest at home. The official in charge of the investigation noted that eighteen landowners had been murdered by their serfs the previous year (1848) and that arson attacks had increased dramatically. The Petrashevsky Circle, officials concluded, was an "all-embracing plan of an overall movement for change and destruction." It was a "conspiracy of ideas." Tsar Nicholas considered the Petrashevists' conspiracy dangerous enough. "Even if it is all just a lot of idle talk," he told the head of the Third Section, "it is still criminal and intolerable in the highest degree."

By the summer, Dostoevsky was consuming little beyond castor oil to relieve his hemorrhoids. He suffered chest pains and "nervous spasms." He had lost all sense of time during months of solitary confinement. Sometimes each minute felt anchored into place, and sometimes days blew past like dead leaves. His five broken hours of sleep each night were filled with "long, hideous dreams." When he was awake, he hallucinated. He felt his entire prison cell tossing violently. "I sit in my room as though in a ship's cabin." This is what it is like to be at the mercy of consciousness. He had thought about this before his imprisonment, about how the mind abhors a vacuum. When the external world retreats, one's ideas and memories, "nerves and fantasy," come rushing in like invading platoons from all sides. And now he was locked inside a vacuum for months. It felt, he said, as if the air were being pumped out of his cell. Sometimes memories forced their way in—the garden of the engineering school, springtime in Estonia with Mikhail—he couldn't keep them away.

He tried to be optimistic. The guards let him walk in the prison garden, which had "almost seventeen trees." After a few months they gave him a candle in the evenings and allowed him to read books. He somehow borrowed ten silver rubles for small purchases (tea, tobacco) and asked Mikhail for the money to repay it. Mikhail had been released after nearly two months of interrogation and had become his brother's primary connection to the world beyond his sea-tossed cabin. Most of Dostoevsky's family was not even aware that he had been arrested. "What are you living on?" he wrote to Mikhail. "What precisely are you doing?" "What do the children think about me?" Surely by now they were wondering where he'd gone. Mikhail sent money as well as a Bible, a volume of Shakespeare ("How did you guess?"), and issues of *Notes of the Fatherland*. He devoured any information about the world beyond the prison. ("What an excellent piece about banks!") Turgenev's new play was awful, but the English novel in the journal was "extraordinarily good." It was Charlotte Brontë's *Jane Eyre*.

He wrote whenever he could. He conceived of two novels and three short stories, one of which he had begun writing. "I have never worked so *con amore* as now," he told Mikhail. Such love helped fill the vacuum. "Work, write— what's better than that!" Yet even that vocational joy could only have reminded him of the nature of his crime, a crime of thinking. "Why was I educated," he asked his interrogators, "why has a desire for knowledge been aroused in me by learning if I do not have the right to voice my personal opinion or disagree with that opinion which retains its authority no matter what?"

One point of learning that he began cultivating in order to help him through his persecution was a myth of self-reliance. "Good spirits depend on me alone," he wrote to Mikhail. He kept convincing himself through the autumn. "It's been nearly five months now that I've been living on my own means, that is, on my head alone and nothing else." Speshnev might have said the same thing. Speshnev's peculiar hold on Dostoevsky was partly why he couldn't sleep. As Dostoevsky plotted the wording of his written confession, he had to wonder what someone might be saying about him, and about Speshnev, in the interrogation room.

```
If you know anything about any criminal conspiracy
going on outside the meetings designated, you are
obliged to give full and frank testimony about
it here.
```

I have no knowledge of anything of the sort.

This was a lie. The truth was that Dostoevsky belonged to yet another circle—smaller and more secretive. The Speshnev Circle. They planned to stoke grievances among serfs, religious schismatics, and conscripted soldiers in order to start a revolution. The circle was small, eight or nine men, mostly agitators hidden within the Petrashevsky Circle—Filippov, for example, Mombelli. Speshnev had reached out to them slowly, carefully, giving them confidence. He needed writers, of course, propagandists who could inspire and enrage, and Fyodor Dostoevsky was perfect.

Their secret circle had become more than a crime of thinking. The conspirators had taken several steps to gather, print, and distribute antigovernment propaganda: essays on serf emancipation, socialism, and Fourierism. A banned Turgenev play, illegal translations, revolutionary poetry. One of them wrote a short story about a serf who pummels his landlord for raping his sister. They created a revolutionary version of the Ten Commandments, each one interpreted to pit God's laws against unjust state laws. Thou shalt not kill—except in self-defense against a landlord.

And then there was Belinsky's letter. Dostoevsky read it partly to test its effectiveness and partly to lure kindred propagandists. The Petrashevsky Circle meetings were, in fact, being co-opted for Speshnev's purposes without Petrashevsky's knowing it. When they had their falling-out, the conspirators needed to use another circle as cover. This is why Dostoevsky reshaped the innocent "cultural" meetings at Durov's apartment. It's why he invited Speshnev and Filippov. And it's why he was so eager to keep the group together when its political tenor began tearing it apart. These were all serious offenses.

The plot became even more serious the moment they began assembling a lithographic press to print their propaganda. Filippov drew up sketches of the machinery. They ordered components from around Petersburg, paid in cash (lithographic stones cost twenty rubles), and brought them to Nikolai Mordvinov, who began assembling it. Just days after their lithograph was finished, they were all arrested. Dostoevsky knew that the longer the investigation continued, the more likely the truth would come tumbling out in a stray comment deep into someone's fourth or fifth interrogation. The Third Section would search Mordvinov's apartment, and when they did—if they hadn't already—the case against Dostoevsky would change completely. Reading an inflammatory letter was problematic. Planning to print and distribute that letter—to say nothing of the rest of their propaganda—was a grave offense. There'd be no debates about motives. They would have a real device, hard evidence of a crime.

The Commission of Inquiry kept circling closer to the truth. Dostoevsky admitted that, yes, Filippov once *suggested* acquiring a lithograph, though nothing more. But there was much more. Dostoevsky had played a substantial role in Speshnev's hidden circle. He had recruited new members. One night, early in 1849, Dostoevsky visited his friend Apollon Maikov and spent the night on his couch. Dostoevsky had met Maikov, a poet, through Belinsky, and they quickly became close. Maikov had occasionally visited Petrashevsky's but stopped after his brother drowned in a pond outside Petersburg.

Late at night, before sleeping, Dostoevsky told Maikov that he had a proposal for him. "Petrashevsky is a fool, an actor and a chatterbox," he said. He was incapable of purposeful action, so the Petrashevists "who meant business" hatched a plan to assemble a secret lithograph, print propaganda, and start a revolution. They wanted Maikov to join them. He was shocked. The whole idea, he told Dostoevsky, is "emptyheaded and disturbing"—the entire group is "headed for certain disaster." "And besides," he told him, growing animated, "you and I are poets and hence impractical folk. We cannot even manage our *own* affairs, whereas political activity constitutes the highest degree of practicality."

Dostoevsky sat there, Maikov remembered, "like the dying Socrates." He called upon Maikov to help him "save the fatherland." Maikov beheld his friend Fyodor Mikhailovich in a nightshirt, unbuttoned at the collar, crashing on his couch, and he started laughing.

"So that means no?"

"No," Maikov said, "a thousand times no!"

The next morning before leaving, Dostoevsky told him, "I do not need to tell you not to breathe a word about this to anyone."

In June, the Third Section searched Speshev's apartment again but found no sign of a press. What they did find was the draft of an oath to a secret society (signatories would swear to give up their lives at a moment's notice) and notes for a lecture about how Russia's censorship made revolutionary violence essential. "Since we are left with nothing but the spoken word," Speshnev declared, "I intend to use it without any shame or conscience, without any disgrace, to disseminate socialism, atheism, terrorism, everything, everything good in this world, and I advise you to do the same."

Speshnev had been pulling the strings. He goaded people into making inflammatory statements at meetings. He fed Mombelli ideas about secret societies so that someone else would bring them to Petrashevsky. Dostoevsky's friends had noticed Speshnev's unusual influence over him, too. They shared books and long conversations. They shared a love of ideas (forbidden or otherwise), a quixotic streak, and a commitment to words as an astringent truth or a cutting blade.

But there was something else about Speshnev's hold on him, something simpler and more tenacious. Dostoevsky owed him money. By 1849, he had been in debt to Kraevsky, his editor, for years with no hope of writing his way out of his "slavery," as he put it. His debts—to Mikhail, his tailor, his landlady—exacerbated his depression, anxiety, and illnesses. When Dostoevsky asked Speshnev for a loan, Speshnev gave him five hundred silver rubles—a small fortune. Even if he could repay the debt, Speshnev wouldn't take it. "From now on I have a Mephistopheles of my own!" Dostoevsky said. He kept repeating it, as if in disbelief or trying to break a spell, but payment was inevitable.

The Speshnev Circle benefited less from diabolical power than from sheer luck. When Mordvinov was arrested, the officers determined that his suspicious possessions were too numerous to seize immediately. One of his rooms was a laboratory filled with mechanical contraptions, arcane instruments, and specialized devices, all of which seemed incriminating. So the gendarmes sealed off the room before escorting Mordvinov to the Third Section. After the officers left, Mordvinov's family managed to remove the door from its hinges and enter the room without damaging the seals. They dismantled the lithograph and eliminated all traces of it. When the gendarmes returned, it was as if the criminal machine had never existed.

But this did not erase the conspiracy surrounding the lithograph, and the commission did not need hard evidence for that. Corroborating testimony from two witnesses was sufficient, which made investigations rather easy. Once an interrogator confronts a conspirator with something the conspirator knows is true, denying it is perilous, and confirming it often yields more details and conspirators. When one conspirator wobbles, the rest fall like dominoes.

One morning a gendarme appeared at the bedside of Apollon Maikov and escorted him to the Peter and Paul Fortress. Maikov had been waiting for this. Everyone who knew the Petrashevists had been arrested or interrogated, and the search kept widening outward until it had reached him, the brotherless poet. Maikov was terrified. He thought back to the details of that night, about Dostoevsky's revolutionary zeal, the lithograph, and the secret circle. He must have rehearsed responses to all the branching interrogative paths as he waited for General Gagarin and the commission to summon him into the interrogation room.

When it was over, Maikov walked out of the bright room and groped half blindly down a dark corridor, trying to find his way out. Then he saw someone in full dress uniform holding a candle and staring at him from above the glow. It was General Nabokov in the darkness. "Who's there?" Nabokov asked. "What are you doing here?"

I n October, after six months in prison, the Petrashevists were each told to make a final statement. "Do you have, in addition to the testimony already given by you under investigation, anything further to present in your defense?" Several admitted their guilt and begged for mercy. Dostoevsky, however, had only one thing to add: "I never acted with malice or premeditation against the government. What I did do was done thoughtlessly on my part and much of it almost accidentally."

The Petrashevists languished in prison until just before sunrise on December 22, 1849. Dostoevsky heard carriages and gendarme squadrons approaching, voices in the corridors, and cell doors opening. The guards came with the Petrashevists' original clothes. They were told to put them on. "What is this for?" one of them asked. "Where are we going? Is our business finished?" He received no clear answer.

Each prisoner was taken into a carriage by a soldier in a gray overcoat. The convoy crossed the Neva, proceeded along the embankments, and traversed the city at a trot. Dostoevsky saw crowds gathered along the streets.

The tsar's verdict had been announced in the press, but the spectacle's significance was clear even for those who hadn't read the proclamation. Mounted gendarmes with unsheathed swords rode along the sides of twenty carriages. There was a platoon of gendarmes ahead of them, another platoon behind, and a general on horseback leading the procession to the Semenovsky Parade Ground. Hundreds of soldiers were already in formation in the plaza—infantry battalions, the Life Guards, cavalry grenadiers. Throngs of spectators stood behind them. In the middle of the plaza there was a large platform covered in black fabric. In front of the platform there were three stakes.

The prisoners stepped out of the carriages into the bitter cold. There was fresh snow on the ground, and the red sun was shining just above the horizon. It was beautiful. The Petrashevists greeted one another. They were gaunt and haggard, but some were smiling behind their feral beards. This was their first real human contact in eight months. Speshnev, once so handsome, looked awful. He was pale and thin, like everyone else, and he had blue patches under his eyes. There were rumors that he had been starved.

A priest in black vestments approached them holding a large cross and a Bible. "Today you will hear the just decision of your case—follow me!" It was then that Dostoevsky realized he was going to die. The prisoners shuffled through the deep snow as the priest paraded them in front of the battalions and halted to display them before the soldiers. They ascended the platform steps, and each prisoner was assigned a place in two rows on opposite sides. A soldier stood beside each of them.

The just decision was arriving. The troops were ordered to stand at attention. The lieutenants and sergeants were ordered to present arms, and the thud of gunstocks against the ground echoed across the parade grounds. The general shouted to the prisoners, "Hats off!" When they hesitated, the soldiers pulled them off. The drummers sounded three drumrolls, and an official began to read the verdict with such perfunctory haste that it was difficult to understand—"involved in conspiracy . . . tried in accordance with the Criminal Field Code for state crimes . . . no distinction is made between the major culprits and accomplices." He proceeded down each row and read out the sentence of each man in turn.

"The Military Court finds the defendant Dostoevsky guilty . . ." The words washed over him. Guilty of reading Belinsky's letter, "a criminal offense against church and government," guilty of disseminating the letter, guilty of not reporting its dissemination. "Hence the Military Court has sentenced him, the retired engineer-lieutenant Dostoevsky . . . to be deprived, on the basis of the Code of Military Decrees, Part V, Book 1, articles 142, 144, 169, 170, 172 . . . of ranks, of all rights to his social estate and to be subjected to the death penalty by firing squad."

"It's not possible that we'll be executed," Dostoevsky said moments later. Durov, standing next to him, motioned to a cart beside the platform. It contained a large cargo concealed beneath straw matting—surely coffins. The general commanded the troops to slope arms. With the firearms poised at the men's shoulders, the lieutenants and sergeants took their places as the drums continued to beat. Two executioners in colorful caftans ascended the platform steps carrying multiple sabers. The prisoners were told to kneel. The executioners broke a saber over each man's head to signify the criminal's exclusion from Russian society. They had lost all rights, all property, all standing.

The executioners gave the convicts long white shirts and caps—their death garments—and the priest reappeared as they finished putting them on. "Brothers! Before death you must repent," he said. "The Savior forgives a repentant's sins." No one moved. "I urge you to confession," the priest implored. Timkovsky walked up, spoke in whispers with the priest, kissed the Bible, and returned to his place. The priest approached Petrashevsky to admonish him personally, and Petrashevsky muttered something in response—it wasn't clear what—but when the priest thrust the cross next to his face, he kissed it. Then all the Petrashevists kissed the cross in turn.

Dostoevsky began talking excitedly, frantically. He told Mombelli, standing next to him, that he had written a story in prison. "A Little Hero," it was called. He talked about Victor Hugo's story *Le dernier jour d'un condamné*, about a criminal's thoughts before the guillotine, a criminal who believes, in the end, that Christ's law would someday replace all the executioners. Dostoevsky embraced Durov and another Petrashevist and bade them farewell. Then he turned to Speshnev and said, "Nous serons avec le Christ." ("We will be with Christ.") Speshnev replied with a grin, "Un peu de poussière"—a bit of dust.

When the priest departed, soldiers grabbed the first three men in line—

Petrashevsky, Mombelli, and Apollon Grigoriev—dragged them off the platform, and tied them to the stakes. Dostoevsky was next. The commander ordered their caps to be pulled over their eyes, though Petrashevsky somehow managed to get his cap off so he could stare down his killers. Fifteen privates, accompanied by sergeants, assumed their positions fifteen paces from the stakes.

"Load weapons!"

The sun was rising above a nearby church's cupola. What Dostoevsky felt at that moment was a sublime and wondrous terror. He was facing the great rift of living, an incomprehensible truth. He thought about his brother, about how much he loved him. He thought about the morning sun rising up.

And then—suddenly—the drummers sounded the cadence for retreat. The soldiers lifted their weapons, and a small detachment came galloping across the plaza. An adjutant presented a document, and the document was read aloud: Tsar Nicholas, in his great mercy, grants the prisoners a last-minute reprieve. Instead of execution, the Petrashevists would be exiled.

"Long live His Majesty!" some began shouting. People in the crowd were crossing themselves, grateful for the tsar's benevolence. The peasant cart did not contain coffins. It contained prison uniforms. The convicts were given foul-smelling sheepskin coats, prison caps, and boots for their long journeys ahead. Some on the platform were less sanguine about the prospect of Siberian labor camps. "It would be better to be shot!" one of them said.

Dostoevsky returned to the fortress prison in ecstasy. He paced the length of his cell, singing at the top of his lungs. He hadn't grasped the nature of life until now, didn't understand that to be alive at all is to be teeming with life, that life is everywhere even in a world of death and executioners. He wrote to Mikhail hours after his ordeal. "When I look back on my past and think how much time I wasted on nothing, how much time has been lost in futilities, errors, laziness, incapacity to live; how little I appreciated it, how many times I sinned against my heart and soul—then my heart bleeds." He could finally feel the full heft of life, even if to talk about it was to wrap it in cliché. "Life is a gift," he wrote to Mikhail, "life is happiness, every minute can be an eternity of happiness!" Still inspired by Victor Hugo's story, he exclaimed, "On

voit le soleil!" Even a convict can rejoice in the sun. Exile would be an opportunity to reflect and repent. "I'll be reborn for the better," he told Mikhail.

This is how Dostoevsky was supposed to feel. Gratitude for his punishment. Gratitude for the tsar. The Petrashevists were never going to be executed, but it was important for the criminals and the public to think so, to
experience the dread of death, the harsh fate that malefactors deserve, and
then to have that fate lifted by the tsar's great mercy. The entire execution
ceremony was yet another display staged by the tsar to showcase his power
and his goodness. Nicholas issued detailed instructions, down to the horses'
pace through the city, the firing squad's distance from the hooded targets, and
the live ammunition loaded into the soldiers' chambers.

And yet Dostoevsky felt grateful for something else. The Commission
of Inquiry never found the lithograph. They never asked Maikov about Dostoevsky, never discovered that he was recruiting people for a propaganda conspiracy already well under way—never discovered the conspiracy at all. Fyodor
Dostoevsky was a member of Russia's first revolutionary socialist organization,
and nearly everything about it has been erased from history. The joy he felt
was, in part, the joy of getting away with his most serious crime.

Dostoevsky nevertheless received one of the harsher sentences for his active involvement in a seditious group and for having read a letter "filled with
impertinent freethinking." The High Military Court recommended sentencing Dostoevsky to eight years in a hard-labor prison camp. The tsar generously reduced his sentence to four years, after which Dostoevsky would be
required to serve in the army in Siberia for an unstated number of years.

After the initial wave of glee, the undertow of reality began to pull Dostoevsky down. As a convict, he had been deprived of all rights, which included
the right to publish. Wasn't that like an execution? "The head that created,"
he wrote to Mikhail, "that lived the higher life of art, that recognized and
grew accustomed to the higher demands of the spirit, that head has already
been cut from my shoulders." He would have to be reborn as someone else.
"Can it be that I will never again take my pen in hand?" It didn't seem possible. "My God! How many forms, still alive and created by me anew, will
perish, extinguished in my brain or dissolved like poison in my bloodstream."
The gift of life was being snatched away all over again. "Yes, if it's impossible
to write I will die."

PART II

---·•·---

Our time can be characterized in these words: that now, especially
in literature, there is no opinion at all; all opinions are allowed,
everything lives alongside everything else; there is no common
opinion, common faith.

—*Dostoevsky to Turgenev, February 13, 1865*

Seven

Exile

Just past midnight, on Christmas morning, the guards nailed Dostoevsky into his leg irons. He was being sent to Siberia in a convoy with Durov and Jastrzembsky. Each of the three prisoners lumbered into an open sleigh with an armed guard and a driver, and a courier guided the convoy out of the city. They left in the middle of the night to avoid drawing attention, and though the streets were empty, Petersburg's houses were lit up for the holiday. The reality of exile hit Dostoevsky when his sleigh passed the glowing apartment where Mikhail's wife and children were having their Christmas party.

As the group traveled through the thinning suburbs, Dostoevsky's emotions became too complex to name. "My heart was caught up in a bustling of some kind," he recalled. After eight months in prison and the terror of the firing squad, the journey east seemed like the beginning of a new life. At daybreak, the drivers stopped to don scarlet sashes in celebration of Christ's birth. Word spread along the route that the Petrashevists were passing through. "Whole villages would run out to look at us," Dostoevsky recalled. They covered about eight miles every hour, day after day, ten hours at a stretch, crossing the Volga at Yaroslavl, passing Nizhny Novgorod, then Kazan and countless settlements clinging to the roadsides.

Dostoevsky initially thought he was being exiled to Orenburg, out on the edge of Europe, possibly because the alternative was too difficult to fathom. Siberia begins on the Asian side of the Ural Mountains, a low, craggy range running from the Caspian Sea to the Arctic Ocean. At the time, Siberia was more than five million square miles—larger than the United States, larger than all of Europe. It was three-quarters of the Russian Empire and the largest land-mass affixed with a political meaning. For Russians, that meaning involved Asia's bearing on their national character, the sense that some outsize portion of their nature had yet to be surveyed.

The road to Siberia was studded with way stations every twenty-five versts (about twenty-six kilometers) where travelers exchanged their weary horses for rested ones that would take them to the next station. The guards took the prisoners inside for warmth and food at every fifth or sixth station. Everyone charged them triple—they were noblemen, after all—but the courier, Prokofiev, insisted on paying nearly half of their expenses. Durov wouldn't stop talking. Jastrzembsky was emaciated and beset by terrifying visions of what awaited them. But Dostoevsky was buoyant, "cheerful," as he recalled it, relishing the food and drink, chatting with Prokofiev, absorbing every detail and insight the journey offered. Wouldn't God be in Siberia? Wouldn't he be alive among human beings?

Prokofiev transferred the prisoners to covered sleighs to protect them against the cold, which was fortunate, because as the convoy began its ascent into the Urals, the temperature dropped to fifty-eight below zero Fahrenheit. The eyes' moisture congeals in cold that severe, making it painful to blink, and the vapor from your breath encases your nose and mouth in a crust of ice that the wise traveler does not wipe away. Thin poles sometimes marked where the road lay buried beneath the snow, and the high winds and freight sleighs packed the snow into rolling waves over which winter travelers climbed and plunged like reckless mariners.

Dostoevsky had it easy. Most exiles walked to Siberia. Anyone traveling along the "road of chains" would come across dozens of figures flanked by guards, led by mounted Cossacks, trudging through snow, mud, or dust in leg irons and manacles. Exiles were chained together in small groups walking from one ramshackle way station to the next. They slept on wooden planks or filthy floors. The guards often pocketed the prisoners' government allotments, so they pooled their money and begged for alms by singing in a haunting, quavering drone, their voices piling onto one another as they shuffled onward. Sometimes the leg irons froze to prisoners' skin. Sometimes they carved wounds into their ankles. Only those who could afford leather under-fetters were free from the fear of gangrene and an amputated foot. One in twelve convicts died en route. In bad years, it was one in four. Convicts exiled to Siberia's outermost limits had to walk more than five thousand miles—it took years. And the day they finally arrived was the day their sentences began.

It took only a few days for Dostoevsky's convoy to reach the cross that marked the end of Europe. Guards customarily stopped to let exiles bid fare-well to the continent, but a snowstorm was raging, their horses got stuck in snowdrifts, and the Petrashevists watched the guards and drivers struggle to pull everything back out. Night had fallen. Dostoevsky stood in the Great Siberian Road, with Petersburg two thousand versts away and all of Asia filling the white darkness ahead, and he cried.

The magnitude of Siberia set in as the convoy ventured farther east and the landscape opened up into the great Siberian steppe, the flat, open grass-lands that stretch across the continent to Mongolia. They were pasturelands for nomads and settlers. The southern steppe is too dry to support many trees, but it's enough for wolves and wild boars. In the warm months, the steppe fills with feathered grasses and great blooms of sage and peonies, goldenrod and monkshood and immense blue fields of forget-me-nots. One can imagine walking for years through Siberia, walking north to the margin of the steppe, where the grasslands shade into deciduous elms, birches, and maples, and farther north into the rugged conifers of the boreal forest, the taiga. You could walk through pines and firs, through the territories of bears, elk, and reindeer for hundreds of miles, and then farther north, to where the shallow roots of larches cling to the veneer of soil on the permafrost, and farther still, past the thinning forests, to where the tundra tapers off to dwarf shrubs and delicate gray mosses beside frozen pools and arctic foxes scratch for earthworms on the roof of the world.

The convoy traveled for sixteen days before they came to a clearing in the woods and saw a steep promontory over a frozen river, the stone walls of a citadel, and an Orthodox cathedral's five rounded cupolas. This was Tobolsk, the gateway of the Siberian exile system. The Tobolsk fortress held the empire's Exile Office, which processed and outfitted nearly all of Siberia's exiles. Dostoevsky was one of 5,574 new arrivals in 1850, which was a slow year. From 1649, when exile was codified, until the fall of the Romanov dynasty in 1917, Russia exiled about 3 million people to Siberia. It was essentially the only serious punitive method. Capital punishment was abolished for all but the most dangerous political criminals after 1753, and Russia did not have a prison system as we know it—jails only held people awaiting judgment. Exile was punishment for a variety of offenses over the years, from murder and "disseminating unrest" to lesser crimes like begging "under false pretenses," driving a horse into a pregnant woman (assuming she miscarried), possessing tobacco, and knocking people's hats into the street.

Exile became more useful as the empire grew. The unfortunates, as they were called, generated taxes and developed land. Convict labor extracted Siberia's massive wealth from mining districts—iron, copper, silver, and gold. Convicts pulled iron ore from marshes and bogs and cut down forests to feed blast furnaces. They hammered through frozen soil to make prospecting holes and blasted away fifteen feet of earth to reach gold. They descended sixty fathoms into the silver mines of Nerchinsk. They were chained to their wheelbarrows.

Siberian wealth had always buttressed Russia. Siberian furs empowered the early tsars. Siberian iron allowed Peter the Great a way to produce seemingly unlimited cannons and muskets to build his empire, and by the 1780s, Russia produced more iron than any country in the world. Siberian silver and gold shaped the empire's monetary system and helped pay for western infrastructure and expansionary wars.

The growing empire expanded its exile system by removing procedural restraints. During Nicholas I's reign, the majority of Siberian exiles were never actually convicted of a crime. They were all punishable by "administrative exile," which involved essentially no judicial procedure whatsoever. The practice allowed serf holders, mining authorities, and local police to control "impudent" or "unseemly" serfs by simply sending them away. Political agitators, striking workers, revolting peasants, and student leaders all received administrative exile. The wives of men condemned to administrative exile were forced to go with them. Sometimes entire communities were summarily banished. Between 1823 and 1845, more than 200,000 Russians walked the roads to Siberia. There simply weren't enough mines, factories, and distilleries for all the hard-labor criminals, and there was not enough known arable land to settle them: less than 1 percent of Siberia's land had been surveyed.

The overburdened system made it easier for those unseemly exiles to abscond from mines and factories or simply leave their assigned settlements. In some districts only about one in five exiles remained in their assigned communities. There were entire villages of runaway serfs hidden in the wilderness, and *brodiagi* (vagabonds) roamed the forest indefinitely. Once an exile started to roam, there was no incentive to return. Officials would brand their faces upon apprehension and strip them of all social status. The result was large swaths of unwanted people—outcasts among outcasts—who banded together as highway brigands or formed roving gangs that stormed villages, raping women and snatching people in the streets with lassos or grappling hooks.

The guards led Durov, Jastrzembsky, and Dostoevsky through a massive hall where hundreds of men, women, and children were getting their heads shaved. Others were being shackled and threaded onto iron rods for their march. Convicts with branded faces—an *O* burned into their foreheads, a *C* and a *K* on their cheeks—were toiling away on documents in the dim Exile Office. Others had their nostrils slit, a punishment officially outlawed decades earlier.

The warden approached them. "In shackles?"

"Yes, sir," they said.

"Search them."

The officials confiscated the prisoners' money and a naïvely purchased bottle of rum, issued the prisoners their uniforms, and hauled them off to a cold, narrow cell with straw-filled sacks on planks. At night they listened to a guard pacing back and forth and detainees shouting drunkenly over a card game. Dostoevsky spent much of the night persuading Jastrzembsky not to commit suicide. When his despair lifted, Dostoevsky produced cigars that had somehow escaped the warden's attention.

Though the officials had staggered the Petrashevists' departure from Petersburg, Tobolsk's administrative bottleneck brought nine of the radicals together, including Speshnev, Mombelli, and Petrashevsky himself. There hadn't been so many political criminals in Tobolsk since the Decembrists, rebels who staged the last serious challenge to tsarist authority back in 1825.

The physician who examined them found the typical signs of frostbite and shackle injuries. Dostoevsky had scrofulous sores on his face and in his mouth since Petersburg, and yet he was "exceptionally calm." The doctor evaluated their mental states: Could they tell him why they were here? Petrashevsky wanted to write out a full explanation, but his disjointed defense of Fourierism and phalansteries seemed disturbed. Later, fearing he might be caught with Petrashevsky's mini treatise, the doctor tore it up. All of the men were dangerous. One of the Petrashevists danced around in his shackles and kept telling the vice-governor that he found the holding cell quite satisfactory, yes, that the tsar had provided them with an excellent space in such a comfortable transfer prison.

Dostoevsky was held in Tobolsk for eleven days, and the hopeful aura surrounding Siberia dissolved into horrifying facts—the stench of human waste, windows plugged with rags and straw, dilapidated walls and caved-in floors, crooked wooden supports sinking into the ground. He saw emaciated convicts chained to walls inside the dark stone barracks. They had been tethered there for years, and their great hope was to complete their time on the chain so that they could one day walk around in the prison yard.

Dostoevsky and Durov were assigned to serve out their sentences in Omsk, a three-day journey by sleigh. While they waited to depart, several women arranged for a secret meeting with the Petrashevists. Alexandra Muravyeva, Praskovya Annenkova, and Natalya Fonvizina were wives of Decembrists and had voluntarily followed their husbands into exile. The meeting was brief—an hour—but heartening. They gave Dostoevsky food and clothing, as well as blessings, sympathy, and counsel. They warned him about the officer in charge of Omsk's fortress prison, Major Krivtsov, a man Dostoevsky would eventually describe as "a petty barbarian, quarrelsome, a drunkard, the most repulsive creature imaginable." The women handed Dostoevsky a New Testament as they left. The leather-bound copy was the survivor of an 1823 edition that Russian authorities had inexplicably burned. Dostoevsky found ten rubles hidden in the binding.

Fonvizina was especially touched by the prisoners' plight. She was related to Western Siberia's governor-general, so she wrote to him in Omsk asking him to provide some clemency for the Petrashevists. The other women wrote letters to the governor-general's three daughters, hoping they might appeal to him directly. When Fonvizina found out Dostoevsky's departure date, she and another woman, Maria Frantseva, drove seven kilometers south of Tobolsk in the early morning, walked another kilometer so their coachman wouldn't see, and waited for Dostoevsky and Durov on the road. Fonvizina and Frantseva had made arrangements with the transport guards beforehand, but something had gone wrong, and the women waited in an open field by the roadside in a nearly forty-below-zero chill. "We paced back and forth," Frantseva recalled, "warming our feet and tortured by uncertainty, not knowing how to explain their delay."

When they finally heard the troikas' sleigh bells, they walked out into the road and signaled to the guards. The convicts wore fur hats with earflaps, and their shackles rattled as they climbed out of their sleighs. Dostoevsky appeared small. Durov had black eyes and hair, and frost already covered his beard. They made their farewells quick in order to avoid trouble. The women told them not to be discouraged and assured them that they would be taken care of. Frantseva secretly gave something to the guard—yet another letter seeking protection, this time to a lieutenant colonel in Omsk—and he dutifully delivered it.

But the guard was carrying another letter as well, a message from the Tobolsk commandant to his counterpart in Omsk. It informed him that Dostoevsky and Durov were "prisoners in the full sense of the word," that there should be no leniency toward them, and, in fact, that "a trustworthy official should be appointed to maintain a strict and unceasing vigilance." Those instructions came from the tsar himself.

Omsk was on the edge of the Kazakh steppe, where Western Siberia's forests thin into small stands of trees amid waves of grasses on a vast plain, the bottom of a prehistoric sea. Across the Irtysh River was where the ancestral lands of the Middle Horde Kazakhs began. Wild horses grazed in the semiarid landscape, and caravans of camels pulled cargo through winter snow or summer sandstorms to and from Tibet and Mongolia.

Omsk's eighteen thousand inhabitants were enough to make it Siberia's second-largest city. It had mostly irregular unpaved streets and one-story wooden houses, but there was a square lined with shops, a Catholic church built by Polish exiles, and a mosque. No bridge crossed the Irtysh at Omsk, and the bridge crossing the stream between the town and the fortress was just an assembly of tethered boats. The town was dominated by Cossacks, soldiers, and cadets. There were four taverns, four liquor stores, and a liquor dispensary. There were no theaters and no local newspapers. "Omsk is a vile little town," Dostoevsky wrote to his brother years later. "It's a filthy army town and depraved to the highest degree."

Vile or not, it was the capital of Western Siberia. It housed the headquarters of the Siberia Corps and a new frontier administration that supervised the "external districts" across the Irtysh. The fortress at Omsk was one of the largest on the Siberian Line, a string of garrisons facilitating the empire's eastward expansion to Kamchatka. By the time Dostoevsky arrived, the garrison housed four thousand soldiers as well as administration buildings, the governor-general's palace, and the hard-labor prison.

Controlling this vast expanse of central Asia was crucial. Peter the Great was said to have called the Kazakh hordes "the key and the gate of all the lands and countries of Asia." Kazakh nomads roamed a million square miles of steppe pasturelands on horseback from the Caspian Sea to the Chinese Empire. They traced their ancestry to Genghis Khan and the Mongol warriors who dominated the steppe for centuries. The Middle Horde was the largest of the Kazakh alliances, and their territory extended north to the Irtysh River at Omsk.

Russia's power in the region had long been tenuous because the Kazakh hordes were among the most restive peoples in Siberia. In the 1830s, Russian officials estimated that two hundred Russians were enslaved annually in raids. They ended up as the Kazakhs' slaves or were sold in markets in Bukhara and Khiva. Russia fought the hordes with a combination of force and bureaucracy. Officials abolished the Middle Horde khanate by decree and claimed their territory for the Russian Empire. They eliminated the title of khan, subjected sultans to imperial approval, and divided the horde's territory into subdistricts designed to restrict nomadic movement and fracture collective identity. They taxed yurts and livestock. They provided government-subsidized bread, hoping it would inspire the nomads to settle on farms.

In 1837, Kazakhs mounted a ten-year revolt against Russian incursions into their ancestral lands. When Russian authorities asked the Kazakh leader, Kenisari, why they were rebelling, he recounted a catalog of sacked villages, plundered property, and the numbers of his people slaughtered in years of raids. The Russians, Kenisari declared, were "leeches sucking the blood of the Kazakhs."

The people who led those raids were themselves resistant to Russian power. One of the paradoxes of Russian imperialism is that the empire's expansion depended on a motley people averse to hierarchy and nationhood: the Cossacks. They originated as a loose array of deserters, schismatics, outlaws, and runaway serfs who gathered on the southern steppe for lives of banditry—*qazaq*. Cossacks organized into self-governing communities of mercenaries securing trade routes, quashing rebellions, and collecting sable pelts. Their tradition of dividing spoils equally made their leaders difficult to bribe, so the tsars influenced them with hereditary titles and elaborate regalia. This strategy had limits. Cossacks often adopted non-Russian ways—living in yurts, eating raw fish and meat, practicing shamanism. They wore Kazakh clothing and converted to Islam. But the tsar needed them. By the mid-nineteenth century there were 200,000 Cossacks in Siberia, many serving in battalions so diverse that Russian soldiers sometimes found themselves a minority population alongside Bashkir, Tungus, and Buryat Cossacks as well as Russia's prisoners of war—Lithuanians, Ukrainians, and Poles.

This assortment of prisoners and Cossacks made the army itself a source of unrest. In 1833, officials uncovered a conspiracy to seize Omsk's fort and mount a large-scale insurrection of exiles and factory serfs along the Irtysh. Polish soldiers, prisoners, and settlers joined forces with Russian exiles, Cossacks, a top Omsk officer, and two Kazakh sultans who controlled tens of thousands of horsemen. About a thousand conspirators were arrested days before the uprising, though the sense that no one had control over the Omsk frontier remained.

I nstead of stone walls, the fortress at Omsk had layers of defenses: a stockade of sharpened timbers, a high earthen rampart covered in weeds, and a waterless moat. The Petrashevists crossed a drawbridge to reach the south gate. Sentries paced back and forth along the rampart. Through the gate was the interior yard, about two hundred paces wide, where supply carts trundled noisily, soldiers performed drills, and prisoners lined up to be counted several times a day. The stockade's perimeter formed an irregular hexagon, and several brick and wooden buildings stood just inside—battalion barracks, prison barracks, imperial departments, houses for administration heads and their families.

Dostoevsky and Durov approached the Omsk fortress in the afternoon. Darkness was setting in as a mustached sergeant opened the gates and led them to the commandant's quarters. Major Krivtsov had a tall, robust frame that seemed stuffed into his uniform. He launched himself at prisoners in bursts of anger and had them beaten for absurd offenses: crying out from a bad dream was unacceptable. He would declare a random prisoner "drunk as a cobbler" and have him flogged, though he rarely needed to invent infractions. The major wore glasses, but he seemed to see everything without having to look. The prisoners called him "Eight Eyes." Unpredictable aggression and uncanny omniscience might not have served him well in life, but the traits were well suited for maintaining control over hundreds of military prisoners. He was unmarried, frequently drunk, and devoted to his poodle, Tresorka.

Dostoevsky recalled seeing Krivtsov approach them "like a malicious spider pouncing on a poor fly caught in its web." He examined the prisoners and asked them their names, though he knew everything he wanted to know already.

"Sergeant!" he called out. "To prison with them at once; give them a civilian shave in the guardhouse, immediately, half the head; fetters to be redone tomorrow."

Then he saw their uniforms. The prisoners' coats typically had a red or yellow diamond in the center of the back to give sharpshooters a clear target if they ever tried to escape, but these men's coats had yellow circles.

"What are these overcoats? Where did you get them?" he asked, turning them around. "It's a new uniform! It must be some sort of new uniform . . . Still in the planning stage . . . from Petersburg . . ."

He addressed the convoy guard. "Nothing with them?"

"Their own clothes, sir."

"Take it all away. Leave them only the underwear if it's white, but if it's colored, take it away. The rest will all be sold at auction. Record the money as prison revenue. A prisoner has no possessions."

Major Krivtsov berated them as fools for their political crimes and made it clear that they'd receive no special treatment. "See that you behave yourselves! That I hear nothing! Or else"—he emphasized—"cor-por-al pun-ish-ment! For the slightest misstep—the *rrrods*!" He meant the birch rods the soldiers used when they beat offending convicts. Nobles were not normally subject to corporal punishment, but he was not above beating noblemen.

Shortly before Dostoevsky's arrival, three Polish insurrectionists, all noblemen, were sent to Omsk for their involvement in the 1848 revolutions. Major Krivtsov immediately began berating the gray-haired elder. "Who is that? He looks like a brigand!" Jozef Zhokhovsky, a former mathematics professor at Warsaw University, had been sentenced to ten years for instigating rebellion among Polish Catholics.

"I am not a brigand but a political prisoner!" he told the major.

"Wha-a-at?! Insolence? That's insolence!" Krivtsov ordered him to the guardhouse. "A hundred lashes, right now, this minute!"

The guards led the old man away. "I'll show you!" Krivtsov kept shouting. "I'll teach you what it means to serve!"

The "Statutory Log of State and Political Prisoners" holds Dostoevsky's details:

Age: 28.
Denomination: Orthodox.
Build: Solid.
Apparent Features and Flaws: "Clear, white face, gray eyes, common nose,
dark blond hair, a minor scar on the forehead over the left eyebrow."

Officials registered the status of Dostoevsky and Durov. "These belong to the category of the most dangerous convicts." When they escorted the new arrivals to their barracks, Dostoevsky recoiled at his new home: blackened timbers, dripping ceilings, mud covering the rotting floorboards, tiny windows covered with frost. The poorly fed furnace emitted soot and heavy fumes that just perceptibly cut through the stench.

Prisoners in bare feet and half-shaved heads, some with branded faces, turned to the arriving noblemen with looks of pure malice. Tallow candles cast dim light on dozens of bodies shivering in sheepskin coats patched with canvas. They wore dual-colored trousers—one leg gray, the other leg navy or black. Some of their heads were shaved on the left or right side. Other scalps were shaved just in the front or the back. Omsk's prisoners were from all corners of the empire, from Riga to Kamchatka. "The devil wore out three pair of boot soles before he got us heaped together!" they'd say. There were Ukrainians, Finns, and Kalmyks. Catholics, Jews, and various Muslims—Chechens, Bashkirs, Lezgins, and three Dagestan Tatars, brothers. The youngest, Ali, had scars all over his body from bayonets and bullets, wounds from a guerrilla campaign against the Russian army that began before he was born.

And then there were the religious schismatics—the Raskolniks, sometimes referred to as the Old Believers. They were Orthodox Christians who had rejected the church's seventeenth-century reforms, no matter how minute. Raskolniks make the sign of the cross, for example, with two fingers instead of three. Involving the thumb is sacrilege. There were four Raskolniks in Dostoevsky's barracks, including a serene old man with wrinkles radiating out from his bright eyes. The prisoners affectionately called him Grandpa and gave him their money for safekeeping. He hid it inside a wooden post with a removable knot. Grandpa was imprisoned for denying Orthodox officials' authority and for refusing to attend a church dedication ceremony—a public display of disobedience. The prisoners had landed in Siberia for a wide array of crimes: theft, counterfeiting, vagabondage. Many were military criminals serving time for desertion or insubordination, or for assaulting officers, or for murdering them. And now they were all living together in this awful room.

What struck Dostoevsky was the general disorder of barracks life. The prisoners roamed around, dragging their chains, singing, arguing, and starting fights. Some played cards. Others were drunk in broad daylight. They smuggled vodka inside bulls' guts. They had contraband tools and weapons, pipes and tobacco. The guards didn't seem to care when prisoners smoked (how else do you fight scurvy?), but all of this was officially prohibited. Pens and paper were prohibited, as were all books except the Bible. Offenders could be flogged or chained to a wall or a wheelbarrow. Bawdy songs were prohibited. Musical instruments were prohibited. Enforcement was capricious, probably deliberately. Dostoevsky soon realized that the guards were integral to the vodka-smuggling business, and for the right price they'd arrange liaisons with prostitutes on the outskirts of town.

The capriciousness came from the top. Major Krivtsov would rush into the barracks in the middle of the night, inspect the sleeping prisoners, and then, in the morning, flog anyone who had been sleeping on his back or on his left side. "Sleep on your right side, as I ordered," Krivtsov would say. That's the side Jesus slept on, he'd say, and everyone should follow the Lord's example.

Krivtsov's arbitrary violence terrified Dostoevsky less than the specter of violence at the hands of the convicts sleeping beside him, a specter made more terrifying by the fact that they took such pleasure in Dostoevsky's suffering. They hated noblemen. One of the biggest prisoners nearly beat Dostoevsky with a kitchen tray almost immediately after his arrival. "You're going to see a lot more unpleasantness here," a Polish nobleman, Alexander Miretsky, told him. Miretsky had been in Omsk for years. "It's terribly hard here for all of us." Dostoevsky felt the convicts' resentment. "You nobles, iron beaks, pecked us to death." That was the relentless refrain. "You used to be a gentleman and torment the common folk, and now you're worse than the worst, you've become just like us."

His new life made that clear. Every now and then a platoon of armed soldiers would march the prisoners to a bathhouse in town. Dostoevsky later wrote about his first bath as a prisoner in such detail that few readers would forget it. He was still unable to walk comfortably in his shackles, he recalled, and he struggled with the puzzle of how to remove his clothes. You have to take off your underfetters first to give yourself some space between your ankles and the iron. Then you stuff one leg of your underwear through that narrow space and around your toes so you can pull the fabric back up through the shackle along your inner ankle. Once that leg is clothing-free, you stuff the entire garment through the space between your ankle and the iron on the other leg. He needed help with all of this.

When Dostoevsky opened the bathhouse door, he saw one hundred naked men packed in a room twelve paces wide. The air was filled with steam and soot, and there was no place to walk without stepping on someone. He squeezed his way forward, across the slimy floor, and purchased a prisoner's space on a bench for one kopeck. He felt the wet shoulders of the men beside him. On the floor at his feet there were more prisoners, hunched over and dousing themselves with hot water from small basins. Everyone was issued a coin-size piece of soap, which was pointless. Sweat and grimy water dripped down from the bodies of seated or standing men onto those huddled on the floor.

Through the haze he caught glimpses of crooked arms and switches of birch branches jerking downward as dead leaves fell to the floor. The prisoners were beating their backs over and over again, "to the point of intoxication," Dostoevsky thought, reddening the skin. The scars on their backs were raised up. He heard shouts echoing all around him, the sounds of chains yanked and tangled, and shrieks of delight from spectral figures deep in the steam. A mustached soldier occasionally slid the window open, checking on things.

A prisoner named Andrei Shalomentsev was always at Dostoevsky's side. He helped Dostoevsky remove his clothes, guided him through the bathhouse ("be careful, there's a step here") and offered to wash him, "so that you'll be all nice and clean," he said. He began soaping Dostoevsky, who felt helpless and embarrassed. "And now I'll wash your *little feet*," Shalomentsev said. Dostoevsky, not knowing what else to do, submitted to his attentions and thanked him later with tea and vodka.

Dostoevsky was famous for writing about poor folk, but he had never been very close to them until now. He had written about would-be murderers, but he had never actually encountered one until Siberia. Murder, for Dostoevsky, was something that he heard had happened out in the country-side to his father, something he had sometimes turned into gothic fantasy, a plot device for evoking chills in late-night readings in St. Petersburg drawing rooms. Now he was living with murderers—fifty-four, in fact—sharing tables and latrines with them, hauling bricks with them, sipping water from the same ladles. The complexities of murder, all the winding paths that might lead someone to take another person's life, were just beginning to become clear.

He wanted the details from the murderers themselves. Dostoevsky heard rumors about a former soldier named Sirotkin who struck him as a meek and rather pretty young man—twenty-three years old, with a smooth face, blue eyes, and reddish-blond hair. It took multiple attempts before Dostoevsky got him to open up. "I came here," Sirotkin said, "because I killed Grigory Petrovich, my company commander." Dostoevsky said he couldn't believe him. Sirotkin never fought. He didn't drink or gamble. He followed the rules, though it was true that Sirotkin strolled behind the other barracks during off-hours and performed services. Sometimes someone dressed him nicely, sometimes in a red shirt.

Sirotkin had been conscripted into the army and found military life unbearable. The officers and soldiers berated him mercilessly, and the company commander began singling him out for punishment. He couldn't endure the loathing and isolation. "I used to slip around a corner somewhere and cry there," he said. One autumn night he was on duty in the guardhouse. It was windy, pitch black. "I felt so heartsick, so heartsick!" He removed the bayonet from his rifle, took off his boot, placed the muzzle against his chest, and pulled the trigger with his toe. "Misfire!" he told Dostoevsky. "I examined the gun, cleaned the touchhole, put in some fresh powder, rubbed the flint a little, and put the gun to my chest again. What then, sir? The powder flashed, but again no shot!" So he put his boot back on, fixed the bayonet, and paced in silence. Sirotkin vowed to escape—anywhere but the army. His commander arrived thirty minutes later. "Is that any way to stand guard?" he shouted at Sirotkin. "I grabbed my gun and stuck the bayonet into him up to the muzzle."

The way the convicts told murder stories interested Dostoevsky as much as the details. Sirotkin recounted his crime with a touch of helplessness. Others would tell them with no emotion or with uncontrollable laughter. That's how the prisoners told Ilinsky's story. Ilinsky was a Russian nobleman who had been an ensign in the Siberia Corps. He was dissolute, had gone into debt, and became estranged from his wealthy father. Then, they said, Ilinsky had gone and killed the old man. His decapitated body was discovered a month later in a sewage ditch with the head carefully put back in place and resting on a pillow. Ilinsky denied any involvement. Dostoevsky remembered him as intelligent but thoughtless and somehow merry, even in prison—"the most excellent of spirits." He didn't seem cruel. Dostoevsky suspected he wasn't the murderer at all, and he turned out to be right.

But many of the murderers surprised him. Orlov, for example, was infamous—a runaway soldier and a brigand who confessed to many homicides. He stabbed old people. He stabbed his own daughters. Dostoevsky imagined a monster, but when he finally saw Orlov, he was surprised by how small and seemingly weak he was. His strength was his astonishing willpower. Dostoevsky had long talks with him, conducting a character study of "a new type," as Petersburg literati might have said. "I can say positively that I have never in my life met a man of stronger, more iron character than he," Dostoevsky declared.

Orlov had incredible drive ("a thirst for activity, a thirst for revenge, a thirst for attaining a set goal") and absolute self-control. His cravings were never physical. Dostoevsky probed him for details about his life, but when Orlov realized that the novelist was looking for signs of repentance, he looked upon Dostoevsky with pity, as if he were a little boy. Then he burst out laughing—genuine mirth. When the laughter subsided, all that remained was contempt. Orlov despised Dostoevsky for how weak and submissive he was while he, Orlov, was indomitable. Orlov was vain, like most prisoners, yet he never boasted or sought anyone's praise. He was handsome. He was contemptuous of everything. He was afraid of nothing.

If Dostoevsky were being honest, he would have to admit that he despised submissiveness as well. He despised it in the slavish, unthinking obedience of a prisoner named Yefim Belikh who slept in the bunk next to him. Belikh was a highly decorated former commander of a frontier outpost. He was tall and lean, cantankerous, dim-witted, and "punctilious as a German," Dostoevsky recalled. "An odd bird." He was handy—a locksmith, a gilder. He could fix boots and shoes. He spent his free time making baskets, lanterns, and toys to sell in Omsk. His profits bought him a pillow, linen, and a folding mattress. He sewed shirts for Dostoevsky out of government linen for just a few kopecks. He sewed him a quilt. He told him where to buy scraps of old prison broadcloth so that he could make him warm trousers and jackets.

Belikh could not countenance rule violations. According to prison logs, he had been convicted of a "faulty . . . understanding of patriotism"—faulty in its violent excesses. Krivtsov made him the "senior prisoner" of their barrack to help keep the others in line. Belikh would scold misbehaving prisoners, who would simply laugh, though that did not deter him. He found contentment in prison, as if being the best of all prisoners awarded him yet another decoration, as if it pleased the tsar. Dostoevsky looked for some hint of bitterness or anger in him—he *wanted* to find it—but there was nothing. Belikh escaped prison by loving it. While gluing his lanterns, he would chatter for hours about his favorite military exercises, highlights from his company reviews, the medals he had received, the names of his commanders, the years they had served, the latest regulation updates. "And all," Dostoevsky recalled, "with such a level, sedate voice, like drops of water dripping."

Never being alone was a great torment to Dostoevsky, and he tried finding solitude by reading the leather-bound Bible the Decembrist wives had given him. He dug his fingernail into the pages beside verses he liked, making small marks in the shape of a cross. There were hundreds of them. He craved the solitude of sleep, whether it brought him dreams or nightmares or a few hours of oblivion. And if sleep wouldn't come, he would lie down on his bed—three wooden planks—close his eyes, and pretend to sleep (right side only!), but this would only amplify the bickering all around him. "You Moldavian plague!" "Go talk to a Turkish saber!" They had elevated swearing to an art, a form of pleasure. "You slurp *shchi* from a bast shoe!" A petty thief was a "pantry whore."

Sometimes Dostoevsky sought solitude by walking behind the barracks during free hours, counting the stockade palings, but Shalomentsev, who had been so helpful in the bathhouse, would spot him from a distance and bolt over.

"Hello," he'd say.

"Hello."

"Am I bothering you?"

No, he wasn't bothering him.

"I wanted to ask you about Napoleon."

His questions were urgent, as if time were running out on the answers. He seemed to have a list saved up.

"Is it true what they say, that there are apes whose arms reach their heels, and who are as tall as the tallest man?"

"Yes, there are such apes."

"What sort are they?"

Dostoevsky gave the answer his best shot.

"Where do they live?"

"In hot countries. There are some on the island of Sumatra," Dostoevsky told him.

"That's America, isn't it? Don't they say the people there walk upside down?"

"Not upside down. You're talking about the antipodes."

Dostoevsky explained America and Australia. They covered a lot of ground together.

"Well, good-bye," Shalomentsev would suddenly say. "My thanks to you."

Some of the prisoners found Shalomentsev terrifying, "the most fearless of all the convicts." He'd knife you without remorse. He was a former soldier sent to Siberia for theft and for insubordination—he tore the epaulets off his company commander. Shalomentsev told Major Krivtsov that he was going to kill him, or if he failed, he'd harm himself. He had a shoemaker's awl hidden in his sleeve. Nothing came of it beyond a flogging for making the threat, and he accepted his punishment stoically. Dostoevsky might have taken his compulsive questioning as a sign of some desperate search for the truth. And perhaps his bathhouse attentions were an artless expression of kindness. In any case, when Shalomentsev asked, Dostoevsky let him borrow his Bible.

Dostoevsky's only genuine companion was a prison dog named Sharik, a large black mutt with white spots and a bushy tail, which survived on kitchen scraps. "Nobody ever petted him," Dostoevsky recalled. He fed him some bread the first day he saw him and began soothing him. Sharik would yelp at the sight of Dostoevsky, put his paws on his shoulders, big tail wagging, and lick his face. One day Dostoevsky returned from a work site with a companion for Sharik, a puppy he had found with shaggy, mouse-colored fur, one ear droopy, and a wide body. He named him Kultyapka (Stumpy). They'd both come bounding around corners when they heard Dostoevsky's voice.

But the companionship Dostoevsky craved most was never just around the corner. Month after month, while other prisoners got letters from their families back in Russia, Dostoevsky received nothing. Not a single letter. No news. No money. No encouragement or love. He felt orphaned. Was it his fault or was time slowly erasing him from everyone's memory? This is what it meant to be a hard-labor convict in Siberia. They were, in prison parlance, severed branches.

To Dostoevsky it felt more like being buried alive. The prison was a living Dead House. At night, the soldiers would lock them into the stifling wooden box swarming with fleas, lice, and cockroaches. Yefim Belikh would make the rounds, telling prisoners to tidy up, to settle down and go to sleep, but who can sleep when the night is filled with raving and crying? "We're a beaten folk," they'd say, "we're all beaten up inside; that's why we shout in our sleep." You'd drift off for a moment and wake up with the shrapnel of someone else's nightmare in your ear, ". . . his head, his head!" One night, Dostoevsky heard quiet, repressed weeping. It was Grandpa, the old Raskolnik, his eyes lit up by the dim tallow candles. He had climbed up to a shelf on top of the hearth of the barracks furnace, where he customarily sat and prayed.

"Lord Jesus Christ, have mercy on us!" was his habitual petition. But that night, he was praying from one of the handwritten prayer books the Raskolniks used. "Lord, do not abandon me!"

Eight

The Social Contract

S ometimes you go looking for thieves—at certain cafés or lodging
houses—and sometimes the thieves find you. It was mid-September
1834 when Lacenaire saw someone hailing him from across boulevard
du Temple. It turned out to be Alphonse Bâton, one of his Poissy prison mates.
He was a tailor by trade, an extra for the Opéra-Comique for fun, and a thief
by vocation. His criminal record must have hampered his acting career because Bâton was an excellent performer with a talent for shedding tears on
command. But he was being forthright with Lacenaire when he suggested
they rob a wealthy merchant in his building. After the falling-out with Vigouroux and the collapse of his literary ambitions, however, Lacenaire had begun
thinking about something much bigger. Why rob a merchant when you can
rob a bank?

He was not suggesting that they storm a bank vault. Rather, Lacenaire
would walk into a bank and ask to see a specific employee—someone who
no longer worked there. The news of his departure would be quite unfortunate because he had worked with that fine gentleman for years, he would say,
and now he needed a favor. He would tell them that he works for a distant
bank—in Lyons or Rouen—and that he has to collect payment for a bill of
exchange due in the next few days. But he's leaving Paris that afternoon and
doesn't have time. Would they mind collecting it for his bank? He would give
them his esteemed client's Paris address and the date the payment is due.

In other words, Lacenaire would ask a bank to collect payment on what was essentially a postdated check. This was how large amounts of money typically changed hands. People transferred funds by exchanging cash for a bank's bill of exchange, which could move across borders and large distances securely, and the payers' and payees' banks would credit and debit each other's balances. Dozens of collection clerks crisscrossed Paris every day carrying satchels filled with cash and banknotes. Lacenaire's scheme was to get a bank to send a collection clerk over to his address, ostensibly so that some esteemed client could hand over whatever amount of cash the bill specifies. But instead of finding the client, the clerk would find two ex-convicts. They would take his money, and they would kill him.

Nothing about the plan was easy. They needed the name of a former bank employee. They needed to rent an apartment at a respectable address. They needed good furniture, too, to complete the illusion of the residence of someone wealthy enough to be holding large amounts of cash. The "out-of-town bank official" would have to play the role well enough to make reluctant bankers act on behalf of someone they had never seen before. And when the collection clerk arrived, Lacenaire and Bâton would have to kill him without drawing the attention of any neighbors. They wanted no witnesses.

Bâton was not the ideal partner. He was neither fearless nor particularly bright, but he was desperate, and he had confidence in Lacenaire—a winning quality. So they started making and selling forgeries to get the money to rent an apartment and acquire furniture. It's unclear how Lacenaire knew the names of former bank employees, but the two years he had spent working at a bank seem not to have been wasted on him.

They rented an apartment under the name Bonin. On September 30, a likely-sounding due date, a clerk for Pillet-Will Bank arrived at 66 rue de la Chanvrerie to collect 1,580 francs, an innocently specific amount. He was asked to arrive late in the afternoon, after a long day of collections. But the name on the bill was difficult to read. He told the doorman he was looking for—a Monsieur Bluet? Or Boulet? No one by either of those names lived in the building, the doorman said, so the clerk left with 91,000 francs still in his safekeeping. Lacenaire and Bâton remained waiting upstairs for nothing.

They tried again about six weeks later. They rented a small fifth-floor room with their diminished funds. Lacenaire posed as an out-of-town teacher needing nothing more than a humble pied-à-terre in Paris, and he would be staying with a friend. Things went worse this time around. The furniture they rented never materialized, and when the clerk from Rougemont de Löwenberg Bank arrived to collect one thousand francs from the teacher, it struck the doorman as rather odd.

"You go like that," he told the clerk, "to people who are brand new here and who don't even have enough to sleep on?"

When Lacenaire opened the door, the collection clerk was there, but so was the doorman, who had decided to usher the clerk upstairs and observe the exchange. Lacenaire and Bâton made up some story about why they weren't prepared to pay, and they vacated the apartment the next day.

The partner Lacenaire really wanted was Victor Avril. He was only eighteen when they met in Poissy—"too young for me to have anything to do with him," Lacenaire later wrote. Avril was a roofer serving five years for theft, and his description in official documents is unremarkable—wide nose, pale complexion, budding beard, smallpox mark. The exception was his gray-red eyes. When Lacenaire was back in Poissy nearly five years later, he found himself in the workshop beside Avril. The young man began telling him everything about himself. His passions and instincts were clearer, and when Lacenaire looked at him now, his gray-red eyes seemed feline. One day Avril told him that he had tried killing a guard with a sharpened file after the guard attempted to take it away from him.

"From that moment I knew he was the man I was looking for," Lacenaire recalled. "He was made for me," he said, "because he had no shadow of reasoning power." Avril was scheduled to be released shortly after Lacenaire's second bank robbery attempt. On November 25, Lacenaire made the trip back to Poissy, thirty kilometers away, and waited for Avril at the prison gates.

Avril knew about Lacenaire's plan and the money it required. He had been filing and polishing machinery in the prison workshops for the past five years, so he came out with two hundred francs in wages. Avril was tougher than Bâton, but he had no self-control. He couldn't wait to spend his money, and he was already thirty francs down by the time they reached Paris. Avril was politely deferential with Lacenaire. Yes, he'd say, Lacenaire knew best, he was the clever one, and yes, he'd save his money for their scheme. But he wouldn't let Lacenaire hold his purse, and shortly after arriving in Paris, Avril left him for wine and gambling.

He came back about a week later when his pockets were empty. Luckily, Lacenaire had some money from skeleton key thefts, and one of his friends—a pimp known as the Cutler—let them borrow an apartment he had on rue de Sartine. They bought a couple of three-edged files (Avril's special weapon), and Lacenaire sharpened them while his partner smoked. Lacenaire was now "Louis Guérin" waiting for a collection clerk to arrive from the Rothschild Bank—his biggest target yet. Everything was set, but the clerk never showed up. All that work for nothing. Avril decided to steal the pimp's curtains, which Lacenaire found rather ungrateful. But that's how desperate they were. They had no money, and nothing was working.

Lacenaire decided it was time to visit "Aunt Madeleine." They would take the money they needed from Jean-François Chardon, one of the "aunts" they knew in Poissy. He was now a con artist going around in a tunic and scapular, selling devotional objects, and pocketing donations to his bogus Charité de Sainte-Camille. An acquaintance told him that there was a large amount of money hidden in Chardon's apartment: ten thousand francs in cash. It was the payoff for Chardon's repeated petitions to the queen to support an alms-house. Chardon lived with his mother, a sixty-six-year-old widow—an actual charity case—and for a small fee the acquaintance would tell him their sched-ules so he could rob them when they weren't home.

Lacenaire decided it was best to kill both of them, the son and his mother. He hated Chardon. Whatever animus existed between them began in prison and escalated after a new affront: Chardon was a blackmailer, and he threat-ened to have Lacenaire arrested, possibly for both forgery and his "infamous habits"—"habits" they shared, a sexuality that made both of them loathed and isolated. After Chardon's threat, Lacenaire channeled his broad outrage at the world's injustice toward the immediate injustice perpetrated by a man who might have reminded him just a bit too much of himself.

Avril acquiesced to the plan but then hesitated. Colluding with Lacenaire, he realized, would mean being at his mercy. The partners were walking down rue Saint-Martin toward the Chardons' apartment when Avril backed out. "I know you," Avril told him. Anyone could blackmail.

It took just a few days for Avril's destitution and hunger to outweigh his qualms. On December 14, he woke up in the morning and told Lacenaire, "Well, if you want me to, today, I'm ready." After planning all the details over lunch at the Big Seven cabaret, they walked up the damp stairwell in the passage du Cheval Rouge. Avril, unarmed, began strangling "Aunt Madeleine" while Lacenaire attacked with his sharpened file. Then Avril grabbed the ax hanging on the door and broke the man's skull while Lacenaire went into the other room and began stabbing the old woman in the face. They moved the bed aside, and Lacenaire heard a nearby clock striking one as he was breaking into the armoire to discover little more than some silverware and five hundred francs. It was not what they were expecting. But how could anyone have believed that the queen had given Jean-François Chardon ten thousand francs for an almshouse?

The next day, Lacenaire took the money, along with what Avril had gotten from selling some of the Chardons' belongings, and started his bank robbery scheme yet again, still hoping to improve his performance. The last collection clerk might not have shown up because he simply did not play the part convincingly enough. This time they would try the Mallet Bank. He would ask the bank to collect on two bills, and then, if they hesitated, he would reduce it to one, a smaller, simpler favor—collecting from a Monsieur Mahossier at a nearby address. They would stay away from the apartment beforehand so their faces would be difficult to describe. They needed a building without a doorman. And they needed to get rid of the body.

They rented an apartment on rue Montorgueil, claimed they were law students, and acquired simple furniture. They asked the landlord for straw for a bed. Everything was going well until a few days later. Avril forcibly interfered with the arrest of his girlfriend, a prostitute, so the police arrested him as well. When Lacenaire tried getting him out, he was nearly arrested himself.

He needed a new partner immediately—the apartment was his for exactly two weeks, until December 31. On the thirtieth, Bâton introduced Lacenaire to a man who claimed he would kill someone for twenty francs: his name was Hippolyte-Martin François—le Grand Hippolyte, people called him, given his height and build. He had been wounded five times while serving in Algeria and Martinique. He had big red sideburns, and he was missing three fingers. Lacenaire wanted to match the impression, so he told François about how he had murdered Chardon and his mother two weeks earlier, how they used an ax and a sharpened file. François told him that he needed money, and he was willing to do anything.

The following morning, December 31, 1834, Lacenaire strolled to 66 rue Montorgueil with a small cane and a book under his arm. When the final preparations were complete, he waited calmly on the landing outside the apartment door, smoking a pipe and reading Jean-Jacques Rousseau's *The Social Contract.*

At half past three that afternoon, an eighteen-year-old clerk named Genevay walked up to the fourth floor and found the apartment at the rear of the building. MAHOSSIER was written across the door in chalk. A gentleman wearing a long frock coat and a red cravat answered the door. He closed it behind them and nudged the clerk toward a back room. Something wasn't right. It was dark. There was a table with paper, quills, and ink. There were two bales of straw and a large wicker basket. There was a big man in the corner wearing a bronze-colored hunting jacket, a cap, black shoes, and black stockings.

When Genevay asked whom he should talk to, Lacenaire pulled out his sharpened file and stabbed him in the shoulder, hitting his right lung, possibly puncturing it. Genevay started screaming. François sprang forward to strangle him, but somehow his fingers got in Genevay's mouth. Lacenaire tried pulling Genevay's satchel away, and Genevay screamed louder—"Thief!" He elbowed François and broke free.

They decided to run. Lacenaire followed François down the stairs, shouting, "Thief! Assassin!" to sow confusion. Genevay, bleeding, staggered out after them. Neighbors gathered on the landings. An old woman grabbed Lacenaire by his coat, and he began dragging her, making eye contact before breaking free. Another neighbor emerged from her apartment and joined the chorus of shouts, but she did not yet know why.

Nine

The Dead Man

Early each morning, the prisoners marched through town in two rows to the beat of a drum, sometimes accompanied by honking geese from the prison yard. The sight of so many men in chains, with half-shaven heads and multicolored uniforms, under armed guard, provoked fear in the towns-people. It was the fear of revenge, that at any moment "a prisoner might throw himself at them with a knife," Dostoevsky noted. Sometimes the spectacle provoked ridicule ("Not enough gray cloth, and not enough black!"), and other times it inspired people to give alms. ("Here's for your geese!") Once, while Dostoevsky was returning to the barracks alone, escorted by soldiers, a ten-year-old girl, "pretty as a little angel," he recalled, ran up to him. "Here, 'unfortunate,' take a little kopeck for Christ's sake," she said, putting a copper coin in his hand. It was a quarter kopeck, and he cherished it.

The prisoners built the government's infrastructure in and around Omsk. They made bricks. They laid foundations. Some worked with wood or metal. Others made the prison uniforms. The retired engineer-litterateur Dostoevsky was given menial, low-skill tasks. He shoveled snow from houses and govern-ment buildings. He turned a heavy lathe in a workshop to help the woodworkers make banisters or table legs. He carried twelve-pound bricks on his back as the ropes dug into his shoulders. He fired alabaster in a kiln and then pounded it with a mallet, crushing the alabaster into a white sparkling dust that filled the air.

After work, he would return to the prison kitchen and eat watery shchi (cabbage soup) fortified with beef, when he had money, or with insects, which were free. Sharik and Kultyapka were his only reliable solace after work assignments. It occurred to him that if the soldiers ever wanted to crush someone's spirit—"to annihilate a man totally, to punish him with the most terrible punishment"—all they needed to do was assign him utterly meaningless labor, day after day. Dig a massive ditch, then fill it up. Then dig it again. Crush stones into sand.

The hard-labor system's primary method of punishment was less creative than Dostoevsky's. It was the gauntlet. They'd strip an offender to the waist, tie his arms to rifle stocks, and pull him through two lines of soldiers holding three-foot birch canes. Each soldier was ordered to deliver a single blow. The gauntlet's length depended on the infraction. There could be fifty soldiers on each side. There could be five hundred. A convict who collapsed would be thrown into a cart and pulled through the rest of the gauntlet that way. A doctor would halt the punishment if death were imminent, but it would resume when the convict recovered.

The commanding officers liked to toy with the men beforehand. One lieutenant would wait for the prisoner to beg for mercy, hoping he would instruct the soldiers to go easy on him. "Be a father to me!"

The lieutenant, tall and plump, would remind the soldier that it is the law that punishes, and that it would be sinful to relax the law. Then he would relent. "Well, all right! So be it, just for you! I know I'm sinning, but so be it," he would say. He would lighten the punishment. "You swear to me that you'll behave yourself in the future?"

The prisoner would give his word. "Lord strike me dead."

Very well, but this would be the last time.

"Take him." The two soldiers would pull the prisoner toward the gauntlet, and the first canes would rise up. The lieutenant would shout out, "Punish him!" and the canes would crash down on his back amid screams. "Burn him!" the lieutenant would shout. "Thrash, thrash! Scorch him! More, more! Harder on the orphan, harder on the rogue! Cut him down!" Each soldier would strike as hard as possible while the lieutenant would laugh hysterically in high-pitched waves. He would double over with laughter, gasping. It never got old.

Virtually every prisoner at Omsk received corporal punishment. Dostoevsky desperately wanted to know what it was like. He drew out their stories, elicited the smallest details of the experience, what the prisoners thought, what the gauntlet felt like. He wanted to know the intensity and quality of the pain, and he always got the same answer: "It burns, it scorches like fire." But this was unsatisfactory. He watched one gauntlet survivor return to the hospital. The other prisoners carefully removed the splinters from his wounds and dressed them in damp sheets. He observed how the survivors' gaze wandered far off, how they bit their lips until they bled, how they paced, how they never moaned or cried or spoke.

Dostoevsky spoke at length to one convict imprisoned for murdering an officer. He had to go through a gauntlet of one thousand soldiers five times. The man knew he could withstand abuse, but five thousand strokes was daunting. He tried getting baptized, hoping they would be lenient if he were a Christian instead of a Kalmyk Buddhist. They were not. He tried parceling out the ordeal by "playing dead," but before long he didn't need theatrics. After two thousand strokes, he collapsed. His face turned blue; he was foaming at the mouth and hardly breathing. They carried him to the hospital repeatedly and repeatedly brought him back for more. But he was alive, he told Dostoevsky. He endured it. It was his great fortune to have been beaten so mercilessly as a child.

The gauntlet was the dignified punishment. It was meted out by soldiers wielding canes. For grave infractions, criminals could be beaten with the rods (ten to fifteen birch switches bound with cords), with the lash (three leather tails knotted at the ends), or with the knout, the most fearsome instrument. The knout had several hardened, three-foot rawhide thongs with metal tips that gouged the flesh.

Only executioners could wield the knouts, lashes, and rods. They mastered their skill like a trade and boasted of their prowess, how they could kill a man with one blow, how they could rip a brick from a wall. Siberian executioners were typically convicts themselves. Punishment was their hard labor. They lived under armed guard in permanent isolation to protect them from revenge and to insulate them from bribes and sympathy-inducing friendships. The distance gave them an aura. They developed an air of superiority, a genteel bearing. It occurred to Dostoevsky that it was their refined manners that made them so terrifying. He believed there was something of the Marquis de Sade in them. They had succumbed to the thrilling pleasure of having absolute power over another person. That pleasure was hidden in everyone, he believed, and he wanted it to remain hidden. Its emergence sickened the executioners, and it would sicken all of society.

Weeks after Major Krivtsov had the older Polish prisoner flogged for his insolence, he summoned the prisoner to his quarters.

"Zhokhovsky! I offended you. I was wrong to flog you, I know it. I repent. Do you understand that? I, *I*, *I*—repent!"

The major's eyes became bloodshot when he drank. His silver epaulets would have glinted had they not been so dirty. "Do you understand that I, *I*, your superior, summoned you in order to ask your forgiveness? Do you feel that? Who are *you* next to me? A worm! Less than a worm: you're a prisoner! While I, by God's grace, am a major. A major! Do you understand that?"

Zhokhovsky answered that he understood that, yes. But Krivtsov wasn't sure he appreciated the magnitude of the event. The major's blotchy face got closer.

"Do you feel it, do you feel it fully, in all its fullness? Are you capable of understanding and feeling it? Just think: I, I, a major . . ."

Nothing encapsulated the imperial regime's self-defeating brutality better than the practice of branding convicts' faces. The tsarist regime carefully regulated the procedure. A doctor would apply a spring tourniquet to pull the skin taut. Then he would heat a standardized copper plate with a blade template of the letters they intended to sear into the flesh. *C П* or *C O K* or *K A T*. He would press the hot brand into the skin to make clear, clean cuts and pour indigo and India ink into the wounds. Anyone who failed to brand someone properly could be prosecuted. Convicts who tried to escape were branded so they could never blend in. There was a brand for thieves (*B O R*, *vor*—thief) and another brand for convicts who refused to identify themselves (*Б*, for *brodiaga*—vagabond). Every brand carried the same essential message from the tsar: *this is who you are.*

Branding was like a table of criminal ranks, tattooed and razor precise, though there was no possibility of promotion, and it actually increased Siberia's disarray. A branded convict was locked into a life of crime (who would hire a convict?), and the growing population of lifelong criminals became uncontrollable. There were at least twice as many exiles arriving each year as officials anticipated. Siberia's infrastructure and civil service personnel were woefully inadequate. The exile system received no state money (it depended on philanthropy), and supplies and funds disappeared on their way across the Urals. Corruption and embezzlement were rampant, and the leadership resisted reform. Basic record keeping was shoddy. Convict laborers were accidentally sent to the wrong destinations, and prisoners could easily switch their identities (and their sentences) with others in their convoy. They called it "changing their fate." Sometimes orders from Petersburg got lost in the paperwork, and sometimes they were simply ignored. The governor-general tasked with reforming Siberia was exasperated. "There is not a country in the world where words correspond less to reality."

And yet Siberia's existence beyond the reach of firm imperial control made the land a refuge for outcasts and misfits and the marginalized—Cossacks, runaway serfs, and (more and more frequently) Raskolniks. They began coming after the great schism—the raskol—of the 1660s. The Raskolniks rejected the Orthodox Church's seventeenth-century liturgical reforms, which were intended to bring Russian practices closer to Greek Orthodoxy. For Raskolniks, it was modern Russian Orthodoxy that was deviant. They insisted upon the traditional seven loaves of bread at the Eucharistic service instead of five, two hallelujah chants after the psalmody instead of three, and no polyphonic singing (only monodic). They preserved original prayers: one must pray for God's blessing "for all of us" (*o vsekh nas*) instead of "upon all of us" (*na vsekh nas*). Once the first Raskolniks broke away from the church, the split widened. Multiple sects emerged over the years. The Spirit Wrestlers rejected icons, the doctrine of original sin, and the divine inspiration of the Bible. (How could a book contain God's word?) One sect was known as the *Skoptsy*—the Castrates. Many Skoptsy had their testicles, genitals, nipples, or breasts ritually removed or scarred. They wanted to be victorious over the flesh, to break with the natural world, to become like angels.

Many Raskolniks saw themselves as the only genuine Russians left in an empire that had lost its way. By the nineteenth century, Raskolniks represented 10 percent of the Russian Orthodox population. They had lived through eras of tolerance and persecution, at times becoming thriving entrepreneurs, at other times hunted down and tortured as loathsome apostates. In an autocracy resting upon Orthodoxy, ritual disobedience is tantamount to political disobedience.

This is why Nicholas's regime subjected Raskolniks to forced conversions and public shaming. Raskolnik merchants were expelled from guilds. Schismatic monasteries and hermitages were destroyed or seized, and sects like the Skoptsy were exiled to Siberia en masse if they hadn't already gone willingly. Raskolniks initially responded to government assaults by capturing and abusing Orthodox priests. They broke into Orthodox churches, stripped them bare, and performed reconsecration ceremonies. Entire communities sometimes locked themselves inside their churches and set themselves on fire. But more often they retreated to rural areas far from wicked civilization.

The most radical Raskolniks believed the tsar was the Antichrist incarnate. They refused to pay taxes, ignored all laws and decrees, and paid heed to no armies. They eschewed the tsar's name and likeness on all documents, including coins and paper rubles—money was an instrument of the Antichrist. They wanted to escape what the world had become. The *Beguny* (the Runners) rejected not only all connections to the state but also to their families. A secret, nomadic life was the only path to salvation. They rejected printed books. They rejected the use of their own names. When the world belongs to the Antichrist, the only way to evade his control is to run. They came to Siberia.

Dostoevsky was fascinated by the ways people found freedom in Siberia. He took a special interest in Grandpa, the old Raskolnik in his barracks, and listened. "At the end of the world the river of fire shall flow, to the doom of sinners, to the cleansing of saints. All cliffs and mountains shall become flat. For mountains are made by the demons." Dostoevsky thought of Raskolniks as dogmatic, but he admired Grandpa's honesty and fervor. Suffering is what kindled it, Dostoevsky realized. Suffering was a strength-giving virtue. A hard-labor prison was a blessing.

Most prisoners pursued another kind of liberation. "Money is minted freedom," Dostoevsky said of life in a Siberian prison. It felt liberating even if it remained in your pocket, like some quantum of power standing by. It promised at least a small measure of comfort and dignity beyond government-issue essentials. This was why the convicts worked so assiduously in the evenings with their forbidden tools, carving, gluing, and hammering by candlelight to fill orders from the townspeople—Omsk had no craftsmen to speak of. One prisoner was making beautiful half boots for an official's wife. Dostoevsky admired the handiwork until he noticed the mouse-colored fur lining the boots and was horrified. It was Kultyapka.

Nothing was safe in the fortress prison. He watched men nearly kill one another over a foot rag. Stealing was a form of freedom, too. There really was a liberating power in taking something, simply making it yours. Major Krivtsov took anything valuable from new prisoners, selling what he could and keeping what he wanted, like wool suits and satin pillows. Dostoevsky paid a prisoner for a small chest with a lock for his valuables. By the time he discovered his empty chest the next day, the thieves were already sobering up from their spree. Prisoners stole from Dostoevsky continually, without hesitation, as if his carelessness deserved punishment.

One day he realized his Bible was missing. He had let Shalomentsev borrow it, he remembered, and so it was Shalomentsev who had to tell him that his Bible—bound in leather, priced at two rubles and twenty-five kopecks—was long gone. And it was such a pitiful sight, really, watching the poor nobleman trying to account for that big book of his. He just wouldn't stop looking for it.

Some men gambled for money. In the middle of the night, a handful of men would squat over greasy cards and little piles of coppers strewn about on a small rug. They'd pay someone a kopeck to watch for guards in the freezing entryway. Throughout the night they'd play three leaves. Anyone who lost could take his miserable foot rag or spoon to the barracks pawnbroker for a fraction of the object's value and retrieve it at ruthless interest if his luck turned. But walking away with money wasn't the only victory. The convicts felt free just getting away with it, seizing the night hours for themselves.

Out here, in Siberia, freedom was not some rational achievement of history. It was not some World Spirit sweeping away chaos and tyranny. Freedom was flinging away all the dirty coppers you'd saved in your chest or had given to Grandpa to hide. A prisoner wants money, Dostoevsky observed, in order to "throw it away like wood chips." Freedom had been whittled down to abandonment. And the greatest, most spectacular abandonment in the hard-labor prison was a rollicking, drunken binge.

Dostoevsky was amazed at how a prisoner would work and save for months so that one morning he could dress up in fine clothes—a Siberian caftan or a calico shirt with a brass-studded belt, borrowed or purchased precisely for this day. He would buy food (beef and Siberian dumplings) and eat it conspicuously. He would get a cup of overpriced vodka from a tapster, drink it down, and buy more, each cup more diluted than the last. He would hire a musician. One of the Polish prisoners would play dances on his violin and follow the reveler as he sauntered through all the barracks. The guards would look the other way. Everyone instinctively respected the ritual's importance. The prisoners would bear the carouser's jibes, steer him away from trouble, compliment his outfit, and give him space until the whole procession slackened into stumbling and the fine clothes got traded for the last, watery cups and the other prisoners finally put him to bed.

The reckless freedom that the prisoners found in binges seemed to echo their criminal histories. There was a pattern. A prisoner would be well behaved for years, and then suddenly—"as if some devil has gotten into him," Dostoevsky wrote—he'd become unruly or turn violent. "Suddenly something in him comes unhinged." Dostoevsky listened to stories of murder that he would never write about (possibly for fear of censorship), but he never forgot them. One convict, a serf, told him about how his landlord raped his wife on his wedding night, so the serf took an ax from the shed, concealed it on his body, and waited. As the gentleman strolled alone in his garden, the serf hopped over a low fence and crept up to him on the grass. But he wanted the lord to see him, to know why it was happening. So he coughed. The lord turned around and felt a flash of recognition before the serf swung the ax down and the blood and the brains sprayed out. Everything changed after that. The serf killed a captain on his convoy to Siberia with a folding knife he had traded for a shirt. The convicts were exhausted, he explained, and he began protesting when no one fed them. "Where's the rioter?" the captain shouted after hearing of the complaints. The serf cut him from his gut to his throat.

During the long evening hours, without a Bible to read, Dostoevsky was left to ply the only craft he knew: ruminating over the lives of the people around him, working his way into the thoughts of killers. A person murders to exact justice, Dostoevsky thought, but once he crosses the line, it's as if all restraints vanish by some demonic fiat, and the murderer can "revel in the most boundless and unbridled freedom." So he begins to murder indiscriminately, "for fun, for a rude word, for a glance, for a trifle." He binges on the intoxicating horror of himself. All that mattered was feeling one brief moment of abandon, something so intense that it could vitalize you by taking you to the brink of your obliteration. Or maybe it was like being buried alive, Dostoevsky thought, like waking up in a coffin and pounding on the dreaded planks, pushing helplessly against the earth. You know you'll never escape, but logic doesn't matter: "It's convulsions."

Weren't many crimes like that? Surely revolutionary fervor could be fleeting, unintended, and illogical. That, after all, is how Dostoevsky had described his own crimes to the Commission of Inquiry. "I never acted with malice or premeditation against the government," he insisted. "What I did do was done thoughtlessly on my part and much of it almost accidentally." Taking someone's life seems like a grotesque act of will, but perhaps it was nearly devoid of any deliberate willpower whatsoever.

The murderous convulsion was difficult to articulate, so paradoxical and intense, but Dostoevsky kept trying. He imagined it as the feeling of standing on the ledge of a tower, longing for the rushing wind, the brief, embracing emptiness, and actually doing it. Stepping off and feeling alive. A person kills, Dostoevsky wrote, out of a "convulsive display of his personality, an instinctive longing for his own self, a desire to declare himself." The serf pulls out the ax so that the lord will look him in the eye at last, so that the final message flitting across his still-intact brain will be a defiant serf's declaration: *I exist.*

Dostoevsky did not go on drunken sprees in prison. Nor did he gamble or steal or lash out. Dostoevsky declared his existence by writing. While the other convicts were fighting over rags or playing cards, he hoarded scraps of paper. He had somehow gotten hold of a pen and ink, and he would jot down a few words whenever it was safe. "The iron beaks have pecked us to death." It had to be fast. "On your word we'll see daylight, father." He wrote down the ingenious curses and insults, like the ones about the Turkish sabers and slurping shchi from a shoe.

The argot helped him sketch convicts' lives. He recorded idioms and expressions, like the devil wearing out three pairs of shoes to gather them all together. There were songs he'd never heard, prison proverbs, and observations. "An old tree creaks but lives." "Nobody sows our kind, the fools, we spawn all by ourselves." He was amassing hundreds of small pieces like tiles for a mosaic. There were bits of arguments and dialogue. "Don't you act like a devil in a suitcase!" "Look at the fatso! The devil must be feeding you cannonballs." One note captured the zeal for bingeing: "Hey, you! You have money, but you're sleeping!"

They would appear harmless if a guard ever found them. "Haven't been home, but I know everything!" was one hastily scrawled line. "Godfather! Timoshka! Executioner!" was another. But they were consequential. He was trying to smuggle the experience of a Siberian fortress prison back to St. Petersburg. He wanted to render not just a "new type" but a new culture—or, more accurately, a rich blend of cultures assembling across one of the largest empires in history—and he had to do it with bits of text small enough to hide from Eight Eyes and all the guards. Each colorful fragment risked severe punishment. The guards conducted surprise searches in the middle of the night, and people caught with *this* type of contraband—an inkwell would've been enough—were typically beaten.

Dostoevsky escaped the searches by writing and stashing his notes in the prisoners' ward of the military hospital, half a kilometer from the fortress, where the medical staff was sympathetic to the exiled novelist, a physician's son. The hospital was a drab yellow building on Sorrowful Street. Armed soldiers stood guard in the corridor and outside the barred windows, and the doors were locked with iron bolts. Each of the two wards was a long narrow room with a couple dozen green wooden beds along the walls. It smelled of sickness and medications. Convicts paced in their slippers, caps, and brown hospital robes. A man with blackened tooth stumps hacked up phlegm and smeared it on his robe so he could preserve his handkerchief. Tubercular patients coughed up blood. Some men had smallpox-disfigured faces. Some were carried into the ward screaming, manic or violent. Some were put in straitjackets or bounced from ward to ward or removed indefinitely to who knows where.

The ward was nevertheless a vacation from the barracks. It was high ceilinged and comparatively clean. It had a stove that the staff actually fed, and the beds had straw mattresses. Most important, the staff would lend Dostoevsky books, though he accepted them only when the temptation was irresistible, like when Russian translations of Charles Dickens—*The Pickwick Papers* and *David Copperfield*—finally made it to Omsk. No English-language novelist was more popular in Russia than Dickens. Reformers admired his compassion and his implicit calls to ease urban hardships, while tsarists and conservatives could feel vindicated by his jabs at Parliament and laissez-faire capitalism. Dickens was just safe enough to be permissible in Russia, and in Siberia a Dickens novel was a rare privilege.

Word got around that the hospital's chief doctor was lenient with the political prisoners (letting them convalesce longer than necessary, slipping them special provisions), and before long a special envoy—a criminal chamber counselor from Tobolsk—arrived to investigate. He interrogated the hospital staff and various prisoners, and at one point his probe turned to Dostoevsky, who was questioned about the suspected laxity in Omsk. Had he written anything in prison or while he was in the hospital?

"I have not written nor am I writing anything, but I am gathering material for future writings."

"And where are these materials stored?"

"In my head."

Someday, he hoped, the tsar would let him be a writer again. That possibility was worth lying for, worth bracing for investigations and night searches. It was worth the trembling fear each time he dipped his pen in ink to jot down an ingenious retort or a scene from a story.

The prison and the hospital were his workshops, where he could read and think, observe and listen. Dostoevsky wanted the prisoners' stories even more than Dickens's. They were reluctant to talk about their crimes, but there was something about the hospital—its eased restrictions, perhaps, or the relief from hard labor, or the proximity of death, or all three—that loosened the tongue. They whispered about the past at night to neighboring patients, who listened or half listened while smoking. Dostoevsky would look at someone for extended periods of time (sometimes a whole hour, he claimed) and imagine what he was thinking. He would jot down a sentence or two whenever he had a chance.

"I look, I see a man who's taken a bad turn (he's all pale)." He wrote just enough to conjure a memory years later.

"Give it all up, and it won't be enough (what would you have of me!)."

"Here, sir, it's the tenth year now since I've gone wandering."

"Changed his fate."

Prison also gave him time to scrutinize himself. He no longer had to rush, and he could pursue ideas to their ends. He replayed his memories, calling forth as many details as possible, scraping the bottom of every moment. The hedgehogs and dead leaves of Darovoe. Standing in Vissarion Belinsky's apartment, and the furrows in the critic's forehead when he implored the young man to cherish his gift, to "remain faithful to it, and be a great writer." He recalled that moment repeatedly. He feared that he would forget himself, that his creativity would "turn cold" after so many years out on the Siberian steppe. He feared that even if the tsar allowed him to be a writer again, it would be too late.

D ostoevsky was in the hospital because he had epilepsy—the "falling sickness" or, in Russian, the "falling." His seizures usually happened at night. They began deep inside Dostoevsky's brain, beneath his left temporal lobe, at the bottom of the Sylvian fissure, in a small neural body called the insular cortex. Its ridges are packed with elaborate neural networks constantly at work. Electrical charges skip across the nodes of axons. Molecules dart across synapses to the branches of neighboring dendrites spreading out like trees in the neuronal forest. From time to time, however, the equilibrium in Dostoevsky's brain would begin to tip. A population of neurons in one of the cortex's anterior ridges would start firing unusually rapidly, charging the neurons around it. Something about the firing would activate distant neurons as well, generating scattered, idiosyncratic activity. Then a dire turn: his temporal lobe would begin firing continuously, relentlessly. And when a threshold was reached, an electrical surge would sweep through the region in an advancing wave front, leaving in its wake a field of neurons firing in synchrony, rhythmically, uninhibited. The wave would roll across both hemispheres, becoming global. Then it would reverse course and ricochet back through Dostoevsky's brain at different speeds, intensities, and scales as his 100 trillion synapses became the microscopic vectors of a complete catastrophe.

A high-pitched shriek was usually the first outward sign—his larynx tightening. The charges would travel down his spinal column to motor neurons throughout his body. His entire frame would stiffen. Then his limbs, face, and torso would contract and relax in rapid succession, convulsing his body for several minutes. His breathing would become labored and erratic, and he would foam at the mouth. It's unclear exactly when Dostoevsky's sei-zures began, but it was likely before his imprisonment. The convicts in the neighboring bunks first witnessed the terrifying spectacle soon after Dosto-evsky's arrival. They would tie him down with their coats, trying to prevent him from battering his own head and limbs, and then, rather suddenly, every-thing would stop.

Bloodletting was about the only treatment the hospital could offer. Some-times they used leeches. Sometimes a doctor approached a patient with a heated, bell-shaped glass in one hand and a small brass box in the other. The box is a scarificator. It has a trigger and twelve slits at the bottom for the spring-loaded blades inside. The doctor cocks the device, places the box on the back of the patient's neck, and pulls the trigger. The blades lash out and retract like claws—it's mercifully quick—and the doctor places the mouth of the hot glass over the incisions. The air inside compresses as it cools, and the resulting vacuum pulls the blood out of the incisions, filling the glass.

For centuries, doctors believed seizures were caused by excess blood in the brain. When bloodletting didn't help, they searched for other causes. Intestinal worms, digestive problems, and poor nutrition. Sleep cycles or lunar cycles. An irregular domestic life could cause epilepsy, doctors thought, as could anxi-ety or depression, fear or shock. Painful impressions or intense mental work might lead to seizures, which could not have been encouraging news for Dos-toevsky. A Siberian labor camp was not a salubrious environment for an epi-leptic, but there was nothing Dostoevsky's doctors could do about that. It would take weeks for him to recover. The seizures left him weak and aching, disoriented and melancholy, and the bloodlettings surely made him weaker.

Seizures taught Dostoevsky about powerlessness in a way that even exile and prison could not. For while all the prisoners had their waking hours ruled by the drum, as they put it, and their activities circumscribed and surveilled, Dostoevsky could not control his own body. This was, to some degree, central to every convict's experience. The unremitting lesson of the fetters and flog-gings, the facial brands, the demeaning uniforms and haircuts, and the endless hours carrying bricks is that your body belongs to His Imperial Majesty. Crim-inals were compelled to bow down in labor and in pain because they had refused to bow down willingly. They would learn to become slaves of the tsar.

But epilepsy made Dostoevsky's body seem fundamentally disobedient, a thing that belonged to no one, not even the tsar, not even himself. He had no direct experience of his seizures—he would lose consciousness before the tremors would start. He wouldn't understand what had happened to him until he began sliding back into a foggy awareness of the broadcloth coats pinned against his torso. And Yefim Belikh, no doubt, would be trying to restore order as thieves and rapists described to Dostoevsky how he was jolting uncontrollably on his wooden bunk. He had woken everyone up—*he* was the one shouting in the night. It was an awakening to a profound helplessness. His body was an automaton, a malfunctioning machine, and no amount of bloodletting or contemplation or strength of will would ever fix it.

What most alarmed Dostoevsky was his suspicion that his seizures were damaging his mind. "I sense that I am losing my memory and faculties," he wrote in one of his first accounts of his epilepsy. He wrote another letter two days after a seizure: "I . . . am now literally not in my right mind. My head is not clear and all my limbs hurt." How could it not be ominous? He had premonitions of his death, and the prisoners shared his foreboding. During an unusually long hospital stay, a rumor began circulating that Dostoevsky had finally succumbed to epilepsy, which made his reappearance, a month and a half later, all the more startling. "Hi! You're still alive!?" one of the prisoners asked. "I was holding a wake for you! I scattered some twenty stones for the dogs." Dostoevsky earned a nickname after his return. They called him "the Dead Man."

His seizures likely filled the prisoners with the sense that there was something uncanny about Fyodor Mikhailovich. The stigma of epilepsy was centuries-deep, and a supernatural aura surrounded the falling sickness. It suggested demonic possession, or prophecy, or a visitation. But his estrangement was greater than that. Dostoevsky had not fully comprehended the distance between himself and the peasant convicts until one summer day, when he saw them assembling in the yard, presumably for a roll call. Dostoevsky went outside to line up, and that's when he noticed it—their anger.

"What are you doing here?" someone finally said. Dostoevsky was confused. Another man piped up. "Really, what are you doing standing here? Go back to the barrack," he said. "This is none of your business." Others joined in. "Iron beak!" "Fly squashers!"—which was a new one. They laughed. An older prisoner, a horse thief, took Dostoevsky by the arm and led him away. "All your kind are in the kitchen, go there."

The noblemen were laughing at him when he arrived. Didn't he know about the protest? The convicts were so upset about the declining food quality that they decided to take their grievances to Major Krivtsov. It would clearly fail, one of the Polish noblemen said, and even if they were to join, they'd just blame the nobles for instigating it. "We'd risk a hundred times more if we came out; and for what? *Je haïs ces brigands.*" The prisoners in the yard stood at attention when Krivtsov came rushing out, red-faced and screaming, running up and down the rows, hurling himself at prisoners' faces, and quashing the protest in minutes.

Dostoevsky hadn't even registered the discontent spreading throughout the barracks, but in retrospect it was clear. For days, little groups had been forming during free hours—resentment incubators. Shalomentsev would pad around barefoot from group to group, his anger building as he absorbed the muttered complaints. Maybe the cooks were cutting costs and pocketing the extra money. Dostoevsky recognized it now, but what he still didn't understand was the rejection: the men didn't even want his help. He eventually asked Shalomentsev about it.

"Aren't your people angry with us?" he asked, referring to the noblemen. "Why should they be?"

"Well, because we didn't come out for the grievance."

Shalomentsev was confused. Why should the noblemen protest? They buy their own food.

"But some of yours eat their own food," Dostoevsky said, "and they still came out. We should have, too . . . out of comradeship."

"But . . ." Shalomentsev said, trying to understand him, "but how can you be our comrades?"

Dostoevsky finally realized: noblemen "are separated from common people by the deepest abyss," he later wrote. You may spend your entire life among the peasants, they may serve you every day, but "you will never know their real essence. It will be an optical illusion, and nothing more."

They seemed so childish from his side of the abyss. These were men given to snowball fights and callous pranks and laughing fits. They butted heads with the prison yard goat and wove garlands for his horns. They strutted around with their coats draped over their shoulders as if they were capes.

Dostoevsky got his clearest view of the convicts' essence at the prison's Christmas theater. He had been hearing stories about their annual theater for weeks. The men would turn one of the barracks into their auditorium. A curtain of old shirts and blankets featured a scene of trees, ponds, and stars painted in oils. They illuminated the stage by cutting tallow candles and lighting all the pieces. The sets were minimal (the backdrop, for example, was a rug), but that hardly mattered, and the real spectacle was the audience. All of the convicts crammed into the building. Some were standing on the bunks. Others were balancing on logs propped against the wall while they supported themselves on friends' shoulders. There were men standing on the furnace's steps. Five more were lying on top of it. Still others were watching from the wings or peering in from the barrack's chilly vestibule.

The crowd parted as Shalomentsev escorted Dostoevsky to a space near the front. The prisoners considered him a connoisseur and wanted his approval along with a donation (they passed a plate around). A small orchestra was set up on a couple of bunks: guitars, accordions, two violins, three balalaikas (all homemade), and a tambourine. The balalaika players ran their fingers over the strings and rapped their knuckles on the soundboards, deftly thrumming alongside the accordion bellows and the tambourine's rustle and punch. Dostoevsky was amazed. "For the first time then I fully understood precisely what was so endlessly exuberant and rollicking in these exuberant and rollicking Russian dance songs."

The acting was even more impressive. One of the performances was a vaudeville routine called "Filatka and Miroshka." The lead, Filatka, had a frock coat, wig, and fake mustache. Sirotkin played Filatka's young bride in a flounced dress with a dainty pelerine and a parasol. She spoke in couplets. Sirotkin's character was the pretty counterpart to a comical lady in a muslin dress, garishly powdered and rouged, fluttering a painted paper fan. Dostoevsky marveled at the performances, especially the man playing Filatka. His lines and gestures were so carefully considered, so precise, and yet so natural. You forgot he was a murderer.

There was no theater in Omsk (though the town's horse arena held occasional productions), so the annual prison performance was a special event.

Fifteen actors had spent weeks rehearsing behind the barracks for three nights of performances. A few chairs and benches were reserved in front for distinguished guests, and officers and nobles attended each night. There was a ballet. There was a pantomime set to Glinka's *Kamarinskaya*, in which a miller drives out his wife's lovers, who are hidden throughout the cottage.

And then they staged a dark comedy called *Kedril the Glutton*, which Dostoevsky had never heard of. A gentleman arrives at an inn with his servant, Kedril, who carries a suitcase and a chicken wrapped in blue paper. The innkeeper warns that there may be devils in the room, and the master mutters offhandedly that, yes, he's known that for quite a while now, which Kedril finds rather terrifying. He's trembling as he unpacks the master's belongings. The master paces back and forth and announces that this is the end of his wanderings. He had appealed to dark forces for help a long time ago, and the devils had come to his aid. Today, perhaps, would be the day they'd come for his soul. This is no comfort to Kedril as he prepares his master's dinner, setting out a bottle of wine and some bread and unwrapping the chicken. The audience laughs as Kedril eats a small piece just to be sure it's been prepared properly.

Suddenly the inn's shutters rattle in the wind. In the commotion, Kedril begins stuffing chicken into his mouth—fearfully, without thinking—while his master continues to pace the room. The crowd's laughter grows.

"Is it ready?" the master asks.

"One moment, sire . . . I'm . . . getting it ready for you"—only now he's actually eating at the table, sitting down. When the master turns to look, Kedril dives under the table and continues stuffing himself.

"Soon now, Kedril?"

"Ready, sir!" At this point there's just a drumstick left on the carcass, but he presents it to his master, who's too preoccupied to notice. Kedril stands behind his master's chair, ready with a napkin. He turns to the audience and laughs, and the prisoners roar.

Just then two figures cloaked in white appear. They have lanterns instead of heads, and one carries a scythe. The master announces that he's ready to be taken. Kedril dives back under the table, snatching the wine on the way. The devils grab the master and drag him down to hell.

"Kedril! Save me!" he yells as they disappear, but Kedril is too busy working on the bread.

The inn settles back into calm, and it dawns upon Kedril that he's finally alone, "no devils, no master," as Dostoevsky put it. He emerges from underneath the table, smiles broadly, and winks at the audience.

"The devils took my master!"

The prisoners are ecstatic.

Kedril pours himself a celebratory glass. But then, just as he's about to drink, the devils return. Only now there are three. They approach silently and grab Kedril from behind. He screams. He's frozen—he can't even look at them—and he's still clutching the bottle and glass as the devils drag him down to hell. The audience still hears him shouting after he disappears backstage. The prisoners love it. No one escapes the devils.

Dostoevsky caught glimpses of the men around him during the performances. Ali, the young Dagestan Tatar guerrilla fighter, was standing with his brothers, and his face was beaming with pure joy. Dostoevsky looked farther back to see the crowd. All those branded faces, red and glistening from the collective heat, laughing without restraint. They shouted encouragement to the actors. They hung on to one another. They clutched the people around them. They pointed and whispered. Their eyes widened when the devils appeared, when the hidden lovers were rustled out from behind the furniture, and when pretty Sirotkin appeared in drag and clinking chains.

This was a wonderful people. He finally saw it. It would come back in flashes. Their souls would open up, Dostoevsky said, and reveal "such riches, feeling, heart." These prisoners were much more than he had imagined— "profound, strong, marvelous." There was "gold under a coarse crust."

It's what he needed. He needed to know that within a callous murderer was a beautiful dancer or a brilliant actor who could play a gentleman. He needed to feel kinship across the deep abyss. He sometimes thought of it as a national bond, but the truth is that he found it in the most heterogeneous group of people he had ever known. The barracks bunked Finns and Bashkirs alongside Russian peasants, Chechens, Dagestan Tatars who hated the tsar, and Old Believers who considered him the Antichrist. These differences intensified the kinship. This was the paradox that now compelled Dostoevsky and his irrepressible desire to write: the feeling of simultaneously knowing and not knowing the people around him, the feeling of distance coiled inside an intimacy, and a bond tightened by vast stretches of emptiness.

One summer, Dostoevsky spent two months hauling bricks from the bank of the Irtysh River to a barrack under construction two kilometers away. He had to climb up over the fortress rampart to the site, and from the top of the rampart in the early morning he could gaze far out into the open steppe stretching beyond the river with waving grasses and forget-me-nots and birds disappearing into nothingness.

Sometimes he saw Kazakh nomads in the distance, wisps of smoke rising up above their yurts and women tending to their sheep. Sometimes he heard the Kazakhs' far-off songs in the distance, creating the perfect tableau of the steppe's wild and simple freedom vanishing on the horizon. Everyone would vanish into this distance. Dostoevsky knew—he must have known—that the steppe was not as free and peaceful as the flowers and grasses suggested, that he was gazing at a byway for mercenaries and slave traders, a space for bandits and kidnappers and Cossacks. He knew that the rampart he was standing on and the very bricks he was carrying were made to end the Kazakhs' nomadic culture and to silence their songs. He knew that the Kazakhs themselves were not inhabitants here from time immemorial but recent arrivals, that beneath the tableau in front of him was another in which the Golden Horde had controlled these lands, in which Batu Khan's 150,000 horsemen were sweeping westward across the steppe, galloping up the frozen Volga River, burning the city of Ryazan to the ground, and slaughtering its inhabitants before destroying Moscow. And before the Mongols it was Cuman horsemen behind iron masks dominating the steppe with war hammers and javelins. And before the Cumans it was the Kimeks, and the Göktürks, and the Khanty, and the Scythians, and the paleo-Siberians. And before that it was the prehistoric sea that had given this landscape its flat expanses by inundating everything, by wiping out every last flower.

After four years on the margins of the steppe, the guards escorted Dostoevsky to the fortress smithy. The blacksmiths placed his foot up on an anvil and struck his ankle fetters off. He wanted to hold the chains in his hands. When he left the fortress prison, he made a vow. "I will no longer write trifles."

Ten

Aunt Razor

The commissioner of Paris's third arrondissement ordered his men to break down the door after they got no response. They found Jean-François Chardon's body in a pool of blood in the kitchen. Dishes, pots, and pans were strewn around the floor, and next to his corpse was a bloodstained ax. The scene was similar in his mother's bedroom—locks broken, furniture moved and smashed, clothing and possessions tossed around. Her body was buried beneath pillows and bedding, as if whoever killed her didn't want to look at her.

The police weren't notified until a large stain had appeared under the Chardons' doorway. No one had heard from the widow or her son in two days. Doctors examined the bodies. Chardon had been wearing a flannel vest at the time of the attack, and his body exhibited eleven wounds from two different weapons—possibly three. The ax fractured his skull. There were five triangular wounds all around one of his eyes, all of them superficial and close together, as if someone jabbed his face playfully after he was dead.

The widow had wounds from a similar weapon, triangular, as well as what appeared to be knife wounds on her neck and in her throat. One of the doctors discovered that her body was still warm. She remained alive, underneath the pillows and blankets, before expiring. The neighbor living upstairs reported hearing groans in the middle of the night but assumed they were coming from the nearby baker.

The police found a sharpened three-edged file with a homemade cork handle behind the widow's chest of drawers. It would have been smarter to toss the weapon out the window overlooking the alley, but perhaps it was thrown in frustration. The end of the file had split the cork apart, and bloodstains suggested the person holding it had been cut. The search of the apartment was not thorough. Days later, while the building's caretaker was washing away all traces of violence, he found a small knife with a broken tip and some bloodstains. The victims' estranged family told the caretaker to bring the evidence to the police.

The police already knew about Jean-François Chardon. They knew where people with "Aunt Madeleine's" loathsome habits lived and congregated, so they arrested half a dozen men of his type to see if they could get a confession or a denouncement. They kept others under surveillance. They tracked down a young man named Brabant who had been staying at the apartment, but he turned out to be nothing more than a petty thief. He arrived at the Cheval Rouge apartment several hours after the murders, late at night, and pounded on the door repeatedly. When no one let him in, he found someplace else to sleep. Arresting and surveilling the neighborhood's "abject beings," as the lead investigator described them, was about the extent of the resources the police devoted to the case, and no one was saying anything.

O n December 31, 1834, an attempted murder took place in the same neighborhood. The victim, a young man named Genevay, was a collection clerk at the Mallet Bank, which made the police rather more diligent. The Mallet Bank was an *haute banque*, one of a network of family banks financing the major institutions of modern French society. They backed Napoleon's 1799 coup d'état and helped found the Banque de France. The Mallets were arguably the most prominent of the high banking families. By the 1830s, the Mallet Bank was financing railways and factories, the nation's first insurance companies, and some of its prestigious cultural institutions, including the Palais-Royal Theatre and the Opéra-Comique.

What was still more disturbing was that the crime resembled other recent bank robbery attempts. So the police swept through Paris's lodging houses and reportedly rounded up about four hundred suspects. When this massive dragnet yielded nothing, the police turned over the investigation to the Sûreté—the

French national police. Both the Mallet Bank case and the Chardon murders were assigned to Chief Inspector Louis Canler. He was young—thirty-seven—but he had been a police officer for more than a decade, and he was effective. The first thing Inspector Canler noticed when he went to the building on rue Montorgueil was the door—MAHOSSIER written in white chalk like that, so distinctively. Canler interviewed the landlord, a fruit seller, who described Mahossier clearly. He and his friend were law students with little money—Mahossier asked for straw to make a mattress—but they paid in advance. Mahossier was slender, nicely dressed, and had a mustache and memorable features. There wasn't much to say. The men were hardly ever home, though he remembered seeing them bringing up a large wicker basket.

Canler had his men remove the chalk-inscribed door so he could seize it as evidence. Because the suspects seemed transitory, he began searching the ledgers of Paris's disreputable lodging houses. Hotels and inns were required to keep "police books" that listed arrival and departure dates for every guest. Canler had nothing but a name and a description, but the description was detailed, and Mahossier was a rare name. Did it even exist? Mahussier, yes, but Mahossier? Any Mahossier would be his.

He eventually found him in a police book entry in Simon Pageot's lodging house on rue du Faubourg du Temple. He checked out in early January, shortly after the crime. Pageot and his wife still remembered him: he stayed with a man named Fizelier. They didn't say much, but Mme. Pageot's description of Fizelier—tall, sturdy, red sideburns—reminded the inspector of someone he had recently questioned for fraudulently acquiring three barrels of wine: Hippolyte-Martin François. Canler went to his jail cell, pulled out his notepad, and pretended to look for a name he had written down.

"I've been racking my brains since yesterday," he told François. "I wonder why you went to stay at Pageot's under the name of Fizelier?" Canler was taking a stab. When François responded that he used the pseudonym because there was a warrant out for him, Canler had what he needed—a suspicion confirmed. Red sideburns and a few nights with a Mahossier were enough to name François a suspect in the attempted robbery of the Mallet Bank. But he wanted more leverage before he'd question him.

Something made Canler return to Pageot's lodging house. Places like that acquired their clientele by cooperating with the police as little as possible.

When he returned, Mme. Pageot was there without her husband, so he seized the opportunity to get more information. Mahossier had lodged there before, she said, but he registered under the name Bâton.

Canler began searching the usual criminal hangouts, armed with a description and now two names. He took two agents with him to Quatre Billards, where the worst of Paris congregated. Some abruptly departed when he and his men arrived. Others watched. Bâton played billiards there all the time, apparently, so Canler had one of his agents surveil the billiard hall while he waited at a nearby wine shop. When Bâton showed up at Quatre Billards at around nine o'clock, he was placed under arrest. But as they escorted him to the prefecture, the inspector began to have doubts. Bâton didn't look anything like the descriptions of Mahossier. They were arresting him for going by a suspect's alleged alias and for playing billiards in an ill-famed establishment. When Canler summoned the fruit-seller landlord and the wounded collection clerk, Genevay, neither recognized Bâton.

So much of an investigation depended upon hunches and luck. Canler had a habit of gathering information constantly, whether or not he knew what to do with it. He got word of something an inmate said when Bâton was brought in—it wasn't much, just a little joke. A prisoner in La Force known as Aunt Razor laughed about how bored Bâton's friend Gaillard would be now that Bâton was in jail, considering how the two *"couldn't be more intimate."* Salacious information was the most useful.

Canler recalled the details of the investigation in his memoirs. After hearing about Aunt Razor's joke about Bâton's lonely friend Gaillard, he decided he needed to know more, even though Bâton himself wasn't a suspect—just a name in a ledger. Canler offered to walk with Bâton for a bit as he was being released. He likely apologized for having wrongfully arrested him—something to set him at ease. Bâton was a good actor, but he wasn't keen enough to see when he was being upstaged. Canler nudged the conversation toward Poissy and prison life, its hardships and colorful characters, until "Gaillard" bubbled up. Ah, yes, Gaillard—what did he look like again? Bâton's description was exactly what Canler was looking for. A match for Mahossier.

Canler found multiple Gaillards in the lodging house registers. On his

second day, one employee mentioned that their Gaillard left something behind. It was a letter setting up a meeting. Canler noticed something when he
examined it. It wasn't a name or an address. It was the way he formed his
letters. The tops of his lowercase *d*s had extravagant curls. He made wide upward swoops before rounding off his majuscule *P*s. He finished off every *t*
with a long, satisfying slash across the entire word. And his capital *M*: two
sharp, narrow peaks flanking a deep plunge, a nadir at the center of the character. It was odd. And it was exactly the way MAHOSSIER was written in chalk
on the door of the rue Montorgueil crime scene. When two experts compared
the handwriting with one of the forged bills of exchange, Gaillard became the
lead suspect.

What did Canler have? A string of names (Mahossier—Bâton—Gaillard)
looped around descriptions from Genevay, the fruit-seller landlord, and Bâton.
Each one brought the man into focus. His slender build, his height, his broad
forehead, his sense of style, the way he spoke, the men with whom he was
close. Facts were scarce. A man stayed at Pageot's lodging house under his
friend Bâton's name and under the name Mahossier shortly after a nearby
crime was committed under that same unlikely name. This man shared a
room with a tall gentleman sporting red sideburns, just like the man in the
hunting jacket who tried to strangle the Mallet Bank's collection clerk, just
like François.

Everything was questionable. A tall man with red sideburns isn't much,
and if the case taught Canler anything, it was that a name could be meaningless. The investigation was built upon a handful of words: descriptions of facial
hair, names written in ledgers, the shape of a letter *M*, and a little passing joke
from a man called Aunt Razor.

After François had a few days in jail to think, he wrote to the chief of the
Sûreté, Pierre Allard, claiming he had useful information for him. Canler escorted the prisoner to Allard's office for questioning and chatted with
him during the carriage ride, thinking he might say something useful about
the attempted bank robbery. But he offered something completely unexpected:
he knew who killed Chardon and his mother. He knew all the details, too.

How? "Because I heard them from one of the murderers"—a friend of his named Gaillard. François repeated the story for Allard and an examining magistrate, at which point Inspector Canler's two most prominent cases—the double murder and the attempted bank robbery—became linked in a single crime spree.

Information about Gaillard was suddenly valuable, which might have been why another prisoner came forward. He told the Sûreté's agents that he knew Gaillard, knew all his aliases and habits, and could track him down if the police would set him free for a week. The new informant's name was Victor Avril, and he had just been sentenced to a year in prison for physically obstructing his girlfriend's arrest. Canler agreed to Avril's proposal—it was not, at the time, an uncommon practice—and he followed Avril to every gambling house, café, and wine shop he knew. Avril never suspected that two undercover agents were following both of them, just in case the convict had designs. Eight days later, Gaillard was still nowhere to be found, and Avril was back in prison.

Avril did, however, provide a crucial piece of information. Gaillard had an aunt who lived in Paris, on rue Barre-du-Bec. Canler and Allard decided to go. She had a small judas door covered by a metal grate so she could see who was there without opening up. She answered after the second ring.

"What do you want?"

"To speak to Mme. Gaillard."

"Myself."

"We wish, madam, to speak to you about your nephew Gaillard."

She informed the detectives that she was afraid of her nephew. He was the reason she had the grate on her door. He had been living with her after serving a prison sentence for stealing silverware. The crime seemed harmless enough, but as her nephew himself said, a young man's first stint in prison might be misfortune or folly, but never the second. She cast him off for good after he had stolen the cabriolet and horse. The final insult must have been how he told that poor driver to walk up to her apartment to deliver a message so he could speed off with the carriage. It was as if he were making her complicit. Then the details of the crime—along with her full street address—were printed in the newspaper for everyone to see. He was a bad man. But his name isn't Gaillard, she told the investigators. It's Lacenaire.

. . .

L acenaire was struggling to stay ahead of the police. On New Year's Day 1835—the day after the attempted robbery-murder—he and François exchanged clothes. Lacenaire put on François's hunting jacket, which was rather large on him. François put on "Mahossier's" red cravat and frock coat. A friend who made hairpieces shaved off his conspicuous red sideburns.

The men had gotten desperate after things went wrong in rue Montorgueil. Lacenaire attempted to kill a woman who threatened to tell the police what she knew. A robbery in Issy was foiled by a maid who wouldn't leave, and they resorted to stealing a clock from a window display. Two days later, after François was arrested for a prior offense, Lacenaire decided to leave Paris. He went gambling, won three hundred francs, and ended up in Dijon with some ill-gotten money and a new scheme. He planned to forge sight drafts, bills of exchange that paid cash immediately rather than on a fixed date. He obtained a genuine bill drawn by a bank in Dijon, payable to one of his false identities. Then he had counterfeits made. He would cash a fake bill in one city and then the real bill in another, as quickly as possible, before the banks could communicate with each other. He'd get paid twice for one bill, and all collection clerks would remain unharmed.

His first bill was to be drawn against a bank in Paris, but when he arrived, he discovered that the police were looking for him, and his description was circulating on all the roads entering the city. He went to the bank as quickly as possible, but it hadn't yet received an advice from Dijon that the genuine bill had been drawn, so when he handed over his counterfeit bill, the staff started scrutinizing it. Lacenaire decided to slip away. Thirty minutes later he was on a stagecoach carrying a passport under his new name: Jacob Levy.

The police caught up with him at a café in early February in Beaune, south of Dijon, after he had dropped counterfeit notes in several cities, including Lyons and Geneva. The lieutenant of the Beaune gendarmerie just sat down at the table next to him. After arresting him, they itemized his clothing—all the coats and vests, hats and handkerchiefs. When officials pieced together his real identity, the Sûreté had him transferred to Paris, suspecting that Jacob Levy was Lacenaire, known as Gaillard, known as Mahossier.

The man of many names was lying on a cot in his cell with iron shackles around his ankles when Canler and Chief Allard first saw him. The shackles were an extraordinary measure, a punishment for insulting a provincial official. But what surprised the detectives most was how polite Lacenaire was, how compliant and pleasant. He was happy to be back. "It was only in Paris that I wanted to die," he wrote later. Allard convinced the prisoner that he wouldn't escape conviction. His only real question was about Lacenaire's accomplices. He wanted their names. "As you can see, I get straight to the point," Allard said. "If I can do something for you, in your position, I will do it." He gave his word of honor.

Lacenaire confessed to the Chardon murders and the Mallet Bank attempted robbery-murder. He told them about his previous bank robbery attempts and how the plan improved over time. He explained the large basket and the straw. He planned to cut up Genevay's body and pack it in the basket so that the straw would absorb the blood. Then he and his partner would get rid of it. Without a body, the police and the Mallet Bank would come to the simplest conclusion: that Genevay had simply run off with the money entrusted to him.

He confessed without remorse, Canler recalled, the way "a merchant would speak of an unsuccessful speculation." It was the same way he confessed to stealing cravats and clothing. He supplied details, dates, and addresses, but he balked at betraying his accomplices. "Gentlemen, though we may be villains, we possess a self-pride."

When Canler told him they already knew his accomplice was François, Lacenaire smiled as he denied it. Canler had more: "And I can tell you also that it was you who murdered Chardon and his mother." François already told them how Lacenaire had boasted about it over wine.

"François told you that, did he?" It wasn't only François, Canler said. "I went around with Avril for a week trying to track you down, with Avril performing the part of the denouncer at his own request."

"Ah, him too," he said, "really, him too."

Lacenaire didn't want to talk anymore until he found out the truth.

"I have only one request to make," he told them, "to be relieved of all this paraphernalia," gesturing to the fetters. "They keep me from walking."

By the time the guards removed the fifteen-pound leg irons the next day, it had become clear that François had betrayed him. After all, they had only met the day before they tried to kill the collection clerk. He remembered following François down the stairwell after Genevay's screams alerted the neighbors. François slammed the building's front door behind him so that Lacenaire had to unlock it from the inside. He was barely able to elude the pursuing neighbors. They met back at Bâton's place, as they had planned, though Lacenaire first decided to stop by a reading room (a small private library). When François arrived, Lacenaire's appearance startled him. "I thought you were arrested."

Was Bâton any different? He sometimes warned Lacenaire not to mistreat him, hinting that he could provide damning testimony. That's when Lacenaire started putting Bâton's name on his forgeries. He was sure Bâton was planning to blackmail him, though he wasn't afraid. "You can only send me to my death," Lacenaire told him. "I can send you to the galleys"—forced labor.

But he refused to believe that Avril betrayed him. Canler's story about Avril's leading him around their Paris hangouts, trying to track him down, must have been a prank—and a rather good one, getting released from jail, having a few days of police-subsidized fun and freedom. It took time for Lacenaire to accept the truth.

Two months later, when the detectives visited him at La Force prison, he stood up and bowed. He was grateful for how graciously everyone had treated him since his return to Paris, from the prison officials to the functionaries and magistrates. The director of La Force, admittedly, insisted on addressing him informally (*tu* instead of *vous*), but that was an unfortunate exception. He counted the amiable conversations he had with one prison official as among the many "charms of my captivity." Lacenaire developed a special admiration for Chief Allard. He was honest and direct, "a sincere, delicate person." In trying to extract a confession, he never once lied to him. He engaged in no trickery. He was devoted to his duty and to reforming the police. "Every one of his days is marked by a new service to Society." It made him think of how difficult it was to be a good policeman. They received scant pay and little credit. Lacenaire was grateful, and he never forgot a kindness.

I n late July 1835, after Lacenaire returned from the Mouse Trap—the underground cavern where prisoners awaited their turn before the magistrates—François caught his attention in one of the prison's common areas. While they were speaking, someone struck Lacenaire's head, and several prisoners attacked him after he fell. The guards managed to stop it in time for him to escape with little more than a wound on his forehead. Chief Allard saw to it that Lacenaire remained in the prison infirmary as long as possible, which was fortunate, because plans were afoot to kill him in his sleep for snitching.

Lacenaire was becoming notorious outside prison as well. Articles about him began hitting the press when he was transferred to Paris in April, and they multiplied as his November trial neared. Newspapers featured sensational accounts of the Chardon murders. Some claimed that Aunt Madeleine's body had been found naked and infamously defiled. Rumors circulated about still more crimes—that Lacenaire approached a wealthy man one night and stole five thousand francs from his pocket while he choked him.

It wasn't long before some of the attention became admiring. Multiple people visited him in prison. Women brought scented notes and wrote him poetry. Allard had his portrait painted. People sought his views on politics, on the justice system, on religion. A few days before the trial, he fielded questions before journalists, lawyers, and a doctor. "How is it that your intelligence did not protect you against yourself?" the doctor asked.

"There came a day in my life when I had no alternatives other than suicide or crime."

"Why, then, not choose suicide?"

"I asked myself whether I was my own victim or society's."

Everything Lacenaire did and said was notable—how he caressed his mustache and ran his hands through his curly black hair, the way his pupils darted around the room, the way he hummed or whistled tunes in the middle of conversations about cannibalism or metempsychosis. Several newspapers deplored the fact that the press was reprinting his every word, spreading his message for profit. The novelist Léon Gozlan, writing for the *Revue de Paris*, claimed the press coverage turned him into a legend or a saint. "This man is immortal," Gozlan wrote. There would be future Lacenaires.

Sometimes he was pressed on the details of his crimes. What would he have done with Genevay's body? The parts in the wicker basket would've been found eventually. Lacenaire said he planned to travel down the Seine to a cottage in Saint-Ouen, and he and François would have cooked Genevay right there, piece by piece, until nothing but the bones remained. He'd break them apart and carry a few of them with him each day when he went fishing. Day by day, he'd drop the fragments in the river.

Visitors often asked him about his near-certain execution. He usually called his beheading in front of a large crowd an "exceptional death." Though one day an unbearable idea crossed his mind. *"Do you think they will despise me?"*

Eleven

The Resurrection

He could tell St. Petersburg had changed before he even arrived. The city's outskirts were dotted with more factories than he remembered. Cotton mills and iron foundries crowded the Neva, and industrial plants churned out specialized goods like wallpaper and porcelain and macaroni. A new railroad connected Petersburg to Moscow, and more smoke obscured the city from a distance. These were the first signs of the unfamiliar energy in Peter's abstract city. New trade relationships, new capital, and new financial networks were pulling peasants in from the countryside. The signs multiplied as Dostoevsky's carriage approached the city. Wooden tenements had sprouted up in the outer districts to house the factory workers. There were six-story apartment buildings where there were once houses, and in the poorer neighborhoods the classical facades of the older buildings concealed increasingly irregular, subdivided interiors. He saw the same streets under different lighting: gas lamps had replaced the oil lamps.

He knew that the first sight of home would be like a scale telling the weight of what he had lost. Dostoevsky had been gone for ten years, and all of Russia had changed. Tsar Nicholas I was dead after refusing treatment for pneumonia. Some considered it a form of suicide after the disastrous Crimean War, which cost the empire half a million lives, control of the Black Sea, several principalities, and immeasurable pride. The empire's power following the Napoleonic Wars had diminished. Alexander II, Nicholas's son, was coronated in 1855 and began an era of liberal reform. Nicholas's most oppressive measures were relaxed. The empire's judicial system was being overhauled. And serfdom was coming to an end. In 1856, the young emperor unexpectedly announced to an assembly of Russian nobles, "It is better to begin abolishing serfdom from above than to wait for it to begin to abolish itself from below." Dostoevsky heard the joyous reports about the new sovereign shortly after he was freed from the Omsk fortress prison. He was thrilled to be a loyal servant of "our Angel-Tsar," as he called Alexander. "I adore him."

Dostoevsky had also changed. He was now a retired ensign of the Seventh Siberian Line Battalion. He had spent five years in compulsory service following his release from prison, and he would remain under surveillance indefinitely. He was nevertheless indebted to the merciful tsar for "resurrecting" him, for restoring his noble status and allowing him to return to Petersburg. Dostoevsky departed the capital as an infamous criminal against the state, and now he was returning as a grateful and loyal subject. He was thirty-eight years old, wiser, more mature. And he was married.

He met Marya Dmitrievna Isaeva in Semipalatinsk, where Dostoevsky was enlisted. The soldier's life resembled the prisoner's life—an endless round of drills and inspections and verbal abuse. He hardly found time to sleep, and when he had a spare waking moment, he wanted to be alone. Semipalatinsk was a small garrison town on the Kazakh steppe with a few mosques, one Orthodox church, and no trees. A large encampment of yurts was typically set up right across the Irtysh River, and sand drifted into piles along the streets. People referred to the town as "the Devil's Sandbox." It was an improbable place to meet a spouse.

Their circumstances were also improbable: Marya Dmitrievna was already married. Her husband was a low-level civil servant prone to drinking. Dostoevsky met them through a mutual acquaintance, and he began tutoring their seven-year-old son, Pasha. Marya Dmitrievna was twenty-eight years old. She was blond and slim, with dark eyes and full lips—"attractive," Dostoevsky wrote to Mikhail, "very well educated, very intelligent." It wasn't long before flirtations began. He liked that she was "cheerful and frisky." He wrote to her about the importance of "a woman's heart, a woman's compassion, a woman's sympathy, infinite kindness." It took an ideal of companionship to break through his misanthropy. Dostoevsky needed Marya Dmitrievna more than he wanted her. "I lived for five years without people, alone, without having, in the full sense of the word, anyone to whom I could pour out my heart," he wrote to her. Before they met, he was becoming isolated and numb, "but now I'm a human being again."

When her husband unexpectedly died, Dostoevsky's feelings grew into an all-consuming passion. He couldn't be without her. "I'll either go mad or jump into the Irtysh," he wrote to a friend. Their yearlong courtship involved confrontations with rival suitors and forbidden out-of-town journeys. "I am ready to go to jail if only I can see her," he declared. The couple were married in a small ceremony in Kuznetsk in February 1857. On their journey back to Semipalatinsk, Dostoevsky had a seizure. The bride witnessed her new husband's convulsions for the first time. The doctor advised him to be cautious during new moons and confirmed beyond all doubt what Dostoevsky already knew: "I have *genuine falling sickness*." He would not have married Marya if he had known for sure, he insisted.

Life with Marya proved rather more complicated than a life warmed by womanly compassion and sympathy and infinite kindness. Her "frisky" nature soon seemed "intensely impressionable," and Dostoevsky had not fully anticipated the responsibilities of providing for a wife and child on his soldier's salary. Pasha was admitted to the Siberian Cadet Academy in Omsk, but they soon heard complaints of misbehavior and poor academic performance. Stress, Dostoevsky thought, made Marya Dmitrievna ill, but over time it began to seem chronic. She was constantly weak, febrile, and coughing. She was always irritated. It was an ill-fated marriage. He craved companionship after years in prison, and she craved stability, a way to avoid being a single mother without means in Siberia. And she pitied Dostoevsky. He was, she would say, "a man with no future." In her angrier moments she would call him a criminal, reminding him what he was. After his seizure, it became clear she had made a mistake.

His family provided little comfort. When he was released from prison, he began his first letter to Mikhail in years, "Tell me please, for the love of God, why have you not yet written a single line to me?" He had feared his brother was dead. The truth was that officials had inexplicably informed Mikhail that contacting his brother was forbidden. When Dostoevsky discovered his older brother was alive, he felt abandoned, and regaining their old connection took years. The rest of the family was nearly silent. "What's with our family?" he asked Mikhail. "Where's brother Andrei, where's Kolya?" His sisters weren't even responding to his wife's letters. But the months between Mikhail's letters were the most painful. "Are you alive? . . . I dream of you every night, I am terribly alarmed." Before long, his letters were silent on his domestic life. "I'm completely alone," was all he would say, and "you are all I have."

He did manage to cultivate a couple of close friendships, including one with a well-positioned public prosecutor, Baron Vrangel, who would eventually become a diplomat. Vrangel had witnessed Dostoevsky's mock execution when he was only seventeen. In Siberia he spent years petitioning officials on Dostoevsky's behalf, and they would remain in correspondence long after Dostoevsky left.

He also developed an unusually ardent friendship with a Kazakh named Chokan Valikhanov. "You write me that you love me," Dostoevsky once wrote to him, "and I declare to you without any ceremony that I've fallen in love with you. I've never felt for anybody, not even excepting my own brother, the attraction I feel for you, and God knows how this came about." Valikhanov was a direct descendant of Genghis Khan and the grandson of the last khan of the Middle Horde Kazakhs. Dostoevsky met him as he was becoming the first Kazakh ethnographer, and he was captivated by Valikhanov's research and stories. Dostoevsky urged him to write about growing up on the steppe, and Valikhanov's split identity thrilled him. "Remember that you are the first Kazakh educated entirely on the European model," he told his young friend. It was Valikhanov's "sacred mission" to interpret the significance of the Kazakhs and to advocate for their just treatment by the Russians. They took a photograph together in 1858. Dostoevsky sits in his officer's uniform while Valikhanov, twenty-three years old, holds a dagger in his left hand—Dostoevsky's gift to him.

I want to write and publish," he wrote to Mikhail in 1856. His release from penal servitude did not restore his right to be a writer, but he was willing to publish anonymously if necessary. "It was not in vain that I took this road," he told Mikhail. "I'm convinced that I have talent and that I can write something good." It wouldn't be easy. He couldn't get his hands on the most basic reading material—"books are life, my food, my future!" Mikhail secured permission to send him books, but parcels took months to arrive. He once waited for the better part of a year for a journal issue.

A decade of literary isolation had stymied his creativity. He would jot down notes, begin sketches, cross out passages, and revise endlessly before stopping altogether. Epilepsy made writing more difficult. He had several seizures while on guard duty and several more in his sleep. He informed Mikhail in September 1858, "Last month there were four attacks, which has never happened before—and I did almost no work." He wrote to an official that he needed to be treated "seriously, radically," or he would die.

Reading kept him going. He recalled holding a journal issue for the first time in years, and it was like seeing St. Petersburg once again: "All my former life rose up clear and bright before me." He'd savor everything, trying to find glimmers of the old literary scene, only to feel more acutely what he'd lost. Gogol was dead, just like poor Belinsky. An entirely new generation appeared. After reading a couple of stories in *The Contemporary*, he wrote to a friend, "Please let me know who *Olga N.* and *L.T.* are." He told Mikhail he wanted "all the *behind-the-scenes secrets* of current literature." He told Baron Vrangel that he hoped to be famous again. He would see Turgenev's name in print and admire something he had written, and his competitiveness would invigorate him. He never got an answer about Olga N. and L.T., but Dostoevsky was still intrigued. He wrote to his old friend Apollon Maikov months later, "I like L.T. very much, but in my opinion he won't write much (perhaps I'm mistaken, however)." L.T. was Leo Tolstoy.

Prison had nevertheless given him more than it had taken away. "I seem to be ripe for something," he declared upon leaving the fortress. There was more to write about now than ever before—the abundance of material tormented him. He had listened to so many stories, he told Mikhail, stories "of the whole dark and wretched side of life! It will be enough for entire volumes." He gathered twenty-eight pieces of paper and cardboard and sewed them together with thick black string. He diluted some precious nut ink and rewrote all of the little fragments he had written in the prison hospital into his makeshift notebook. He numbered the entries, and he would return to them for decades.

Dostoevsky spent years not knowing if he would write again, but before he made the journey back to Petersburg, the merciful Angel-Tsar finally granted him permission to publish. He was sincere when he closed one of his petitions to Tsar Alexander, "With feelings of reverence and passionate, infinite devotion I make bold to call myself the most loyal and grateful of Your Imperial Majesty's subjects."

But his return to Petersburg was not triumphant. A novel he wrote, set in Siberia, garnered little interest. Mikhail Katkov, the editor of *The Russian Herald*, offered him a small advance of five hundred rubles for it. The opportunity was promising—*The Russian Herald* had become one of Russia's leading journals—but when Katkov saw the unfinished manuscript for *The Village of Stepanchikovo* in 1859, he rejected it outright and demanded his money back. "The ass!" Dostoevsky said of Katkov. "He thinks he's Jupiter." Dostoevsky's standing was not what it used to be.

He was forced to offer his manuscript to *The Contemporary*, to Nekrasov, the man who had helped drum him out of Belinsky's circle and who mocked him as a "new pimple" on Russian literature's nose. *The Contemporary* had openly derided him while he was in Siberia. The journal's co-editor, Ivan Panaev, wrote about that bizarre time when everyone in Petersburg was enamored of a brand-new author, "our little idol," before he got too arrogant for his own good. "Poor fellow! We killed him, we made him ridiculous." Happily, the idol was removed from his pedestal "and completely forgotten." Panaev didn't name Dostoevsky, but he didn't have to. "Dostoevsky is finished," Nekrasov said after reading *The Village of Stepanchikovo*. "He will no longer write anything important."

D ostoevsky kept staging his comeback. He was filled with ideas. He wanted to self-publish his collected works. He was rewriting *The Double* to prove the critics wrong. "They will finally see what *The Double* is!" he exulted to Mikhail. And he had another idea. He would write about his experience in a Siberian fortress prison and call it *Notes from a Dead House*. There was the problem of censorship—they'd surely ban details about his penal servitude—but he developed a strategy. "My person will disappear. These are the notes of an unknown person," so, technically, it could sell as fiction. People would see his name on the cover and know the truth. He had another idea, too, something he came up with while lying on his plank bed in Siberia: *A Confession*, a novel that would be "striking, passionate." He thought of it in the depths of his despair. It was the germ of *Notes from Underground*. "All my heart and blood will go into the novel," he told Mikhail. And he had yet another idea—something else he imagined in prison—a novel about a young man who ends up in Siberia.

Mikhail had an idea as well. He had been struggling in the tobacco business for years, and on a whim he applied for permission to publish a journal. The Petersburg Censorship Committee granted that permission in October 1858. Mikhail had decided that it was too much work, but now that Fyodor was back, perhaps they could pull it off together. Dostoevsky always wanted to edit his own journal and attack the oligarchs. He wanted a publication with "more energy, passion, wit, staunchness—that's what is needed now!" He was sick of *the statistical movement in literature*," the vogue for making it scientific and programmatic. He wanted a platform to write "about the futility of *directions* in art."

Owning a journal was a way to escape the trap of inequality. Wealthy writers could take their time to produce better writing that would fetch more money, whereas writers like him—"I'm a Proletarian Writer," he declared—were stuck in a cycle of low payments for rushed work. Gentry writers with large estates were getting more per page than he was. "Why do I, with my needs, charge only 100 rubles, when Turgenev, who has 2,000 souls, gets 400?" If he were an editor, he'd pay himself what he was worth, and he wouldn't have to rush. The more Dostoevsky thought about it, the more he wanted to do it. He and his brother were smarter and more talented than Russia's reigning litterateurs. "They're peasants in literature," he said, and yet they were getting rich.

It was an excellent time to start a journal. Alexander II's loosening censorship standards revitalized the literary scene. One hundred fifty new periodicals were founded in the second half of the 1850s, five times as many as the previous five years. Book publications were increasing rapidly, buoyed by rising literacy rates: Petersburg now had a majority-literate population. So the Dostoevsky brothers set up a small office in Mikhail's apartment and hired a handful of friends to recruit contributors and to help write, edit, and advertise.

Dostoevsky would write *Notes from a Dead House* during the day, begin editing around midnight, and continue until dawn. Staff meetings were in the afternoon and normally involved scouring periodicals and arguing during tea breaks.

They circulated their mission statement widely. "We live in an epoch in the highest degree remarkable and critical," it began. "Russia is in the midst of a great transformation," the combination of European and Russian culture, the "fusion of enlightenment" with "the people's life." Their new journal would help Russians navigate this transformation. It was a monthly, and they called it *Vremya* (*Time*). Dostoevsky wrote the statement, but his name did not appear below it. His name was not on *Vremya*'s masthead, either, because ex-convicts were not allowed to edit journals.

The first issue (January 1861) included an excerpt from Casanova's memoirs, an overview of 1860's biggest political events, and Dostoevsky's encomium to the Russian character. He praised "its talent for universal reconciliation, universal humanity. The Russian character does not possess the European angularity, impenetrability, inflexibility. He gets along with everybody." He also admired the Russian's "absence of any self-exaltation." The issue opened with original translations of three Edgar Allan Poe stories: "The Tell-Tale Heart," "The Devil in the Belfry," and "The Black Cat"—tales of inexplicable violence and murder, unexpected choices for a journal devoted to "universal reconciliation." "The Black Cat" is told by a man who kills his beloved feline out of "the spirit of perverseness," which the man claims is central to human nature. The cat "had given me no reason of offence," the narrator confesses. He hanged it from a tree simply because it was forbidden. Dostoevsky's introduction praised Poe's psychological insight.

The journal was hard work. The subscriptions were "so-so," but it was worth it. "I understand what the first step means, and I love it," Dostoevsky said. But it was better than so-so. The Dostoevskys had twenty-five hundred subscribers in their first year, which made it one of Russia's premier journals. The immediate success of *Vremya* owed partly to *Notes from a Dead House*, which created a sensation when it was serialized. No one had ever read anything like it, even under the thin veil of "fiction." *Dead House* informed everyone that Dostoevsky had returned from Siberia, and he brought the truth back with him. He was an ex-convict, a political prisoner exiled for his beliefs, which earned him a special regard among radicals and moderates alike. "It revived my literary reputation," Dostoevsky wrote a few years later. When Leo Tolstoy read Dostoevsky's account of Siberia, he quickly wrote to his cousin, "Get hold of *Notes from a Dead House* and read it. *It's essential.*" His impression was undiminished when he reread it decades later. "I don't know a better book in all modern literature, Pushkin included," Tolstoy wrote to a friend. "If you see Dostoevsky, tell him I love him."

Russian society was fracturing into "two hostile camps," Dostoevsky announced in *Vremya*. Though he was exiled for testing the limits of political discourse in 1849, he returned ten years later to find himself a moderate in a polarizing environment. Petersburg now had a wider array of perspectives, including several new writers moving toward radicalism.

The most important of these new writers had lurked on the edges of the Petrashevsky Circle but had escaped arrest. His name was Nikolai Gavrilovich Chernyshevsky. He was bookish, shy, and slight. He was poorly dressed but incredibly ambitious. When he was young, he worked on creating a perpetual motion machine that would eliminate all material need, win him the tsar's praise, and make him a "second Savior."

Chernyshevsky took over *The Contemporary* in the late 1850s and brought back Belinsky's thundering style. "In literature," Chernyshevsky wrote, "we still need an iron dictatorship, to make them tremble as they trembled before Belinsky." He was the heir of 1840s radicalism. He discovered Feuerbach and Fourier—materialist atheism and utopian socialism—through the Petrashevists and intended to take them further. He considered Russian autocracy the pinnacle of brutal class hierarchy: "The sooner it collapses the better." His vision of large-scale destruction and renewal derived from Hegel's philosophy of history and the "eternal struggle" he thought it depicted.

Chernyshevsky believed that history's movements could be defined precisely. He fetishized precision. It was a verbal tic in his essays—"precise methods," "exact solution," "precisely solved," "exact scientific analysis." When he was young, he recorded everything in a diary. He counted the minutes he spent walking. He drew the floor plans of his friends' houses. He made a diagram of the scene of his first dance. Chernyshevsky's aesthetics were a corollary to his empiricism: Beauty is life itself. Art merely imitates it. The purpose of art is to help people understand reality, which would inspire bold political action. Chernyshevsky attacked a Turgenev story, "Asya," because of the protagonist's fussy indecision, which Chernyshevsky called "trashy weakness." The best artworks, he argued, provide models for clear judgment and political efficacy.

Turgenev did not take this evaluation well. He complained that the new critics at *The Contemporary* were trying to eliminate all aesthetic principles. They are "literary Robespierres," he claimed, who would chop off the heads of poets the first chance they got. He considered Chernyshevsky's grand aesthetic treatise (*The Aesthetic Relation of Art to Reality*) *"worse than an evil book; it is—an evil deed."* Privately, Turgenev called him a "stinking cockroach." Tolstoy had the same visceral reaction. He bristled at Chernyshevsky's "unpleasant, reedy little voice" and warned that he was ruining *The Contemporary* with his insolence and malice. He was, Tolstoy added, a "gentleman who smells of lice."

The growing divides in Russia were social as much as ideological. Chernyshevsky was a member of the *raznochintsy*—people of miscellaneous ranks, the sons and daughters of priests, for example, or low-ranking military officers, people without estates, people with different values. As the phalanx of raznochintsy began taking over *The Contemporary*, gentry writers began leaving it. But what was happening with *The Contemporary* was a sign of things to come. Its subscriptions more than doubled in Chernyshevsky's first five years, and it had become one of Russia's most influential periodicals.

Across the divide was Mikhail Katkov, "the ass" who had unceremoniously withdrawn his publication offer to Dostoevsky. Katkov's primary task in *The Russian Herald* was "liberating the Russian mind from the foreign yoke." He was a conservative Hegelian who believed the Russian language would unite all Slavic peoples. The language's strength and beauty made Russia "predestined for something great and universal," Katkov declared. The only thing Russia needed was a literature to fulfill its world-historical importance.

Katkov was the closest thing to an establishment journalist that Russia had. By 1861, his journal had a circulation of six thousand, which rivaled *The Contemporary*. He was a skillful businessman who had developed extensive government connections during editorial stints at semiofficial newspapers, and he knew how to pull strings. He kept tight ideological control over his journal, dismissed writers who didn't toe the line, and paid his loyal contributors well. He had the means to outbid the competition and the judgment to know when to do so. When Tolstoy and Turgenev left *The Contemporary*, they went to Katkov.

Katkov worked hard to be an establishment editor partly because he felt marginal—he, too, was a member of the raznochintsy. His father, a low-ranking civil servant, died when Katkov was five years old, leaving him to spend part of his childhood living in the Moscow prison where his mother became a linen keeper. As a young adult, he fretted about social minutiae, and he masked his anxiety with wild antics, drunkenness, and at least one challenge to a duel. Katkov's youthful antics evolved into a petulance that left him isolated. None of his extensive connections brought any warmth.

When *Vremya* burst onto the scene, Katkov mocked the first issue's naïveté and high-flown rhetoric ("universal reconciliation," "universal humanity," "universal meaning")—never mind that it resembled his own. His mockery might have been payback. Dostoevsky had penned an invective against the "golden mediocrities" directing Russian discourse. They were "the first to throw stones at every innovator," Dostoevsky wrote, and terrified of new ideas. Addressing equal rights for women or the despotism of husbands sent them into a panic about the future of matrimony. The golden mediocrities were "'businessmen' who make use of the fashionable phrase," Dostoevsky wrote. They profit from the geniuses they once persecuted. "They vulgarize everything they happen to touch."

Dostoevsky wanted *Vremya* to take the high road, but that didn't last long. When Katkov referred to Dostoevsky as "a fop perfumed with patchouli" (the two had clearly never met), Dostoevsky hurled insults back, calling Katkov conceited as well as "incontinent and quick-tempered." He suffered from "childish irritability" and, simultaneously, "a kind of senility." Dostoevsky saw personal attacks as essential to developing an idea. "You need to lash out sometimes," he later told a friend starting a journal. Angry disputes clarify thought. For an idea to thrive, it needs "the most personal, current, everyday particulars."

And vulgar as it may be, sharp disputes were good business. Now that there was a little room for debate in Russia, readers subscribed to journals for ideological battle, and the debates became heated because journalism was the closest thing to politics that Russians could enjoy safely. Fiction and poetry— and arguments about them—became proxies for dangerous political opinions. As politics were squeezed, reading and writing expanded. Tsarist oppression inadvertently helped create the golden age of Russian literature.

Dostoevsky's ideological niche in the crowded literary ecosystem was somewhere between moderate conservatives like Katkov and radicals like Chernyshevsky. "Beauty is useful because it is beauty," he argued, bypassing the false choice between radical action and conservative aesthetics. It was a sign of things to come that his call for reconciliation between hostile camps devolved into a fight.

Russia was at an inflection point in 1861. Alexander II and his government were in the midst of a great era of reforms that would modernize the empire's judicial system, its banking and financial sectors, its schools and universities, its administration and infrastructure. This was the "great transformation" that Dostoevsky mentioned in *Vremya*'s announcement. It was motivated not by any reformist zeal on Alexander's part but by a general sense of crisis following the Crimean War. What began as a campaign to protect Orthodox Christians in the Holy Land led to the disastrous siege of Sevastopol. Russia fought the war in the name of Christianity and Russian nationalism, only to be defeated by Ottoman Turks allied with European powers. For a nation whose pride stemmed from the centuries-old myth of its military strength, the defeat was humiliating. The new tsar took the loss as an opportunity to make sweeping changes.

The most consequential reform was the emancipation of the serfs. Building a modern empire on feudalism simply wasn't tenable anymore. The economic arguments for emancipation proved more persuasive than the moral ones. An agricultural system sustained by peasant farmers who could not leave a plot of land discouraged investment and innovation, and farming productivity suffered. Serfdom also hampered the development of an industrial labor

force, which consisted largely of serfs from countryside estates working tem-
porarily in factories and mills. Industrialists needed something more reliable.

The only thing serfdom did efficiently was transfer wealth from the peasants to the hereditary nobility. It stratified society. Hereditary nobility made
up about 1 percent of Russia's population, and its power became dominated
by an ever-smaller group of elites, none of whom paid taxes. In 1858, the
gentry's wealthiest 1 percent held nearly a third of all seigneurial serfs. The
average estate had more than two thousand tax-paying souls. Only serfs were
conscripted into the army, and their service requirement was fifteen years.
The burden of supporting the empire led to widespread peasant revolts.
There were twenty-five uprisings in 1856. In 1858, there were more than two
hundred.

When Alexander issued his emancipation decree in 1861, the long-awaited
moment of liberation was greeted with confusion, dismay, and anger. The
decree was written in arcane, bureaucratic language that peasants and local
officials could barely understand. Disputes erupted during public readings
over the proper interpretation of the text, and dissatisfied peasants often recruited people who could supply the "correct" reading. But the correct reading
was that emancipation was neither immediate nor free. Serfs had to buy themselves out of their bondage by paying for the land they had cultivated—plus
interest. It worked, in theory, as something like a forty-nine-year mortgage.
Landlords and serfs negotiated the land's value and the size of each buyer's
allotment. The government would issue bonds to the landlords and collect
annual payments from the peasants. In practice, however, land prices were
inflated, sometimes to two or three times their value. Refusing to purchase
the land was not an option, and only one-third of redemption agreements were
reached amicably. The government provided no financial assistance—not even
for emancipation's administrative costs. Most serfs would remain obligated to
their landlords through the end of the century.

Confusion quickly turned to anger. The largest act of disorder took place
in a village called Bezdna, where a Raskolnik announced that he was the
emancipation decree's true interpreter. Serfs had been granted complete emancipation, he declared, they should obey neither the authorities nor the gentry,
and they should pay no obligations. Peasants throughout the region took him
for a prophet, and after a standoff with thousands of the Raskolnik's followers,

soldiers fired into the crowd, killing hundreds of people. Within days, the Raskolnik was sentenced to death and shot.

The question that loomed over these tumultuous years was whether modernizing Russia was the same as westernizing it, thus destroying its essential character. Some trade-off seemed unavoidable. "Our task is to create a new form of ourselves," Dostoevsky wrote in *Vremya*'s announcement, while warning, "We cannot be Europeans." European principles, he wrote, "are alien and opposite to us." Becoming "modern" meant incorporating advances in science and technology into agriculture, industry, governance, and education. For Alexander's reforms, it meant teaching the natural sciences in secondary schools. It meant building railroads and modern factories. It meant rationalizing the state administration, the legal system, and the economy. It meant using statistics and data to design and implement clear statutes, transparent procedures, jury trials, and an international system of trade.

Being modern and rational could easily seem like being "alien," and the modern Russian economy seemed to embody the apparent trade-off. It had struggled for decades, partly because of scarce capital and an anemic banking system. This meant that any large initiative—in industry or in the tsar's government—was likely financed by foreign lenders. And the financiers who especially troubled many people (including Dostoevsky) were Jewish, people who were seen to be stateless agents of an international order. The empire had gone to dreadful lengths to quash Jewish culture in Russia—bloody pogroms, forced conversions, traditional clothing bans, strictly delineated settlement areas—but in the era of modern and rational reform some of those practices were beginning to change, at least for a time. Several large Jewish-owned banks were just being established in Petersburg, including the Ginzburg Bank and the Stieglitz Bank, which helped Russia draw from banks in Amsterdam, Paris, and London. Petersburg saw an influx of wealthy Jewish entrepreneurs who held sway in industry, commerce, and securities. And so the city's status as the center of Russia's rapidly growing banking industry, the home of its stock exchange, and the largest port for its foreign trade made it a testing ground for whatever "alien and opposite" version of Russia the future might bring.

Dostoevsky despised predatory usury and international finance too much for his hatred not to search for human targets. His anti-Semitism was still mild in these years—he attacked anti-Semitic screeds and advocated for legislation expanding Jewish rights in several *Vremya* issues—but his prejudice was growing. The more he believed that Russians were destined to play a messianic role for humanity, the more the Jewish people seemed like enemies of Russia's essential national character. And the less he thought about it, the more it made sense.

Most 1860s radicals, however, were indifferent to national character and to what counted as alien or native. Instead, they pinned their messianic hopes on the power of reason and the discovery of an essential human nature. Societies ought to be rational, they believed, and they ought to be rational because human nature is rational: it obeys unalterable laws all around the world. The natural law that most captivated the radicals' imagination was the premise that humans seek pleasure and avoid pain. "All people are egoists," Chernyshevsky wrote. He renovated Max Stirner's egoism by tethering it to altruism. Virtuous acts provide more pleasure than vicious ones, so the true egoist would never slide into a selfish, violent abyss. A person needs only to experience altruism to live a life of benevolence.

Chernyshevsky referred to this as *rational* egoism. Where Stirner saw the ego as doing what it wills—taking what it wants and murdering, if necessary—Chernyshevsky claimed that we are the slaves of the pleasure we seek. We have no free will whatsoever. Human nature, he believed, is simpler than we think. There is no complexity or mystery to people. There are no internal conflicts. There is no morality because humans make no choices. Some people are good and others bad because their circumstances and environment dictate it. Carbon, depending on its environment, can become diamonds or coal. Chernyshevsky estimated that 90 percent of all crime would disappear if we simply fed everyone—having no free will did not diminish his conviction that we have the power to change everything.

The genealogy of Chernyshevsky's ideas is important. His rational egoist is the unlikely progeny of Max Stirner and Jeremy Bentham, whose ideas were popular in 1860s Russia—it was Bentham who made the ego seem slavish but efficacious. The moral goal, he believed, is to maximize everyone's pleasure, not just one's own ego, and so where Stirner's inward turn made him free for bombast, Bentham's aims forced him to be calmly empirical. To maximize everyone's pleasure, Bentham argued, a person must "sum up the values" of all the pleasures an action causes and subtract all the pains for every person affected. The resulting number is the score of an action's virtue. The philosophy of maximizing happiness by summing pleasures and pains is called utilitarianism. It was not clear what unit of measurement Bentham had in mind, but the implication was that if individuals, groups, or governments want to know how to act, all they need is good data. The emergence of statistics was not just a helpful advancement. It was a great moral tool.

This means that the ultimate authority for Chernyshevsky and the radicals following him was not philosophy or literature or political theory. It was science. All the "new ideas" they advocated, he informed his readers, "are based on the truth discovered by the natural sciences by means of a most exact analysis of facts." Russian radicals had good reasons to rely upon science. While European radicalism began to flower in the 1848 revolutions after decades of intellectual ferment (Bentham, for example, developed utilitarianism in 1780), Russians had a scant tradition of radicalism to rely upon. They drew their authority from science partly to bypass qualms about "alien" ideas and partly to bypass politics altogether—a crucial asset to reformers in an authoritarian state. A purely empirical framework for social change gave Russian radicals the hope that the days of political factions, secret circles, and ideological conversions—the days of the "instability of views," as Chernyshevsky put it— were coming to an end. Society was entering a new era of statistics, natural laws, and certainty. Philosophy was now based on science, Chernyshevsky declared, and "present-day science" was "beyond all dispute or doubt."

The science that most inspired Russian radicals was physiology. They found great social promise buried within detailed examinations of the human body and treatises on the ways desires and actions are determined by external inputs and electrical impulses traveling across nerves. One 1855 physiological study, Ludwig Büchner's *Force and Matter*, became known as "the Bible of Materialism." When Russian officials banned it, copies couldn't be smuggled in fast enough, so ardent fans (mostly university students) made illegal translations and secretly lithographed thousands of copies.

Materialism became a byword for a form of scientism, a radicalism ostensibly without chauvinism or compromise, and it spread. In 1863, a Russian physiologist, Ivan Sechenov, published *Reflexes of the Brain*, which details a series of experiments he performed on frogs. Decapitated frogs, electrocuted frogs, frogs that are pinched or smeared with sulfuric acid, all demonstrate that their movements are inevitable and mechanical, like the hands of a clock. Sechenov performed experiments on himself as well (Question: How do large amounts of alcohol affect metabolism?), and he drew ambitious conclusions. Everything that goes on in a brain (human or amphibian) "can be reduced *to muscular movement*." Voluntary movements are essentially mechanical reflexes. Choices are reflexes. Emotions are reflexes: "Animation, passion, mockery, sorrow, joy, etc., are merely results of a greater or lesser contraction of definite groups of muscles"—"a purely mechanical act." Every thought we have, everything we know, everything we do, is the inevitable response to an external stimulus, a series of electrical impulses coursing through an intricate network of nerves and muscles, and all the lofty ideas we build on top of that—free will, self-consciousness, morality—are unreal. Russian radicals were enthralled. All the ghosts were finally dead, vanquished by science at last, and what remained was machinery.

An overarching theory seeming to support this understanding of human nature came in 1864, with the appearance of the first Russian translation of Charles Darwin's *On The Origin of Species*. Garbled versions of Darwinism gained traction among radicals almost immediately. Human beings became machines programmed for survival and reproduction, and survival became a sign of supremacy. Superior animals stride atop the wreckage of extinct species. Extraordinary people dominate by natural law. The World Spirit trampling innocent flowers became evolution.

Dostoevsky could see where Russian radicalism was heading. Materialism was promising to be a solution to politics rather than another instance of it. It was expanding to become a catchall for rationalism, egoism, physiology, and social Darwinism, and it completely missed what it meant to be a human being. It was blind to anything it could not measure, and it could measure very little. Dostoevsky did not want to dismiss science—he thought "enlightenment" could go hand in hand with Russia's "native soil"—but he wanted *Vremya* to put materialism into perspective. Humans are more than nerves and electrical impulses. People are not rational. They are horrible at maximizing their own pleasure, and sometimes they sabotage it. A person could kill a beloved thing out of "the spirit of perverseness," as Edgar Allan Poe wrote, for essentially nothing. A person could champion "exact scientific analysis" with zealous faith and questionable evidence.

Dostoevsky was determined to remind the world that every perceived law of human nature and every carefully gathered statistic crashes on the shore of innumerable details. "Reality is infinitely diverse compared to all, even the cleverest, conclusions of abstract thought," Dostoevsky wrote in *Dead House*. Years of exile in a land where no law reigned and no theory sufficed made this clear. People squander their money on drunken binges. They gamble everything away. They kill for trifles. There were dark mysteries that materialism would never touch, and any path forward for civilization would have to take up those mysteries and carry them forever.

Twelve

Ferocious Materialism

While hunting for new material for *Vremya*, Dostoevsky came across a collection of accounts of infamous trials, mostly in France: *Causes célèbres de tous les peuples*. One of the first stories was about a man named Pierre-François Lacenaire. The opening page featured an illustration depicting an old woman cowering in her bedclothes, looking up, eyes wide, at a slender man in a frock coat lunging forward with something sharp—like an ice pick—above his head. A top hat sits on a nearby chair. Through an open doorway in the background, someone on the floor pleads for his life as the man standing over him is about to swing his ax.

Dostoevsky read about Lacenaire, how he and an accomplice brutally murdered a man and his mother, took what little money they had, and then tried robbing the collection clerks of large banks like the Rothschild and the Mallet. The account of Lacenaire's crimes and trial was written by Armand Fouquier, not a name Dostoevsky knew, but it was well written and thorough—thirty-two pages that included several engraved illustrations. There's one of Lacenaire in profile wearing a cravat and high collar, vest and wide-lapeled coat. He has a prominent nose, brow, and sideburns. His hair billows and falls over his ears. He's wearing his top hat in other illustrations—while stealing a clock, while huddling over drinks with his accomplice. In the final image, the top hat tumbles to the ground as prisoners attack him. And now he's the one pleading.

The murders were gruesome, but Fouquier's volume was filled with sensational crimes like this—a murder for love, the murder of a priest, cannibalism. What caught Dostoevsky's eye was Lacenaire himself. The elegant man with large, deep-set eyes gazing off to the right with an expression somewhere between thoughtfulness and boredom. He had come from a good family. He had a good education and "a lively taste for studying," Fouquier noted, but lack of funding scuttled his plan to study law, and he turned, improbably, to literature. He published an article about the justice system. He wrote poetry. When his literary career stalled, he became bitter and isolated until his relationships dwindled to one faithful friend and a mother who still sent him money from afar. He craved his own punishment, seemingly from the beginning, though he never expressed remorse, and the stated reasons for his crimes kept shifting. At one point, Fouquier noted, Lacenaire claimed that he would have abandoned crime altogether and lived a tranquil bourgeois life if only he had succeeded in one grand, triumphant coup.

Fouquier reprinted several of Lacenaire's poems and songs, enough to capture his voice, which was at turns melancholy, playful, and aggrieved. "Banned, chased, proscribed, and crushed under offense. / One happiness remained to me, that of vengeance." He cultivated another voice in prison. "I kill a man as I drink a glass of wine." Nothing he said seemed entirely true, and he seemed to be reabsorbed into a culture degraded enough to admire him. The article noted that admirers visited him in prison, that the press reported on his every word, that he wrote poetry and dashed off his memoirs, and that one fashionable lady asked him to write something "on the subject of imagination," to which he responded, "I am not at the mercy of the people of the world!"

It was difficult to get a handle on Lacenaire's motive. Money was the obvious reason. "Gold, lots of gold," Fouquier wrote, "to satisfy his vain conceit." He wouldn't work for it, Fouquier observed, because in addition to his "taste for studying" Lacenaire "had a taste for easy living." But that did not explain his ruthless indifference, or why he intended to kill people when robbery would suffice. When someone asked Lacenaire why he felt no pity for his victims, he answered philosophically. "Man does whatever he wants," he observed, though "the means had to be in harmony with the purpose." What was his purpose? Fouquier's answer was clear: Lacenaire "systematized ferocious materialism." He sought refuge from his poverty in "atheism and materialist philosophy." Fouquier borrowed this perspective from the press accounts he had gone through. Several newspapers declared that Lacenaire's poetry amounted to a defense of "egoism and materialism." But big labels hang loosely, and Lacenaire's words make him seem sometimes much more than an egoist-materialist and sometimes much less. Fouquier concluded that Lacenaire was "essentially incomplete in nature."

Dostoevsky thought it was Lacenaire's trial—the proceedings themselves—that clarified things the most. He read Lacenaire's advocate trying to solve the enigma in his final defense. The murderer's misfortunes, the advocate argued, triggered a fever of despair. His fever gave way to delirium, harmful theories, a mania for literature, an all-consuming egoism, and a numb disregard for all laws and all people—"a cruel illness," he called it. Yes. It was not a philosophy so much as a swell of ideas, an illness, a potential plague.

Only a careful examination of the proceedings could make that apparent. Fortunately, Fouquier was able to draw upon a stenographic account of the trial. Stenography allowed the proceedings to be "transmitted with the exactness of a daguerreotype," Dostoevsky marveled, "a physiological drawing." And that's exactly what people needed to see.

On November 12, 1835, a crowd packed into the Assize Court in the Palais de Justice. A well-known actor was in the audience (he had once met Lacenaire backstage—the criminal had made an impression). The reserved benches in the front were filled primarily with women. There were at least two stenographers preparing. Several lawyers in their black robes and white frilly jabots eagerly awaited the advocate general's eloquent, veteran representative, Jean-Isidore Partarrieu-Lafosse. Lacenaire's advocate, Gustave Brochant, was twenty-four years old and had been practicing for only three years.

Lacenaire was smiling as the two gendarmes ushered him into the courtroom. He was wearing black pants and a blue frock coat with a velvet collar. He had a silky mustache, a pleasing face, and a calm demeanor. He seemed to glide toward the dock reserved for all three of the accused, and he gazed at the assembled audience before sitting down. Extra guards had been assigned to keep the prisoners apart, and Lacenaire chatted with them while his advocate circulated copies of one of his well-known songs. This was the way to die.

Lacenaire was facing thirty charges, ranging from two counts of murder to one count of stealing a clock. He would be tried with both of his accomplices, and the prosecutor's case was aggressive. Fifty-five witnesses were scheduled to testify over the next two days—detectives, doctors, victims, family members, former prison mates, and acquaintances. Even the pimp (the Cutler) offered testimony. The evidence displayed on the magistrates' desk included a three-edged file, a rusty and bloodstained ax, and an apartment door bearing a name written in chalk. It was covered with battens to keep it pristine.

Président Dupuy, counselor of the Royal Court, presided at the dais in his black robe and cap, with two assessors—fellow judges—seated at his sides. The président of the Assize Court, as always, posed all questions to the witnesses directly. After swearing in the jurors, he turned to the accused.

"Accused, stand up. What is your name?"

"Pierre-François Lacenaire."

"Your age?"

"Thirty-one years."

"Your job?"

"Former traveling salesperson."

Trials in France began with a presumption of guilt based upon testimony and evidence gathered by the examining magistrate. As the président was about to begin his questioning, Lacenaire stood up and bowed gracefully. He was a cooperative witness, and his crimes unspooled as a series of questions and answers.

"So it was Avril who took the ax?"

"Yes, to finish off Chardon, who was still moving."

"Did you strike several blows?"

"Yes, when I saw Avril finishing up, I went to the Chardon woman. I struck her several times, and when I thought she could no longer defend herself, I pushed the mattress over her."

There were gasps from the audience.

"Did Avril help you with the second assassination?"

"No, I did everything this time."

Lacenaire supplied every detail in a clear, steady voice. What did they take from the armoire? What did they do afterward? When he said they went to see a comedy show, the audience was aghast.

"At what time was the assassination of the widow Chardon and her son committed?"

"At twelve fifty-five."

He recalled the clock striking one while rifling through their belongings. He recalled dates and addresses, the precise furniture arrangements, the way a lock was broken. When the subject turned to his murder weapon, he helpfully displayed the scar on his finger and pantomimed how he was stabbing the widow when the file broke through the cork handle.

He was a stickler for facts throughout the proceedings. He spoke freely and out of turn. He finished witnesses' responses. He corrected them. One doctor testified that a small knife with a broken tip was found in the Chardon widow's room, but the accused pointed out that it was in the son's room. He noted contradictory testimony and faulty suppositions. The prosecution insisted that the knife was a third murder weapon. Three weapons, Lacenaire noted, don't necessarily mean three killers. Besides, the knife they found was too small for the body's wounds, and wouldn't the doctors have found the broken knife tip inside her? He corrected the chief of the Sûreté ("M. Allard is confused") and the président himself—about where he slept on a certain night and where he had dinner.

Every intervention aided his conviction. A collection clerk from one of Lacenaire's first bank robbery attempts testified about how he tried to collect money on a bill of exchange from a Monsieur "Bluet or Boulet." The courtroom audience was astonished when Lacenaire, finally seeing what had foiled his plan, said quietly, "The bill was signed *Bonin*."

Avril, on the other hand, was defiant. He admitted he was a thief, of course. He had spent five years in prison for it, and thievery was the sort of thing he did with Lacenaire, who had all the schemes. One idea was to order a large amount of clothing from a shop. When the woman arrived with the merchandise, Lacenaire would take her elsewhere to fetch the money for it. Then Avril would swoop in from another room, take the clothes, and run. That plot was foiled when two women showed up.

Avril knew about Lacenaire's bank robbery scheme, but he testified that he never realized it involved murder—he had only agreed to cover a clerk's nose and mouth while Lacenaire took the money. When the time came to rob the Rothschild collection clerk in the Cutler's apartment, Avril testified, Lacenaire showed up with two files and started sharpening them. He was stunned when Lacenaire told him it was for killing the clerk.

"Then I said I didn't want to, and I left."

"Come on!" Lacenaire shouted. "It failed because the cashier didn't come."

"No, sir, that's wrong!"

What seems to have infuriated Lacenaire the most was that Avril claimed that Lacenaire was the one who stole the Cutler's curtains. More often, though, Avril's testimony made him laugh. Avril testified that he was already under arrest the day the Chardons were murdered. Then he claimed he was physically incapable of committing violent assaults. "I had paralysis and could not grab a man around the neck. Even now I cannot raise my arm." He eventually admitted to being with Lacenaire on December 14. He often had lunch with him at the Big Seven cabaret, and he often joined him at the Variétés and the Turkish baths, but he couldn't remember if they had done any of these things on the day in question.

"Lacenaire," the président said, "do you remember that Avril went with you to the Turkish baths that day?"

"Perfectly, M. Président. I even had Chardon's coat on my shoulders."

"Avril, wouldn't you have gone to the Turkish baths to wash bloodstains from your pants and waistcoat?"

"No. Have there ever been any stains on my pants or my waistcoat?"

Lacenaire was making up stories out of revenge, Avril insisted, and possibly for money or favors. Prisoners were bribed for testimony all the time, he said, to avoid the galleys or solitary confinement, to get a sentence commuted or a commutation pardoned. This surprised the président.

"How do you suppose that the authorities wanted to bribe prisoners to denounce their comrades?"

"It's the truth," Avril said. "There are thousands of examples at Bicêtre."

Hippolyte-Martin François was one of the prisoners hoping to trade information for leniency, but his testimony in court was mostly obfuscation. He kept adjusting dates and names and did what he could to undermine Lacenaire's story. He insisted that he was far too big to have traded clothes with Lacenaire in an alleged attempt to avoid recognition. Lacenaire admitted that François's hunting jacket was somewhat embarrassing, though he added that hunting suits have forgiving tailoring.

François was bitter. "Lacenaire has much greater means than I do," he said. "I can neither read nor write, and he can arrange his defense in order to compromise me. He will turn me over like a glove, but it's not proof."

L acenaire spent much of the trial's second day reading press accounts of the previous day's proceedings. His advocate handed him several newspapers before the session, and as he sat with them in the dock, the coverage of the testimony became more interesting than the testimony itself. By the time the doctors had begun testifying about the wounds on the Chardons' bodies (the rough puncture in the mother's throat, her son's ax-fractured skull), Lacenaire was jotting down notes in the margins of the newsprint. His attention would occasionally alight on a juror or one of the ladies or the widow Chardon's estranged second son who helped clean up his mother's apartment, and then he would return to the newspapers, pencil in hand.

He asked his advocate to fill him in when he heard the audience laughing, but some witnesses caught his interest. A laundress testified about how Lacenaire dragged her halfway across her landing as he was fleeing the rue Montorgueil building. The scoundrel didn't even have the courage to face whoever was grabbing him until he realized she was an old woman. "He made me twirl around and fall on my face," she said, and Lacenaire chuckled.

"Do you recognize the person who allegedly mistreated you?" the président asked.

"It's the one who just lowered his head."

"Was it you, Lacenaire?"

He began laughing openly. "Probably." The audience laughed as well.

Entering and exiting the courtroom delighted him. He'd salute the court on his way in and scan the crowd, pleased with the number of ladies in the reserved benches. He'd carefully adjust his clothing and put on his gloves before departing. But the testimony was like watching children taking turns with long division. He'd study the faces of the jurors and run his hand through his hair. He'd pull out his fine linen handkerchief, the latest fashion. He'd rest his head on the railing in front of him. At one point, he was seen with a manuscript—neatly handwritten pages displayed on his knee.

Lacenaire was the only person bored with the capital proceedings against him. The jurors heard details of attempted bank thefts, forgeries, and narrow escapes. They examined the bloodstained weapons and watched the dirty looks and recriminations among the three accused sitting together in dangerous proximity. And there were surprise twists. The lodging house keeper, Pageot, was arrested in the courtroom shortly after his testimony because a juror had noticed that he had altered the dates in his guest register. Then a last-minute witness was summoned. Lacenaire pointed out that Alphonse Bâton, who had introduced Lacenaire and François in the first place, had been imprisoned fifteen days earlier and would be easy to track down in the prefecture jail. Hours later, two gendarmes and a bailiff brought the stunned Bâton into the courtroom to testify, which sealed François's fate.

B eneath the violence, the treachery, and the grudges among the three prisoners, there was another intrigue emerging, something that shaped the way everyone interpreted the testimony.

It started during Avril's examination. The président wanted to clarify a small detail—a phrase he used. When Avril referred to Chardon as "my aunt," he meant it as a slang term for someone with "infamous habits." It was not a question, really. He was pointing it out for the jurors. A few minutes later, Avril admitted that he stayed with Lacenaire before, during, and after the Chardon murders and that he knew about Lacenaire's crimes. The président found it strange that Avril would keep Lacenaire's company knowing what he knew.

"Avril," the président asked, "did you sleep with Lacenaire in the same bed?"

"Yes, because there was only one room available."

That slight, embarrassed turning aside—from "bed" to "room"—was perhaps when it clicked. Aunt Madeleine and Avril and Lacenaire. They were all of a piece. Sleeping in the same bed didn't necessarily mean that something "infamous" was happening between them, but it was suggestive, and it became more suggestive as the nature of these men became clearer. The président pursued the matter with François.

"You said in your preliminary examination," the président reminded François, "that it was January 1 that you received this confidential information"— Lacenaire's boast about the murders—"yet you continued to sleep with him until January 6. How can we suppose that, with such a secret, you would have continued to sleep with him?"

François was unmoved. "It would be very unfortunate to be an accomplice in an assassination for having slept with Lacenaire."

By the time Bâton testified about introducing Lacenaire to François and the discussions they had the day the collection clerk was nearly killed, the président seems to have formed his opinion.

"Do you know the accused?" he immediately asked Bâton, who was still getting his bearings.

"I know all three of them."

"It even seems that you know all three in a particular way," he said. Bâton became embarrassed. For those watching, the courtroom testimony seemed to be uncovering the sort of tragedy that unfolds among intractably infamous people.

The advocate general emphasized the criminals' nature when he stood on the platform to make his closing argument. Who was Lacenaire? he asked the jury. He was Avril's bedmate (*camarade de lit*) at two apartments. "When Avril is taken to the police station on the twentieth, who goes to reclaim him? Always Lacenaire, his *inséparable*." And what sort of person would share a bed with a man who had just committed double homicide?

Homosexuality was not itself a crime at the time, though French law enforcement criminalized it indirectly through charges like adultery, sexual assault, public indecency, and incitement of youth to debauchery. Aggressive police tactics (surveillance and entrapment, sweeping roundups and interrogations), as well as the blackmail and recriminations that ensued, led to frequent arrests of homosexual men, and those high arrest rates reinforced the public impression that they were somehow naturally criminal.

The prosecutor tacitly relied upon this prejudice. He reminded the jury that under French law jurors are instructed to follow their deep beliefs about the case before them. They did not need proof, "only an intimate conviction." Lacenaire's moral degradation was self-evident, the prosecutor argued, and it compelled him to commit horrible acts. For him, murder was just business. He killed Chardon and his mother, robbed a widow of her last savings, in order to rob banks—"Pillet-Will, Löwenberg, Rothschild, Mallet!" Lacenaire was a symptom of a deeper problem. Here was a man who had everything—a good family, a good education. He was an intelligent man, a poet. Why would he throw away his pen for a sharpened file? "This is what happens," the pros-ecutor said, "when one does not have a calm faith in the future, which trusts work and patience, when one wants to conquer everything in one day, a too-common disease of our century."

Maître Brochant had his own story to tell. The man sitting before the jury had been blessed with a "beautiful nature." He was a man of "gentle and peaceful manners" who had been destroyed by misfortune. He returned from the army one day to discover that his father had gone bankrupt and that his family had departed France. He was unprepared for his future. His education made him ill suited for manual labor, and his "ardent and fiery soul" rebelled against any career in commerce. The young man grew increasingly bitter and impoverished until one day he fought a duel with Benjamin Constant's nephew. The fatal outcome marked him as a murderer and left him utterly alone— without friends or family. He drifted into petty crime, and a one-year prison stint corrupted him.

It was around that time that one of his great gifts—his intelligence—led him further into the abyss. Brochant argued that Lacenaire developed a cyn-ical philosophy in which life is merely the pursuit of pleasures at all costs and death is just "a cessation of movement, sensitivity, activity, pain, a return to nothing." Our brief interval of existence amounts to a war between the wealthy and the impoverished. "These ideas became second nature," Maître Brochant intoned.

He kept describing the philosophy as an illness. Lacenaire suffers from "delirium" and a "fever" that burns away every emotion. He submits his entire existence to logic and becomes a man who does as he pleases and remains unfeelingly serene. Yes, the jurors could indeed follow their convictions. They need only observe Lacenaire's courtroom behavior to see the symptoms of his "sick mind." His indifference to witness testimony, the way he sits in the dock during his own trial, reading and writing: "this confidence in atheism, this composure in front of the scaffold, and then this passionate love of letters." It's a toxic combination. Listen to Lacenaire telling you that he experiences no remorse for what he's done, he advised the jurors, "then ask yourself if this man has not suffered from a cruel disease!"

Brochant was not trying to convince the jury that Lacenaire was innocent. He was only trying to save him from the guillotine. Lacenaire, the advocate claimed, had no choice. His delirium made him believe that he's driven by a "superior force," that he is merely obeying the fate awaiting him. "The fever that consumed him did not leave him this free will which one must possess to be guilty." That is why the jury did not have the right to execute him—"That would be cruelty!"

Finally, after pleading for mercy, Brochant suddenly turned to Lacenaire.

"And you!" he said. "In the midst of your cruel sufferings, of your ever-increasing miseries, you will finally open your eyes," he declaimed, "and, in your misfortune, you will know the finger of the God whom you have blasphemed; you will bow your head before its power, and you will accept your evils in expiation for all your crimes."

When Maître Brochant sat down, Lacenaire leaned over the railing to congratulate his advocate on his performance. It was magnificent.

Lacenaire's story was perfect for *Vremya*. Dostoevsky helped translate Fouquier's account, and in *Vremya*'s second issue (February 1861), after the Domestic News section (featuring articles on steamships and remotely managed corporations), readers found "The Lacenaire Trial." The journal devoted fifty pages to it, and Dostoevsky introduced it to his readers in a note. Lacenaire "is a remarkable personality," Dostoevsky wrote, "enigmatic, frightening, and gripping." His cowardice and base instincts in the face of poverty made him turn to crime, but the criminal himself did not see it that way. "He dared to set himself up as a victim of his century," Dostoevsky wrote. Some might consider this an enlightened individual's humbling recognition of the force of history and environment, but it was really something else—"boundless vanity." Criminal trials like these, he wrote, are "more exciting than all possible novels because they light up the dark sides of the human soul that art does not like to approach."

Thirteen

The Birth of Nihilism

nonymous leaflets began appearing in Petersburg in the summer of
1861. They were stuffed in mailboxes, nailed onto walls, and scattered on major streets. They bore impressive titles: "Great Russia"
and "What We Want" and "To the Citizens." They were putting common
complaints in writing: the government should bear the costs of serf emancipation, for example, the government was "stupid and ignorant." Occasionally,
they included vague calls for reform. The leaflets were a nuisance, small in-
trusions into everyday life. A manifesto would be slipped in between the pages
of a theatrical program lying on a seat, a little sting before the curtain. But
over the next several months, the messages became more difficult to ignore.
And over the next several years, similar messages would shape mid-nineteenth-
century culture in Russia and beyond.

The first serious warning sign was a leaflet called "To the Young Generation." "Imperial Russia is in dissolution," it declared, and it was time for the
people to overthrow the oppressive tsars forever. It demanded elections, freedom of speech, the nationalization of the land, and the end of private farming.
The underlying attitude was alarming and yet familiar to anyone who remembered Chaadaev. "We have no political past. We are not bound by any tradition," it said, "that is why we move boldly forward to the revolution, why we
long for it." Russians could wipe everything away. "Imagine that suddenly, on
one single day, all our ministers, all our senators, all the members of our council of state were to expire, and at the same time all our governors, all our

officials, Metropolitans, Bishops—in a word, all our present administrative aristocracy—were to die too. What would Russia lose? Not a thing." Writers, scientists, and artists were all that Russia had. "To the Young Generation" was explicitly violent: "If to achieve our ends—to divide the land among the people—we had to kill a hundred thousand landlords, even that would not frighten us."

There were other signs of trouble. Alexander's university reforms were creating a restive student body. Admissions previously had been restricted almost entirely to nobles entering government service, but Alexander opened universities to anyone who could pass qualifying examinations. Now the sons of nobles were studying alongside the sons of soldiers and clergymen, merchants, Jews, and peasants. Women were still barred from enrollment, though they could audit Petersburg University lectures, which was a bold step—Moscow University faculty voted against female auditors almost unanimously. One Petersburg law student remembered seeing his first female auditor in 1860. A young woman in a simple black woolen dress and provocatively short hair walked into the lecture hall carrying a notebook. The rector escorted her to the front and gallantly seated her in an armchair as the students stared. Before long there were many women like her. In some departments the auditing women outnumbered the enrolled men.

The women in the lecture halls were among the most visible signs of university reforms. Disciplinary action was less severe. Uniforms and military training were abolished. Bans on foreign scholarship were eased. Universities taught philosophy again. Students were permitted to run their own libraries and publish their own magazines and newspapers (*The Herald of Free Opinion*, *The Spark*, *The Unmasker*). Some were meager—handwritten—but they were valuable forums for criticizing faculty, administrators, and university rules. Students smoked despite the rules. They wore long hair and mustaches despite the rules. And small rebellions grew. Students began circulating petitions for university and city officials. They began forming student governments modeled after western democracies. They set up funds to subsidize the poorer students. They set up "Sunday Schools" to teach their compatriots how to read.

In 1861, the government began cracking down—abolishing student organizations, restricting student publications, taking control of student libraries. Fees were reinstated. Censorship was tightened. The Third Section trained a new cadre of "outside agents" to conduct surveillance. When students began to protest the new rules at mass meetings during the fall 1861 term, the administration ordered a partial lockout. So students broke down the door of a main auditorium, held a meeting, and vowed to reject the new rules formally. The new hard-line minister of education responded by closing the university entirely.

The situation escalated. A thousand students assembled in the university courtyard, and incendiary speeches led to a procession through the streets. Onlookers gawked as two long files of students and sympathizers, monitored by policemen, crossed the Neva with a list of demands for the university's curator. Nothing like this had ever happened in Petersburg before. That night, dozens of students were arrested and locked up in the Peter and Paul Fortress. When students and allies gathered in the university courtyard the next day, they were surrounded by troops. Administrators expelled student protesters, but after they reopened the university, the expelled students stormed the main building and halted lectures. Soldiers pummeled the protesters, but they remained defiant. "Carry me off to prison too," they shouted. Five students were exiled, and the university remained closed for the rest of the year.

D ostoevsky was sympathetic—he sent the imprisoned students beef and cognac—but Russia's scant activist tradition made the sudden arrival of leaflets and demonstrations difficult for the public to tolerate, and opinion soon began to turn against radicalism. One of the catalysts for this change was a new novel. In March 1862, Katkov's *The Russian Herald* published *Fathers and Children*, Turgenev's most influential work. It features a character named Bazarov, Turgenev's mouthpiece for the young radicals. Bazarov is a militant empiricist who turns skepticism into a rallying cry. "We act on the basis of what we recognize as useful," he tells one of the older men. "Nowadays the most useful thing of all is rejection—we reject."

"Everything?"

"Everything."

God, ideals, principles, aesthetics, rules. Lofty terms like "liberalism" and "progress" and even "emancipation" are vaporous illusions—ghosts. "We were being oppressed by the most primitive superstitions," Bazarov declares, but now a new sensibility is liberating young people, and Bazarov had a name for it. He called it "nihilism." "A nihilist," Bazarov's friend explains, "is a person who doesn't bow down before authorities, doesn't accept even one principle on faith." Turgenev wasn't the first person to use the term "nihilism," but it was his portrait that stuck.

Turgenev's depiction of Bazarov helped define the new generation of Russian radicals. Bazarov is coarse and arrogant, and he takes materialism to its logical extreme. The only things a person can know are perceived through one's own senses—learning from others is bowing down—so Bazarov starts from scratch. He undertakes his own physiological investigations, repeating old experiments so he can witness the results firsthand. Soon, however, Bazarov falls in love. He becomes ruled by his lofty passions, and he stumbles uselessly through an awkward, unrequited love. Bazarov is rebuffed and soon dies from an infection after accidentally cutting himself while dissecting a corpse.

Dostoevsky loved Turgenev's novel. He saw what few other people did: that Bazarov is tragic, a good-hearted person who has lost his way. Beneath the calculating rationalist, he is, as Turgenev described him, someone "grim, wild, huge, half grown out of the ground, powerful, sardonic, honest"—and doomed. The radicals reacted differently. *The Contemporary* ran a scathing review that lambasted Turgenev's novel as a nobleman's hateful caricature of an entire generation. Chernyshevsky agreed, claiming that Turgenev offered his readers demons: "gaunt, green, with roving eyes, with lips contorted by malign sneers of hatred, with unwashed hands," villains who reject and destroy everything.

The person who should have hated *Fathers and Children* the most was Dmitri Pisarev, the chief critic of Russia's most radical journal, *The Russian Word*. Pisarev was twenty-one years old and a Chernyshevsky acolyte. Turgenev's portrait of a young physiologist as a Büchner-loving dilettante carrying a sack squirming with frogs for dissection might have insulted Pisarev, who had written extensively about physiology and Büchner in the previous months, and yet Pisarev loved Turgenev's novel. He especially loved Bazarov, and he was willing to adopt the term "nihilist" with pride. When Pisarev reviewed *Fathers and Children*, he declared Bazarov an unintentionally accurate portrait. "Turgenev himself does not fully understand his hero," Pisarev claimed. So

Pisarev took the opportunity to explain the hero himself, supplying unwritten facts, including Bazarov's hidden motives, his upbringing, and relationship details. Fruitlessly pursuing a love interest is not Bazarov's mistake. Rather, Pisarev declared, "this capacity consciously to behave stupidly is an enviable virtue of strong and intelligent people."

The fact that an artist like Turgenev could not understand his own character was, for Pisarev, evidence of just how extraordinary a nihilist is. The novel's timeless tragedy is that a great man must live and die alone. Every epoch has a handful of elite people—world-historical people—who are dissatisfied with civilization while the masses remain content and refuse to "make discoveries or commit crimes." The elites rise above all social constraints. "Nothing but personal taste prevents them from killing or stealing," Pisarev declared. "If Bazarovism is a disease, then it is a disease of our time, and must be endured to the end," he informed his readers. "You will not be able to stop it."

Pisarev was the rising voice of the radicals. *The Russian Word* was relatively obscure before he began turning it into a journal that would rival *The Contemporary* by taking materialism further than Chernyshevsky would go. Pisarev was perhaps Russia's most prominent advocate for the social promise of physiology and evolution. He declared evolutionary biologists like Darwin "the philosophers, the poets, the aestheticians of our time." He was captivated by Sechenov's experiments: "In this very frog lies the salvation and renewal of the Russian people." Pisarev delighted in describing people as machines running on elaborate chemical reactions, and he could see the influence of physiology everywhere. Charles V, the Holy Roman emperor, ruled erratically because he had a deformed jaw. The Protestant Reformation happened because the tea in northern countries enhances critical thinking (Catholics, unfortunately, drink coffee). The radicals' dispute over *Fathers and Children*—the question of whether Bazarov is an insult or an archetype—was the beginning of what Dostoevsky would call the "schism among the nihilists."

And as with the Raskolniks, that schism was the result of a zealous devotion to an older dogma. "I know only what I see," Pisarev wrote, or "what the evidence of my senses can convince me of." Any abstraction or belief did not exist for him, which was functionally the same as not existing at all. Once he began targeting abstractions, they seemed to be everywhere. Reason is an abstraction, just like God. Generalizations are abstractions. While *facts* and *proof* were essential to materialism, any theory built upon those facts was abstract, unreal. Being a nihilist meant training your attention on small facts so that you will not lose yourself in bewildering fantasies. It meant trapping real rabbits in imaginary forests.

Pisarev was not philosophical by nature. Classmates remembered him kicking and beating a classroom wall during an 1858 university protest against disciplinary measures. When friends reported his increasingly erratic behavior (quarrelsomeness, depression, delusions), he was committed to a psychiatric hospital. After a few months, he escaped from the institution and fell in love with his first cousin. When she got engaged, Pisarev burst into her fiancé's apartment and struck him with a whip. He later attacked him on a train platform while wearing a false beard and peasant clothing, and the two men brawled until police arrested them. It was around that time that he began studying Chernyshevsky and other materialists. "I began to construct for myself an entire theory of egoism, admired it and considered it indestructible," he wrote to his mother. "Love your personality," he urged her. "This is the purest and highest source of joy." It would never let you down.

The further Pisarev went into egoism, the more popular his writing became, and the government took note. Young people "not only read his works but *study* them," one official wrote. His power was his ability to turn the self-affirmations of materialism into a form of vengeance. Abstractions weren't just unreal. They were pernicious. "Poison," "slavery," a "nightmare," a "cage," a "phantom," a haunting "specter"—no single description could cover their depredations against the individual personality. A commitment to scientific truth had become a crusade for the self.

"Here is the ultimatum of our camp," Pisarev announced in 1861: "That which can be smashed should be smashed: that which withstands the blow is fit, that which can be dashed to smithereens is trash. In any case, strike to the right and the left, no harm will come of it." Russia found its own Max Stirner.

N ow Pisarev has gone further," Dostoevsky wrote in his notebook in 1862. Something important in Russia was being filtered through Pisarev, something diffuse and acrid, something that would compel people to abandon the era of reform and smash everything breakable. Much of the intelligentsia had hoped serf emancipation would trigger a peasant uprising that would usher in democracy or socialism or both. "Only the peasants' axes can save us," as one radical put it. By 1862, it had become clear that none of that was going to happen. Emancipation now seemed like a ploy to avert a revolution by appeasing the peasants with crumbs. Reform-era optimism turned into frustration. Frustration soured into resentment.

This was fertile ground for the idea that Chaadaev planted years earlier: that Russian culture did not exist. Long-standing insecurity resurfaced. Was Russia meant only to be a military power and anemic in all other aspects of life? "In that case," Chernyshevsky wrote, "it would be better not to be born at all than to be born a Russian." The empire had spent decades trying to fit itself into the myth of having saved Europe twice, first from the Mongols and then from Napoleon. Maintaining its gargantuan army required a constant cycle of foreign debt, fiscal austerity, inflation, and the overtaxation of its peasants. It came at the expense of infrastructure, education, public health, and industrial development. Decades of losses ensued. Per capita income in Russia (adjusted for inflation) was *one-third* of what it had been in 1810. Every year, Petersburg filled with more tenements, more drunks, and more foundlings. Peter the Great's abstract and premeditated city had the highest mortality rate of any city in Europe. The empire sacrificed so much for military dominance, and now, in the aftermath of the Crimean War, it was clear that it was all for nothing.

The feeling distilled in Pisarev was the feeling of generational bitterness, the feeling of having been dispossessed by decades of failures after the Napoleonic Wars. Everyone had failed—the peasants, the bureaucracy, the military, all the writers and artists. Bitterness that intense is isolating. It is natural, when everyone has failed, to turn inward, to rely upon a tiny elite, at most, or upon yourself, at least, and to smash everything else.

And so nihilism spread in the 1860s as a quest for world-historical greatness not through military domination but through a mixture of science and extravagant individualism. There were no nihilist organizations, but in certain Russian cities, particularly around universities, one could spot a nihilist. They had a style. The most conspicuous element was blue-tinted spectacles, which normally signified studiousness (blue light was supposed to be healthier for reading), but when they were worn on the street, it was as if the bespectacled passerby, a woman as likely as a man, were filtering out large swaths of the world, keeping it aloof in order to examine it properly.

Nihilist men often wore long hair, though this was not new. What was new was that it was unkempt, unwashed. They sometimes had dirty fingernails. They carried gnarled walking sticks and wore shirts without collars or cuffs. They wore baggy pants tucked into unpolished boots. Nihilist women were more alarming. Just when crinoline hoop skirts were at their largest— massive cages of whalebone and wire—nihilist women cast them off for simpler, freer skirts. They treated their bodies not as opportunities for decorative display but as functional organisms requiring freedom of movement. You could spot a radical woman by the way she rejected ribbons and ruffles for plain clothing and muted colors. Or by the way she wore her hair short. Or if she smoked cigarettes. The nihilist style was a pattern of little infrapolitical cuts and sartorial gestures toward revolution: Scottish plaids, Garibaldi ties, wide-brimmed Fra Diavolo hats, or, more daringly, a four-cornered hat that alluded to a Polish insurrection against the Russian Empire. But the rebellions would not remain infrapolitical.

One morning in May 1862, Dostoevsky found a crudely lithographed leaflet wedged in his door handle. **YOUNG RUSSIA** was emblazoned at the top. It announced that Russia was on the brink of "a bloody and pitiless revolution, a revolution which must change everything down to the very roots, utterly overthrowing all the foundations of present society." It was a manifesto signed by something called the Central Revolutionary Committee, and it attacked religion, family structures, and the social order. Russia's ruling class, the leaflet proclaimed, was separated from the people. "Under this regime a small number of people who own capital control the fate of the rest." The coming revolution would establish a socialist republic with national and regional assemblies, universal suffrage, universal rights, and progressive taxation. The program would be enacted by a dictatorship of revolutionary elites.

The "Young Russia" manifesto was recklessly violent. "We will move against the Winter Palace to wipe out all who dwell there," the manifesto declared.

We will cry "To your axes," and then we will strike the imperial
party without sparing our blows just as they do not spare theirs against
us. We will destroy them in the squares, if the cowardly swine dare to
go there. We will destroy them in their houses, in the narrow streets
of the towns, in the broad avenues of the capital, and in the villages.

Dostoevsky was aghast. A villain had written it, he said, "to cause maximum offense." It was difficult for him to believe that Russians could produce
something so absurdly violent. "Rivers of blood will flow," the manifesto read,
and "perhaps even innocent victims will perish." What frightened Dostoevsky
most was that the impulse motivating such violence was "something utterly
trivial," smaller than trivial, actually, an appalling "nullity."

Then the fires started. They began a day or two after "Young Russia"
appeared. An uninhabited building burned down first, which concerned no
one. A house burned the next day. Then another, and another. Then a much
larger fire erupted, fed by strong winds, and consumed about a dozen buildings every hour before it could be contained. Fear set in when five large fires
broke out in different neighborhoods across the city—afflicting the wealthy
and the poor alike. Five days later, on May 28, an inferno tore through a
massive market in the center of the city. It was a half-mile-square labyrinth
of alleyways lined with thousands of wooden stalls and storehouses filled with
old furniture, secondhand clothing, pottery—all the paraphernalia of everyday life. It was the center of Petersburg's book trade. No one knew how the
fire started, but it spread rapidly. One survivor remembered the terrifying
flames rising up moments after the initial smoke. "Like an immense snake,
rattling and whistling, the fire threw itself in all directions, right and left,
enveloped the shanties, and suddenly rose in a huge column, darting out its
whistling tongues to lick up more shanties with their contents."

Whirlwinds of heat and smoke whipped debris through the air. The timber yards across the canal caught fire. Vendors began piling their goods in the
adjacent streets, braving periodic explosions and waves of heat to salvage what
they could, but the falling embers turned what could've been escape routes
into tracks of merchandise bonfires.

No one was prepared. Petersburg's only steam fire engine was at the ironworks forty kilometers outside the city—they had to haul it in by rail—and the fire raged through the night. By the time the blaze was contained, little remained beyond "heaps of metal and skeletons of houses," according to one official. Thousands of families were homeless. Petersburg suffered more than a dozen serious fires in less than two weeks, and there were more to come.

Authorities railed against the "savage audacity" of the arsonists. The press spoke broadly of the "terror" sweeping the city, and the lack of reliable information amplified fears. Criminals were to blame. Or Poles. One rumor circulated that a rogue general covered his uniform with a substance so flammable that all he had to do was rub his back against a building to make it burst into flames. Others believed arsonists were slathering walls with a fluid that could ignite under sunlight. One Petersburger recalled seeing a small crowd of people scrutinizing the neighborhood's fences and scraping away suspicious stains. People in poorer neighborhoods—those most vulnerable to fires—had suitcases packed and belongings piled into baskets so they could flee at a moment's notice. Volunteer watchmen patrolled neighborhoods at night. People on the streets who looked as if they could be arsonists were searched for suspicious concoctions, sometimes beaten, sometimes dragged to the nearest police station.

Radicals were the obvious culprits. The "Young Russia" manifesto promised exactly this kind of wholesale destruction, and the market blaze was adjacent to the State Bank and the Ministry of the Interior, which held the serf emancipation records—clerks had rushed out of the building with armloads of documents. The market fire was still burning when someone approached Turgenev on Nevsky Prospect. "Look at what your nihilists are doing! They are setting Petersburg on fire!" The police arrested scores of people. Some officials proposed using torture to get straight answers.

Whatever modest support the liberals and student activists enjoyed crumbled as people began craving stability. It was Katkov, more than any other journalist, who took advantage of this craving. He used his publications—*The Russian Herald* and *The Moscow News*—to blame the fires on radical Russian expatriates, to promote economic nationalism ("Russia for the Russians"), and to reject "foreign" ideas like free trade and universal male suffrage ("The people is not a herd of heads"). He defended the reigning order. "Destroy the natural aristocratic element in society," he warned in 1862, "and its place will be taken either by bureaucrats or demagogues."

Katkov denounced nihilism as a "social disease" and a "religion of negation." He described physiological dissections as rituals celebrated by writers who have "never been inside an anatomical theater" and "cannot distinguish hydrogen from nitrogen." His conservatism was making him one of the empire's most influential men. Tolstoy referred to him as a "terrifying, omnipotent force in Russia." The government supported his journalism financially, and in the aftermath of the fires the tsar invited him to a ball at the Great Kremlin Palace to thank him publicly for his service. Katkov felt secure enough to criticize lax government policies in print. He had powerful allies—including the minister of war and the minister of foreign affairs—who would shield him from punishment, an exceptional status for a Russian man of letters.

Dostoevsky's reaction was quite different. He paced the room as *Vremya*'s editorial staff weighed the possibility that revolution was afoot. The discussion was heated, but everyone fell silent when Dostoevsky began to speak, almost in a whisper. It was impossible, he said, that the Russian people would take part in a revolution concocted by a handful of radicals ripping ideas from the pages of western books. He was trying to convince himself.

Dostoevsky rushed to see Chernyshevsky as the Petersburg fires raged. They were little more than acquaintances, but Chernyshevsky admired Dostoevsky, and when his servant announced Dostoevsky's unexpected arrival, he cordially greeted the esteemed writer in the hall, took him into his study, and sat beside him on his sofa. Dostoevsky was holding a copy of "Young Russia."

"Nikolai Gavrilovich, what on earth is this?" he asked. "Is it possible that they are so stupid and ridiculous? Is it possible that they can't be stopped and that an end can't be put to this abomination?"

"Do you suppose that I support them?" Chernyshevsky asked, ready to take umbrage. "Do you think that I could've had a hand in putting together this wretched leaflet?"

No, he didn't think so. Dostoevsky shifted tack. "You are well acquainted with the people who burnt the Old Clothes Market and have an influence on them. I beg you, stop them from any continuation of what they have done."

Chernyshevsky kept distancing himself, but Dostoevsky persisted. "They must be stopped somehow," he said. "Your word means something to them, and of course they're afraid of what you might say."

"I don't know any of them." Chernyshevsky had heard that illness had upset Dostoevsky's nerves, and he did what he could to calm his guest down, but Dostoevsky persisted.

"You certainly don't need to know them or speak to them personally. You need only express a word of censure publicly, and they'll hear about it."

"That may not have any effect. And, indeed, things like this, as extraneous facts, are inevitable." Calming people was not among Chernyshevsky's gifts.

The Third Section arrested Chernyshevsky for political agitation several weeks later. Pisarev was arrested the same week for advocating the overthrow of the Romanov dynasty in his own anonymous leaflet (the typesetter denounced him). "What is dead and rotten must of itself fall into the grave," Pisarev wrote. "It remains for us only to give a last push and throw the dirt over their stinking corpses." Arrests seemed constant. *The Contemporary* and *The Russian Word* were both suspended for eight months.

It is to Russia's credit that it produced so many writers dogged enough to withstand its government. Chernyshevsky was eventually sentenced to seven years of hard labor and indefinite exile in Siberia. Soon after his arrest, he began writing a novel called *What Is to Be Done?* As a work of fiction, it is nearly unreadable, but as a how-to manual for radicalism and rational egoism it was powerful. Chernyshevsky's readers would learn how to maximize utility, how to set up a workers' collective, how to manage communes and polyamorous marriages, how to create gender and sexual equality, and how to remake civilization. The novel culminates in a vision of a massive glass and steel building inspired by London's Crystal Palace. It has floor-to-ceiling windows and mirrors, aluminum furniture, and electric light. Russians dance in loose Athenian clothing, feast at large tables (with aluminum plates), and disappear together in adjacent rooms for amorous delights. It was Fourierism with updates. The old world—the world of surveillance and starvation—was simply forgotten: "There are no such memories here, no danger of grief or need, only the recollection of free and willing labor, of abundance, goodness, and enjoyment."

Pisarev also found his voice in prison. He was sentenced to be locked up indefinitely in the Peter and Paul Fortress. He spent years in almost complete isolation, seeing little more than his mother and his interrogators—an arrangement he enjoyed inordinately well. When he was brought before the

Senate for questioning, senators claimed he looked "as though he had some-how just arrived from a ball." When Pisarev was granted permission to pub-lish again from his cell in April 1863, he wrote more than ever and developed his distinctive style. He became more incisive and more creative. These years were quite possibly the happiest of his life.

I t wasn't long before the Dostoevsky brothers were in Katkov's crosshairs. They wrote an article in *Vremya* pointing out that while everyone blamed the authors of "Young Russia" for the Petersburg fires, no one had any evi-dence for it. The Dostoevskys derided the rampant fear and the wave of de-nouncements, which is exactly the position a radical journal would take. To make matters worse, they seemed to know who the authors of "Young Russia" were (they referred in passing to "three scrofulous schoolboys"). The censors banned the article before publication, and they banned the more tactful revi-sion as well—the tsar himself reviewed the proof sheets. Mikhail was called in for questioning (who exactly *were* these schoolboys?), and *Vremya* was nearly suspended for eight months.

The vise tightened after Poland's January Uprising in 1863. Years of Polish demonstrations, sometimes violent, became more serious when thousands of men who had been hiding in the forests to avoid Russian army conscription began fighting a guerrilla war against the empire. Katkov depicted the upris-ing as a direct attack upon Russia by a sworn enemy. "The question between Russia and Poland is a state question: whether or not a Polish or a Russian state is to exist." At stake, Katkov warned his readers, was "the very existence of the Russian state." His fears were genuine. Katkov warned a government official, "Revolutionary agents are being sent throughout Russia."

When Katkov came across the April 1863 issue of *Vremya*, he was incensed. The Dostoevskys published an article describing the Polish insurrection as "a civilized people" rebelling against "barbarians." The author might have been ventriloquizing the insurrectionists' perspective, but the superiority of Polish civilization was not a point about which a Russian writer should be unclear—Polish nationalists touted their European identity while denigrating Russian rule as "Asiatic." Katkov's *Moscow News* ran a blistering attack that accused both the article's author and *Vremya* of disloyalty and "a perfidious design."

Two days later, the tsar himself banned *Vremya* permanently for its "harmful tendency." Dostoevsky insisted that his journal was the victim of clumsy prose and a hostile interpretation, but the decision was final. *Vremya* had accumulated more than four thousand subscribers—nearly double the size of its inaugural list two years earlier and rivaling the long-established literary journals—and now, in a single day, with a single decree, it was over. Katkov was happy to see it go. The journal supplied "fog and emptiness," he wrote, when what Russia needed was "living reality."

For the Dostoevsky brothers, however, living reality was always closing in. The ban on *Vremya* was hard on Mikhail. He had sold his share of a cigarette factory at unfavorable terms and had taken on substantial debt to fund the journal, and now they had nothing. "His family will practically have to go begging," Dostoevsky wrote to Turgenev. And Dostoevsky's wife, Marya Dmitrievna, was increasingly ill. She was febrile and coughing up mucus and blood. Dostoevsky was also ill. The falling sickness "keeps intensifying and drives me even to despair," he told Turgenev. "If you only knew how depressed I am sometimes for entire weeks following attacks!" He couldn't pick up a pen for a full month. Which was just as well, for the latest living reality was that his journal, his literary independence, had become a casualty in the government's war against radicals whom he himself opposed.

Fourteen

A Gambling System

Winning at roulette is easy. The secret is to maintain complete control over your emotions at all times, to be a machine. You must have no feeling for all the francs and guilders and napoleons raked in and shoveled out across the table. You must remain indifferent to the deliciously clinking gold and silver and the rising or falling stacks in front of you so that when you see the wheel spinning and hear the ivory ball coursing around the track as the wagers accumulate, following it as it noses down into the wheel's bowl, *tick-tack-tack*ing across the numbers—red-red-black-red—you can remain calm, and whether it hunkers into thirty-one or skips belatedly to twenty-seven, you will not be disturbed. You will keep your head.

For days, Dostoevsky watched hundreds of gamblers muscling their way through the crowd to place bets. *Rouge, impair, manque.* Some of them recorded the results in notepads and scanned for patterns. A streak of reds, two elevens, a full hour without a single zero. This was helpful. But most gamblers are impetuous—they come and go like pebbles on the shore. To win, you have to play for days, endure hundreds of spins, thousands. You have to ride out the bad turns patiently so that you can take advantage when momentum shifts. Resolve like that requires an iron constitution. It requires determination and faith. Dostoevsky learned the secret to roulette by studying a stoic Frenchwoman and an English lord who nearly broke the bank. If you could keep their level of imperturbable control, Dostoevsky explained in a letter, then "it's impossible to lose, and you're certain to win." He called it his "system."

One difficulty of adhering to the system is that everything about a casino heightens people's emotions. The clinking coins—all stakes must be in coins—the frenetic action, the jolting outcomes, the weight of people's bodies pressing forward, women in Garibaldi blouses and necklaces with diamond crosses, men in white linen suits, uniforms from every army in Europe. The croupiers call out "Faites le jeu!" as the ball spins and coquettes laugh with duchesses. The croupier closes betting—"Le jeu est fait!"—as the ball audibly decelerates, and the sound around the table settles down to whispers, a ruffle of crinoline, a saber tip touching a boot. When the ball finds its place, you hear cheers, gasps, moans, and curses—the full spectrum of emotions in one relieving burst. But what if you could ignore everything around you?

Dostoevsky's response to Russia's turmoil, to *Vremya*'s banning and its lingering debts, to his brother's hardships, to his wife's health, and to their troubled marriage was to flee to a casino in Wiesbaden, Germany. It was clear by now that his marriage with Marya Dmitrievna had been born of necessity and marred by their futilely concealed illnesses. It had also become clear that her coughing and fevers were symptoms of tuberculosis. She had been fighting the disease since before their wedding in Siberia. Each of them found medical reasons to part ways for the summer of 1863. She went to Vladimir, a town east of Moscow, for treatment and for its healthful climate, and he requested a passport to Europe to seek treatment for his epilepsy. He gave Marya Dmitrievna the proceeds from the first book edition of *Notes from a Dead House*, took a loan of fifteen hundred rubles from a Russian writers' association called the Literary Fund, and on his way to Paris, he detoured to Wiesbaden.

He had been to this casino once before, the previous year—on his first trip to Europe—and he had won thousands of francs (Rhine casinos paid in francs). This is how he knew that once he walked through the colonnade, past the restaurant and the velvet divans in the corridor's alcoves, and stepped into the great gaming hall, it would feel like drifting into a fantasy world. Damask and gleaming mirrors, glass chandeliers, a high, gilded ceiling. And so many people to watch. Velveteen coats, gold-embroidered tunics, scarlet cuffs and collars. Top hats, hats with feathers, hats with entire birds. All the continent's languages jostled together. A factory owner would elbow his way toward a table after strolling around the garden's miniature lake, where his children could feed the swans. A shopkeeper would wait for his moment, stake everything on one spin, and leave to see the dancers or the comedians or the magicians. Soldiers make way for clerks. Priests place bets alongside unchaperoned young women. The flow of money washes away decorum and flattens all hierarchies into a soft green field. All rules beyond the rules of the game become meaningless. The hall's closed shutters suspend time. Memories fall away and all hopes concentrate on a tiny ball. Everything spins around the wheel.

At some point, Dostoevsky started winning. He had amassed 10,400 francs in just one hour. There comes a point when the stacks of money loom large enough that you begin searching for other ways to measure their value so that you can fully appreciate the dimensions of your triumph and keep it in mind for future reference. Ten thousand francs can warp time. Dostoevsky won in just a few moments what a high-level French civil servant would make in seven and a half years. Or he could have weighed it in words, or in manuscript pages, or in copies of books. Ten thousand and four hundred francs was nearly three and a half thousand rubles—the same amount he had just received for the first edition of *Notes from a Dead House*, his greatest accomplishment since his return from exile. Hundreds of hours of work and years of experience matched an hour of steeled nerves.

That is power. That is what it means for rules to be meaningless. The normal boundaries, the normal order of things dissolves before you. You feel the significance of your winnings in the way the other gamblers begin to watch you—the same way you had once watched others—the way they whisper about you, the way they begin to place their bets wherever you place yours. Dostoevsky described the throbbing excitement of winning, how a winner at roulette becomes fearless and acquires "the air of a conqueror." You bet on red when you shouldn't bet on red, and you win—of course you win—because at some point during a winning streak the game shifts. Victory begets victory. You mock fate, you insult the mathematical odds, and you understand that the rolls of napoleons lying next to the croupier and the Friedrichs d'or wrapped in dark blue paper belong to you. A loss becomes an affront to your charismatic power and to the tribute displayed in all the piles in front of you.

This is why it is so hard, as Dostoevsky knew, to maintain the steadfast composure that guarantees victory. To withstand the excitement of conquering power or the shame of defeat, one must be chillingly, inhumanly cold, and he had not quite perfected that. Ten thousand four hundred francs was not as much as Dostoevsky wanted—"not 100,000," he lamented—so he kept playing, and the ebony rake began dragging his money away. He had the presence of mind to walk away, fortunately, and he managed to leave Wiesbaden in 1863 with 5,000 francs. He sent 1,250 francs back to his ailing wife and his stepson, Pasha. He sent the money through his sister-in-law. "Don't tell anyone about this," he wrote to her.

D ostoevsky knew Europe would be a good place to escape, whether or not he could send his casino winnings home. Back in the summer of 1862, shortly after the Petersburg fires, he had toured London as well as cities in Germany, France, Switzerland, Austria, and Italy, and there were too many impressions to register. He had spent eight days in London overwhelmed by its howling machinery, its drunken masses, its factories and pollution: "Everything is so huge and abrupt in its individuality."

Dostoevsky was terrified when he saw the Crystal Palace. It was a latticework of thousands of tons of glass and iron forming a barrel-vaulted nave and transepts, like some brittle cathedral. It had been built for London's International Exposition, and now it seemed to be a pilgrimage site for millions of people eager to worship a pagan god of industry and materialism. It was more than twice the length of St. Peter's Basilica in Rome, and it appeared, Dostoevsky wrote, like "something out of Babylon, a kind of prophecy from the Apocalypse fulfilled before your very eyes." Just looking at it, Dostoevsky wrote, would make a person feel "that something final has been accomplished, accomplished and brought to an end."

Visitors strolled through history as they saw exhibitions devoted to the Egyptians, the Greeks, and the Assyrians. There was a Byzantine Court, a Nineveh Court, a Renaissance Court. The palace showcased cultural triumphs from every era—Greek friezes, Roman busts, and French portraiture—and now, the palace seemed to say, the triumphs of civilization are machines. The ground floor displayed massive arrays of engines and mills, threshers, reapers, and plows. There were centrifugal pumps, brick machines, and tile machines, and they were all for sale.

The highlight of his first European tour was Paris. France was the looking glass by which educated Russians often judged themselves. Nearly every important Russian writer had spent time in France, the country that produced Hugo and Balzac, Racine and Corneille—the literature Dostoevsky had loved since his days at the Academy of Engineers—and yet it was a country, he began to believe, where great literature was evaporating into airy bourgeois eloquence. He observed a civil trial and sensed that eloquence alone won or lost cases. Eloquence was a dimension of Parisians' obsession with fine clothing and shoes. Appearances, for the bourgeoisie, were synonymous with essence. "Everything shines with virtue," Dostoevsky wrote of Paris. It is "the most moral and most virtuous city in the whole world. What order!" The city itself was their glimmering temple to apocalyptic finality.

French complacency, Dostoevsky believed, drew upon nothing deeper than material comfort. The bourgeoisie had no need for ideals. *Liberté?* "What liberty?" Dostoevsky asked. "When may you do anything you want to? When you have millions." The notion of *egalité* before the law was laughable, and *fraternité* had been overtaken by isolation, vanity, and self-interest. The bourgeoisie had no need for ideals because it embodied the ideal. The Frenchman's core belief, Dostoevsky claimed, is "that he is the foremost man on the face of the earth." The bourgeoisie saw itself as "the image of ultimate beauty and the greatest possible human perfection."

But material comfort has a steep price. The more we love what we have, the more we fear losing it. "He who fears most," Dostoevsky wrote, "is the one who prospers most." The bourgeoisie was afraid of losing everything, and that fear was what lay beneath its obsession with appearances. For what is orderliness but a tight grip upon things as they are? Things as they might be, absences or abstractions, reforms or ideals—especially revolutionary ideals—could be nothing but vicious threats. The French patriot once fought for *fraternité*. Now, Dostoevsky observed, the revolutionary aim has shrunk down to the individual. The individual stands in opposition to "all of nature and all other people." The individual claims to be of "equal value to everything that exists outside itself." The bourgeoisie was devolving into egoism, and Stirner's fierce selfishness now had an elegant facade of virtue.

.   .   .

Dostoevsky was eager to return to Europe in 1863. He suspected there was much more to discover, particularly in France, which was where he took his winnings from the Wiesbaden roulette tables. "I like Paris this time because of its exterior, that is, its architecture," he wrote to his younger brother Nikolai. "The Louvre is a superb thing, and all that embankment, right up to Notre Dame, is an amazing thing." Perhaps his warmer impressions derived from his own weakening resistance to appearances, or perhaps they were softened by his gambling wins.

Or perhaps it was the young woman he had come to see in Paris. Apollinaria Prokofievna Suslova. She had submitted a story to *Vremya* about a young woman who flees a loveless marriage and finds a career as a teacher. Though she succumbs to tuberculosis, she dies knowing that she never compromised her independence. It was an archetypal narrative for those advocating women's rights in Russia. *Vremya* published it in the October 1861 issue, and the journal's new contributor—one of only a handful of female contributors—eventually met Dostoevsky and made an equally strong impression in person. He would soon be calling her Polina.

Suslova was the daughter of a serf who had purchased his own freedom from one of Russia's wealthiest families and had gone on to manage some of their holdings. Her sister, Nadezhda, would eventually become Russia's first female medical doctor. The family moved to Petersburg, where the sisters received their secondary education and became nihilists. Apollinaria was among the daring women attending university lectures, and she taught peasants in the Sunday Schools.

Many of the details of their relationship are unclear, but their romantic involvement likely began near the end of 1862, after the lecture halls were closed and the Sunday Schools banned. Suslova had been in Paris since the spring of 1863—they hadn't seen each other for months—and his gambling in Wiesbaden delayed their reunion a few more days. She wrote to him on the eve of his arrival:

> You are coming a little too late . . . Only very recently I
> was dreaming of going to Italy with you, and I even began

to learn Italian: everything has changed within a few days. You told me one day that I would never surrender my heart easily. I have surrendered it within a week's time, at the first call, without a struggle, without assurance, almost without hope that I was being loved. I was right to get angry with you when you began to sing my praises. Don't think that I am blaming you, but I want only to tell you that you did not know me, nor did I know myself.

Goodbye, dear!

She hoped the letter would spare her from seeing him, but he had rushed to Paris with his roulette windfall, so he hadn't received it. She was trembling when he finally saw her face, her slightly upturned nose, and her dark eyes and hair, which she often braided. When she said, "How are you?" he knew something was wrong, and she knew that he knew.

"It is too late," she told him.

"I must know everything, let's go somewhere, and tell me, or I'll die."

He was Spanish, a medical student named Salvador. Whatever happened between them happened quickly. She would read his palm. They talked about poetry. He dreamed about immigrating to America. He would ask if she was thinking of him and badger her about taking her medicines and cleaning her teeth. She would visit him at his hotel, sometimes unannounced. Once she sat in his room and waited for him for a full hour until she could no longer bear it. She left a note. "Don't you know that your absence causes me pain?" At some point she realized she would never go to America with Salvador. She planned to return to the Russian countryside, to become a Raskolnik and join the Runners.

Dostoevsky knew this would happen. She was young—twenty-three years old—and passionate. "You fell in love with me by mistake, because yours is a generous heart"—too generous. She was careless.

A few days later, Suslova received a letter informing her that Salvador had contracted typhus and couldn't see her until he recovered. She wrote to him repeatedly, thinking he might die, telling him it was barbaric to be kept away, begging for a reply. Dostoevsky tried soothing her. The doctors are so good in Paris, he'd say, and the city has the best air. Days later, while walking near the Sorbonne, she spotted Salvador from a distance, alive and healthy. He smiled as he approached her—it was his first time out in days! "Yes, you are very pale," she said. She thought she could see spots on his cheeks. It wasn't until she was alone in her room that she came to terms with what had happened. "I'm going to kill him!" she screamed.

She burned compromising letters and diary entries, and after a sleepless night she told Dostoevsky everything. He assured her that they were both young and foolish. She was tall and slender and beautiful—beautiful "to all tastes," he said—and when she made herself available to Salvador, he simply took advantage. She knew, and he knew that she knew.

"I'm only afraid," he told her, "that you may come up with some foolishness." Something violent. She shouldn't ruin her life for such a loathsome pest. She looked at Dostoevsky. "I would not like to kill him," she said, "but I would like to torture him for a very long time."

They decided to travel to Italy together, posing as siblings. But first they went to Baden-Baden, a resort town on the Rhine with baths, of course, and a casino. He registered himself as an "*Officier*" at their hotel and immediately started gambling. "He plays roulette all the time and is generally very carefree," Suslova wrote in her diary. It was an unlikely description of Dostoevsky at any time, but especially so now. He won six hundred francs in his first fifteen minutes and then began losing, spectacularly and relentlessly, day after day. He couldn't stop. Every outcome, every emotion—exhilaration or fury—propelled him forward. Losing is "like sliding down a snowy hill on a sled," he later wrote, "it all goes faster and faster." Losing is gambling's greatest thrill.

Dostoevsky lost everything he had—three thousand francs. He wrote to Marya Dmitrievna asking her to return some of the money he had given her before his departure. He wrote to his sister-in-law asking her to intercept the portion of his Wiesbaden winnings still on its way to his wife. He begged Mikhail for money as well. He had won so decidedly in Wiesbaden, Dostoevsky told his brother, "how could I fail to believe that if I follow my system strictly, luck is in my hands?" Every loss challenged his faith in his system, and he overcame every doubt by staking more money. Winning was his just reward. He was doing it for them, after all. "I need money, for me, for you, for my wife, for writing a novel. . . . I came here with the idea of saving all of you and of shielding myself from disaster." He imagined that the winners at the table were somehow sacred, favored by God. To lose was to be abject, to be a loathsome pest.

One night, after another round of losses, Suslova and Dostoevsky drank tea in her room. She asked him to sit close to her. "I felt good," she recalled in her diary. She held his hand and admitted that she had been unkind to him in Paris. When he finally got up to leave, he stumbled over one of her shoes. He quickly turned around, looking at her tormentingly slender foot and sat down, as if overcome. "You don't know what just happened to me!" he said. "I was just going to kiss your foot."

"Ah, why that?" she asked, tucking her feet out of sight.

"I just got the urge, and decided that I'd kiss it." But he didn't. She wanted to sit with him some more but found his longing gaze too difficult to bear, so she told him to return to his room so she could sleep.

"Right away," he said, but he lingered. Then he kissed her—"very ardently," Suslova noted in her diary. She was silent about how she responded, but it seems he did not find her receptive. He got up to light a candle and retreated into his adjoining room without closing his door. Moments later he came back, ostensibly to close her window. He suggested that she get undressed.

"I'll get undressed," she said impassively, waiting for him to leave, and he left. But he returned again, under some other pretext, and finally he left for the night. He apologized the next day. He had been drunk and had acted foolishly, he explained, but his foolishness, he insisted, was out of his control. Everything goes faster and faster.

Suslova vaguely sensed their financial predicament. "F. M. has lost some money gambling and is a bit worried about not having enough money for our journey," she wrote in her diary. Was she obliged to help pay? "No," she decided, "this is nonsense." But it wasn't long before they began pawning possessions—his watch, one of her rings.

Mikhail somehow managed to send 1,450 francs, so Dostoevsky and Suslova toured the Colosseum of Rome, walked the narrow streets of Genoa

As a young man, Fyodor Dostoevsky was a celebrated writer, but he became involved with the radical politics of his day. In 1849, over a dozen members of a group known as the Petrashevsky Circle faced a firing squad in the middle of St. Petersburg for discussing and conspiring to spread unlawful ideas. The first three men were tied to the stakes, and Dostoevsky was next in line when Tsar Nicholas I spared the prisoners' lives.

Their death sentences were reduced to terms of exile and hard labor in Siberia. A hard life lay ahead. Siberian convicts sometimes had their faces branded as punishment.

Corporal punishment was pervasive in Russia's hard-labor fortress prisons. Fritz Eichenberg depicted the gauntlet, rows of soldiers wielding canes, for *Notes from a Dead House*, Dostoevsky's account of his prison life in Siberia.

Dostoevsky and convicts from across the empire were crammed into small, filthy barracks. His description of their communal steam baths reminded Ivan Turgenev of Dante's *Inferno*.

After years of hard labor, Dostoevsky was sentenced to serve in the Siberian army. He posed for a photograph in 1859 with a Kazakh friend, Chokan Valikhanov, who holds a knife— Dostoevsky's gift to him.

In Siberia, Dostoevsky married Marya Dmitrievna Isaeva, a widow struggling to raise her son, Pasha. The marriage was troubled from the start.

Dostoevsky returned to Petersburg in December 1859, after a decade in exile. What followed was the most important and productive decade of his career. This lithograph depicts the "resurrected" novelist in 1862.

Dostoevsky's brother Mikhail helped him mount his literary comeback. Together they started two journals, *Vremya* (*Time*) and *Epokha* (*Epoch*), before Mikhail suddenly died in 1864, three months after Dostoevsky's wife died of tuberculosis.

While searching for magazine material, Dostoevsky came across an illustrated account of Pierre-François Lacenaire, convicted of murder in Paris in 1835. Lacenaire claimed he was attacking an unjust society. "I come to preach the religion of fear to the rich," he wrote, "for the religion of love has no power over their hearts."

Lacenaire.
Condamné à Mort par la Cour d'Assises de la Seine

Dostoevsky translated and published Lacenaire's story in *Vremya* in 1861. Cases like his, Dostoevsky told his subscribers, are "more exciting than all possible novels because they light up the dark sides of the human soul that art does not like to approach." He was particularly disturbed by the boundless vanity masquerading as an ideology.

In 1865, Dostoevsky was destitute from roulette losses, hungry, feverish, and trapped in his German hotel—unable to pay his bill. He began filling notebooks with ideas and scenes for a new story: two brutal ax murders told from the murderer's perspective, crimes that he insisted would benefit society.

———

Throughout his notes, Dostoevsky made detailed sketches, including repeated renderings of his murder story's characters, as if he could summon them by drawing them.

———

While rushing to meet *Crime and Punishment*'s deadlines and struggling to fulfill an exploitative contract, Dostoevsky hired a stenographer to increase his pace. In October 1866, a young woman named Anna Grigorievna Snitkina began working with a novelist she had admired for years.

In April 1866, as *Crime and Punishment* was being serialized, Dmitri Karakozov tried to assassinate Tsar Alexander II, but his pistol shot went wide. The manifesto in his pocket declared, "It's the tsars who are the real culprits in all our misfortunes."

Anna Grigorievna became Dostoevsky's first reader and his first critic. The two fell in love while working on the final chapters of *Crime and Punishment*. They married weeks after the novel's completion.

("roofs overgrown with grass"), and watched children in Naples doing somersaults for coins. Her demeanor toward him alternated between indifference and affection, irritation and sympathy. Sometimes she would hold his hand or look at him "caressingly." Sometimes she would rebuff him or maintain her distance. She kept certain things unspoken. He would bring up the possibility of rekindling their love, and she would say nothing. She would upbraid him, feel remorse, and offer him hope-kindling tenderness. During one affectionate moment, she recalled, "he responded with such joy that I was moved by it, and I became twice as tender."

Dostoevsky tried being defiantly cheerful, but it felt as if she were torturing him. "I am unhappy," he told her in Rome. "I look at everything as though it were my duty, as though I were learning a lesson."

What was the lesson he was supposed to learn? Once, during dinner, he watched a girl at an adjacent table completing school lessons. "Well, imagine," Dostoevsky told Suslova out of the blue, "there you have a little girl like her with an old man, and suddenly some Napoleon says, 'I want this city destroyed.' It has always been that way in this world." He knew Suslova harbored an unconquerable desire to murder Salvador. Was it Napoleonic? "I'll poison him with a slow-working poison," she confided to her diary. "I'll take away his happiness. I'll humiliate him." Dostoevsky thought of Suslova as a "sick egoist." She had a "utilitarian attitude," he told her, and it would be her ruin.

She felt the same way about him. He understood his obligations, but he "would not miss his pleasures either," she wrote in her diary. He pursued them in his high-minded way, behaving "like a serious, busy man." He was the sort of man who would extrapolate out from a girl sitting right in front of him. "I was never ashamed of my love for you," she wrote to him in a letter she apparently never sent, "it was beautiful, even grandiose." But *he* was ashamed. He would never be frank with his wife, never admit that he loved someone else, never defy matrimonial conventions. He let their love become dirty.

Pondering Suslova's egoism distracted Dostoevsky from his own. He had escaped to Europe while his brother struggled with *Vremya*'s debts and his wife became increasingly ill. He hadn't heard from her at all. Was she too weak to write? "Let me know immediately if you hear anything about Mama," he wrote to Pasha, then in Petersburg. He craved Suslova's judgment, and he deserved to be tortured.

Summer turned to fall. Dostoevsky had spent everything Mikhail sent, and now he had nothing left for his trip home. He started jotting down an idea for a story on scraps of paper. It was about a gambler, spontaneous and passionate, someone "much developed but unfinished in everything." He turns to gambling because he has no opportunities in Russia. Dostoevsky sketched the gambler's character for a friend in Petersburg who had helped edit *Vremya*: "All his life juices, energies, violence, boldness have gone *into roulette*." He begged his friend to find a publisher for a "GRAPHIC and very detailed portrait of the game of roulette." He asked him to approach various journals, "not *The Russian Herald*, of course"—considering Katkov's animosity—and not *Notes from the Fatherland*. He'd likely have problems with *The Contemporary*, too, but he needed to hurry. "The whole deal needs to be concluded in two or at most three days." Otherwise, he warned, "I'm done for, literally done for."

Somehow Dostoevsky's friend managed to find a publisher willing to advance Dostoevsky three hundred rubles. Shortly after receiving the money, Suslova went to Paris, and Dostoevsky went gambling—this time in Homburg. Days later, Suslova received an urgent letter. He had lost everything at roulette and needed three hundred francs to get home, so she borrowed money and pawned her watch and chain to get it for him.

D ostoevsky returned to Marya Dmitrievna in early November 1863, after more than three months abroad. He was taken aback by how awful she looked—skin and bones, yellowish pallor, weary. She had endured a more or less continuous fever for two months, and she coughed so much she could barely speak. "Her former doctor doctored her to death," he wrote to his sister-in-law, "now there's a new one." Dostoevsky had two seizures in his first few days back. The couple moved from Vladimir to Moscow for better treatment, but her health declined as fall turned to winter. A persistent fog hung over the city. He tried consoling her with trinkets—little handbags, for example, piggy banks—and she pretended to be pleased with them. Distraction seemed to be the best palliative for her exhaustion, irritability, and distrust. She was suspicious by nature—she long believed, according to Dostoevsky, that Mikhail was her "secret enemy"—and illness enhanced her instinct to draw inward. By January, grief and despair had settled in.

Dostoevsky tried to be optimistic for Pasha's sake. "Who knows, perhaps she'll survive the spring," he wrote to his stepson, "and if she survives the spring, then she'll survive the summer, too, and perhaps even get better." He brought Pasha from Petersburg to help console Marya Dmitrievna, but the boy's presence agitated her. Dostoevsky shared her impatience and regularly upbraided him once Pasha was back home. "You don't pay the slightest attention to what she says." Pasha had been expelled from his school for a prank, and now he was cycling through a series of tutors. "At the age of seventeen you still don't know multiplication and even brag that you have dull capacities." He was selfish, slothful, and vain. He wrote just one letter in two months. "Either you are ill, so that you can't write a couple of words, or you are hopelessly stupid." He seemed insufficiently affected by his mother's deteriorating health. It was time for him to begin weighing "other thoughts, more magnanimous and noble." Pasha eventually wrote to say that he was learning about polygons and to ask for a twenty-eight-ruble coat. Dostoevsky responded that they could afford only twelve to fifteen rubles.

Throughout all of this, Dostoevsky and his brother were trying to start a new journal, and he encouraged Mikhail to borrow nine thousand rubles from their aunt ("letting a really brilliant enterprise go under is nearly a crime"). The idea was to extend the work that *Vremya* had begun. Dostoevsky wanted to call it *Pravda* (*Truth*), which he thought captured the faith and naïveté that their readers valued. The brothers were indeed naïve enough not to anticipate the authorities' swift rejection of such a presumptuous title, so Mikhail named their new journal *Epokha—Epoch*.

They tried learning from past mistakes. They found a government official to serve as a nominal editor in chief in order to help shield them from powerful rivals like Katkov. They embarked upon the now-familiar work of creating and printing advertisements ("We need to repeat them, to wear people out with advertisements") and finding contributions, including a story from Turgenev, "Phantoms," and another from Suslova, "One's Own Way." It is "no worse than her earlier ones," Dostoevsky told Mikhail.

Dostoevsky began working on a novella to help boost the new journal's subscriptions, but he was struggling. "The whole story is junk," he wrote to Mikhail in February. His seizures continued, and the onset of another illness made matters worse. He wasn't quite sure what was wrong with him. "Hemorrhoids have attacked my bladder," he told Mikhail. A doctor later informed him that his prostate was inflamed and that he might have an abscess. His treatment involved enemas and leeches. The strict diet the doctor prescribed was useless; he had no appetite, he was always tired, and he suffered painful spasms. Sitting was so excruciating that he tried writing in bed. "I can scarcely hold a pen in hand. Constant pain." He wanted Mikhail to know how much he was trying. The inaugural issue of *Epoch* was delayed for months, partly because Mikhail was himself overwhelmed and grieving. One of his daughters died of scarlet fever in February. Her death brought Marya Dmitrievna to tears and rattled Dostoevsky. "Look after your health," he implored Mikhail, "and don't go out if you don't feel entirely well."

By March 1864, any optimism he had harbored for Marya Dmitrievna's health was gone. She talked once about spending the summer in the countryside, but that was just a quick break in the clouds. The doctor "doesn't vouch for even a single day," he told his brother. Pasha would need a black frock coat, pants, and vest at a ready-made clothing store (*"the cheapest price"*) so he could be ready to take the train to Moscow at a moment's notice. Dostoevsky would mention Pasha to his wife occasionally, and she would take it as a veiled reference to her impending demise. She would summon her son for a blessing, she declared, when she sensed her moment was imminent, but under no circumstances did she wish to see him before then. He wrote to Mikhail in despair, "The fact that I'm not with you in person troubles me awfully. Every day I have some thought or other—and I'd like to talk about it and tell you." He was not prepared for how lonely this would feel.

He began writing intensely. In one week, the story he was working on had become nearly twice as long as he had planned. "I am writing with ardor," he told Mikhail. "I don't know how it will turn out—it may be trash, but I personally have great hopes for it." He hadn't written anything like it before. The first part had no plot, just pages and pages of "chatter," a searching,

buzzing voice, someone's mind at work like an insect meandering with uncertain purposes, possibly benevolent, possibly harmful. The action ("unexpected catastrophe," Dostoevsky hinted) would not begin until the second
part. How long can a story progress without a plot? What if a mind at work
carried all of a narrative's dramatic load? He worried that people would laugh
at it, but he kept going. He called it *Notes from Underground.*

During an intense week of writing in April, in the middle of the night,
Marya Dmitrievna Dostoevskaya asked for a priest. Her priest, her doctor, and
her husband sat by her side through the night. She received the Eucharist
before dawn, asked for forgiveness for those she might have wronged, including Mikhail, and made her peace. "Don't abandon Pasha," she told Dostoevsky. He promised he wouldn't. After mid-morning she had a pulmonary
hemorrhage. He did not spare Mikhail the brutal details when he described
the end. "Blood gushed from her throat and started to flood her chest and
suffocate her."

Dostoevsky kept a vigil for his departed wife. He had no illusions about
their relationship. "She and I were absolutely miserable together," he confessed
to Vrangel, his old friend from Siberia. "The more miserable we were, the
more we became attached to each other." But sitting in silence beside the
washed corpse inspired bigger questions. "Will I ever see [Marya] again?" he
wrote in his notebook. Dostoevsky tried reasoning his way toward solace. It
was clear that humans are "not finished but transitional"—climbing up from
animalistic egoism toward divine selflessness. It is "completely senseless," he
wrote, for humans to cease to exist once they attain a state of completion.
"Consequently, there is a future paradisiacal life."

Dostoevsky was trying to prove immortality through logic, even though
the story he was writing, *Notes from Underground*, was a sustained rejection
of rationalism, a fictional stone hurled at nihilists like Pisarev and Chernyshevsky. The story's main character is a way of thinking, a conviction regarding science and natural law that swerves toward thoughts of bloodshed and
mad spontaneity and the charm of two times two equaling five. It is a man
having a prolonged conversation with himself or with a tricky ghost popping
up in strange places, rearranging the furniture. Or maybe, he realizes, he's
just chattering, pouring nothing into nothingness.

In July 1864, less than three months after his wife's death, Dostoevsky wrote a brief note to Pasha. "My brother is dying. Don't tell anyone about this." He had gone to visit Mikhail and his family at their summerhouse outside Petersburg. Mikhail's appearance was horrifying. He had been intermittently ill with a liver ailment for the past two years, but it never seemed serious. He could edit. He could walk around. In late May, however, he had abdominal pains and began vomiting. He felt weak, but he continued to work on *Epoch*. Dostoevsky's alarm spurred Mikhail to see a doctor, and he was diagnosed with an abscessed liver. Days later, Mikhail collapsed as bile began hemorrhaging into his bloodstream. The doctor told Dostoevsky there was no hope. Mikhail fell into a calm, heavy sleep. He died four days later without ever waking.

"That man loved me more than anything else on earth," Dostoevsky said. His past life and everything he had lived for was gone. "Ahead are a cold, lonely old age and my falling sickness."

Fifteen

An Evil Spirit

In just a few months, Dostoevsky's life had been chiseled down to a stump. "Out of the whole stock of my powers and energy all that's left in my soul is something disturbing and vague, something close to despair," he wrote to Baron Vrangel. "Alarm, bitterness, the coldest vanity." And yet gazing directly at the deaths of his wife and his dearest brother somehow made him feel alive. It was like seeing the sun rising up over the firing squad. "I am only just preparing to live. It's funny, isn't it? Feline vitality."

Dostoevsky's artistic vitality often manifested itself as a sudden, powerful recoil. He kept thinking about Chernyshevsky's novel *What Is to Be Done?*, which he had read shortly after its 1863 publication. He mulled over its depiction of dogged revolutionaries hoping to change the world and its vision of a rational paradise inspired by London's glass and iron Crystal Palace, the pagan temple of reason and machinery that Dostoevsky found so horrifying.

He considered how Turgenev combated nihilism in *Fathers and Children*. His tight, straightforward plot and the way his characters became mouthpieces for two generations of liberals were effective to a degree, even if it directly inspired Chernyshevsky's novel. He also thought about "Phantoms," Turgenev's story that Dostoevsky and his brother published in *Epoch* the previous year. It was so different: a lyrical story about a female spirit who whisks the narrator off on nightly flights—above Petersburg, Paris, the Black Forest—and back through history as well, to ancient Rome. But the phantom is a vampire, and the more the narrator sees and knows about the world, the more he is drained of blood, until he is emaciated, his heart sucked dry. Turgenev thought it was too much of a fantasy to be published, but Dostoevsky reassured him in a letter. Over the past few years, Dostoevsky wrote, realism had become banal, the "ennui" of sophisticates. People needed amazement, something to jolt them out of nihilistic complacency.

In fact, Dostoevsky insisted, "there is *too much* of the realistic in 'Phantoms.'" The whisked-away fantasy seemed to rankle him, as if it were another way for Turgenev to deliver his full convictions expressly. Something about the story, upon rereading, seemed to be "*lacking faith*," Dostoevsky had written to Mikhail, and the impression held. The narrator's heart was sucked dry, and yet Turgenev never delved fully into his psychology.

Dostoevsky must have been thinking about building upon *Notes from Underground*. He had recently been working on a novel about drunkenness and destitution. A civil servant clutches a bottle in a tavern as he tells someone his story. He's unemployed. His wife beats him. His daughter registers herself as a prostitute to support his family. Each humiliation plunges him further into drunkenness, which deepens his humiliation and his destitution. "Poverty is nothing, but destitution, dear sir,—destitution is a vice. If you're destitute they drag you off to the police station . . ." The hallmark of destitution is a hopelessness so profound that it reduces social interactions to rituals of abasement. Dostoevsky planned to call his novel *The Drunkards*. He thought it would sell—Russia's epidemic of drunkenness was a major public topic—and he was determined to finish it quickly. He had no choice.

He struggled to keep *Epoch* afloat after Mikhail's death. He pored over proofs, pleaded with contributors, cajoled censors, and employed three print shops simultaneously. He worked day and night, sometimes until five in the morning, suffered two seizures, and somehow turned out five issues in seventy-five days. "I'm a machine of some sort," he told Turgenev. His brother Nikolai put it differently: "He is the unhappiest of mortals."

He intended to salvage his "brilliant enterprise" with Mikhail and establish a legacy for his brother. Mikhail had hoped *Epoch* would provide his family with ten thousand rubles a year, but his widow and four surviving children had nothing—his funeral cost them their last three hundred rubles. *Epoch* was tens of thousands of rubles in debt to printers, paper suppliers, and contributors, and profitable days were not on the horizon. The journal's entire first year was destined to operate at a loss. This was because the Dostoevskys offered *Epoch* at a nearly 60 percent discount to former *Vremya* subscribers as recompense for the eight *Vremya* issues that were never published due to the government's ban. The discounted subscriptions were the majority of *Epoch*'s subscribers, and getting new readers was a perpetual challenge. Fyodor Dostoevsky's name could never be on the masthead, and he was so busy editing that his writing stopped appearing. When Mikhail passed away, people thought that Fyodor was the one who had died.

Mikhail left his family more than twenty thousand rubles in personal and business debts. Dostoevsky took all of them voluntarily, relieving Mikhail's family, and he signed promissory notes officially transferring much of it into his own name. It was his debt of honor to his brother. He was determined to preserve Mikhail's good name and to repay him for everything he had done for him. "Thank you, thank you for not abandoning me," Dostoevsky once wrote to Mikhail in Siberia, "without you what would I be!" "I'll repay you someday" was his refrain. Now he would have to repay his grieving family. "It goes without saying that I'm now a servant to them," he wrote to Vrangel. "For the sort of brother that he was I would give up both my head and my health."

Dostoevsky spent ten thousand rubles he had received from his aunt on keeping *Epoch* afloat. When that wasn't enough, he asked his brother Andrei for another three thousand, but he simply couldn't lend it. When the journal garnered only thirteen hundred subscribers for 1865 (half of what it needed to stay in business), Dostoevsky had no choice but to cease publishing *Epoch* after the second issue of the year.

He blamed the economy and a "universal journal crisis." He blamed the government for the family's hardships and for Mikhail's death. The debts were unbearable after *Vremya* was banned, and it was no coincidence, Dostoevsky believed, that Mikhail collapsed the day after hearing that an upcoming *Epoch* article would be banned. Unpleasant news for such a sick man—"that's poison." But Mikhail's family blamed Dostoevsky alone for mismanaging their only asset. One of his nephews was going around Petersburg saying as much: "My uncle managed things so badly that he ruined us."

And something odd happened. Dostoevsky was fifteen thousand rubles in debt—five thousand "on my word of honor" and ten thousand in promissory notes. Creditors had assured Dostoevsky leniency in exchange for the legal security of the debt documents, but toward the end of May 1865 several creditors began demanding their money simultaneously. One was named Gavrilov, an agent at one of *Epoch*'s print shops. "He's a so-so person," Dostoevsky later said, "elderly, not without certain merits, somewhat wily, and possessing money." After Mikhail's death, Dostoevsky casually asked if Gavrilov would lend him a thousand rubles. "Be pleased to," he said. They signed a promissory note the same day, as simple as that. On May 27, Gavrilov wrote to remind Dostoevsky that the term of his loan, per his promissory note, was set to expire on June 1. "Everything would be fine," Gavrilov wrote, if *Epoch* were still being published and he were still contracted, but he wasn't, so "now it's a completely different matter." Gavrilov was giving him five days' notice. And suddenly several creditors were demanding a total of about three thousand rubles in promissory note debt. "My business affairs keep getting worse and worse," Dostoevsky wrote to Pasha as the month drew to a close.

Around the same time, a notorious publisher named Stellovsky presented Dostoevsky with an offer. Stellovsky was a bookseller and a publisher known for exploiting writers in need. He initially gained prominence as a music publisher, and he somehow managed to buy all of Glinka's back catalog from the deceased composer's sister for twenty-five rubles. Stellovsky offered Dostoevsky two thousand rubles to publish a three-volume edition of his collected works—everything he had ever written. He was giving Dostoevsky ten or twelve days to think it over.

He could not have thought about it very long. Stellovsky was offering Dostoevsky just a little more than half of what he had received for the first *Dead House* edition alone. But then, days later, a stranger named Bocharov appeared demanding money from him. Bocharov was a high-ranking gentleman, a lawyer who dabbled in poetry. He had translated and published a volume of Goethe decades earlier (Belinsky hated it), and now he was presenting Dostoevsky with a promissory note that Dostoevsky had given to one of *Epoch*'s old paper suppliers. The supplier sold the note to Bocharov, and now the gentleman was demanding payment. But that wasn't all. Bocharov had also bought Gavrilov's promissory note, as if he were in the market for Dostoevsky-branded assets.

Dostoevsky panicked. He "knocked at doors everywhere" for help repaying the notes, but he had no luck. He went to Bocharov's home about eight times to plead for more time, but Bocharov was never home. Dostoevsky had not anticipated this dire possibility. Every time he had signed a promissory note for one of Mikhail's debts, he was turning a personal obligation into a transferable asset, something that could be bought, sold, and traded among strangers and institutions. A commercial bank could give an impatient creditor cash at, say, 90 percent of the note's value, and suddenly the obligation he had to a paper supplier he'd known for years would belong to a company he'd never heard of.

Dostoevsky might even have felt powerful when issuing those promissory notes because the ability for someone like him to do so was new. The use of notes had long been restricted to certain people, such as merchant guild members, but three years earlier, at the end of 1862, the government allowed virtually everyone to issue them. Dostoevsky instinctively felt bound and protected by the culture of debt he'd always known—informal agreements built on promises, strengthened by social ties, renegotiated with handshakes, enforced by honor—only to discover that he had slipped into a new realm of formal, anonymous debt built on contracts and legal proceedings and enforced by property seizures and debtors' prisons. The easy transferability of debt enabled the system's harshness because enforcement would only begin with a creditor willing to trigger it—likely not someone you'd worked with for years, but perhaps a high-ranking stranger, a dilettante poet who would never be home and who cared nothing for your plight or the plight of your brother's family.

Dostoevsky knew exactly what debtors' prisons were like. He recently had to redeem his brother Nikolai from debt prison for an old 120-ruble debt. Petersburg's House of Confinement for Delinquent Debtors stood next to Trinity Cathedral and alongside rows of Imperial Guards barracks. It held more than five hundred prisoners in 1862—about a quarter of Russia's debt prisoners. All ranks of Russian society were housed together. The staff interrogated new prisoners. How do you earn a living? What are your expenses? Why haven't you paid your debts? They questioned family members, friends, and acquaintances to corroborate the answers and gather details about the debtor's way of life.

A few days after Bocharov's unwelcome appearance, Dostoevsky found himself visiting Petersburg's debt prison again. He received a letter from one of *Epoch*'s former contributors begging Dostoevsky to pay him the forty-five rubles *Epoch* owed him. Dostoevsky met him in the prison's visitors' room, and the trip must have been disturbing. That same month, a moneylender visiting one of his debtors in Moscow's debt prison was beaten by several inmates while the guard simply watched. Dostoevsky gave the writer what he could spare, but it wasn't everything. He explained his own pressing situation in enough detail that the debt prisoner began feeling bad for *him*. "I even feel sorry that I wrote you about this matter," he wrote to Dostoevsky. If one wanted to be optimistic, life in debt prison was not entirely bad. They ate cabbage soup with beef and had unlimited bread and salt.

Three days later, Gavrilov's boss at the print shop, Eduard Prats, demanded payment for a promissory note of nearly 1,000 rubles. It was as if they smelled blood in the water. That same day, Dostoevsky received a notice from his police precinct regarding promissory notes held by a solicitor named Pavel Lyzhin and a "peasant," as Dostoevsky identified him, named Semyon Pushkin. The notice informed F. M. Dostoevsky that the authorities would be taking an inventory of his assets at 12:30 p.m. the following day because of his "nonpayment." It ordered him to wait for the police in his apartment; "otherwise the inventory will be conducted without your presence." The first step began with such trifling amounts! Dostoevsky estimated that by now his promissory notes totaled 13,000 rubles. He owed Lyzhin 450 rubles. He owed the peasant Pushkin just 249. But if their money was not soon forthcoming, Dostoevsky's inventoried possessions would be seized and auctioned off. If his debts exceeded the value of his possessions, he could be taken to prison, where he would remain until his debts were paid.

Second Lieutenant Makarov arrived at Dostoevsky's small apartment the following day. The ritual was familiar enough. One or more officers search a debtor's apartment and rifle through belongings while a scribe compiles the inventory. Sometimes appointed witnesses are present, sometimes the creditors are present, and sometimes there are skirmishes. Dostoevsky, however, was exceedingly friendly. He charmed the second lieutenant, befriended him. To some degree he was probably looking for levers to pull, but Dostoevsky was genuinely curious about the police, and he began asking the officer questions about how investigations work. He provided valuable answers. At some point Dostoevsky started telling him about his other debts and almost certainly mentioned his departed wife and brother, his banned journal, his failed journal, his litany of creditors, his dim publishing prospects—how it had all come to this humiliating accounting of his meager possessions.

The second lieutenant, after listening, began asking questions of his own. Did Dostoevsky know who Bocharov was? He did not. Well, Bocharov happened to be a good friend of that publisher, Stellovsky. He was a man who "undertook business for him."

And that's when it dawned upon him. Bocharov was buying up Dostoevsky's debts and demanding payment because Stellovsky had instructed him to. He might even have been coercing Lyzhin and the peasant Pushkin to initiate proceedings against him to maximize the pressure. He was tightening the financial vise so that Dostoevsky would sign away the rights to his works for as little as possible. Stellovsky was orchestrating his financial woes. He couldn't prove it, but he was certain it was true. Stellovsky was a rogue. He was a scoundrel and a pettifogger.

Dostoevsky started writing *The Drunkards* "under the lash," as he described it. An advance for a new novel was the only escape left. Two days after the inventory of his possessions, Dostoevsky offered *The Drunkards* to Kraevsky, his old editor at *Notes of the Fatherland*, another man who had ensnared him in debts. Dostoevsky asked him for an advance of three thousand rubles—enough to satisfy his most impatient creditors. He pledged to deliver a novel of more than three hundred pages (or at least the first few chapters) in less than four months. If Kraevsky didn't like it, he would pay back the advance at 10 percent interest. A publisher could hardly receive a more favorable offer. Kraevsky rejected it anyway.

Dostoevsky had no choice but to return to Stellovsky, and Stellovsky was waiting for him. This time, however, his terms were rather different. Stellovsky would give Dostoevsky the three thousand rubles he needed in exchange for an edition of his collected works, but now he wanted the right to include any new material he would produce for the next three and a half years.

He also wanted a new novel from Dostoevsky—a small one, mind you, a story of at least 160 pages—and he wanted it by November 1, 1866. Dostoevsky would do well to keep that date in mind because Stellovsky required one more brutal stipulation: if Dostoevsky failed to meet that deadline for his new novel, Stellovsky would own the right to publish anything Dostoevsky wrote for the next *nine years*—and he would pay Dostoevsky nothing.

The contract was unprecedentedly bad. Dostoevsky was gambling nearly a decade of his future work just to keep his possessions and stay out of debtors' prison. He knew he could get two to three times as much for his publication rights without any strings attached, but the only interested publisher wouldn't have that kind of money until the fall. Dostoevsky needed the money now. So he signed Stellovsky's contract and subjected himself to what he called "the most humiliating and impossible conditions." And there was one final insult: Stellovsky issued a portion of Dostoevsky's advance in promissory notes.

After signing the contract, Dostoevsky settled his most pressing debts, got another loan from the Literary Fund, and escaped once again to Europe with 175 rubles in his pocket. It wasn't much, but it was enough for him to change his fate at the casino.

W inning at roulette is "terribly stupid and simple," he insisted. All one has to do is remain calm for an hour or two. Even years later he swore it was true: "If one is as though made of marble, cold, and *inhumanly* cautious, then definitely, *without any doubt*, one can win *as much as one wishes*." It was all about "composure and calculation." Dostoevsky returned to the Wiesbaden casino, where he had been so lucky before, and he was not greedy. He intended to turn his 175 rubles into 425, just enough to sustain himself for three months in Europe.

He began winning—the system was working. There were, admittedly, a few blind spots. It's not exactly clear, for example, what one should calculate so calmly in roulette, so you calculate whatever you can. You look for streaks and patterns, missing numbers, hidden influences, momentum, and hot players, as if each spin of the wheel were not an isolated event but a scene in a narrative. And in this particular narrative, Dostoevsky was alone, a novelist of some repute gambling with the only money he had left, money taken from a villainous publisher and wrested from his departed brother's creditors, and he was on the verge of overcoming his great misfortunes until the croupiers began to rake his winnings away.

And this narrative turn highlighted another rather large blind spot in Dostoevsky's gambling system: it never told him when to stop playing. When you are in the middle of a story filled with unexpected twists, you keep reading until there are no pages left. Who knows if this string of losses is the arrival of a protagonist's doom or merely a dramatic setback before his final triumph? So you keep going. You play every spin, you turn every page until you have lost and borrowed and pawned everything you own down to your last paragraph. Dostoevsky's closing sentence was his silver watch. He pawned it in Wiesbaden's lone pawnshop, and he lost that money, too. He lost everything in three days.

He had to ask Turgenev for a loan. Turgenev was in Baden-Baden at the time, so the money could arrive quickly, and he had no other choice. "I am disgusted and ashamed to trouble you. But except for you I have absolutely no one at the present moment to whom I could turn." He tried explaining what had happened, to himself as to others. "I went off my head" is how he described it to Vrangel. But it was more than that. A gambling win is like biting into hollow fruit. The expected satisfaction instead leaves you with a deeper hunger. The desire becomes "ever stronger and stronger," Dostoevsky later wrote, "to the point of utter exhaustion." To play roulette was to dive down into a whirl of excitement and need. "The moment I hear the clink of spilling money—I almost go into convulsions." People are not coldly rational, calculating machines. They are irrational. He thought he already understood that.

Turgenev sent half of the money Dostoevsky asked for. Luckily, Polina Suslova was arriving in Wiesbaden, just when he needed her most. They had kept in touch—he had hoped to see her in Paris—but her appearance here could not have been much comfort. She was in town with another man, a young Russian physician whose youthful manliness she admired. There was "golden down" on his upper lip. To make matters worse, he seemed to be a nihilist physician straight out of Turgenev. He told Suslova how he admired animals much more than humans. "He felt that horses were saints," Suslova recalled, and "nerves" were the only things he respected in nature. What happened between Dostoevsky and Suslova is a mystery, but Dostoevsky's pre-dicament was clear and familiar to her. She gave him whatever she could. After she left, he thought about how she must've gone hungry.

Suslova's money was not enough to get home. It wasn't even enough to pay his hotel bill. He was staying at the Hotel Victoria, a somewhat small, mid-level inn situated among beer houses across from the railway station, and his bill grew larger every night. He tried keeping up appearances, though the staff must've been used to Russians without their watches hurrying to their rooms. And European hoteliers were inveterate spies. Dostoevsky was convinced they reported details about foreigners to the authorities. It wasn't just the registra-tion forms they gave you, which gathered basic information ("who, how, from where, with what intentions, and so on," as Dostoevsky explained). He noticed them monitoring him. They recorded his physical features—his height, the small scar on his forehead. A proprietor once asked him to step toward a win-dow so he could get a better look at his eyes ("more a shade of gray," he noted). And these were the *French* hotels. Wiesbaden was a scrupulous town, and when dealing with guests like him, they were pitiless. "For a German," Dos-toevsky wrote to Suslova, "there is no higher crime than to be without money and not pay on time."

Eventually, the staff was given orders not to serve him dinner. He sought an explanation, and "the fat German proprietor" told him, quite plainly, that he did not "deserve" dinner. "Since yesterday I have not been eating and have been living on tea alone," he wrote to Suslova. "And the tea they serve is aw-ful." They refused to clean his clothes and boots. The servants began ignoring him when he called. They refused to give him a new candle even when the one in his room had burned down to the smallest stump. He was worried they would seize his possessions or that he would be thrown out or arrested. Until then, he was stuck in the Hotel Victoria.

He read as much as possible and tried to stave off hunger by remaining stationary. In mid-September, he was leafing through *The Voice*, one of the Russian newspapers available in Wiesbaden, and came across a story about a man named Chistov—a Raskolnik—who killed a cook and washerwoman with an ax. They were older women employed by Chistov's wealthy relatives. It was the cook who let him in, but the washerwoman appeared unexpectedly.

The three of them drank vodka and snacked on pickled cucumbers, and when the cook went to the kitchen to fetch more food, Chistov pulled out his ax, which was hidden under his coat, and he attacked the washerwoman.

The article included detailed descriptions of the bodies and the crime scene. The washerwoman was lying on her back, her head inclined to the left, her feet facing the window. She had three head wounds, including a four-inch gash in her neck. There were blood splatters under the table and on the furnace tiles. The cook's body was facedown by the stove. There were ax wounds on her face. There were multiple large, smooth-edged wounds across the back of her neck and running diagonally down to the right side of her body nearing the waist. She had hemorrhages "on the surface and base of the brain." Beneath her body was an earthenware plate and two pickles. After the murders, Chistov went methodically through the house and stole more than eleven thousand rubles in cash and property—silverware, gold and diamond jewelry, a lottery ticket. It was such an astonishingly gruesome murder. And yet such a commonplace motive.

After several days without dinner, Dostoevsky began losing his appetite, and he developed a fever that went on for days. The proprietor kept threatening to summon the police. He tried to get money from Suslova again. "Polya, my friend, help me out, save me!" She did not send anything. He wrote letters to friends and acquaintances—people he barely knew, people he hadn't seen in years, anyone who could bail him out—but he had no money for the postage (the recipients would have to pay to open his letters), and he counted the days that he didn't receive replies. It was humiliating. He wondered if the German proprietor was right, that he didn't "deserve" help, and maybe everyone knew it. Every detail, every sign, every absence of a sign, caused his mind to race. "In inaction the imagination runs so very wild," he wrote to Suslova, but she did not respond.

Dostoevsky would leave the hotel for a few hours every evening so people would think he was eating dinner somewhere. He found himself wandering around Wiesbaden as the darkness raked away the city's sheen. Beyond the artificial fishponds and manicured groves, vestiges of older eras would peek out from centuries of renovations. The medieval fountain in the marketplace, the clock tower, a small section of the town's ancient Roman wall. To be in

Wiesbaden in late September was to feel a resort's late-season emptying. The gamblers and the infirm who had swept into town for the casino and the healing baths began drifting back to far-off homes. What remained were the locked doors of the apothecaries and mineral water dealers, a stand of donkeys and saddle horses available for excursions, the trumpet blast announcing evening feeding time in the wild boar park, the steam still rising up from the hot spring on the northern edge of the old town, and the old town itself, with its narrow, winding streets cutting through a jumble of buildings wrenched out of joint.

One night, as he wandered through Wiesbaden, hungry and ill, an idea for a new story came to him, suddenly and with great clarity. He went back to the Hotel Victoria and began writing in a hardcover notebook bound in dark maroon cloth. Sometimes he filled the pages with narration and dialogue, and sometimes there were just snippets jotted down on whatever page was available, notes to himself, glimmers of characters.

"That was an evil spirit," he wrote at the top of the first page. "There's an evil spirit here," he wrote a few pages later. "How otherwise could I have overcome all those difficulties?" The meandering, insect-buzzing voice in *Notes from Underground* was diving down into the voice of a criminal. He would write a murderer's story from the murderer's perspective. How would he think? Suspicions would arouse his thoughts. Everyone around him would be a potential accuser. "Scoundrels, torturers, scandalmongers! scandalmongers! scandalmongers!" He crossed it out. The narrative itself has to be paranoid. It has to mimic a suspicious mind. Dostoevsky made a note for himself: "Completely unneeded and unexpected details must leap out at every moment in the middle of the story."

He saw many details clearly. An old, dilapidated top hat from Zimmerman's. A homemade sling for the ax. The blood in the water after he washes the blade. The noxious air in the stairwell leading up to the police station. The sickening, oppressive atmosphere of all of St. Petersburg bears down on the murderer. "The heat was terrible," Dostoevsky wrote, "stuffiness, crowds, plaster from the scaffolding, sand, dust, stench from the shops"—later he added, "and particularly from the taverns"—"shouting hucksters and drunkards, who were falling down on the street at every moment." The sunlight blinds him and makes him dizzy. He was ill. He had a fever. "It seemed to me that my head would burst like a bomb," he says.

But there's something wrong with the details. The facts of the crime have been terribly misallocated somehow. Complete strangers know disturbing particulars about his crime—things that he himself doesn't know—as if they were somehow watching him do it. And yet they're also blind to his involvement, as if they had been passing around a photograph with a hole burned through the middle. The publicity surrounding the murder is central to the story. Nothing works without that. He overhears his friends discussing early rumors of the crime he committed, and that's how we begin to hear details. The murderer stole a few odds and ends but missed fifteen hundred rubles in notes, possibly "because he lost his head," one of his friends guesses. He was nervous, inexperienced. He even left the door open. Then the other woman entered—Lizaveta—and he got scared. "The whole business took about 5 minutes or so."

The murderer wants to read all about it in the newspapers. He asks for a copy of *The Voice* at a café, and it's the anonymous fame that makes it surreal. Seeing yourself from far away. Dostoevsky jotted down another note. He would write letters to the public—in the press, perhaps, or in scattered leaflets—"to make a bit more famous."

Dostoevsky began writing day and night by the candle nub in his room. The words filled his notebook pages alongside doodles and drawings. The outlines of leaves are strewn in the corners of several pages. Gothic arches and cupolas. A strutting figure emerges from a block of text on another page. He wrote the names of characters repeatedly in calligraphy. He drew their faces. On one page, in the middle of several snatches of writing—boxed-off notes, sudden passages, horizontal and vertical, marginal additions, additions to additions—Dostoevsky sketched the murderer's face in shadow. He looks downward, eyes obscured, a blond head of hair swept back, emphasizing his furrowed brow. He has compressed lips and a chin stiffened into the grimace of a man whose skull is about to detonate. Below the face he drew another one with a similar grimace. But this face is hairless, smaller, in deeper shadow— a sketch of a sketch, perhaps, or a double. Above the murderer's face, Dostoevsky wrote some numbered notes.

Remarks

1) I didn't look into the purse.

2) I gave it up so easily: Why did I do the murder?

3) How easily was such a hard deed accomplished.

The ideas were coming rapidly. Dostoevsky wrote nearly fifty pages of material, and then, in just a few days, nearly one hundred. When he ran out of sheets, he would turn his notebooks upside down and continue writing from back to front, from the bottom up.

What he also saw with great clarity was violence. The murderer returns to his cramped fifth-floor room near the Haymarket, trembling from weakness. He takes off his clothes (keeps his socks on), lies down on his ragged divan, and pulls his coat over himself like a blanket. Some time later he wakes up to the sound of screaming. He sits up, terrified in the deep dusk of a Petersburg summer night. "God, what a scream! I had never heard such unnatural sounds, such yelling, grinding of teeth, sobs, curses, and blows." It's his landlady. He can't make out her words, but she's begging for the man to stop.

He can hear the attacker. He's irate and unintelligible, but the voice is familiar. It's a police officer. A man nicknamed Lieutenant Gunpowder who had recently summoned him for questioning. The lieutenant drags her out into the stairwell as the murderer upstairs listens, frozen on his couch, piecing it together. "He must have been beating her with his boots, with his hands," he tells us. "He trampled her; and grabbing her by the hair he slammed her head against the staircase. There was no other way he could have beaten her to judge by the squeals and desperate cries of the poor woman." He can hear the other tenants on the landings, opening and closing doors, their voices barreling up and down the stairwell, the sounds of running, knocking on doors, doors slamming, more running. Why is he beating her? "Fear like ice penetrated me," he says. Dostoevsky added in the notebook's margin, "Soon they will come for me also."

The noises eventually die down. He can hear the landlady moaning in pain on the stairs and the lieutenant cursing her as he leaves. The people in the stairwell, shouting, then whispering, gradually withdraw and close their doors. Somehow the landlady drags herself up and locks herself back inside her apartment. The murderer sits silently in his small room on the top floor.

"Wasn't he asking for me?" Dostoevsky crossed it out. But still the murderer wonders, "And can it be that all this is possible? How could he dare beat her."

Dostoevsky wrote to a friend in Petersburg. He said he was working on a story that was "widening out and becoming richer" every day. He gave a basic sense of the idea and asked him to find a journal to publish it. "People will pay attention to it, talk about it," he wrote. "Nothing of this kind has yet been written among us; I guarantee its originality, yes, and also its power to grip the reader." His friend likely thought he was trying to talk his way into a contract. Enthusiasm sells, after all.

But Dostoevsky knew he was seizing something powerful from his dire circumstances. On some level, he had been playing a game of brinksmanship with himself, engineering a moment of literary salvation. He had pretended that escaping to Europe and winning at roulette would be his salvation. The hand of God would rescue a virtuous, long-suffering man through the un-likely instrument of a tiny ivory ball. And when that salvation didn't come, when he was utterly ruined, his eyes would be opened at last, and he would realize that he could be saved only through writing. So by the time he picked up his pen in Wiesbaden, the ink that flowed onto the page had become the product not of a secular profession but of a genuine calling. The story taking shape in his notebooks was God's true saving instrument.

The only problem was that no one wanted it. *The Reading Library* and *Notes of the Fatherland* both declined. The editors of *The Contemporary* wouldn't even entertain the proposal. They believed Dostoevsky had insulted Chernyshevsky in a short story called "The Crocodile," and now that Cher-nyshevsky had been sent into exile, they wanted nothing to do with anyone who disrespected him.

Though there was no promising news from Petersburg, he continued writ-ing, putting all his faith in it. In September, after more than a month in Wiesbaden, a princess came to his rescue. He had met Princess Shalikova through a Russian Orthodox priest whom he had befriended. She was herself a writer, sometimes publishing under pseudonyms—Narskaya, Gorskaya. She listened to Dostoevsky talk about his predicament and then, eventually, about the details of the new novel he was writing. We don't know exactly what he said—or if she had gotten a chance to read some of his notebook pages—but she was intrigued. At some point she suggested that he send his story to her brother-in-law, the editor of *The Russian Herald*, Mikhail Katkov.

The name must've made Dostoevsky wince. Katkov's role in getting *Vremya* banned hastened the decline of his fortunes and made the past two mournful years even more difficult. Dostoevsky must have been mindful of the way Katkov swiftly rejected one of his novels. He must have been mindful of calling Katkov childish, incontinent, and senile. He must have been mindful that Katkov surely was not too senile to have forgotten those words. "Katkov is such a vain, conceited, and vengeful person," Dostoevsky wrote to Vrangel. Even if he were to like his new story, Dostoevsky believed, Katkov would likely reject it out of pride.

The princess's advice prevailed nevertheless. Dostoevsky sat down and drew up a detailed proposal for the esteemed editor of *The Russian Herald*. "It is the psychological account of a crime," Dostoevsky wrote. It would be told from the perspective of an intelligent, well-intended young man, "one of the new generation."

> A young man, expelled from the university, petit-bourgeois by social origin, and living in extreme poverty, after yielding to certain strange, "unfinished" ideas floating in the air, has resolved, out of light-mindedness and out of the instability of his ideas, to get out of his foul situation at one go. He has resolved to murder an old woman, a titular counselor who lends money at interest.

The "unfinished" ideas are utilitarian. Dostoevsky sketches out the murderer's reasoning, his justifications and psychology. "The old woman is stupid, deaf, sick, greedy, charges Jewish interest, is malicious and preying on someone else's life by tormenting her younger sister, whom she keeps as a servant." Her life, in other words, offers no utility to anyone. She is crude, exploitative, and childless, and how much longer would she live anyway? "Is she of any use to anyone at all?" the young man asks. So he decides to murder her and take her money. He would use it to make his mother happy and to save his sister, employed by a gentry family, "from the lascivious attentions of the head of the landowner household—attentions that threaten her with ruin." After saving his family, he would earn his degree, go abroad, and begin a career "fulfilling his 'humanitarian duty to humanity.'" All would be justified.

The young man somehow pulls off the murder, and no one suspects him, but this is when the drama begins. Perplexing questions, unexpected emotions, and torments begin hounding him. Eventually, the murderer confesses. He willingly denounces himself "so as to become linked to people again," Dostoevsky explained—even if it means being exiled to Siberia. Punishment doesn't deter a criminal, he insisted. The criminal demands punishment.

The story had contemporary appeal, Dostoevsky claimed. Recent events demonstrated that his plot "is not at all eccentric" and that "unfinished" ideas do in fact lead people to horrific acts. And yet something curious happened as Dostoevsky conjured examples for Katkov. Different types of crimes—different psychologies—started bubbling up. He informed Katkov that he had heard about an expelled Moscow University student who resolved to kill a postman, but this was a matter of sheer pride and indiscriminate vengeance rather than utility. Dostoevsky also insisted that several incidents recently reported in the newspapers bore out his idea. For example, Dostoevsky wrote, "that seminarian who murdered the girl in the shed by arrangement with her and who was arrested an hour later at breakfast, and so on." But that unfeeling calm was exactly the opposite of his own fictional murderer's prolonged torment and eventual confession. If he were being honest, he would have to admit that it was rather difficult to think of an example of a utilitarian murderer.

"It is difficult for me to explain my idea completely," he wrote to Katkov, and the story was growing so quickly. He nevertheless assured Katkov of the story's quality. It was true that pressing deadlines had forced him to write regrettable things in the past. "I have written this piece, however, unhurriedly and with ardor." It would be around ninety pages long, and he could finish it in about two weeks. He left the question of payment up to Katkov, though he requested that *The Russian Herald* at least match the lowest pay rate he had received—half of what he had gotten for *Dead House*. What he really needed, Dostoevsky explained, was three hundred rubles immediately to get him out of his own rather foul situation. And he needed a quick reply "For me, in my straitened situation, every moment is valuable." Looking back over his proposal, he realized how little he had actually conveyed. "I have passed over the whole plot." He didn't even mention the title, if he had one.

The story would be called *Crime and Punishment*. He imagined it as an introspective murderer's diary, and he kept writing while he waited for Katkov's answer. "We'll examine why I did it, how I decided to do it," the murderer explains. "There's an evil spirit here." The diary would reveal the "bitterness and destitution" lying beneath that evil spirit, and Dostoevsky decided that the murderer would conclude that "he had to do it." It was logic at work.

The murderer describes how he returns to his room after the deed, how he hides the loot in a small space behind some removable bricks underneath his windowsill. The next day he's unexpectedly summoned to the police station, though it turns out the summons is regarding an unpaid promissory note that he signed for his landlady so long ago that he barely remembers it. He was a law student when he first rented the apartment, but he was expelled for failing to pay his student fees (fifty rubles per year). After leaving the university, he began tutoring to make ends meet, but eventually he lost his students and became mired in destitution. He hasn't paid his rent in four months, and his landlady has stopped serving him dinner.

When the murderer reports to the district department, Lieutenant Gunpowder is repelled by his appearance. "Take a look, please, a gentleman writer," he announces, pointing out the young man for the district chief. Nothing but a former student who doesn't pay his debts. "He is a pretty sight!"

"Poverty is not a vice!" the district chief reminds Gunpowder.

The police require him to sign a statement declaring that he won't leave the city or sell property before repaying his landlady. As he's doing this, a couple of officers nearby are talking about how last night's killer must've been in the apartment when two other men knocked on the old woman's door. He must have escaped while the men went downstairs to get the building's superintendent.

The police clerk watches our protagonist carefully because he notices he can barely hold the pen. Then he faints. When he regains consciousness, he sees the district chief, with his black handlebar mustache, holding a glass of yellow water out for him.

"What's the matter with you, are you sick?" Nikodim Fomich asks sharply.

"'Yes . . . ' I answered, looking around me."

"Have you been sick for a long time?" Lieutenant Gunpowder yells from his desk across the room, pretending to sort through papers. He has been sick since yesterday.

"Didn't you go out yesterday"—Gunpowder doesn't ask, exactly, he leads.

"I went out."

"May I ask where you went?"

"Walking."

"Hmmm."

The murderer manages to escape the department. He needs to hide the loot somewhere far away. He ventures out to one of the Petersburg islands until he comes across a decrepit yard beside a large building. He pushes open the rickety gate. There's a wooden gutter running along the edge of a yard and a few sheds with piles of lumber. Someone wrote in chalk on the fence, "It is forbidden to stop here." There's a large stone beside the gate, near the gutter, just steps away from the sidewalk. He pushes the stone a bit, places the purse in the hollow beneath it, rolls it back in place, and walks away. "No one, no one noticed me!" the murderer thinks.

The plot centered on the drama of escaping capture. "They hunt me like a rabbit, like an animal," the murderer writes in his diary. He develops a fever and falls into a delirium for days. A man with a bulldog is waiting behind his door. People seem to crowd around his bed and argue or come to take him away. With "animal, beastly cunning," he listens to his friend Razumikhin and a doctor talking at his bedside while he pretends to sleep. Details about the murder tumble out second- and thirdhand. Traps seem to be everywhere. He suspects Razumikhin is a spy, or that they're using him as a spy and the fool doesn't realize it. He plans to flee to America or to lock himself up in another apartment where no one could find him or torment him, "and it would be like that forever."

He swerves from fear to audacity. He runs into the police clerk at a café and confounds his suspicions by voicing them—by more than voicing them.

He scatters clues. He walks right up to the edge of a confession. He says he knew the pawnbroker quite well.

"I pawned things at her place," he says, tying himself to the victim. Then he asks the police clerk, "What would you think if I were the one that snatched her money and put it under a stone. Suppose it were me."

Confronting one of his hunters like that, seeing the expression on his face, feels like "animal cowardly joy"—no, not cowardly. Dostoevsky crossed it out: "*instinctive* joy of self-preservation." Yet even fending off suspicions is galling. "How I would like to take them all and slaughter them all to the last one." Even Razumikhin's kindness enrages him. At one point he worries if he harbors some hidden malice even toward his mother, whom he intended to help in the first place. "Can it be that I want to tear apart her heart?" He pushes this possibility away. "No. I will be worthy!" He was at the nexus of emotions and ideas tugging in opposite directions.

Dostoevsky settled on a name for the murderer: Raskolnikov.

Dostoevsky's strategy was to let Raskolnikov's confusion undermine the supposed logic of his crime, but he found this contradiction increasingly difficult to sustain in the form of a diary. He wanted the murderer's bewilderment to pervade the narrative. He wanted a haze of uncertainty to surround basic facts, what's real and not real. This is why Raskolnikov falls into delirium and fever dreams. It's why details arrive as rumors and overheard discussions. And it's also why, when Raskolnikov's landlady is being beaten, she is not being beaten. The reader discovers it later. Lieutenant Gunpowder did not, in fact, storm into Raskolnikov's building in the middle of the night. He did not drag his landlady into the stairwell. He did not pummel her mercilessly in front of alarmed tenants. It was all part of Raskolnikov's fever dream.

It's exasperating to have events unmasked as delusions, but Dostoevsky used it to establish the narrative's paranoid rules. If this meticulously detailed event is a hallucination, then everything is suspect. The reader recalibrates, becomes suspicious. The "unneeded and unexpected" details leaping out in the story could portend the hunted criminal's capture, or they could be toothless ghosts. Raskolnikov is never sure, and now neither are we.

"Of General Importance," Dostoevsky wrote in his notebook, taking a step back. "In all these six chapters, he must write, speak, and appear to the reader in part as if not in possession of his senses." Dostoevsky himself was recalibrating. Each step Raskolnikov takes toward uncertainty led Dostoevsky to another. He was beginning to let uncertainty drive the story forward until it resolves—but how? At one point, he imagined Raskolnikov suddenly seeing his demonic character and the true motives for his crime. He would realize he wasn't being logical or utilitarian, and he would confess. But by now that resolution seemed implausibly neat.

Somehow, beneath Raskolnikov's paranoia and delusion, the reader and the murderer will have to touch down on some bedrock reality. The sight of a dead body, perhaps. Locking eyes with a dying woman. But Dostoevsky kept his distance from the violent deed at the center of the story, as if it were too awful to narrate directly. His notebooks sketch details before and after the crime (Raskolnikov hiding the loot, getting rid of the ax), but the murders themselves come only in flashing glimpses. One idea was to have the police clerk piece the scene together forensically. In another sketch, Razumikhin deduces how the murderer must have hidden in the apartment that the painters left open. Then there are sketches in which Raskolnikov briefly remembers the crime, or explains it, or confesses to it, but we are never really there in the pawnbroker's dim apartment.

And the pawnbroker herself never ceases to be more than the two-dimensional figure that Dostoevsky sketched for Katkov—"stupid, deaf, sick, greedy"—but there's another woman in that apartment. Raskolnikov does not just murder the pawnbroker. He also murders her half sister, Lizaveta Ivanovna. He doesn't plan to kill her, but her unexpected arrival on the scene leads to the bedrock reality—personal details. Lizaveta is a peddler who does odd jobs. "I knew her and she mended my linen," Raskolnikov says in an early sketch. "She's an idiot. The old woman beat her when she was pregnant. I saw it myself. Pregnant, pregnant, sixth." Dostoevsky crossed it all out. He tried it another way, in a dialogue with the landlady's servant, who has to remind Raskolnikov that Lizaveta once mended his shirts.

"She was murdered pregnant," the servant informs him, "they used to beat her for nothing, and whoever wanted to could outrage her." Dostoevsky imagined it several ways. In another version the baby belongs to the doctor, and the dead baby is—was—a boy. In the end, all direct references to the baby were crossed out.

D ostoevsky soon realized that the story was much larger than ninety pages, and he wouldn't be finishing it in two weeks. The murderer's story was a novel, and it was big enough to encompass Dostoevsky's ideas for the other novel he had been planning, *The Drunkards*, about the destitute civil servant talking in the tavern. The drunkard is talking to Raskolnikov. They resemble each other. They share a volatile blend of pride, humiliation, and destructiveness. The "destitution" that the civil servant bemoans also lies beneath the murderer's evil spirit. They both dream of money saving their families. They both believe that providing that money is a way to love them. Dostoevsky started weaving the plots together in small ways. The district police chief, for example, seems to comfort the civil servant from across story lines when he reminds Lieutenant Gunpowder, "Poverty is not a vice!"

Dostoevsky drafted several pages of the drunkard's monologue. "We are the poor, the fallen, the lost. Let it be, let it be, let it be that we are lost!" He cannot grasp his misfortune other than as a part of who he is. "But, dear sir, who will take pity on us?" Dostoevsky gave the drunkard a sweet, childlike name to contrast with his world-weary bitterness: Marmeladov. "We are God's children," Marmeladov says, "we live in hell." Raskolnikov finds the drunkard's abjection alluring, even enviable. But who will pity a murderer? Raskolnikov craves pity because that is the way compassion circulates in a hierarchical society. Pity compels patronage because it fixates on the suffering itself. It is a compassion that sticks to people. That's the form of goodness he instinctively understands, but it goes wrong so easily. Raskolnikov's altruism is really pity that sours into contempt. Most people seem "low and vile" to him until he catches himself. "No: gather them up in one's hand, and then do good for them."

Doing good is, for Raskolnikov, "simply a matter of arithmetic," a Benthamite accounting of costs and benefits, pleasures and pains. He would use the old woman's money to help his mother and sister, as well as others. Money is perfect for arithmetic. In a couple of drafts, Raskolnikov uses the loot as seed money for stock market investments that would increase the yield of his benevolence. "And then when I become noble, the benefactor of all, a citizen, I will repent." It was simple. His crime would amount to nothing next to his "mountain of good and useful deeds."

D ostoevsky didn't know it, but his proposal was exactly what Mikhail Katkov needed. *The Russian Herald* had recently had a falling-out with Tolstoy, and Turgenev wasn't writing anything. The journal was hungry for fiction, and Katkov could take Dostoevsky up on his minimum offer and get a rather unusual murder story for a bargain. And Dostoevsky's story was timely. It was landing in Katkov's lap just as the first wave of Russian crime writing was cresting—the public was hungry for tales of lurid offenses. So Katkov quickly accepted Dostoevsky's proposal and sent three hundred rubles to Wiesbaden.

By the time the money arrived, Dostoevsky had already left. The Orthodox priest who had introduced him to Princess Shalikova lent him what he needed to get back to Russia and took responsibility for his bill at the Hotel Victoria. Dostoevsky arrived in Petersburg in October 1865. The snows had come early. Sleighs replaced carriages on the streets, the Neva was freezing over, and the Summer Garden's statues were encased in little structures that would shelter them from the elements.

Everything Dostoevsky had tried to escape in Europe was waiting for him in Petersburg. He suffered a powerful seizure his first night back. Five days later, just as he had begun to recover, he had another one, stronger. Shortly after that he had a third. And then a fourth. By mid-December, it was clear that his seizures were coming more frequently than ever. And his Wiesbaden gambling spree left him with no money. The priest forwarded Katkov's three hundred rubles, but this barely met the immediate needs of Mikhail's family. When Dostoevsky heard that his brother Nikolai needed hospital treatment, Dostoevsky had only one ruble to send him. He started borrowing money again. When he asked a writer friend about getting financial assistance to start yet another journal, his friend just shook his head and advised him to "renew" his name by writing another novel. It had been more than four years since he had published one.

To change his fortunes, Dostoevsky tried proposing marriage to Polina

Suslova—repeatedly. "For a long time now he has been offering me his hand and his heart," Suslova wrote in her diary in November. It made her angry. "I simply hate him. He made me suffer so much," she wrote earlier that fall.

Dostoevsky could feel her anger. "You can't forgive me that you gave yourself to me, and so you are avenging yourself," he told her.

She judged him unworthy of her love—he knew that—and yet despite her disapproval, despite her contempt, her "egoism and vanity," he told Suslova's sister, "I love her even now, love her very much." He couldn't help it.

Suslova's answer to his proposals was always the same. A part of her wanted to leave everything, to float away from the world. She told him that she was going to become a holy woman, that she would walk through the Kremlin gardens barefoot and tell people she speaks with angels. The idea was indeed appealing.

T he rejection encouraged Dostoevsky to throw himself into *Crime and Punishment*. He would have to submit the first few chapters to Katkov soon because journals like *The Russian Herald* typically began serializing new novels in their January issues. Time was running out. In November he began filling a second notebook with passages and notes and doodles. There was a man's screaming face on one page. In the margins of another he wrote the name "Lizaveta" in calligraphy, three times. Beneath her name he repeated the word "Mankind."

Dostoevsky was still struggling with basic narrative problems. He had a delusionally confused character narrating the aftermath of a heinous crime motivated by radical philosophy. The murderer somehow has to write his way through idealism, bewilderment, fear, rage, and remorse. He began to sketch the murderer's philosophy. *"There is no free will, fatalism,"* Raskolnikov reminds himself. It soothes him not to have a free will. "A Nihilist is a lackey of thought," Dostoevsky wrote. Raskolnikov was beginning to act like the machine he believed himself to be. His feet take him through Petersburg, seemingly of their own volition. "I was drawn, somehow drawn mechanically to do it as quickly as possible," Raskolnikov says.

The crime is inevitable. Raskolnikov has essentially nothing to do with it. "It happened so completely by chance," he explains, "that I didn't think really that I myself would have to do the killing." If everything is preordained—if free will is nothing but an illusion pulsing through your nerves—then the fact that it is *you* who murders the two sisters with an ax is incidental. You are cosmically thrown in their direction. "The whole thing was done almost accidentally," Raskolnikov insists. The sisters were born to be murdered.

The more Dostoevsky wrote, the clearer it became that simply keeping a diary could not make his character remorseful, so he began to imagine the murderer writing out a full confession after his arrest. "I am on trial and I will tell everything." Raskolnikov could simply declare everything freely for his judges and for the public to behold—like Lacenaire. His story could lay bare the monstrosities lurking in Russian society. "Five days ago, I was walking around like a madman," Raskolnikov's confession begins. "I even began to fall into a kind of unconsciousness." But this narrative method was also problematic. Aside from the fact that announcing your mad behavior is a poor way to evoke madness, Raskolnikov's turn toward sanity and contrition happens in just five days, as if he has suffered from temporary insanity, and that was all wrong. Raskolnikov's behavior is not an aberration or a fit of madness. It is a gradual descent, and it is more reasonable than it should be.

"A New Plan," Dostoevsky wrote in his second notebook. "The Story of a Criminal." He would confess eight years later—"in order to keep it completely at a distance," Dostoevsky noted to himself. Raskolnikov would gain clarity after slowly recognizing his guilt. But this plan was also problematic. A belated confession still made Raskolnikov's fear and confusion remote. His delusions and fever dreams, the bulldog just behind the door, the landlady pleading on the landing below. The reader must experience these things just as the murderer does.

"Rummage through all the questions in this novel," Dostoevsky noted to himself. At some point in late November, one question must have occurred to him: What if the most intimate perspective isn't actually the first person? What if we could be even closer to the murderer by lurking a half step behind him, looking over his shoulder, close enough to hear his quickening breath, to see his eyes darting, to think and feel what he thinks and feels not because the murderer narrates it but because we hear it slantwise from someone more lucid, someone who could be Raskolnikov's double. The narrator would be "invisible but omniscient," Dostoevsky decided, someone "who doesn't leave his hero for a moment." The half-step distance from Raskolnikov allows the reader to follow all his actions, thoughts, and emotions, without being overtaken by them.

This intimate third-person perspective changed everything. Dostoevsky later wrote to Vrangel, "At the end of November much had been written and was ready; I burned it all. I didn't like it myself. A new form, a new plan excited me, and I started all over again." It's unclear if he actually burned anything, though it surely felt that way. Dostoevsky had finally found a portal into his character, and it led to new possibilities. If we are going to get so close to a murderer—if we are going to witness his delusions, eavesdrop on his fears and rage, follow him as he evades capture—then why not go further back into that midsummer evening, before Raskolnikov rushes up to his room, trembling and weak, before he takes off his clothes and pulls his coat over himself like a blanket? Why not peer over Raskolnikov's shoulder while he's face-to-face with the stupid, deaf, sick, greedy pawnbroker, waiting for his moment? Why not be startled by the sudden appearance of her pregnant "idiot" sister, Lizaveta, standing in the doorway?

Sixteen

An Ax

H e rushed to the door, listened, snatched his hat, and started down
his thirteen steps, cautiously, inaudibly, like a cat." Rodion Roma-
novich Raskolnikov stalks down the street in a loose-fitting coat
and a ragged top hat with holes and stains. He is poorly dressed yet remarkably handsome. Tall and slender, dark blond hair and beautiful eyes. He has
an ax inside his coat. It's dangling from a homemade sling—a long strip of
fabric torn from an old shirt, doubled over, and stitched under the left armhole
inside his coat. He slid the handle through the loop, and now he steadies it
with his left hand in his pocket. No one can tell.

He crosses a small footbridge over a canal, slips through the western edge
of the Haymarket, and turns west. He imagines tall, refreshing fountains as he
passes the Yusupov Garden. He avoids eye contact with passersby but catches
a glimpse of a clock in a shop. Already 7:10 in the evening. He should hurry,
but he can't. He's taking a roundabout route so he can approach the building
from the far side. At some point he reaches the embankment of the same canal
he crossed earlier. He turns right and hears a clock striking half past seven. It's
taking longer than it should. He presses his thumping heart, adjusts the ax, and
slips through the gate of a large house facing the canal. He climbs the dark
stairwell. The building is divided into small apartments for petty clerks, cooks,
locksmiths, and young single women. He was here about six weeks ago pawning his father's silver watch and a ring his sister gave him as a keepsake. That
was the day the idea began hatching in his head like a baby bird.

She lives up on the fourth floor with her abused sister. He's still breathing heavily as he listens at her door, carefully and more carefully. Everything is silent. He feels for the ax again, and his heart pounds harder. He rings her tin doorbell—a feeble jingle, then nothing. He rings it louder. Again nothing. He presses his ear to the door. He's fairly certain he can hear her hand touching the latch and her dress brushing against the door. He's fairly certain she is also listening, pressing her own ear against her side of the door, just inches from his own.

He regroups and rings the bell again as a normal person would. A moment later, he hears the latch being lifted. The door creaks open, and two sharp eyes peer out. He pulls hard, jerking her skinny arm and torso forward—she's still holding on to the handle. He barges through the doorway as she moves aside, saying nothing, staring. The pawnbroker's yellowing fur coat and flannel rags lend her some semblance of bulk, but her neck and legs are thin. Her hair is streaked with gray and heavily greased.

"Good evening, Alyona Ivanovna." His voice barely functions. "I've brought you . . . an article . . . but we'd better go over there . . . near the light . . ." He walks right through the room toward the window. Her apartment is dim, with yellow wallpaper, muslin curtains, and an old woman's spotless clutter—geraniums, chairs against the walls, prints of German ladies holding birds, heavy furniture, an icon in the corner.

"Lord! What is it? . . . Who are you? What is your business?"

He reminds her that they've met before, and he's brought something else to pawn. She glances at the wrapped object but focuses on him. He wonders if she's figured everything out. He considers running.

"Why are you looking at me like that, as if you didn't recognize me?" Raskolnikov says. "If you want it, take it—otherwise I'll go somewhere else. I have no time."

"But what's the matter, dearie, so suddenly . . . what is it?" she asks.

"A silver cigarette case—I told you last time."

She takes it from him.

"But why are you so pale? Look, your hands are trembling! Did you go for a swim, dearie, or what?"

"Fever," he says. "You can't help getting pale . . . when you have nothing to eat."

She asks again what's in the package, and he tells her. "But it doesn't seem like silver . . ."

She turns and walks toward the window while working on the funny knot. He unbuttons his coat and slides the ax out of the sling. He looks at her braid of graying hair and the tortoiseshell comb sticking out.

"Look how he's wrapped it up!"

Raskolnikov lifts the ax over his head with both arms. He swings it down mechanically, and the ax head's blunt end strikes the top of her skull. She cries and reaches for her head, still holding the tied package. She falls to her knees. He bashes her skull again. And again. Battering the same spot. He steps aside to let her body fall backward to the floor. Blood spills out of her as if from a toppled glass.

He bends down and looks at her face. Her eyes are bulging out as if trying to escape, and her expression is distorted in its final spasm of agony. He lays the ax down next to her and reaches into her right pocket while trying to avoid getting her blood on his trembling hands. He pulls out a steel ring of keys, runs into her bedroom, and starts on her chest of drawers. But the sound of the jingling keys makes him halt. No, it's too late to leave—but is she really dead? He runs back to the pawnbroker's body, grabs the ax, raises it over his head, and stops. He bends down and inspects her again, closely. Her skull is shattered, and he's on the verge of probing the wound with his finger when he jerks his hand back. Of course she's dead. She's in a pool of blood.

He notices a blood-soaked string around her neck. He tugs at it, but it's not loose. His hands start getting sticky with blood as he fusses with it. Finally, he manages to cut the string with the ax blade and pull it out. He's right. It's her purse. Suede with a steel clasp—stuffed. It's connected to a small icon and two crosses. He shoves the purse into his pocket, throws the trinkets on the body, and takes the ax to the bedroom. As he sets back to work on the chest, he notices a large notched key. It has to be for a trunk. He looks under her bed, and there it is: upholstered in red leather, studded with nails, nearly three feet long. The key fits.

Inside is a white sheet, a red silk coat with rabbit fur lining. He keeps digging. A silk dress, a shawl, some old clothes. It's frustrating. He begins wiping his bloody hands on the red coat when a gold watch falls out. There's jewelry hidden among the clothing—earrings, bracelets, pins. Some are in cases. Others are wrapped in cloth or newspaper and tape. He starts stuffing his pockets with the pawns.

He thinks he hears something—someone moving in the other room. Silence. Then, yes, a half-muted cry. He's squatting by the open trunk, listening, hardly breathing. Complete silence. He jumps up with the ax and runs to see.

Lizaveta is standing in the middle of the room. She is remarkably tall. She is pale, holding a small bundle, and staring at her murdered sister, the body and all the blood. Her whole body starts shaking when she looks at him. Even her face. She half raises her hand, and her open mouth is silent as she backs slowly into the corner. He charges forward with the ax. Her lips contort like a frightened child's, and she cannot even bring herself to raise her arms up in self-defense. She just watches him swing the ax. The blade splits the top of her forehead like wood, and she falls.

He grabs her bundle. Then he drops it and runs toward the entryway. He tries gathering himself together, but he keeps losing sight of the larger picture.

He spots a bucket of water on the kitchen bench, grabs the sliver of soap from the cracked soap dish on the windowsill, and begins washing his sticky hands in the bucket. He washes the blade and the handle, getting all the blood out of the grains in the wood. He dries the ax and his hands on a garment hanging from the kitchen clothesline. He inspects the ax by the window and slides it back into the sling inside his coat. He checks his clothing and dips a rag into the bucket to clean his boots by the kitchen's dim light.

Then he just stands there in the middle of the room, trying to think. Maybe this is all wrong. Maybe his carefully wrought plan is just a grotesque puppet jerking on a more substantial figure's strings.

"God! I must run! Run!" he says. But when he turns to leave, he realizes that the front door has been ajar the whole time. He slams it shut and fastens the latch.

"But no, again that's not it! I must go, go . . ."

When Raskolnikov tries to leave, he hears two voices near the stairwell entrance, then someone whistling idly on the landing below, then footsteps slowly ascending the stairs. The steps get closer until he can hear the man's labored breathing. Raskolnikov is paralyzed in the doorway. It isn't until the footsteps begin climbing to the fourth floor that he slips back into the apartment, eases the door closed, and silently slides the hook into the latch.

He crouches just inside the door, holding his breath, gripping the ax. He's inside listening the same way she listened. This is exactly like a dream.

The stranger rings the doorbell, waits a moment, and rings again loudly. He starts tugging forcefully on the door handle, and Raskolnikov watches in horror as the little hook jumps around in the eye, about to pop out.

"What's up in there, are they snoring, or has somebody wrung their necks? Cur-r-rse it!" The voice is booming. He's yelling their names. "Has someone done them in? Damned women!" he roars.

He tugs on the bell over and over again, as hard as possible. Then there's another set of footsteps and a younger voice. "What, nobody home?" And then, "How do you do, Koch!" They've played billiards together. They both have appointments; they both need money. They start speculating about where the sisters could be, and the younger man suggests asking the building's caretaker.

"But she never goes anywhere . . ." Koch says, tugging the door again.

"Wait!" the other shouts. "Look: do you see how the door gives when you pull?"

It was latched from the inside.

"So?"

"But don't you understand? That means one of them is home. If they'd all gone out, they would have locked it from outside with a key and not hooked it from inside." He pulls again.

"There, can you hear the hook rattling?" He can.

"But what are they up to in there!" He starts pulling violently.

"Wait!" the younger man shouts. "Don't tug at it! Something's not right here . . . you rang, you pulled . . . they don't open the door; it means they've both fainted, or . . ."

"Or what?"

The younger man persuades Koch to stay by the door while he gets the caretaker. He's studying to be a public investigator, he tells Koch, so he knows what to do. Koch waits a bit but loses patience and heads down. Raskolnikov unlatches the hook, rushes down the stairs, and is almost free when he hears voices below. As he starts running back up, he hears a commotion coming from one of the apartments.

"Hey, you hairy devil! Stop him!"

"Mitka! Mitka! Mitka! Mitka! Damn your eyes!"

Several men's voices echo in the stairwell. The younger man shouts, "It's them!" Raskolnikov decides there's no other choice but to confront them all. But as he charges back down—one floor away from the approaching men— he finds the door to the second-floor apartment wide open. The floors have just been painted, but the painters are nowhere in sight. Raskolnikov slips into the apartment and presses himself against the wall just as the men reach the landing and continue up to the pawnbroker's apartment. He waits for them to pass, slips out of the apartment, down the stairs, through the gate, and into the street bustling with citizens. "He effaced himself among them like a grain of sand."

By December 1865, Dostoevsky had sent the first section of *Crime and Punishment*, which ends with the graphic ax murder scene, to the editorial office of *The Russian Herald*. He received no response, neither to the pages themselves nor to his requests for money. He was selling the last of his books and pawning his clothing. He was working quickly to finish the novel's second part: Raskolnikov falls ill, and Razumikhin nurses him to health. Marmeladov gets crushed under the wheels of a carriage, and Raskolnikov carries the mortally wounded drunkard back to his apartment, where he meets Sonya, Marmeladov's daughter from his first wife, and the half siblings she's now supporting by prostituting herself. The plot was advancing rapidly, but Dostoevsky was getting worried. Were they even going to publish it? The journal would start running the novel in its first issue of 1866, which was due to be out by the end of January. He could have expected to see proofs by now, or at least some plan for publication, or simply an acknowledgment of receipt.

Fed up with the silence, he wrote to Katkov asking for seven hundred rubles and a confirmation of the journal's intentions. "I do not know when my novel will be published," he wrote to Katkov, "and in fact whether it will still be published by you." Being ignored was humiliating and nerve-racking.

Getting clear answers, he wrote to Katkov, "is very important for my equilibrium." If *The Russian Herald* had decided not to publish *Crime and Punishment*, time was running out to find another journal that would. "If you do not like my novel or if you have changed your mind about publishing it, I ask you to send it back to me." He was pinning all his hopes on it—"too many hopes," he conceded, but he stood by his writing, odd and disturbing though it may be. "I ask one more thing," he concluded his letter, "if you intend to publish my novel, I ask the editorial board of *The Russian Herald* most earnestly not to make any corrections in it. I cannot agree to that *under any circumstance*."

Dostoevsky was right to be worried. It was quite possible that *The Russian Herald* might alter his novel or refuse to publish it altogether. A new censorship law was just handed down that made Russian journalists and editors subject to criminal punishment for violating guidelines that the law itself did not even name, and Dostoevsky's novel was testing whatever new limits were now in effect. A newspaper could describe a murder scene, but such stories were forensic reconstructions of violence. Crime reporting was a form of journalism not unlike the physiologies of the 1840s. It was sensational, admittedly, but justifiable as an examination of society's persistent problems—drunkenness, poverty, violence—the exposure of which could spur public action.

Even if this is what Dostoevsky wanted—even if this is *exactly* how he imagined *The Drunkards* before Raskolnikov hijacked the story—the manuscript he had sent was entirely different. Dostoevsky was narrating the act of murder, not reconstructing a crime scene. It was unseemly for any serious literary journal to publish a story that follows a man up a stairwell and reveals every detail as he commits two bloody ax murders. And the fact that it was a novel made the project even more unseemly. It smacked of sadistic indulgence.

And *The Russian Herald* might have been surprised by the pages they received. Dostoevsky promised Katkov a "psychological account of a crime," but the novel's first section featured more violence than nuanced psychology. His proposal barely mentioned the murders.

Katkov had no indication that Dostoevsky would narrate the scene at all, let alone in such vivid detail, because the author himself did not plan to. But then Dostoevsky began to circle closer, allowing himself to imagine the murders, letting them come into focus. In one notebook entry, the pawnbroker's surprise visitor—the young man studying to be an investigator—"tells how they entered the room and saw the bodies." In another note, Raskolnikov says, "it's horrible to kill," after which Dostoevsky writes, "Picture of spilled blood, the old woman, poor Lizaveta." It would not stop there.

Dostoevsky's imagination was insatiable. If there were a darker, more sinister place, something more painful or morbid, some indication that he could go deeper into the abyss, his mind took him there—he couldn't help it. He had a compulsion not just to open a wound but to examine it, to probe it with his finger. It was this compulsive curiosity that made him seek out the Siberian prisoners' most disturbing stories in the middle of the night in the hospital, the same curiosity that demanded detailed descriptions of what it feels like to be beaten with birch rods, that made him want to know why Sirotkin killed his company commander with his bayonet and how Orlov could kill so wantonly yet maintain such self-possession, like a Speshnev, like a Lacenaire. He never tired of the subject. One must study so many murders to write just one murder story effectively.

What is it like—what is it really like—to murder someone? It is inappropriate to ask such a question, and yet the most callous and despicable thoughts somehow find their way in. How would a murderer look at his victim before sliding an ax out of his loose-fitting coat? What sound does a dead body make when it hits the floorboards? It must be wicked to think about things like this, and to dwell upon them is surely corrupting. It can be nothing other than the devil's work to sit down at a desk, to light a candle, to arrange your notebooks, your pens and ink, and to imagine how a woman's skull would crack open when an ax splits her forehead apart. And yet the moment Dostoevsky placed the idea of a murder somewhere off in the far margins of his story, it was only a matter of time before he would move it to the center.

So in the late autumn of 1865, as he started rewriting *Crime and Punishment* through an attached third-person perspective, Dostoevsky began narrating the murders in excruciating detail. His oblique note—"picture of spilled blood"—became one detail in a fully imagined act of violence. The ax crashes down on the pawnbroker's skull, and, Dostoevsky writes, "blood poured out as from an overturned glass." He imagined the weapon's weight in the concealed sling made from the fabric of an old shirt that Lizaveta might have mended. He imagined the murderer's thoughts as he walks up the stairwell, the pawnbroker's stubborn grip on her door handle, how Lizaveta stares, how she barely moves as she tries warding him off, how the warm blood feels on his hands.

It might not have been clear to the editors of *The Russian Herald*, but Dostoevsky's painstaking narration of the brutal crime was crucial to the novel's philosophical goals. The vivid details dispel Raskolnikov's "strange, 'unfinished' ideas floating in the air." Any reader who believes we should weigh pleasures against pains—or who thinks that murdering a "useless" person is justifiable if it produces a mountain of useful deeds—would reconsider once the act is no longer a matter of entries in a ledger, once we see its impact on fully fleshed human beings. It's essential to hear Alyona Ivanovna breathing, to see the comb in her greasy hair, to listen to her asking Raskolnikov why he's so pale. It's essential that Raskolnikov confronts the women as full bodies pointedly alive. It's essential that the murders are visceral, that Raskolnikov slaughters them with an ax instead of poisoning or suffocating them, and that he has to scrub their blood out from under his fingernails.

A good novel is an excellent rebuttal to a vague theory. Dostoevsky wanted the murder scene to pull readers out of the floating world of ideas and thrust them into a swamp of details: the doorbell's jingle, the bloody string around the pawnbroker's neck caught on something he can't see, Lizaveta's unexpected arrival. Raskolnikov's plan crumbles. There are too many keys to test. He spends too much time washing his ax and hands. He leaves the door open. He's wearing his dilapidated top hat despite having reminded himself how conspicuous it is. Raskolnikov intends to be calm and logical, but his emotions are unruly. He can't steady his pounding heart. "Am I not pale . . . too pale?" he thinks. "Am I not too excited?" He can't stop sweating. ("Did you go for a swim, dearie, or what?") His hands go numb. Unexpected thoughts intrude. He finds himself standing in the middle of the crime scene, bewildered, amazed at how he "forgot the main thing and clung to trifles." A spot of blood can bring down a mountain of good.

And something else was happening in the pawnbroker's apartment. As Dostoevsky continued to imagine what it was like to be Raskolnikov, another, deeper motive began to swing into view: Raskolnikov craves absolute power over someone. He does not, after all, have to kill the pawnbroker to take her money, but he never considers any other way. Dostoevsky drafted a scene in

which Raskolnikov meets Razumikhin and several others, including the police clerk. They are at a tavern when the conversation turns to the law, and
Raskolnikov asks, do they even realize that "no one who has power ever obeys
these laws? Napoleons trampled on them and changed them." Razumikhin
has just warned him that everyone thinks he's gone mad, but it makes no
difference. "I take power," Raskolnikov declares, "I seize strength, whether
money or power, but only for a good end."

And yet how much does the good end matter? How much did it ever
matter? Dostoevsky was not adding another motive to Raskolnikov's psychology. He was changing the motive. Raskolnikov's altruistic plans are vague
because they are just a pretense for his despotic spree. In early 1866, Dostoevsky stepped back, as he would from time to time, and wrote a large heading
in his notebook: "The Idea of the Novel." Beneath the heading, we see the
author revising Raskolnikov's fundamental nature mid-sentence:

> *In his portrait* the thought of immeasurable pride, arrogance, and
> contempt for society is expressed in the novel. His idea: assume power
> over this society ~~so as to do good for it.~~ Despotism is his characteristic
> trait.

It was clearer to Dostoevsky, now that he was fully imagining the murders,
how easy it would be to seize despotic power over people. You walk up the
stairwell. You ring the doorbell, and she opens the door for you. It was also
clearer that the barriers keeping us from committing heinous acts are primarily
of our own making. Raskolnikov is baffled when he thinks he hears the lieutenant assaulting his landlady downstairs in the middle of the night. "How is
it that she permitted it?" She doesn't, of course. In a later notebook, Raskolnikov
answers his own question: "I permit myself." This is the despot's mantra.

It had long been clear to him how despotism was a pleasure. Raskolnikov
embraces his thirst for power in subsequent notebook sketches. "I'm a despot;
I hate everyone," he admits. "I know that I want to wield power over others
and that's enough." It's not that Raskolnikov has given up on philosophy. It's
that he now stands on different philosophical grounds. Dostoevsky began
reaching back beyond Chernyshevsky and Pisarev, beyond the 1860s radicals

and nihilists, to the eminence who had been hovering over the Russian intelligentsia for decades: Hegel. Dostoevsky was convinced that radicals would use
Hegel's idea of a world-historical individual who "must trample down many
an innocent flower" as a way to justify their violent, domineering egoism.
Murder the tyrants to move history forward. Murder the exploitative pawnbrokers to facilitate the emergence of Spirit. It's no coincidence that Raskolnikov's model is also Hegel's apotheosis of the world-historical leader: Napoleon.
There are many Napoleons—Raskolnikov thinks *he* could be a Napoleon, and
Napoleons like himself *trample* on laws, take power, grant permission to themselves because they want to—"and that's enough." The danger of ideas is their
malleability. It's easy to make Hegel's idealism serve the solipsistic, destructive
egoism of Max Stirner. And it's easy to swing an ax.

Crime and Punishment had a tumultuous start. In three months, the sensational tale that began as a means to escape gambling debts in Wiesbaden grew from a ninety-page story to the longest, most ambitious novel
Dostoevsky had ever written, and even when it was supposedly just weeks
away from appearing in *The Russian Herald*, so many things remained fluid.
Nothing—not even the "floating" ideas the novel would attack—could be
nailed down. Dostoevsky began letting his own uncertainty drive the story
forward. In a way, he had no choice (the first chapters, after all, were due),
but his insistence upon continually revising the plot, the narrative perspective,
and his central character began to give *Crime and Punishment* its distinctively
unsettling character.

Dostoevsky was writing an inverted murder mystery. The reader knows
who the killer is, and yet knowing the perpetrator only increases the mystery
surrounding him. The murderer's motives would be the narrative's central
mystery. "Why did I do the murder?" That question in Dostoevsky's first
working notebook loomed ever larger. In his second notebook, even as he
reconsidered his overarching plan (under the heading "Chief Anatomy of the
Novel"), Dostoevsky marked out an unfinished task: "Explain the whole murder one way or another." The problem went beyond settling on what motivates
Raskolnikov. Dostoevsky was also struggling with how to turn something

straightforward—why someone does something—into a dramatic puzzle, a funny knot that Raskolnikov himself cannot untie.

That's when Sonya started to emerge in Dostoevsky's drafts, as if she had been waiting for Dostoevsky to notice her in the margins—a stepdaughter, a prostitute, the tragic victim of Marmeladov's drunkenness, a meek woman with flashes of vulnerability and strength. Sonya thinks of herself as a sinner "beyond salvation," which makes her somewhat brittle. "Once insulted she is beside herself," Dostoevsky wrote in one note. She is quiet, and "then suddenly she would burst out laughing terribly at trifles." Bearing the burden of supporting her three half siblings after Marmeladov's death is not sufficiently redemptive. In one sketch, Sonya is taking care of one of Lizaveta's children, a girl named Sassia. "Auntie," the girl calls her.

Sonya's combination of compassion and social marginality makes her particularly appealing to Raskolnikov. Dostoevsky originally imagined him confessing to Razumikhin, but surely Sonya would be the one to draw him out; surely, Raskolnikov thinks, she could pity him and forgive him for his crimes. Dostoevsky began drafting scenes of Raskolnikov confessing to Sonya, but now the murderer's confession shifts from the story's resolution to the moment the story begins in earnest. She listens to him and asks, rather simply, "But why is it that you haven't even glanced into the purse?" If the money is so crucial to his arithmetic, why isn't he even curious about how much he took? Raskolnikov does not have an answer.

Sonya attempts to pierce Raskolnikov's isolation, and it is clear he's been adrift in Petersburg. His mother and sister arrive from the provinces and comment on how strange he is, how different he appears. "Don't talk to me about the way I look. Don't ask me about my health."

He rebuffs Sonya as well. "Why do you come to me?" he asks.

"*You can't live without people!*" she says, holding Lizaveta's baby in her arms. He insults her repeatedly, trying to push her away, though she is undaunted, continues to visit him, and draws him into conversation.

"What does happiness consist of?" she asks him.

"Happiness is power."

The most important thing is silent. "Not a word between them about love," Dostoevsky noted to himself. "This is a *sine qua non*." Falling in love feels like a defeat to him, as if it drains his despotic power. "Sonya and love broke him," Dostoevsky wrote. Her questions made him think.

But how could someone love a murderer? There is, admittedly, some element of his pride that appeals to her—his defiance of conventions and prejudices, his insistence that she need not feel shame for selling her body. Dostoevsky experimented with different ways for her to feel that love after his awful confession. "She rejects him and is afraid." He imagined the relationship culminating in a letter Sonya writes to Raskolnikov. Dostoevsky writes the gist of it and reminds himself to compose it skillfully. "I love you, I will be your slave."

But that wasn't right. In another planned exchange, he's the one who says it, and she is far from slavish.

"I love you."

"Give yourself up," she responds.

Dostoevsky improved upon the exchange in his third working notebook.

"I love you and that's why I told you," he says.

"You need me and that's why you love me."

Raskolnikov philosophizes, but she's the perceptive one, and Dostoevsky did not imagine her as brittle anymore. Raskolnikov tries persuading her of the logic of his crime.

"She's a louse," he insists, referring to the pawnbroker.

"*No, not a louse*. And if she's a louse, why are you suffering so?"

"Well, it's arithmetic; whoever will prevail."

"Perhaps you're not so strong," Sonya says.

"Don't torment me with that nonsense. Don't you think I haven't thought this and suffered over it? Others do it, Napoleon, etc." She is unmoved by this. "Listen," he says, "there are two kinds of people. Those who are superior can cross over obstacles."

The more impervious Sonya is, the more his arguments seem to wither.

"Napoleon, Napoleon, but perhaps it's not that."

"Not that."

PART III

———— • ————

But I shall tell you that you do in fact believe me, you've already believed me for a foot, and I'm going to get you to believe me for a whole yard, because I'm genuinely fond of you and sincerely wish you well.

—Porfiry Petrovich

Seventeen

Headsmen and Victims

L acenaire wrote in a dark cell in the Conciergerie, a centuries-old prison overlooking the Seine. It had been good enough for Marie Antoinette, though his cell was much smaller, eight by twelve, in the Caesar Tower at the end of a vaulted gallery. They had given him a table and a lamp along with quills, ink, and paper.

> *Dear Public,*
>
> *Your curiosity has been so captivated by my latest capers, and you have been so keenly interested in the least thing connected with me, that it would be more than ungrateful of me not to gratify you. What have I to gain by holding my tongue, anyway? I foresee a whole shower of phrenologists, cranium-feelers, physiologists, anatomists and I don't know what—birds of prey that live on cadavers, hurling themselves on mine without even letting it get cold.*

Lacenaire's cell had a stove for warmth and four chairs for visitors. He smoked a pipe stuffed with cheap tobacco, his favorite kind, and a guard slept on a small bed next to his own in case he tried to kill himself. Sometimes he wrote late into the night. He filled pages with small, clear script and used the margins for corrections and additions. He had to write quickly. His lawyer had filed an appeal, but there wasn't much time before the guards would come to take him. He was not afraid of death—he said this repeatedly—but he wanted to tell his readers everything: his motives, his reasoning. "I have decided that I, while definitely in the land of the living, sound in mind and body, will perform my autopsy and dissect my brain with my own hands."

Lacenaire had at least three phrenological examinations in the weeks before his execution. The theory of phrenology is simple. Different "organs" in the brain control different faculties and behaviors, from the perception of time to the capacity for wit. A developed organ expands and therefore pushes the skull outward, leaving an indicative bump. Atrophied organs leave indentations. Phrenologists charted thirty-five different cranial organs, turning the human skull into a map of the tendencies of the brain inside it. They deduced a person's capacity for hope by examining a spot where the frontal and parietal bones meet. Did it bulge? Was it flattened? The love of exquisite things is just below the temporal ridge. The love of children is high on the occipital bone, and language is in the eyes.

Lacenaire had a large protrusion just above his ear, the sign of an overly developed organ of destructiveness. Other bumps suggested cunning, firmness, and vanity. The only perplexing discovery was at the center of Lacenaire's forehead, right at his hairline. Word shot through the press that Lacenaire had a rather large organ of benevolence—all of the phrenologists agreed. Skeptics had a field day, but one phrenologist clarified everything: Lacenaire's organ of destructiveness was so massive that it "restricted his free will" and canceled out his virtuous features. People were focusing on one organ's size rather than on the entire skull's proportionality. Classic phrenological mistake. Lacenaire considered phrenology nothing but a science of falsehoods. "Do you know what I love above all?" he asked an old friend while in prison. "The truth." And there wasn't even an organ for that.

When word leaked out that Lacenaire was writing his memoir, many worried that it would spread his revolutionary philosophy to anyone with fifteen francs to spare—"certainly many women will read it," one newspaper lamented. Yet it was less a diatribe about systemic injustice than a detailed chronicle of the most important struggle Lacenaire knew: the injustices committed by his family, his teachers, his employers, and his friends against himself. Readers would understand why he turned to crime if they knew who he was, and he would never change. He had stood alone against society since the age of eight.

Lacenaire claimed he had no real interest in money. Had he known that there were only a few francs hidden in the widow Chardon's armoire, he still would have taken his sharpened file to that apartment with Avril. It was a protest written in blood, he said, a protest "against the appalling order you have set up in Nature for yourselves." Poverty and prisons were the order of the world, and he knew it well. His schoolmasters were the first to imprison him. About two weeks before completing his studies at the College of Chambéry, Lacenaire objected when one of the masters, a priest, was about to punish one of the school's youngest boys. He insisted it was unjust, so the master decided to punish Lacenaire as well, which he resisted violently. The college was not forgiving on the matter of students raising their fists against priests, so they locked Lacenaire in a disciplinary cell for the rest of the term. "I broke down three or four doors at different times to get out," he wrote. He strolled through the headmaster's garden in the middle of the night, and sometimes he walked into town. During the day he wrote poetry to pass the time. It was only out of respect for Lacenaire's devout father that the school did not expel him, so his father put things in perspective when he received a bill for the broken doors and forced locks.

The family had grown used to Pierre-François's problems at school. His father had to remove him from the College of Saint Chamond after he exposed other students to a heretical Protestant book. He was always getting into unassigned books. He would skip school during the day and read novels at night, shielding his candle so he wouldn't get caught. *Don Quixote*, *Robinson Crusoe*, *Gil Blas*, *Tristram Shandy*. He adored Molière and recited La Fontaine by heart. At twelve years old, he was reading Rousseau, Voltaire, and Diderot. Helvétius, Volney, and d'Alembert—philosophers he was drawn to specifically because he was told to avoid them. "What reading!" It was a miraculous time, he recalled, a time when he absorbed "great and powerful ideas."

His enthusiasm for extracurricular reading was, according to one of his teachers, the root of Lacenaire's problem. One of the Chambéry priests remembered him as a talented, intelligent young man who "wallowed in evil readings," including the philosophes. His wicked readings made him not just indifferent to God but *unholy*. "All authority was odious to him, all law tyrannical, all morals unjust."

It was the assigned readings that Lacenaire found disturbing. When they began studying ancient history, he was horrified by the scale of the injustice. Centuries seemed reducible to a brutal binary. "Headsmen and victims—had I only the choice of one of these two parts?" And the more he considered it, the more it seemed as if the binary had seeped into daily life—the way people heaped abuse upon beggars, or the way they treated animals. Who gave humans the absolute rights they claimed over other creatures' lives? It troubled Lacenaire not just that people routinely hunted and slaughtered animals but that they made them suffer. He hated to see any living thing in pain. "Shame on the first philosopher who declared from the height of his learning that animals are machines and thus gave man the right to torture them at will, as a child amuses itself by twanging the springs of a clock!" Hunters felt justified cutting up their game while the animal was still breathing just so they could better satisfy their delicate palates. "You materialize animals," Lacenaire told his readers, "and I materialize you."

The only real law in history's appalling order was the ruthless pursuit of gratification. Egoism. "It is a knowledge," he said, "which dries up the heart." Were there any exceptions? What was friendship other than an advantage-seeking arrangement where each party dupes the other? Christianity was one of the purest and most beautiful expressions of egoism, a religion designed to make people happy until the churches corrupted it. And there was a righteous pleasure in punishment. Society will decapitate him, Lacenaire believed, because its entrenched egoism deemed him a threat to its existence, and surely a crowd will watch his decapitation with satisfaction. There was a pleasure in hatred, too, in the public's hatred for him and in his own hatred for every new injustice. We dress up our hatred as virtue so we can love it unashamedly.

Lacenaire explained how the crucial turn in his life came in 1829, when he deserted from the army and came home to find that his family had lost its fortune and had left the country without him. He spent a month wandering the streets of Paris, trying to find a job, a place to stay, some bread. He tried writing. He asked for help and got nothing. He begged. It was humiliating. When he eventually found work as a scribe, the wages were minimal, his employers took a third of his fees, and they tyrannized and belittled him. It dawned upon Lacenaire that he was now on the other side of the binary—no longer a headsman but a victim. "I saw on one side a society of rich ones, sleeping amid their delights and shutting their hearts to pity; on the other, a society of the poor, begging the necessities of life from those swollen with superfluity."

That's when he made his decision. "The social structure must be attacked," not superficially, but at its foundations. And who better to do this than him? One month later, he stole a horse and cabriolet so that he could get thrown into prison, form alliances, and begin his onslaught upon society in a spectacular criminal career. It never occurred to Lacenaire to turn to politics. He was "one man alone against the world," he said. He himself was all he needed. In fact, all those nights he spent reading Rousseau and Diderot by candlelight, all those ideas he was absorbing—they were ideas he had already known. That was why reading felt so familiar, he concluded. The truth was within him. Justice was within him: "Only I can decide whether I have done wrong or right to Society." And upon what unbreakable facts did he decide to build his new structure? He knew he was hungry. He knew that he was wealthy and then he wasn't. He knew he had a family and then his family left. He knew his parents preferred his older brother. He knew they never loved him. "My birth gave my parents no pleasure."

As ideas and ideals faded into ghosts, so did the margins that defined his enemies. The callous, egotistical wealthy blended with the Mallet Bank and the Rothschild Bank, and the banks blended with their collection clerks, and the clerks blended with Chardon (Aunt Madeleine, Lacenaire's enemy), and Aunt Madeleine blended with his mother, the poor "widow Chardon," who was never more than exactly that. Not once during the trial or in any of the press accounts covering the murders did anyone ever refer to her by her name. It was Anne Marie Yvon Chardon.

Individual people faded. The margins of his motives faded, too. His protest against society would bob and plunge in the welter of hunger, humiliation, and rejection that he had endured since the day he was born. "I wanted my revenge to be as huge as my hatred," he wrote in his memoirs. The magnitude of the destruction became the only thing that mattered. He dreamed of the guillotine. He had dreamed of it so often that he worried when his beheading actually happened, it would no longer have "the charm of novelty." But this was a small sacrifice, for he knew his annihilation would blaze forth as a great lesson to everyone.

Eighteen

Diseased Imagination

Whatever qualms Katkov had about *Crime and Punishment, The Russian Herald* decided to publish it. Part 1 appeared in the January 1866 issue, alongside an account of Tsar Alexander I's childhood, an essay about the modern schismatic movement, and an installment of Wilkie Collins's novel *Armadale*. The opening section of *Crime and Punishment* took up eighty-five pages. The sheer size of it is part of what worried Katkov. Dostoevsky was now imagining six parts, and the story was growing far beyond his original proposal. Though they were getting Dostoevsky relatively cheaply (125 rubles for every sixteen pages), they weren't sure they could pay that rate for such a large novel. So Katkov sent emissaries to persuade Dostoevsky to reduce his price. "They're terrible skinflints," Dostoevsky wrote to his friend Vrangel. He was in the midst of a "smoldering battle." "With God's help," he wrote, "this novel may be a superb thing." All he needed to do was refrain from taking further advances and renegotiate after completing the first half, which he knew would "produce a sensation among the public."

Crime and Punishment was already producing a sensation. New subscribers flocked to *The Russian Herald*. Everyone, it seemed, was reading it—or at least trying to. One of Dostoevsky's friends recalled how the murder scene "caused people with strong nerves almost to become ill and forced those with weak ones to give up reading it altogether." Dostoevsky writes "with a truthfulness that shakes the soul," one reviewer announced. Another claimed that the novelist was taking on "enormous tasks," tasks "of unrivaled importance"—charting a soul's return to humanity from the most extreme perversion. It could only be accomplished by a writer with "exceptional skill," possessing a talent defined by its "depth and distinctiveness."

Others were appalled. One reviewer wrote that Raskolnikov is a wild man, the "product of a diseased, also partly delirious imagination." The review in the liberal *Contemporary* was scathing. "Who conveys the very act of murder in a most exhaustive picture with the minutest details?" Artistically, it was "pure absurdity, for which no justification can be found in the annals of either ancient or modern art." The reviewer was offended that *Crime and Punishment* linked "scientific convictions" to murderous impulses. The only people well served by the novel were "obscurantists" who see "light as the reason for all the evil in the world." Dostoevsky was promoting ignorance.

"What is this thing," another reviewer asked, a novel or a "psychological exploration"? It was generating "so much uproar and commotion," not to mention faux intellectualism, especially among provincial ladies (never a good thing!). They got together, spoke of the novel in whispers, and used the word "analysis" like a new scientific talisman. It would be far better to read about real trials rather than tales about crimes concocted by an author's "perverted tastes." Even readers who did not find it perverse found it disconcerting. Turgenev loved the novel's first part, but after the murder scene he thought the story devolved into "fusty introspection." It was difficult to get a handle on the novel. Reviewers offered wildly different assessments of Raskolnikov's basic nature. He was either a sick man (for whom nothing is as it seems) or a dastardly villain or a warmhearted intellect who had gotten lost in his ideas, who had become a nihilist and suffered for it.

Among the most anticipated responses was from Dmitri Pisarev, the chief advocate of the nihilism that Dostoevsky appeared to target. Pisarev had just been released from prison for his insurrectionist pamphlet when *Crime and Punishment* began appearing. He wept while reading it. His doctor, seeing the effect the novel was having on his nerves, forbade him to continue. Pisarev continued nonetheless. Dostoevsky's readers "have been deeply shaken" by the novel, he wrote in his review. *Crime and Punishment* has created a world in which "everything is happening inside out and our usual ideas about good and evil cannot have any binding force."

Dostoevsky's novel depicts a virtuous person turning wicked, and Pisarev elaborated on that depiction, just as he did for Turgenev's Bazarov. He imagined Raskolnikov's humiliations—rainwater seeping into his boots, noisy neighbors, tutoring a spoiled boy. Raskolnikov is not insane, Pisarev concluded. He is an "educated and highly developed" young man "drowning in a muddy swamp." His destitution made him a slave to damnable dreams. "He who cannot feed and dress humanly should not also think and feel humanly," Pisarev claimed, and nihilists needn't be offended by the novel because Raskolnikov's theories have nothing to do with the murder—he murders just for the money. Pisarev found Raskolnikov's theories unrecognizable in any case. The murderer conflates *all* crime with greatness. He links Kepler and Newton with killers and thieves. His ideas are "vague," "tangled and confused," a symptom of mental atrophy and perversion. Killing a pawnbroker would never alter a society of pawnbrokers, and declaring "open war" on society and its morals all by oneself is simply dangerous. Where could Raskolnikov get an idea like that?

Pisarev kept finding ways to dismiss Raskolnikov's theories. His review is well over twenty thousand words, and as it unspooled, the firebrand nihilist critic himself became unrecognizable. Pisarev rejected violence as an engine of history, and he rejected the notion that "a few select geniuses" could advance it. "Extraordinary people" bring about change "as calmly as possible"; history progresses by reason and persuasion alone. "I sharply disagree with his ideas," Pisarev said of Dostoevsky's implicit warning about nihilism's violent core, "but I cannot help recognizing in him a powerful talent." Following Raskolnikov's thoughts somehow changed Pisarev. Dostoevsky was more than just a "keen observer of morbid mental states," the critic concluded. He seemed to experience those states himself. And the effect was profoundly disturbing.

Years later, Tolstoy bypassed all these disputes. *Crime and Punishment*, he claimed, is not about analysis or nihilism or the vise grip of poverty. Even the murders are secondary. The novel's decisive moment is not when Raskolnikov lifts an ax up over his head. Rather, it takes place at some quiet, undisclosed instant long before, when Raskolnikov is struggling, idle and alone, thinking about accepting money from his mother and moving to Petersburg, and when a trifling stupefaction—"one glass of beer, one smoked cigarette," Tolstoy wrote—tilts him toward a long trajectory leading to his fatal decision. *Crime and Punishment* is not about how philosophy shapes our lives. It is about how consciousness shapes our lives. "From barely perceptible changes which take place in the arena of consciousness," Tolstoy wrote, "the most unimaginably important, limitless consequences follow." Raskolnikov's specific ideas are irrelevant. What matters is the frightening power of consciousness, that its gossamer threads can become lethal, and that its tiniest movements can change the world.

And the world seemed turned "inside out" for other reasons, as well. *Crime and Punishment* demolished the assumption that criminals are fundamentally different from everyone else: insane or recalcitrant, ineducable, phrenologically doomed, perhaps, or corrupted by circumstances, or perhaps just inherently evil, people with their crimes branded into their faces—surely nothing like anyone reading *The Russian Herald*. It disturbed them that Raskolnikov did not seem fundamentally different, that he might murder not because he was evil but because he, like them, wants to do good, and that he, like them, wants to take ethical ideas to their logical end. It was disturbing to walk beside a criminal and see that he, too, has virtues. Raskolnikov marvels at how easy it is to murder someone, and it terrified readers to understand what he means. Maybe the story of such a murder was more than just the ravings of a "diseased imagination."

I n late January, just days before the opening chapters of *Crime and Punishment* appeared, news reports of a similar homicide in Moscow began to circulate. A law student named Danilov murdered a pawnbroker in his apartment. He knew the place, having pawned a ring there weeks earlier. The men spoke briefly, familiarly, before Danilov killed him. As he was ransacking the place, the pawnbroker's servant unexpectedly arrived, so he murdered her, too. Then he washed his hands in the pawnbroker's bedroom and wiped them on his bedsheets and pillowcase. The investigators found a chaotic scene: drawers pulled out, items strewn across the floor, blood everywhere—on the steps and walls of the stairwell, on a five-ruble bill left behind, in boot tracks by the

front door. The murderer's galoshes were still on the landing, lined up innocently next to the pawnbroker's.

People commented on the similarities between Dostoevsky's novel and the
real-life crime. Danilov was well dressed in a blue frock coat—a "handsome
dandy," one journalist called him. He was "of fortunate appearance and great
intelligence," as the prosecutor later described him to the jury, "and yet, where
are his friends?" Dostoevsky thought his novel was indeed prophetic, that
what seemed like the product of a diseased imagination was, in fact, "real
realism," as he wrote to a friend, a realism deeper than what realists see. "With
them it's shallow sailing."

Many assumed Danilov's crime was ideological, like Raskolnikov's, and
there were good reasons to suspect that any pawnbroker's murder might be
an attack upon a principle. Private, informal lending had always been central
to the Russian economy. It was the way capital flowed in a country with a
small and unstable banking system, and informal lending networks strengthened Russian society. Borrowers typically solicited loans from friends or family
members—spouses or siblings, if possible, or in-laws and distant cousins, if
necessary. Lending tightened kinship ties. It created aristocratic patronage
networks and helped knit together Russia's social strata. Laborers borrowed
from merchants. Nobles borrowed from their serfs.

But pawnbrokers were different. They operated outside the networks of
honor and kinship. They were strangers. They were strictly transactional and
often predatory. They charged exorbitant—and illegal—interest rates to the
people who could least afford it. The typical rate in Petersburg was 10 percent per month, compounded. This amounts to an annual rate of more than
200 percent interest. If a borrower couldn't find the money to redeem his pawn
soon, it was likely lost for good. And pawnbrokers had little incentive to wait.
They lent only a small fraction of the pawn's worth and could sell it whenever
they pleased. Paperwork was minimal or nonexistent, and most pawnbrokers
knew not to ask about an item's origins.

Pawnbroking was legal but regulated, and abusive practices were growing
fast enough that the Third Section conducted sweeping investigations of Petersburg's pawnbrokers using informants, surveillance, and undercover agents
to compile records of their terms and practices, whom they dealt with, who

they were, where they came from. Officials already knew that pawnbrokers often belonged to marginal groups—Greeks, Poles, Jews, and, recently, a rapidly growing number of women—people with less social standing to lose and fewer ways to earn a living. The 1866 investigation found that there were dozens of pawnshops in Petersburg—too many to count, according to a Third Section agent. More than twenty advertised in the newspapers, which is how Danilov found his.

The story of a murdered pawnbroker reads like a story of retribution, an attack on financial predation and the growing precarity that made it possible. The glut of pawnbrokers in an informal lending society suggests that Russia's social fabric was fraying, that too many people lacked adequate social connections, and that even well-connected people were vulnerable. And so a new economy was emerging, and a new set of people was working at the ragged edges.

Dostoevsky was all too familiar with the world of debt profiteers, the Wiesbaden pawnbrokers who would lend on his watch, the Petersburg pawnbrokers who took his clothes and furniture, the debt speculators who bought up his promissory notes at a discount, people like Bocharov and Stellovsky, lying in wait.

And they are coming for Raskolnikov. Even as he slips back into the street with the cleaned ax hidden in his coat, disappearing like a grain of sand, Raskolnikov's creditors are pursuing him. When he is summoned to the police station the next day, he's thrilled to discover that he isn't a murder suspect, but his joy quickly drains away.

"There are complaints against you! You owe money!" Lieutenant Gunpowder informs him.

"But I . . . don't owe anyone anything!"

The police clerk presents him with a demand for 115 rubles—"overdue and legally protested"—from a promissory note that the widow Zarnitsyn offered in payment to a man named Chebarov (a name close enough to "Bocharov" to hurt).

Raskolnikov is astonished. "But she's my landlady!"

"So what if she is your landlady?"

"I absolutely do not understand what this promissory note is! She's now demanding that I pay, but how can I?" He launches into his history with his landlady, how he promised to marry her daughter, and when the daughter died of typhus a year ago, yes, it's true she made him sign a promissory note, but she swore she'd extend his credit indefinitely.

"All these touching details, my dear sir, are of no concern to us," Lieutenant Gunpowder says.

Raskolnikov cannot wrap his head around the fact that his personal debt is a circulating asset, and it's a crucial detail in the novel, a more subtle instrument of power than he can imagine, and a more cunning method of predation. Dostoevsky initially imagined Razumikhin explaining how promissory notes and debt speculators work. "There are, brother, such sharks in the world, which swim in the sea." They hunt for prey and disguise their greed as moral outrage at profligacy. The manipulation works. The shame of unpaid debt oppresses Raskolnikov. On the novel's opening page, he slinks past his landlady's door like a cat, and it isn't long before he imagines her being beaten on those same steps. But debt cannot be evaded. His unpaid rent is probably what forced his landlady to sell his promissory note in the first place.

D ostoevsky was writing *Crime and Punishment* in his study at night, which helped him approach the story with "a certain mood." His landlord would notice the novelist's light still burning in the early morning. Dostoevsky paid twenty-five rubles a month for a small flat at the top of a five-story building on Stolyarny Lane, just north of the Haymarket. His desk was a painted table in the corner. There was a ragged divan. The ceiling was low, and the study was six paces wide, like a cell.

He imagined Raskolnikov living in a room like this, waking up on the divan, gazing with hatred upon the dismal furniture, the peeling yellow wallpaper, and the dust floating in the long sliver of mid-morning light coming through the window. His circumstances become almost comically public. Raskolnikov receives a parade of uninvited guests throughout the novel, each of them struck by the room's shabbiness. Razumikhin routinely bumps his head on the lintel. It's like a "ship's cabin," he says. Descriptions throughout the novel shrink the room further. It is a "closet," a "cupboard," a "kennel," a "trunk." Raskolnikov's mother calls it a "coffin." And yet Raskolnikov doesn't want to leave it. He prefers to lie on his ragged divan, thinking, nurturing his spite. "I hid in my corner like a spider," he eventually tells Sonya.

Dostoevsky cloistered himself in his study in order to meet his monthly deadlines. "I never go anywhere, not to see a single acquaintance." It made him anxious and irritable. "My character has been ruined," he wrote to Vrangel. "I don't know what this will lead to." From time to time, his thoughts would circle around his deeper loneliness. "My kind friend, you are at least happy in a family, but fate has denied me that great and *only* human happiness."

His health deteriorated. He suffered from hemorrhoids so intense that he couldn't write for two weeks. When he recovered, he wrote while lying on his divan because sitting or standing caused painful cramps. And he was having seizures again. "Attacks of falling sickness torment me," he wrote to one of his sisters-in-law. The more intensely he wrote, the stronger they became. In February he wrote to his sister-in-law that he hadn't seen a doctor in two months: *"There is no time."*

And the longer he worked on *Crime and Punishment*—the more he let it grow—the nearer his most onerous deadline approached: the November 1 submission date for the novel he owed Stellovsky, a novel he had not even begun to think about. But focusing on *Crime and Punishment* was worth it. A resounding success in *The Russian Herald* would lead to lucrative volume editions. He'd reestablish his literary name, command more money for future work, and finally pay off his debts. "But here's the problem," he told Vrangel. "I may spoil the novel, I have a premonition of that. If I'm put in prison for debts, I'll spoil it for certain and won't even finish it; then everything will be wrecked."

D ebtors were exempt from Petersburg's House of Confinement if they owned property that could cover their obligations. Property seizures always preceded prison—hence the police inventory of Dostoevsky's possessions. Several regulations curbed Russia's system of debt imprisonment. The creditors had to pay for all confinement expenses, and though the fees were as little as five rubles per month, it was enough to discourage about half of Petersburg creditors from invoking their powers. After 1864, debtors owing less than one hundred rubles were exempt from confinement, and anyone owing less than two thousand rubles couldn't be confined for more than six months. Once the time was served—or when the creditor stopped paying the maintenance fees—the debt was canceled forever.

And yet even with these reforms, Dostoevsky's fear of debt prison was well founded. He owed more than two thousand rubles, and he was pawning the possessions his creditors might otherwise seize. The sight of his meager room was hateful in part because it indicated just how close he was to prison. And the fact that he owed so much money to so many people strengthened his creditors' leverage. They could split Dostoevsky's prison fee among them if they chose, or, as Stellovsky had shown him, one enterprising debt speculator could buy up more than two thousand rubles in his promissory notes and imprison him for up to *five years*. In fact, the reforms likely encouraged speculators to buy up a person's debts because now only the largest debt holders could threaten extended prison stays. And a high-profile borrower like Dostoevsky was an excellent opportunity for debt sharks like Stellovsky because there was a good chance someone would pay his debts for him—a wealthy aunt in Moscow, perhaps, or the editor of a major journal who now depended upon regular installments of a sensational new novel. Paper, ink, and quills were forbidden in debt prison.

Imprisoning debtors and depriving them of employment is a questionable method of securing repayment from them, but the practice continued partly because punishing debtors was a grand tradition. For centuries, Russian debtors were turned into forced laborers—galley oarsmen in the navy, for example, or spinners making linen—and the work was as much punitive as it was reparative. The presumption was that debtors deserved punishment. Repayment was an afterthought. Only the most extraordinary circumstances made chronic debt forgivable. A flood or a fire counted, as did theft and foreign invasion. Unemployment and severe illness did not. Most debtors had been designated "negligent" or "malicious," and eighteenth-century officials recommended that they be hanged so as to serve "as an example to others." Debt prison was a gentler example.

By the 1860s, it was easier to condemn the creditors. Lending once stitched the social fabric together, but now it seemed like a way to profit from the misfortune of strangers. The entire debt regime—the speculators, the circulating promissory notes, the property seizures, and the prisons—seemed a lot like the new, financialized economy in miniature. Tsar Alexander's reformed economy, now more than ever, was an economy dominated by investors funding remote concerns through larger banks or on growing stock exchanges, all of which further enriched the people getting paid for doing nothing. And for someone like Raskolnikov, mulling all of this over on his ragged divan, the magnitude of the injustice makes it easier to vilify while the absence of any legitimate means of protest in Russia made it even more difficult to stop, heaping helplessness upon helplessness. So it is easy to see how someone like Raskolnikov might decide to single out just one individual who could personify that injustice, to target an old pawnbroker who lives a ten-minute walk from his room, and to kill someone like Alyona Ivanovna.

It is no coincidence that Raskolnikov targets a woman. By the late eighteenth and early nineteenth centuries, Russian law granted women an unusual amount of economic power. Married women controlled their own property (including their dowry) and could shield it from their husbands' creditors. It did not take long for Russian women to use their property rights to build up their wealth. Women owned about a quarter of all businesses in nineteenth-century Russia, and many of the property owners throughout Dostoevsky's fiction are female. Raskolnikov resents his dependence upon women, resents their power. It's humiliating to slink past his landlady's door. It's humiliating to receive loans from his impoverished mother. It is humiliating that someone like Alyona Ivanovna exercises some measure of the despotic power that he believes belongs to him, and the fact that she is a woman infuriates him. That fury encourages him to take everything she has.

It is a cowardly despotism. It's easy to overpower an old woman, alone, with a twiggy neck and limbs. Surely there were better personifications of whatever grand injustice led him to his coffin of a room on Stolyarny Lane. While readers found Raskolnikov's crimes despicable, surely it must have occurred to some that the moral calculation might be different if an idealistic young man were to have a more consequential, more despotic target. Murdering a target like that would be a good rebuttal to Dostoevsky's novel unspooling in *The Russian Herald*.

. . .

Dmitri Karakozov wandered through the streets of Petersburg in a loose, disheveled peasant's coat, a red belt, and ragged pants tucked into high boots. His blond hair flared out from beneath a hat with a leather brim. It was early April, and he had been wandering for days, "machine-like," as he later put it, though his head "burned like fire." In his coat pockets he had morphine, strychnine, and a vial of cyanide. He also carried a letter addressed to someone in Moscow. "The results would be different if we had more money," it read, "if our strength were less restricted." He had gunpowder, five bullets, and a double-barreled flintlock pistol. He had a scrap of paper with one word on it, a name: "Kobylin."

Karakozov had been adrift in the city for about a month. He drank vodka. He worked occasionally at a factory for thirty kopecks a day. He had to avoid the police because he didn't have a passport to be in Petersburg. He started calling himself "Vladimirov." Sometimes he slept in hostels. Sometimes he slept under bridges. He had gone missing like this before. One time he went on a pilgrimage to a monastery north of Moscow. At other times he left suicide notes: "If God doesn't help, the devil will."

He had been a law student at Moscow University. He came from a poor provincial gentry family and had tried to make ends meet by tutoring, but it wasn't enough. The university expelled him for failing to pay his tuition. For days he sat alone, his face in his hands. He would lie on his bed and think, and he began to despise people. He developed various illnesses—stomach pains, chest pains, insomnia, and some sort of recurring fever. "Kobylin" was his doctor. He prescribed the morphine and administered electroshock therapy. Karakozov's nerves, after all, seemed to be part of the problem. When treatments failed, he began to wonder how a hopelessly sick man, a wrecked man like himself, could salvage something useful from his life. He wanted to "bring good to the people," he said. He wanted to summon their anger. He wanted to conjure widespread terror and unrest.

On April 4, 1866, he donned his disguise—the peasant's coat, the tattered pants, and the high boots. On top of his white shirt he wore a loose red one—a *rubakha*—that made him look more like a tradesman. One of his coat pockets contained two copies of his manifesto. He railed against the "gentry parasites, a horde of officials and other rich people" who "suck the blood of the peasant." Factory hands and laborers suffer while "others who do nothing live in luxurious houses and palaces." And the crimes came from the top. "It's the tsars who are the real culprits in all our misfortunes," he declared. It wasn't just Alexander II. It was all of them. He wanted to end the myth that the tsars were power, truth, and justice incarnate. His beloved people needed more than a manifesto, so he was going to give them "factual propaganda."

Karakozov walked along the ornate iron railing of the Summer Garden in the late afternoon. It was overcast and somewhat cold. He joined a small crowd at the garden's north gate. "My death will be useful to my dear friend the Russian peasant," his manifesto declared. Even if he doesn't succeed, his great deed would help the Russian people. "My death will be an example for them and inspire them."

Tsar Alexander II was finishing his walk through the garden's paths lined with statues of nymphs and dryads and the old gods. It was his daily ritual. His Imperial Majesty passed through the gate, and as he approached his waiting carriage, Karakozov emerged from the crowd. He drew his flintlock pistol, aimed for the tsar-villain's head, and fired.

He missed. Karakozov panicked and started running, but he was chased down by the police and bystanders. Moments after his apprehension, the tsar confronted his would-be assassin. The emperor said something that just a few people could hear, and Karakozov gave a brief answer.

Fear swept across the capital, which stirred up rumors of conspiracy: mysterious carriages were waiting near the garden gates, people said, multiple suspects fled the scene. The gunman was a "*blind weapon* of some secret machination," according to one newspaper. More sophisticated enemies were lurking all around, continually plotting destruction, slipping in and out of crowds. The government's silence regarding the investigation fed the rumors. In some accounts, he was a socialist. "Fools! I did this for you!" the assassin reportedly shouted out to angry onlookers. "And you don't understand."

Some said the gunman was drafting eloquent—even literary—confessions. Clearly he was educated. Clearly this was the beginning of the nobles' revolt against the tsar who had freed their serfs. The nobles, fearing a backlash, tried to nationalize the threat by insisting the criminal was a foreigner, but other rumors about just what was said between the tsar and his enemy indicated otherwise.

"Are you Polish?" the emperor asks.

"No," the assassin says, "pure Russian."

Motives were easy to conjure. The assassin was aggrieved for the peasants rather than the nobles, and assassination was vengeance for the tsar's onerous terms of emancipation.

"What do you want?" the tsar asks.

The response, some said, was, "What kind of freedom did you make?"

There were so many ways to imagine it.

"Why did you shoot at me?" the tsar asks.

"Because you promised the people land but did not give them any."

Or simply, "You cheated the people."

D ostoevsky burst into his friend Maikov's apartment shrieking, "The Tsar has been shot at!"

"*Killed?*"

"No . . . he was saved . . . Fortunately . . . but shot at . . . shot at . . . shot at . . ."

Dostoevsky was shaking, and the color had drained from his face. Maikov and his friends, worried he would collapse, gave him something to calm him down. Moments later, he ran back outside to commiserate with the crowds in the streets.

Dostoevsky's reaction was understandable because the very concept of tsaricide was terrifying. To kill a tsar is not like killing a president or a prime minister. The tsar is above all politics, all legislation, and all reform. Alexander II was the earthly authority sheltering the people, the state, and its institutions. For the tsar to be murdered by a single person acting alone—a law school dropout, a madman with a gun—was absurd. It was like coming home one day, opening the front door, and discovering that someone had stolen the roof— a bird alighting from an armoire, dew on the lamps, leaves blown into corners, under furniture, between pillows. Every sheltered thing felt preposterously exposed. When the news about Karakozov spread, Russians from Petersburg to Archangel to Iakutsk wondered how they would ever sleep peacefully under any roof again. This is the jarring fear that Karakozov wanted. He wanted to reset all of Russia's political machinery with one jarring act of violence and a manifesto amplified by the mass media. It was a program of terrorism.

For some, Karakozov's assassination attempt suggested that history might not be a pageant leading inexorably toward Hegelian Reason. To imagine a single bullet from a madman killing the emperor was to imagine history ruled by chaos rather than Reason. He might have failed, but would every assassin fail? Or maybe Reason is more devilish than anyone anticipated. Maybe the people who move history forward are not all emperors leading nations or Napoleons on horseback. Maybe they are unheard-of people, dropouts, eccentrics, the sick and impoverished, the insulted and injured carrying pistols and a few bullets. Maybe history catches on the gossamer threads of a single consciousness. What was clear after that April afternoon was that the premise of Dostoevsky's novel—a young man who murders for the greater good—had gone from being an eccentric representation of Russian radicals to being a harbinger of a new world.

The tsar appointed an investigative commission to uncover the extent of the plot against him, and it was clear that everything was about to change. The head of the Third Section and Petersburg's governor-general both handed in their resignations. The new Third Section chief was a hard-liner and "terrifyingly able." He consolidated the empire's disorganized antiradical measures under his command. Authorities began arresting, interrogating, searching, and imprisoning thousands of people in an empire-wide crackdown against radicalism. The most prominent nihilists were exiled. Suspicious students and intellectuals were tracked and surveilled. Dissenters referred to the repressive aftermath of April 4 as the White Terror.

The Third Section created a census of Russian nihilists. How anyone earned their place on the rolls was unclear, though investigators relied upon Russian fiction and journalism to sort out what a nihilist actually was. Internal documents cataloged their identifying features and paid particular attention to nihilist women: they had cropped hair, according to documents, and wore little round hats. Third Section spies tried going undercover as nihilists, though they had the habit of strolling in tight groups, as if in a detachment, and their "nihilist" attire was suspiciously identical. The authorities had better luck with brute force. Officers ordered women to remove their blue-tinted glasses and brought them in for questioning. The Petersburg police shamed nihilist women by giving them the yellow cards issued to licensed prostitutes. In Moscow, officials forced nihilist women to sign pledges that they would grow their hair long and wear crinolines instead of the plain dresses they favored. Women who broke their pledges were banished from the city for twenty-four hours.

The White Terror exploited the nationalism and xenophobia following the assassination attempt. Nihilism became a foreign disease. The enemies were Polish Catholics or members of Raskolnik sects like the Runners. The most comforting myth was that a peasant had saved the tsar's life. A man named Osip Ivanovich Komisarov, an apprentice hat maker, supposedly shoved the nihilist assassin just before he pulled the trigger on his double-barreled pistol, foiling his aim. The story was irresistible. Komisarov was made a noble and assigned a bodyguard. In a matter of days, his image was reproduced on posters and embossed on medallions and brooches. There were odes to Komisarov. There were Komisarov cigarettes, Komisarov pies and drinks. His portrait was paraded through the streets, and those who didn't remove their hats were vilified or beaten. His image reminded Russians that the tsar's greatest protection is the Russian peasants, who would always love him. The idea was endlessly soothing. There were Komisarov chocolates. There was a Komisarov beer. Someone wrote a "Komisarov Polka."

In May, Alexander issued an imperial decree vowing to protect the Russian people from any "false and harmful doctrines" that would "shake the foundations of society." The edict implicated the press in the spread of wayward ideas, and a special council began rooting out the evil lurking in literary circles. Booksellers were carefully monitored. Russia's largest liberal journals—*The Contemporary* and *The Russian Word*—were shut down indefinitely, and several people affiliated with *The Russian Word* were arrested. The Third Section began rounding up writers in the middle of the night. One writer remembers being so paralyzed by fear that he considered asking the police to put him in prison just to end his insomnia. The message was clear: Russian writers would fall in line or face consequences. Even Kraevsky—hardly a figure of dissent—was sentenced to two months in jail for printing an article that passingly referred to certain Russian Orthodox Christians as "unthinking."

The only writers who could feel safe in the spring of 1866 were those affiliated with Katkov. He had become a virulent critic of constitutionalism, federalism, and any reform that would weaken the tsar's power. He had become so aligned with tsardom, in fact, that a show of support for the esteemed editor of *The Russian Herald* amounted to a show of support for the state itself. Patriotic students gathered at Katkov's office to sing the national anthem repeatedly. He had the tsar's ear: Alexander read one of his publications, *The Moscow Gazette*, every day. Katkov later boasted that it was "the fortuitous organ of state activity." His publication didn't just cover policy, he insisted, it made policy.

A few weeks after the assassination attempt, Katkov advocated for more aggressive censorship measures. "What! Will freedom of thought suffer if the power to plot evil is reduced?" he asked. "Since when does liberal politics mean allowing the terrorization of society by evildoers aiming at the destruction of the state?" Katkov was advancing his politics and quashing rival publications simultaneously.

Katkov's bullying bothered Dostoevsky. As an ex-convict under government surveillance, and as a novelist lucky enough to write for perhaps the only editor who could protect him, Dostoevsky had every incentive to stay quiet, and yet three days after Katkov's article Dostoevsky sent him a letter. "Everyone is afraid," he wrote. People are "now fearfully awaiting a clamping down on word and thought" just when the government should be adopting more liberal policies. "How can you fight nihilism without freedom of speech?" he asked his editor. Silencing nihilists only increases their allure—it turns them into "sphinxes, enigmas"—and Russians would laugh at their ideas if they could read them.

He didn't want Katkov to villainize nihilists. They were, by and large, simply naïve. They believe in "enthusiasm for goodness and the purity of their hearts," he wrote. They believe in it so much, in fact, that they believe everything else is an obstacle—tradition, religion, all received wisdom, centuries of experience. Dostoevsky understood radicals better than Katkov did. He remembered what it was like to listen to the impassioned speeches at the

Petrashevsky Circle, to indulge the fantasies of Fourierism. He remembered the thrill of plotting a revolution, the power they felt in writing and printing incendiary words. He recognized his own youthful impulses in Chernyshevsky's Crystal Palace dreams and Pisarev's bold pronouncements: "That which can be smashed should be smashed." They want to sever all ties, he wrote to Katkov. "They are absolutely certain that they will immediately construct paradise on a tabula rasa." The great dream was to wipe everything away.

Nineteen

The Investigator

Dostoevsky submitted part 2 of *Crime and Punishment* about two weeks after the assassination attempt. He was late, and by way of apology he wrote to Katkov and referred vaguely to "bad health and domestic circumstances." Part of the difficulty might have been the way his novel was shifting ground. With the blood washed away, the loot hidden under a stone, and the last bloody scrap of fabric torn to shreds, Raskolnikov feels confident he's gotten away with it, but now the murderer's story is about to begin in earnest.

Raskolnikov wants to recover two items he pawned to the recently deceased pawnbroker: his sister's ring and the "two-penny" silver watch—"the only thing left of my father's," he says. Instead of reporting it to the police, he asks Razumikhin, wouldn't it be easier to get them directly from the inspector? Yes, that's a fine idea. The inspector happens to be a distant relative of Razumikhin's, and he's been busy tracking down the pawnbroker's former clients.

Porfiry Petrovich is standing in the middle of the room when the two friends enter his apartment. He's pug-nosed and clean shaven, short and heavy-set. Even his head and face seem puffy and round. He has a cheerful expression and yellowish skin. He is unimpressive. He's a bachelor in his mid-thirties, living alone at public expense. He's dressed casually and wears shoddy slippers, though his appearance has a feminine quality that makes him far more serious.

And there's something unsettling about his eyes—limpid, gleaming, and surrounded by nearly white eyelashes. He "blinked as though winking at someone." The inspector is pleased by Raskolnikov's visit. "I've been sitting here a
long time waiting for you."

Why has Raskolnikov come here? He's like a moth flying directly into a
candle flame, he thinks. Porfiry Petrovich invites Raskolnikov to the sofa
while he sits attentively at the other end. Raskolnikov explains that they've
come to collect the items he pawned to the unfortunate murder victim, and
the inspector tells him that he'll have to file an official statement. But there's
something odd about the inspector. Perhaps it's his jocular familiarity. At one
point he looks at Raskolnikov "with obvious mockery," the narrator tells us,
"narrowing his eyes and as if winking at him." Could that be right? "Raskolnikov would have sworn to God that he winked at him, devil knew why."
Then the thought suddenly comes to him: "He knows!"

"Your two things," the inspector says, "the ring and the watch, *she* had
wrapped up in one piece of paper, with your name clearly written on it in
pencil, together with the day and month when she received them from you . . ."

He has tracked down nearly all of her clients. "In fact," he said, "you are
the only one who has not been so good as to pay us a visit." And this is rather
surprising, given how important those keepsakes are. The conversation is suddenly hazardous, so Raskolnikov watches his footing.

"I was not feeling very well."

"He was in delirium and almost unconscious until yesterday," Razumikhin offers. He could barely even stand up, and then, when no one was
looking, "he got dressed and made off on the sly, and carried on somewhere
till almost midnight—and all that, I tell you, in complete delirium, can you
imagine it!"

"Really, in *complete delirium*? You don't say!" Porfiry shakes his head, the
narrator says, "with a sort of womanish gesture."

Raskolnikov explains that he went to rent an apartment where no one
would find him. He can afford it, he says, because he found "a treasure somewhere," though he gave it to the Marmeladovs for the poor drunkard's funeral.
He knows he should not have said any of this, but he's losing his self-possession.
His thoughts spin; his lips twitch. He apologizes to the inspector for boring

him with such trifles, but the inspector is not at all bored. "You have no idea how you interest me! It's curious both to look and to listen . . ."

His suspicions are so blatant it's insulting, and Raskolnikov can't shake the feeling that they are closing in. "Did Porfiry wink at me just now, or not?" The answer is crucial. "Either it's all a mirage or they *know*!"

One measure of Dostoevsky's talent is that he could make something as small as a wink turn all the gears in a complex relationship. Porfiry's tiniest movement is either an involuntary twitch or a cunning signal. Either it means nothing or it spells Raskolnikov's doom. He doesn't know how to read it, and he can't even tell if it happened. Raskolnikov wonders if *all* of his blinks look like winks, if the inspector's eyes always gleam on a horizon between empty sky and unsounded fathoms. He begins to scrutinize every detail: the way the inspector positions his body, the tone of his voice, the way he emphasizes the word "*she.*" In Dostoevsky's murder story, the detective is the mystery.

Yet the inspector's uncanny power is more precise than his ability to confound Raskolnikov. It's his ability to get so close to him so quickly. A wink is the perfect device for Porfiry. A wink intrudes. It draws a person into a brief, unasked-for intimacy, like a handshake held too long or a palm on the small of your back leading you through a doorway. It is a flirtation. Raskolnikov thinks the inspector's head moves with a "womanish gesture" and that his feminine figure makes him "more serious" because he senses that he has to read this man more carefully than other men.

But it's more complicated than flirtation. Even the plainest thing about Porfiry Petrovich is perplexing. He shambles and shifts. His laughter can be merry or mischievous or nervous or unnerving. Porfiry Petrovich is a trickster. At one point, Raskolnikov watches his facial features stretch and flatten, his eyes narrow to slits, and his body rock with laughter, all while keeping his eyes locked onto Raskolnikov's. His voice and posture might suddenly change. He can appear much older than he is, seemingly at will. The inspector is artless when he should be sly. He can be insincere seemingly on a whim. He once announced his intention of becoming a monk and kept the ruse running for two months. He pretended to be engaged, an elaborate joke occasioned by his purchasing a new suit. Razumikhin recalls how annoyed everyone was "There was no bride, nothing—it was all a mirage!"

"Are you really such a dissembler?" Raskolnikov asks him.

"And did you think I wasn't? Just wait, I'll take you in, too—ha, ha, ha! No, you see, I'll tell you the whole truth!"

The inspector initially played a bit role in the novel. Dostoevsky imagined a pragmatic, newly appointed official conducting a straightforward interrogation ("Why were you in the apartment with the old woman?") and Raskolnikov easily escaping it. The feckless inspector of Dostoevsky's drafts thinks several people are involved in the murders, including the two men pounding on the pawnbroker's door and a painter working in the apartment below. Dostoevsky imagines the inspector finally finding evidence and confronting the suspect. "Why was their blood in your apartment?"

But what if the investigation were different? Being captured by traces of physical evidence is a bit like Bazarov dissecting frogs under a microscope, and Dostoevsky wanted nearly the opposite of that. What if the inspector investigates Raskolnikov rather than the crime? Dostoevsky's great challenge was dramatizing what goes on in Raskolnikov's mind as he begins to understand what he has done. What if Porfiry draws it out?

Dostoevsky began to see him as a heterodox investigator who doesn't follow regular procedures or apply himself to normal sorts of evidence. "After you've lived a while," he tells Raskolnikov in one notebook sketch, "you'll see that there's something more than arithmetic in a crime." He begins following his instincts. Dostoevsky rethinks the inspector's simple response to Raskolnikov's declaration of innocence: "He's not the murderer then, he thinks." He crossed that sentence out for a new idea: "Porfiry remains convinced that he is the murderer." Porfiry sees criminals differently. Rational self-interest—the fear of punishment—does not deter them. "Be assured," he tells Raskolnikov in another sketch, "that up to now this alone has restrained society: Voices." Weightless thoughts slipping into a person's head. This is what Porfiry Petrovich begins to investigate.

So in the pages Dostoevsky finally submitted to *The Russian Herald*, he gives the inspector a window onto Raskolnikov's thoughts. Porfiry Petrovich mentions that he happened to read Raskolnikov's journal article a couple of months ago. Raskolnikov is taken aback. He submitted an article shortly after he withdrew from the university, but he didn't realize it was published. His article is called "On Crime." Porfiry is especially interested in a brief passage in which Raskolnikov claims that there are two types of people, the "ordinary" and the "extraordinary," and the law does not apply to the extraordinary people. Razumikhin can hardly believe his friend would write this—*entitled* to commit crimes? Not compelled by their circumstances?

This is the idea Dostoevsky initially imagined Raskolnikov telling Sonya, and now the murderer clarifies his ideas in dialogue with the inspector. An extraordinary man has the right to "step over certain obstacles" if "the fulfillment of his idea" demands it, he argues. If Newton or Kepler had to sacrifice a hundred people to bring about their discoveries, they would have had the right—the duty—"*to remove*" them. Extraordinary people are "destroyers." They're criminal by nature. History's great lawmakers—Lycurgus, Muhammad, Napoleon—shed blood mercilessly and broke old laws to create new ones. Every law has criminal roots.

Porfiry seems skeptical, so Raskolnikov tries to reassure him by claiming that any destructive obstacle-clearing must be proportional to the idea's value. And yet the Benthamite accounting problems—how to measure an idea, how many lives it's worth—seem thornier than ever. How useful is discovering the elliptical orbit of the planets? Or is it enough that it is true? And how true are Newton's laws if they themselves will ultimately become obstacles to be removed for newer laws?

Porfiry asks about distinguishing ordinary and extraordinary people. Don't people get mistaken? "Oh, it happens quite often!" Raskolnikov admits, but this shouldn't be alarming, because ordinary people never get far. And when they're caught, they needn't even be whipped, because the ordinary crave punishment. They repent publicly and whip themselves; it is "beautiful and edifying." Porfiry asks how many people have the right to go around stabbing others. "You'll agree, sir, it's a bit eerie if there are too many of them, eh?"

"Men of genius," Raskolnikov assures him, are "one in millions." Some law of nature—"some interbreeding of stocks and races"—ensures it. The greatest people, "the fulfillers of mankind," are one in billions. Raskolnikov values this degree of originality. The extraordinary may be destroyers, but he thinks of them as creative. He describes them as something like artists or writers with "the gift or talent of speaking a *new word*." Porfiry says he's heard most of these ideas before, but he grants the young man one thing: "What is indeed *original* in it all—and, to my horror, is really yours alone—is that you do finally permit bloodshed *in all conscience* and, if I may say so, even with such fanaticism." That idea, Porfiry says, is "more horrible than if bloodshed were officially, legally permitted."

"Quite right, it's more horrible," Raskolnikov responds.

Porfiry continues to press him. Wouldn't an ambitious lawgiver need money to execute his ideas? Might he not steal it? Raskolnikov considers it especially likely. He in fact seems happy to leap into every trap the inspector lays, so Porfiry sets a more blatant one.

"Now then, sir, it really cannot be—heh, heh, heh!—that when you were writing your little article you did not regard yourself—say, just the tiniest bit—as one of the 'extraordinary' people, as saying a *new word*—in your sense, I mean . . . Isn't that so, sir?"

"It's quite possible."

And could it be that he himself might step over an obstacle for the sake of humanity? That he himself might "kill and rob . . . ?" The inspector laughs as he says it, and his left eye winks.

Raskolnikov's encounter with the inspector triggers something ominous in the narrative. Later that day, Raskolnikov sees his building's caretaker pointing him out to a tradesman in a smock and a dirty cap. The man is older—slightly hunched, with a stern, wizened face. The tradesman looks him over carefully, sidelong, then slowly walks away. He asked about Raskolnikov by name, the caretaker says, so Raskolnikov runs after him, catches up, and asks him why he came. The tradesman just continues walking.

"But why do you . . . come asking . . . and say nothing . . . what does it mean?"

The man looks up at Raskolnikov. "Murderer!" he says, softly, clearly.

Raskolnikov goes cold. His heart seems to stop and then begins pounding. He feels weak but keeps walking alongside the man until he can no longer bear the silence.

"What is this . . . ? What are you . . . ? Who is a murderer?"

"*You* are a murderer," he says, loudly this time. His smile is filled with hatred, and Raskolnikov watches him turn a corner and walk away.

It is horrifying to be known. What made him think he was extraordinary? "Those people are made differently," he thinks as he lies on his divan at night. He is nothing next to Napoleon, a man who destroys much of Europe, squanders half a million soldiers in Russia, "and when he dies they set up monuments to him." Men like Napoleon are made of bronze. For them, "*everything* is permitted." But not for him. "An aesthetic louse is what I am, and nothing more." It occurs to him that maybe he decided to kill someone to prove he *wasn't* extraordinary. Maybe he secretly knew he'd be caught and committed this crime to punish himself for his arrogance. "Can anything compare with such horror!"

Raskolnikov finds himself walking through Petersburg in twilight under a full moon. The streets are crowded and smell of dust and stagnant water. A man waves to him from across the street, and when he approaches, he realizes it's the tradesman. Raskolnikov follows him down a side street. The tradesman waves again at a gateway, so Raskolnikov follows him up a familiar stairwell. He hesitates at the third floor, but he keeps going and finds the door of the top floor apartment wide open.

He steps through the dark entryway and tiptoes into the living room. It's filled with moonlight, and everything is silent. There's a sudden snapping sound, like a twig. He can hear his heart pounding and a fly buzzing at the window. In the corner, between the window and a cupboard, there's a woman's coat hanging like a curtain. He draws it aside, and there she is. The pawnbroker. She's hunched in a chair with her head down like she's trying to hide."

He pulls out his ax and swings the blade down on her head, over and over again, but it's like chopping timber. He bends low to look at her face, but she bends down as well, farther and farther. He has to get onto the floor to get low enough to see her, and when he does, he goes numb. She's laughing at him. Laughing silently, trying not to let him hear, as if she were playing a prank. Then the bedroom door creaks open. Whispers and laughter trickle out, and Raskolnikov is furious. He begins axing the old woman mercilessly, with all his strength, chopping her down at the head, but the laughs from the bedroom and from the old woman just get louder. Her body is shaking with hilarity. People are crowded into the entryway—he can't even leave now. There are people in all the doorways of the building, on all the landings, on all the stairs. Everyone is looking and waiting. This is not a dream Napoleon would have.

The novel swerves when we enter the inspector's apartment—the motive is switched on us. Until now, readers have been led to believe that Raskolnikov murders to create a mountain of good, but upon direct examination we discover that the consequences of an action do not concern him. What concerns him is the nature of the actor. Raskolnikov grabs the ax to prove he is extraordinary. Every utilitarian is an elitist at heart.

Twenty

Double-Edged Evidence

"My novel is an extraordinary success and has raised my reputation as a writer," Dostoevsky wrote in a letter at the end of April 1866. Only two of the six parts of *Crime and Punishment* had been published, and booksellers were already competing to publish the first book edition. He nevertheless knew that when the year was finished, the value of his work (in rubles and reputation) would be judged by the narrative's full arc, which had barely begun. Dostoevsky's eccentric inspector, Porfiry Petrovich, had not yet appeared in print, nor had Raskolnikov's mother and sister, soon to become prominent characters. The mystery of Raskolnikov's motive was just starting, and Dostoevsky was about to introduce a character more sinister than Raskolnikov, as if he were determined to test his readers' tolerance for evil.

Dostoevsky was living on kopecks so that he could repay thousands of rubles in promissory notes to three of his brother Mikhail's old creditors. They had begun demanding payment in February, possibly in response to *Crime and Punishment*'s initial success. But repaying a handful of creditors was a trap. "The more money you repay," he later wrote to Suslova, "the more impatient and stupid the creditors are." Two more creditors initiated legal proceedings against him soon after he paid the first three, so he filed a "statement of illness" with the court requesting a deferment. He had reached a point, he claimed, where he couldn't sit up at night without risking a seizure. He hoped illness would keep him out of debt prison ("it's impossible to write in prison"), but by the end of April he was still waiting for the court's decision and writing *Crime and Punishment* as fast as he could. "All my future depends on doing a good job finishing it," he wrote to the priest who paid his way out of Wiesbaden.

For someone with so much staked upon the novel's success, Dostoevsky was taking substantial risks with its direction. We shift away from Raskolnikov to a subplot involving his sister, Avdotya Romanovna Raskolnikova—"Dunya." She has worked as a governess on an estate and has escaped the indecent advances of her predatory employer, Arkady Ivanovich Svidrigailov, but we suddenly see him stalking her on the street in Petersburg. He is hard to miss—tall, broad shoulders, stylish clothes, and new gloves. He has thick blond hair with touches of gray and a beard shaped like a spade. He taps a beautiful cane as he walks. He sees ghosts.

"Violation of a child," Dostoevsky wrote. It's one of the first traces of Svidrigailov in his notebooks. Dostoevsky initially imagined him as a gentleman of leisure, "an *unoccupied* man," but he decided to make Svidrigailov a gambler—a cardsharp, to be precise—and an indebted nobleman. He has been sprung from debt prison by a woman named Marfa Petrovna for thirty thousand pieces of silver. She married him and kept a promissory note against him in case he ever thought of leaving her. But now he's a widower, his wife having died under mysterious circumstances.

Raskolnikov encounters him at his bedside just as he's waking up from his nightmare about the laughing pawnbroker. He sees the smooth white face, scarlet lips, and impossibly blue eyes. He's waiting patiently, his hands on his cane, his chin on his hands, until Raskolnikov is fully awake. He wants Raskolnikov to help him see Dunya again. He intends to save her from her new fiancé, an unsavory lawyer with a taste for vulnerable women.

What is Svidrigailov doing here—not just in Raskolnikov's room, but in the novel? A new villain seems poised to upstage Raskolnikov's villainy. Svidrigailov is intelligent, like Raskolnikov, and similarly taken by new ideas. ("I now place all my hopes in anatomy, by God!") He knows what Raskolnikov has done—knows it immediately, instinctively—and he knows Raskolnikov will help him because, he suggests, "we are apples from the same tree." And yet where Raskolnikov's evil is feverish, Svidrigailov's is a lassitude. He expresses his thoughts without emotion, as if they've been hollowed out by years of boredom. "He is not even interested in his own opinions," Dostoevsky wrote in his notebook. Depravity feels to him like life's last ember, "a small piece of coal in the blood continually burning." Eventually the depravity burns down to bloodlust, "a convulsive and bestial need to tear apart and to kill, coldly passionate," as Dostoevsky described it in a draft.

"The rape is done accidentally," Dostoevsky wrote in his notebook—a bewildering way of putting it. He imagines Svidrigailov telling the story almost accidentally, too, as if it were just a passing thought. Intentions and plans, theories and justifications simply do not matter for him. It was time for Raskolnikov to come face-to-face with someone for whom *everything* is permitted"—not a history-book Napoleon made of bronze, but a Russian made of flesh. Dostoevsky imagined a character so comfortable with his egoism that he did not even consider offsetting his heinous act with a mountain of good or a revolution.

Details about Karakozov, the attempted assassin, began trickling out in mid-April, two weeks after his crime. Anyone following Raskolnikov's story in the pages of *The Russian Herald* would have noticed similarities. The news broke that Karakozov was a law student expelled for not paying his fees. He tried tutoring to make ends meet before drifting into poverty and politics. He wanted to "bring good to the people," to be "useful." His manifesto touted all the good his crime would achieve: one death would destroy all tyrants and tsars, "deliver all Russia from the plunderers and scoundrels," and inspire a socialist revolution. But what Karakozov really wanted was to wield Napoleonic power, to change history through an extraordinary act of will and egoism. It would happen if Russia's peasants would only follow his example and, according to his manifesto, "rely upon nobody but themselves, conquer their own happiness."

The Third Section's investigation uncovered more similarities between the assassin and Raskolnikov. He had been part of an organization that planned to rob and murder rich people in order to fund their revolutionary activities. The group occasionally discussed tsaricide. "Don't talk about it—do it," Karakozov said. He took to writing—something called "Notes of a Madman," which he later offered to a friend as kindling. He would isolate himself in his room for days. He developed a recurrent fever and fell into depression. His clothing became disheveled. He became suicidal and procured enough opium to poison himself. It was while wandering "machine-like" through St. Petersburg that he decided that he would have to act alone, that the only escape from his demoralizing circumstances was to load his pockets with the poisons, the pistol, the gunpowder, the bullets, and the manifesto and commit an act so drastic that it would transform everything.

The resemblance between Karakozov and Raskolnikov is not exact, of course, but it was strong enough that when Pisarev wrote his review of *Crime and Punishment*, he had Karakozov in mind. A single murder cannot amount to a revolution, Pisarev insisted. Revolution never requires bloodshed, he argued (uncharacteristically), and the "extraordinary" people wield science and reason rather than knives and axes. It took the horrifying reality of violence for Pisarev to embrace the power of rationality.

Investigators arrested Karakozov's friends and associates and interrogated them in the Third Section building until three or four in the morning. Karakozov himself was unrepentant. He wrote to the tsar days after the crime, "If I had a hundred lives, and not one, and if the people would demand that I would sacrifice all hundred lives for their well-being, I swear to all that is holy that I would not for a minute hesitate to make such a sacrifice." The future, he wrote, would be shaped by people like him, extraordinary men and women inspired by nihilism, emerging from crowds to sacrifice their lives just as he was sacrificing his.

Karakozov was imprisoned in the Peter and Paul Fortress. For the first few days, he insisted he was a peasant, but that didn't last long. He was tortured—denied food, water, and sleep. He was forced to stand for days at a time. The head of the investigation was a man known as the Hangman of Vilna for his brutal suppression of Lithuanian and Polish rebellions. It's unclear what the Hangman did with Karakozov once he took over his interrogation, but the prisoner's handwriting quickly became illegible.

The government's official report indicated that Karakozov joined a group calling themselves simply the Organization. Its dozens of members intended "to spread socialism, overthrow the government, and wreck the foundations of religion and public morality." There were likely many more young men like Karakozov waiting to strike. The report blamed the "moral depravity" spread by the media, universities, and foreign books. Propaganda about equality and freedom would always lead to tsaricide.

It was Karakozov's charismatic cousin, Nikolai Ishutin, who brought up the idea of tsaricide, and by 1865 he was spearheading the Organization's activities. What distinguished the Organization—even among other 1860s radicals— was the members' fervor and their submission to strict hierarchy. Wealthy members pledged to donate all their money. Several lived austere lives, restricted their diets, and slept on floors without blankets. Chernyshevsky's *What Is to Be Done?* was their radical handbook, and Ishutin compared Chernyshevsky to Jesus Christ. They began discussing ways to punish wavering members (poisons and daggers were mentioned) and how to start an armed uprising. They'd rob merchants and mail carriers for funding. One member offered to poison his father so he could donate his inheritance.

At some point Ishutin formed a secret circle within the Organization composed of the group's most radical members. They lived together and invisibly guided the Organization's activities. One among them would assassinate the tsar. But who? The assassin must "feel hatred for hatred," Ishutin said, and yet "an infinite love and devotion for his country and its good." The secret circle was called Hell.

I t was late at night, midsummer, and silent. A fifteen-year-old boy was trying to sleep in an upstairs room of a small stone cottage in Lyublino, a tranquil town outside Moscow with thick forests and a large lake. There were so many guests in the main house that the boy had to sleep on a divan out here. The cottage was mostly empty—the downstairs rooms were vacant, not even fully furnished—but Fyodor Dostoevsky, the famous writer, occupied the next room. The boy could hear faint noises, sighs, and whispers. It was unnerving; he could feel his heart beating. He liked Dostoevsky, admired him. The novelist was working on *Crime and Punishment*, but he spent his afternoons with the children. He was good-natured, and his gray eyes looked right into you when he spoke. Occasionally, though, the boy thought he saw a sinister light in them. There was something hidden inside him that he was trying to understand.

After a sleepless hour or so, he heard footsteps approaching. The boy startled as his door opened. Dostoevsky stood in the doorway holding a candle.

"Listen," he said, his voice trembling. "If I have a seizure tonight, don't be afraid. Don't raise an alarm, and don't let the Ivanovs know"—his sister and brother-in-law in the main house.

He closed the door. The boy listened to Dostoevsky pacing back and forth in his room, and then, eventually, turning the pages of a book without incident.

Dostoevsky could tell when a seizure was near—sometimes hours in advance, sometimes days. Sometimes he would have heart palpitations. Sometimes he thought he could feel his heart seizing up. Weeks earlier, in June 1866, he was visiting a friend, Milyukov, in a town south of Petersburg. He had known Milyukov for decades: he was loosely affiliated with the Petrashevsky Circle and contributed to both of Dostoevsky's magazines. He was one of the last people to say goodbye to Dostoevsky before he was exiled to Siberia, and he was waiting at the station when his train returned to Petersburg a decade later. Just as the two old friends were sitting down to tea, Dostoevsky jumped up from the table. He was pale and unsteady. After Milyukov helped him over to the sofa, Dostoevsky had a seizure. Milyukov was horrified by his contorted face. Fifteen minutes later, Dostoevsky was able to speak in a low, hollow voice. "What was it that happened to me?"

Milyukov asked him to stay the night, but Dostoevsky refused. I have to get back to Petersburg, he kept saying, I have to get back. He couldn't remember why, but he had to. He insisted on walking to the train station ("fresh air will do me good"), and as they walked through a large park on the way, Dostoevsky whispered, "I'm about to have a fit!" It was evening—the park was empty—and Milyukov sat him down on the grass. Nothing happened. They continued, approaching stairs leading down to a river, and Dostoevsky stopped again. His eyes looked hazy. "A fit! Right now, a fit!" They sat on a bench, and again it passed. When Milyukov visited the next day, Dostoevsky couldn't recognize him.

By 1866, Dostoevsky had been suffering seizures for about two decades. They began in his temporal lobe and quickly generalized. They had always been punishing on his body—every attack left him weary, his arms, legs, and neck aching, his head throbbing—but as time went on, his falling sickness began wreaking havoc on his mind. He would spend days after each seizure wading through a fog, as he described it, trapped in a half sleep from which no one could wake him. His brain simply wasn't functioning properly. It wasn't just his memory. His sense of reason, he wrote to a friend, was "coming unhinged."

His letters might have sounded hyperbolic to his friends and family, but decades of seizures might have been altering Dostoevsky's brain in ways that we are only now beginning to understand. For a fraction of people with temporal lobe epilepsy, the illness generates a complex syndrome of behavioral and personality changes. Patients become preoccupied with religious and philosophical matters, "hypermoralism" and guilt, paranoia and obsessive attention to detail. Sometimes they develop hypergraphia—the need to write constantly, voluminously. Sometimes they gamble compulsively both because changes in the brain's dopaminergic pathways make gambling more pleasurable and because hyperactivity in a specific structure near the temporal lobe impairs several types of perceptions and judgments. Assessing risk becomes more difficult. "Near" losses are perceived as wins. An irrational feeling of control predominates. It seems impossible to lose at a game like roulette.

It may never be possible to know whether epilepsy altered Dostoevsky's behavior or personality, whether it enhanced already established traits, or whether it did neither, but Dostoevsky was convinced that the effects of the disease were deepening over time and that his life was becoming a series of tapering interludes between grand mal attacks. He kept a log of his seizures in an effort to identify what was causing them. He would note the dates and times of seizures, whether he was sleeping or awake, whether there was wind or fog or frost or humidity. He was hunting for patterns. He noted stomach pains, hemorrhoids, sexual activity, and whether he had recently traveled by train. He noted bad dreams before a seizure, the state of his nerves, and the phase of the moon. There were so many potential causes. He noted that he had a seizure nearly the same hour that a murderer was guillotined in Paris.

His depressions after seizures became deeper. "There's *blackness* in my soul!" he once wrote. One evening it seemed to him as if everything in the room had a blood-red tint. And yet every now and then, just before a seizure, Dostoevsky would be lifted up out of his gloom, and he would be bathed in a feeling of pure, unimaginable ecstasy. Voluptuous and divine bliss. It lasted only a second, but the impressions were permanent. He once described them to a friend as a feeling of "perfect harmony with myself and the entire universe." Years later, he would try describing it in a novel, *The Idiot*. His character Prince Myshkin recalls how "his brain would momentarily catch fire" before epileptic seizures, how "his mind, his heart were lit up with an extraordinary light." But the ecstasy was beyond Dostoevsky's descriptive powers— it was incommensurable with everything else he knew. "For a few seconds of such happiness," he told his friend, "one would give ten years of one's life, perhaps even one's entire life." But the feeling was too powerfully beautiful to bear for more than an instant. Just as soon as Dostoevsky could touch it, he would lose consciousness.

We often think of Dostoevsky as melancholy, but he experienced bliss in a way few of us ever will. He thought of his falling sickness as a dialectic of misery and ecstasy: whatever depression he suffered was the inevitable consequence of his split second of sheer joy. He believed that touching the limits of human experience was something he shared with the Prophet Muhammad, who was also reputedly epileptic. Dostoevsky's Prince Myshkin notes that Muhammad's ecstasy took the form of a mythical white creature who whisked the prophet away "to survey all the dwellings of Allah" in the split second it took a jug of water to spill to the ground. That experience, Prince Myshkin says, is how he first grasped the biblical verse *"time shall be no more."*

Dostoevsky was describing an "ecstatic aura," a phenomenon that researchers now realize affects some people with temporal lobe epilepsy. The overwhelming feelings and perceptions emanated from his anterior insular cortex, the island of furrows beneath the temporal lobe—the same part of the brain whose hyperactivity can cause so many behavioral changes. The insular cortex is involved in a wide array of functions, from attention and empathy to the perception of time. It produces the feeling of knowing, the feeling of being present, and the feeling of a "presence," an overwhelming power hovering nearby. It generates self-awareness. It allows us to recognize our own reflections and makes us cognizant of our bodies, of being thirsty or full, of our movements and our heartbeats. It uses a high concentration of unusually extended neurons to perform complex functions like integrating thought and emotion, and there seem to be few emotions that are not linked to it. It's the left insular cortex that activates during joyful experiences: a sensual touch, a piece of music, smiling and seeing someone smile, maternal love, the taste of wine. The structure does not generate these emotions so much as it makes us aware of them. And as it makes us aware of ourselves, it makes us aware of others and our place in our surroundings, in the "entire universe." That was the insight embedded in his bliss. Feeling a stranger's smile and recognizing our own heartbeat are two elements of the same marvelous capacity.

And so in his brief ecstatic auras, Dostoevsky was more intensely conscious than he was at any other time. He understood that the clarity and fullness he felt, the synthesis of all things, were symptoms of a serious illness rather than offerings of a divine epiphany. But in the end, he thought what Prince Myshkin thinks: "So what if it is an illness?"

S tress was exacerbating his epilepsy, and he kept searching for ways to escape it. He planned to settle into a Moscow hotel for the summer, but within a week he found it impossible to work: his room felt like an oven, and he had only one friend in town. His sister Vera's family (the Ivanovs) had a Swiss-style country house in Lyublino, so he joined them when a nearby cottage became available.

He instructed his stepson Pasha in Petersburg not to tell his creditors where he was. When the boy didn't respond to his letters, Dostoevsky worried that he had cholera, which was sweeping Russia again: ninety thousand Russians died of the disease in 1866. "I don't understand what could have happened to you, Pasha. Didn't I tell you, didn't *I order you, NO MATTER WHAT,* to write me every Saturday, without waiting for letters from me?" He wanted Pasha to come to Lyublino, where it was safer. Dostoevsky himself was taking additional anti-cholera measures. "I've been drinking vodka," he reassured a friend.

There was a beautiful park in Lyublino as well as boating and fishing on the lake, but Dostoevsky spent much of his time playing with his nieces and nephews—all nine of them, from infancy to twenty years old. He felt a rare sense of ease among the younger people. He dressed elegantly in a loose blue jacket and starched collars. His nieces teased him about his thin beard, and he, in turn, wrote and recited mocking poems. He and the children put on skits and pantomimes and even a mock trial, which he somehow turned into an opportunity to play a polar bear. When they performed scenes from Shakespeare's *Hamlet*, Dostoevsky played the ghost of the murdered king. He wrapped his head in a white sheet, hid, and stalked around their makeshift stage. In the evenings he told ghost stories that left his seventeen-year-old niece sleepless. Did they want to experience something truly frightening? They should go into an empty room, he said, look into a mirror, and stare into their own eyes for five minutes. It is terrifying, he told the children, and nearly impossible.

He spent most of his free time with the family, but every now and then, in the middle of a game, he would rush back to his cottage, telling the children to fetch him in ten minutes. Later they would find him writing arduously, and he would drive them away.

Keeping up with the installments of *Crime and Punishment* was not his only source of stress. As the summer wore on, he became increasingly anxious about another creditor whose bill was coming due: Stellovsky. Dostoevsky still had to submit a novel to Stellovsky by November 1 or else cede all income from his book editions for the next nine years. The deadline was impossible to escape. At times, the sheer adversity of his circumstances was invigorating. His plan was to spend the summer working on one novel in the morning and another at night in order to produce 480 pages in four months. It would be an "unprecedented and unconventional thing," he boasted in a June letter, a monumental feat, something no one else had ever done in Russian literary history. "Turgenev would die from the very thought."

But things were not going as planned. By the middle of July, he still hadn't written a single page of Stellovsky's novel. All he had was an outline of a story. It was about an incorrigible gambler, a roulette player stuck in a German spa town—he could see the characters so clearly—but an idea was worth nothing. "Stellovsky worries me to the point of torture," he wrote to Milyukov in mid-July, "and I even see him in my dreams."

In his less confident moments, Dostoevsky believed that epilepsy was taking away the only thing he had: his ability to write. The fear would remain with him forever. "My star is fading," he would say to a friend in 1867. "I don't recognize people any more; I forget what I read the day before." He had trouble concentrating. His perceptions were sometimes distorted. He would claim his imagination was spilling over its proper boundaries, flowing over into nightmares. Sometimes he would find himself writing in a state approaching madness.

One night the Ivanovs sent a footman to sleep in Dostoevsky's cottage in case he suffered a seizure. When night fell, the servant could hear Dostoevsky pacing up and down in his room all night. He was muttering something—something ominous. He was plotting to murder someone, the servant reported the following morning. He was sure of it. The footman refused to go back to that cottage.

Crime and Punishment began as a crime novel, but by the summer of 1866 it was splitting into a melodrama and a detective story, with narrative lines that run roughly parallel: Dunya is pursued by predatory suitors, and Raskolnikov is pursued by an inscrutable inspector. Detective stories had been growing more popular over the previous two decades. The genre lets readers imagine a city's criminals squaring off against its institutions so they can witness depravity before watching order and reason defeat it. A moment of brutality yields to procedures and evidence. The detective story showcases the evolving power of modern states: how law enforcement officials were becoming less like executors of the sovereign's will and more like scientists finding ways to make use of every data point they can find—a dropped item, a scrap of clothing, a tuft of hair, a stain.

There were many detective stories from French, English, and American writers whom Dostoevsky admired—Victor Hugo, Charles Dickens, Edgar Allan Poe—but only a handful of Russian detective novels. This is partly because Russia lacked the institutions that made detective fiction work: a highly professional police force and judicial system, formalized procedures and clear laws. Russian police officers were typically former soldiers whose local departments gave them neither specific training nor specialized roles. The closest position to a detective in Russia—a "judicial investigator"—didn't exist until 1860. Before then, investigations were little more than interrogations. Lawyers weren't present, and they weren't likely to be helpful in any case. The legal profession had few regulations and no bar. Nearly any man could be a lawyer, including serfs, including men often found loitering outside administrative buildings and drafting petitions in exchange for vodka.

Until the 1830s, there was no formal legal code at all—no clearly organized set of statutes to which lawyers, judges, and authorities could refer when administering justice. The system sometimes seemed deliberately obscure. When a law professor tried to publish a *Practical Guide to Russian Criminal Court Procedures*, the government's censors banned it.

At the center of the confusion were a few spare principles. A system of "formal proofs" provided a universal rubric for who should be deemed guilty. A confession, for example, amounted to full proof and automatically merited a guilty verdict. The same was true for two eyewitnesses—three if they were women. It was a matter of arithmetic. There were half proofs, three-quarter proofs, one-eighth proofs. Russian judges had virtually no discretion, and Russian juries did not exist. A trial in Russia was effectively the process of certifying the contents of a case file compiled by the police. This meant that most cases were effectively decided in interrogation rooms, and confessions were easy to get because coercion, indefinite detention, and (unofficially) torture were common.

Porfiry Petrovich is a creature of this system. Though his office is in the police department, the judicial investigator is an official of the court, independent and legally trained. But just what sort of creature an investigator would be was changing while Dostoevsky was writing *Crime and Punishment*. A series of judicial statutes enacted in 1864 amounted to the most sweeping reforms of the era, and many provisions were implemented in 1866. There would be a more independent judiciary. Judges would be professionally trained, and most would be elected to lifetime posts. Criminal investigations would no longer be inquisitorial. More than two thousand pages of procedures outlined how investigations would be pursued, how charges would be brought, and how evidence would be heard in actual trials, with actual lawyers making adversarial arguments in public, sometimes before juries. The legal reforms began to lay the foundation for the rule of law (rather than rule by tsar), for government accountability and Russian citizenship.

Even as Russia's judicial system was modernizing, Dostoevsky was imagining how all the grains of evidence might slip through an investigator's fingers.

No amount of reform would alter a case as peculiar as this one. Raskolnikov walks into the police station to retrieve his pawned belongings from the head of the department of investigations. Porfiry Petrovich sits him down on a sofa upholstered in oilcloth. The inspector's office is meager—the back wall is just a partition with a closed door—and Porfiry is unusually animated, moving like a ball bouncing around the room while he talks. Raskolnikov says he must be employing some professional tactic: divert a suspect's attention, lull him a bit, and then "stun him right on the head with the most fatal and dangerous question."

"So you think I'm trying to get you to . . . eh?" Porfiry Petrovich winks and nearly turns purple with laughter before composing himself. It is true that inspectors have their methods, but Porfiry insists that official form is nonsense. A friendly conversation is much more productive than formal techniques. He pauses occasionally while he speaks, as if listening for something, and then he offers a small piece of advice for the former law student.

"Evidence, my dear, is mostly double-edged." What he needs is "mathematical clarity," he says. "I would like to get hold of a piece of evidence that's something like two times two is four! Something like direct and indisputable proof!"

That's why it's foolish to lock up a suspect too soon. Far better to let him roam free and grow increasingly uncertain, increasingly fearful. "He might come himself and do something that would be like two times two, so to speak, something with a mathematical look to it."

Porfiry keeps borrowing Raskolnikov's phrases. At one point, he even uses one of Raskolnikov's unspoken metaphors. "Have you ever seen a moth near a candle?" he asks. His little victim will keep circling and circling, he tells Raskolnikov, getting closer. Freedom will become meaningless. He'll start entangling himself in thoughts, "narrowing the radius more and more, and— whop! He'll fly right into my mouth, and I'll swallow him, sir, and that will be most agreeable, heh, heh, heh!"

Porfiry turns Raskolnikov's theory against him, exploiting his fear that he is somehow born to be captured and sent to Siberia. But then Raskolnikov remembers that the inspector has no physical evidence, and he becomes so indignant that he's afraid he'll start strangling Porfiry in his office. While it's true that the inspector has no evidence, he insists one could gather clues from human nature—fainting in a suggestive place, for example, and turning pale in front of an investigator *too naturally*. It's always curious, Porfiry says, when something is "too much like the truth."

He stands silently for a moment and then bursts out laughing. Raskolnikov, exasperated, leaps up from the sofa and demands to be arrested if that's what the inspector intends to do. "But to torment me and laugh in my face, that I will not allow!" He says it again and again, pounding his fist on the table. Porfiry becomes awfully concerned for his friend. He opens the window for fresh air and fetches a glass of water, which Raskolnikov sips mechanically.

"Yes, sir, a fit, that's what we've just had, sir!" Why doesn't he take better care of himself? Raskolnikov has been agitating his nerves. He knows all about what happened the other night ("I've been informed of everything, sir!"), how Raskolnikov went to the pawnbroker's apartment, to the scene of the crime, just as it was getting dark, how there were workers already hanging new wallpaper—purple flowers, white background—how they watched him walk through the empty rooms ("What do you want, sir?"), how he rang the doorbell repeatedly, listening to the tinny jingle, shuddered at the horror, enjoying it more each time, how he told the workers he wanted to rent the apartment, and how perplexed they were when he asked if there was any blood on the floor. Antics like that are no good for one's nerves. "Sometimes it can drive a man to jump out the window or off a bell-tower, and it's such a tempting sensation, sir." Surely he was in the midst of delirium, Porfiry says.

"I wasn't delirious! I was fully awake!" Everything the inspector says seems like a lie or a contortion. He doubles back over his words, switches meanings around, imputes significance, agrees with things Raskolnikov never said. Porfiry insists he's telling the young man the truth when he tells him that he has nothing to fear. If he suspected him, surely he would have followed official procedures. He would have heard the workmen's testimony, conducted a search, arrested Raskolnikov, and interrogated him. Why were you at a murdered woman's apartment at ten o'clock at night? he would have asked. Why did you keep ringing the bell? Why were you asking about blood? But he has done none of these things. Clearly, he does not suspect him.

"You're lying!" Raskolnikov shouts. He forswore official forms just moments ago. Was he under suspicion or not? "Don't taunt me! I won't have it." He begins banging the table again. "Do you hear! Do you hear!"

Suddenly the inspector warns him, quite seriously—as if breaking character—to be quiet.

"They'll hear you!" he whispers.

Raskolnikov starts walking out, and Porfiry grabs him by the arm. "But don't you want to see my little surprise?" It is waiting for him behind the small door in the partition. Raskolnikov tries to open it, but it's locked. "Show me your facts!" Raskolnikov demands.

And just then they hear a commotion outside the other door, the front door. "We've brought the prisoner Nikolai," someone announces. After a violent struggle, a gaunt young man with a bowl haircut bursts through the door into Porfiry's office. A guard rushes in and grabs him, but he wrenches himself free and goes down onto his knees.

"I'm guilty," he shouts breathlessly. "The sin is mine! I am the murderer!"

A confession will do when all other evidence is absent. Dostoevsky did not just abandon his idea of Porfiry's finding blood. He decided that Porfiry wouldn't find anything—not a shred of physical evidence. By the time Raskolnikov is in Porfiry's office, Porfiry has already had Raskolnikov's room searched "down to the last hair" while Raskolnikov was delirious on his divan. They found nothing.

But Porfiry is an inspector who need not rely upon physical evidence. Even a bloodstained scrap of clothing in Raskolnikov's apartment would be "double-edged." Dostoevsky wanted Porfiry to contrast with the scientific trends in European criminology, particularly in France. The French Ministry of Justice began collecting the first national data on crime in 1825, and by the 1830s researchers were applying statistical analysis to larger and more detailed tables of information. The statisticians' aim was to detect laws governing human behavior—it was a macroscopic counterpart to physiology, seeing human nature not in nerves and reflexes but in data sets of large populations.

One of the pioneers of modern statistics was Adolphe Quetelet, whose sweeping treatise, *Man and the Development of His Faculties*, made an immediate impression when it was translated into Russian in 1865. Crime rates, Quetelet argued, are constant because human behavior is determined by social forces acting upon unchanging aspects of human biology, including race—"the Pelasgian race" along the French Mediterranean, Quetelet noted, is "particularly addicted to crimes against persons." For Quetelet, the most irrational acts were logical and predictable. Virtually everything about murder—the perpetrators, the rates, the methods and instruments employed—was constant over time. The wanderings of criminals in the streets were like the movements of the stars across the sky.

But Porfiry Petrovich is just an "unworldly and unknowing man," as he tells Raskolnikov, and he dismisses all attempts to see an individual as part of a set. "The general case," he says, "the one to which all legal forms and rules are suited, and on the basis of which they are all worked out and written down in the books, simply does not exist." This is what leads him to dismiss all forms and procedures.

Instead of evidence, procedures, and statistics, Porfiry pieces together a psychological profile of Raskolnikov. The little surprise hiding behind the partition in Porfiry's office is a crucial element: it's the tradesman in the smock and dirty cap, the old man who appears like a phantom and calls Raskolnikov a murderer. The tradesman first encounters him outside the pawnbroker's apartment. Two workmen tell him and other passersby all about Raskolnikov's bizarre behavior at the crime scene. Raskolnikov goads the witness, "Scared to go to the police?" The tradesman barely gets his illuminating story out to the inspector when Raskolnikov himself arrives outside his office. So Porfiry hides the tradesman behind the partition, where the man overhears the entire confrontation with Raskolnikov.

The little surprise is a bluff. Porfiry and Raskolnikov both know that a secondhand account of someone babbling about blood and ringing a doorbell to feel the spinal chill cannot count as evidence. Nor would it matter if Raskolnikov merely spills some incriminating information, because Porfiry is still bound by Russia's old system of formal proofs; new standards had yet to be implemented. This is why Raskolnikov becomes so confident. ("Show me your facts!") It is also why Porfiry resorts to such elaborate psychological tactics. Without eyewitnesses and physical evidence, the only "mathematical" evidence remaining is a confession from Raskolnikov. But only a *judicial* confession suffices, a confession presented to an official. Raskolnikov could confess to his mother, to his sister, to Sonya—someone could overhear him confessing—and all those witnesses could report to the police, and it would still be insufficient. Porfiry is doing everything he can to get Raskolnikov to confess to him openly, officially.

And so when Nikolai bursts through his door, it's as if the investigation's only remaining key has been turned by the wrong person. Nikolai is one of the workmen painting the second-floor apartment when Raskolnikov kills the women. He inexplicably offers the investigator a full judicial confession, and he wasn't even tortured. Even confessions are double-edged. The pursuit at the heart of Dostoevsky's novel has become an investigation with no forms or procedures, no evidence, and a false confession. It is an investigation with no foundation beyond an unworldly man's conviction.

N o crime could have been clearer than the one still on everyone's mind: Dmitri Karakozov's attempt to assassinate the tsar outside the Summer Garden gates in the middle of the afternoon. There was a crowd of eyewitnesses—the tsar himself was a witness. The criminal's pockets were filled with physical evidence. The gunpowder, the manifesto, the bullets and poisons. There were six thousand files of damning testimony from dozens of friends and associates. Karakozov himself confessed multiple times—under interrogation, in writing, in multiple letters to the tsar. He fell into despair in the Peter and Paul Fortress. He tried biting through the arteries in his wrists. He refused to eat. After a week, the guards began force-feeding him. One day he tore off a plank in a fortress latrine and threw himself in, but the water was just too shallow.

Dostoevsky wanted the trial to be public. Political crimes weren't subject to legal reforms, but he believed "official secrecy" would deplete patriotic sentiment, sow distrust, and spark fears that the entire judicial system was about to regress. Karakozov's trial was held in the fortress commander's private quarters in late August 1866. The minister of justice was the prosecutor. A Supreme Criminal Court was formed with a panel of five judges, a secretary to keep minutes, and the first stenographer for a Russian trial. There were, in the end, hundreds of pages of trial transcripts, but all documentation of the proceedings was indeed kept secret, and the outcome was never questioned. Karakozov's trial had barely begun when the Petersburg chief of police started building the gallows.

Though most Russians imagined a well-organized conspiracy, the Hangman of Vilna's investigation found the crime to be primarily the work of one man breaking away from the fractious and chaotic Organization. Members resented Nikolai Ishutin's formation of a secret inner circle, and the resentment devolved into open resistance as members threatened to have one another locked up in lunatic asylums.

By early February, Karakozov was suffering from depression and hypochondria. He had spent weeks in a Moscow clinic with an array of ailments: relapsing fever, some sort of a valvular heart disease, intense stomach pains, urethritis, an earache, and a strange sensation of heat along his spine. He was exhausted. Karakozov decided that the time was ripe to kill the tsar and himself. Several Organization members, including Ishutin, tried to dissuade him. When they realized there was no stopping him, a few began to prepare for the inevitable. One associate gave him money to buy a revolver. Another supplied him with poisons.

Crucial details surrounding the crime remained obscure. The investigation suggested that the Organization's inner circle, Hell, was beginning to wage a coordinated campaign of terrorism against the government and the landowners. They were behind the detailed assassination plot and guided Karakozov's steps: The assassin would sever all ties to family, friends, and society. He would assume a false identity. He would descend into the underworld and disappear like a grain of sand until it was time. He would carry a manifesto in his pocket to clarify the meaning of his deed. He would carry two poisons—one to end his own life, the other to disfigure his face beyond recognition.

And yet Hell's alleged members denied any strategy of terrorism. A secret circle providing Karakozov with the means, the tactics, and the motivation to kill Alexander II was just idle talk, a joke. Hell did not exist, they insisted, and there was little to suggest it did. The court avoided ruling on the subject altogether, and so officially it would remain unknown.

And as obvious as Karakozov's guilt was, the man himself became increasingly enigmatic. Investigators found a scrap of paper among his possessions that read "Great is the Christian God." Was he religious? He told investigators it was meaningless, that he wrote it "absolutely mechanically." He asked the tsar to forgive him, and the guards noticed him praying on his knees in his cell for hours at a time. Whether he was experiencing a genuine conversion or in the throes of some hopeful panic at his life's bitter end was never clear.

Clarity may have been the only thing people wanted from Karakozov other than his death. The gravity of his crime compelled Russians to push beyond the bare facts surrounding it—the accomplices, the planning—and to understand this strange man's motives, to see inside his soul, to probe the wound. But while he readily testified about what he had done, he offered little insight as to why. In his final statement to the court, Karakozov could only state that the thing he wanted in the days before he approached the tsar was to "disappear."

The tsar himself immediately needed to know why. And in that brief exchange between Alexander and his would-be assassin, just moments after the gunshot—the confrontation that generated so many rumors and inventions—His Imperial Majesty received his answer from the man who wanted him dead. And what the gunman actually said was far different from what anyone had imagined and more disturbing than what the public was prepared to entertain.

"What do you want?" the tsar asked.

And Karakozov answered, "Nothing."

On August 31, 1866, the Supreme Criminal Court found Karakozov guilty of attempted tsaricide and sentenced him to be hanged in Smolensk Square. Three days later, Karakozov walked slowly to each corner of the platform and bowed to the thousands of onlookers. Some were praying, though nearly everyone was silent. They blindfolded the prisoner, dressed him in a white hooded shroud, and tightened the rope around his neck.

Karakozov was buried in an unmarked grave on Hunger Island, one of Petersburg's outer districts. In the weeks that followed, under cover of night and risking arrest, people tracked down Karakozov's resting place and covered his grave with flowers.

While the Supreme Criminal Court concealed virtually all the evidence, the published verdicts emphasized the threat of a plague of radical ideas. "A circle of young people infected with socialist ideas" sought revolution through tsaricide and the "extermination of governments in general," the court declared. The criminals believed that "the end justifies the means" partly because they came under the "destructive influence" of Chernyshevsky's novel *What Is to Be Done?*

Most of the defendants were exiled to Siberia, and the court read verdicts for the last of them on September 24. That same day, *The Russian Herald* published another installment of *Crime and Punishment*, and it includes a climactic scene in which Raskolnikov confesses his crimes and lays bare his soul. Dostoevsky had struggled to imagine how it would come about. The bedeviling inspector hacks away at the suspect's guilt, his fear, the holes in his theory, but that would only clear the ground. What would drive a man arrogant enough to believe he possesses the exceptional right to murder—a man who has concealed all evidence and left no witnesses—to throw away his freedom and confess to the authorities?

Dostoevsky's notebooks are filled with abandoned possibilities. Raskolnikov offers a simple confession to Lieutenant Gunpowder—"as base, foul and prosaic as possible," the novelist noted to himself. In nearly every scenario, the murderer confesses to someone he knows before turning himself in. He gives an anguished confession to his mother, sometimes in writing, sometimes in person. In one sketch he just sobs and kisses her feet. In other drafts Dostoevsky imagined the catalyst to be an awful fire in which Raskolnikov becomes a hero, as if acting on his virtuous instinct could trigger his remorse and his need for reconciliation. He imagined Raskolnikov confessing to Razumikhin or to Razumikhin and Sonya together.

Over time, the idea of Raskolnikov's confessing to Sonya began to take hold. "He kneels down before Sonya. 'I love you.'" "Give yourself up," she tells him. Dostoevsky had to remind himself: "Fundamental and Most Important," he wrote in large letters. Not a single word about their love for each other. The silence between them fosters their affection. "He needed her as he needed air, as he needed everything," Dostoevsky wrote in his notebook. There's something desperate about Raskolnikov's love—he needs her to save him. "You are the only person who is left for me," he tells her in another sketch. "We are both *damned*, society's pariahs." She is a prostitute, and he is a murderer. The comparison is absurd, as if he still doesn't fully grasp what he's done, as if he doesn't fully grasp what love even is. He confesses because he thinks she'll understand, and that the prospect of being pariahs together might convince her to love him.

But she loves him already. It happened the night her father died, the night they met. Raskolnikov helped carry her drunken father's bleeding, mangled body to their apartment after he was struck by a carriage. He enlisted the help of the police and passersby. He cleaned Marmeladov's bloodstained face and gave the family what little money he had—twenty rubles—to help pay for the funeral. She loves him not because he is guilty but because he is good.

Raskolnikov feels compelled to go to Sonya after the dramatic scene in Porfiry Petrovich's office. She lives somewhere down a dark corridor in an old green building beside a canal. Room 9 is low ceilinged and poorly lit. The fraying yellow wallpaper—everyone has yellow wallpaper—is blackened at the corners, where the walls meet at disturbing angles: acute, obtuse, as if the room has been squeezed and forced into place. Doors on opposite walls lead to neighboring apartments. Raskolnikov broaches the subject under the guise of bandying philosophical principles with her. Shouldn't someone die rather than be allowed to commit abominations? As he sits next to her on her bed, about to say it, he remembers standing behind the pawnbroker with the ax in his hand, staring at her head and knowing he needs to act.

This time, however, he feels powerless. Does she know who did it? "Guess," he tells her with a twisted smile. She starts trembling while looking at him. "Take a good look." Her face suddenly looks like Lizaveta's when she was backing away from him, unable to scream. She pushes him back, stands up, walks away, returns, looking directly into his eyes, knowing it's true, as if she had known all along. "You've guessed?"

"What, what have you done to yourself?" She embraces him tightly.

He tries to explain his motive, but he's meandering and evasive. He doubles back and spins like Porfiry Petrovich—rejecting previous statements, contradicting himself. He insists the money is irrelevant, that he didn't even open the pawnbroker's purse. Moments later he claims the money is crucial, that he needs it to begin his benevolent career "on a new, independent path."

Sonya dismisses all these vague utilitarian plans. "No, that's not it, not it!"

And she's right. "I'm lying, Sonya," he admits. "I've been lying for a long time . . . There are quite different reasons here, quite, quite different!"

He confesses the theory underlying his supposed utilitarianism. "I wanted to become a Napoleon," he says, and a Napoleon going to battle in Egypt or Toulon surely would not hesitate before conquering an "unmonumental" old crone.

"You'd better tell me straight out . . . without examples," she says. She's a guileless investigator.

"You're right again, Sonya. It's all nonsense, almost sheer babble!"

But he doubles back again, defending the babble, emphasizing what's supposedly at stake. He wanted to determine whether he was ordinary or extraordinary, he says, though with Sonya he's more candid about his contempt. "I wanted to find out," he tells her, "whether I was a louse like all the rest, or a man."

There is, however, one anchored idea amid all of Raskolnikov's twists, something so simple and direct that it's almost lost among all the theories. It's something he has never admitted before. The idea begins with his familiar rhetoric about the masses: "He who can spit on what is greatest will be their lawgiver, and he who dares the most will be the rightest of all!" The person with power is simply "the one who dares to reach down and take it." He's rehearsing the ideas in his article "On Crime," but then he makes a crucial turn:

> And then a thought took shape in me, for the first time in my life, one that nobody had ever thought before me! Nobody! It suddenly came to me as bright as the sun: how is it that no man before now has dared or dares yet, while passing by all this absurdity, quite simply to take the whole thing by the tail and whisk it off to the devil! I . . . I wanted to dare, and I killed . . . I just wanted *to dare*, Sonya, that's the whole reason.

A reckless gamble. A leap from a tower. It is Sonya who solves the mystery of Raskolnikov's motives, not the inspector. He doesn't murder to be a Napoleon or to be a lawgiver or even to rule over others. Raskolnikov's idea—the idea that no one, not even Napoleon, has ever thought—is entirely different: to kill simply to cast everything off to hell, to wipe it all away. Raskolnikov seems progressively philosophical until it is clear that he is not philosophical at all, that all those ideas and all those theories were noise, sheer babble, nothing poured into nothingness. Raskolnikov does not want a tabula rasa for a new society or a new legal regime. "I just wanted *to dare*, Sonya, that's the whole reason." Raskolnikov doesn't kill for an idea. Raskolnikov kills for nothing.

"Oh, Lord!" Sonya exclaims. "Nothing, he understands nothing!"

Twenty-One

Little Dove

On October 1, a few weeks after returning from Lyublino, Dostoevsky was pacing in his apartment, smoking a cigarette.

"Why are you so gloomy?" Milyukov asked. He was visiting Dostoevsky and likely disturbed that his friend did not seem healthier or more relaxed since he saw him last.

"You would be gloomy too if you were hitting bottom," he said, still pacing.

"What! What's the matter?"

"Well, do you know my contract with Stellovsky?" Milyukov didn't know the details. Dostoevsky went over to his desk and handed him the contract. "Take a look."

He was obliged to deliver to Stellovsky a new novel of ten signatures (160 pages) by the end of the month, and several clauses were baffling: how little he had received from Stellovsky, and the penalty for failing to deliver the manuscript on time—giving Stellovsky all reprinting rights for the next nine years.

"How much of the new novel do you have written?"

Dostoevsky stopped pacing and spread his arms wide. "Not a single line!"

Milyukov couldn't believe it.

"Do you understand now why I am hitting bottom?"

"But what shall we do? Something has to be done!"

"What can I do when the deadline is in a month?" He had spent his summer writing *Crime and Punishment* and lost precious time revising a chapter that *The Russian Herald* refused to print. Sonya reads Raskolnikov the Gospel story of Jesus raising Lazarus from the dead. It gives Raskolnikov the hope that even he could be redeemed, yet the *Russian Herald* editors insisted they saw "evidence of *nihilism*" in it, which was absurd. He had to travel to Moscow repeatedly, pleading with the editors, hoping to keep the changes to a minimum. And now he had just four weeks to write a small novel. "You can't finish off ten signatures in four weeks," Dostoevsky said.

"Listen, you can't enslave yourself forever," Milyukov responded. "We must find some way out of this situation."

"What way out! I don't see any."

Milyukov was more optimistic. Katkov was allowing Dostoevsky to postpone *Crime and Punishment* work for one month, and Milyukov reminded Dostoevsky that he had drawn up a plan for a novel about a gambler. Dostoevsky had originally conceived of it a few years earlier for another publisher. Nothing came of it, and he had since repaid the advance. So Milyukov had an idea.

"Let's gather several of our friends now," he said, "you'll tell us the plot of the novel, we'll outline its sections, divide it into chapters and write it together. I'm sure no one will refuse." Dostoevsky could compile the sections and smooth out whatever irregularities or contradictions arise. Then "you will give the novel to Stellovsky and break out of his bondage."

"No," Dostoevsky said, "I shall never sign my name to someone else's work."

So Milyukov offered another solution. "Hire a stenographer and dictate the whole novel yourself." The writing would go four times as fast.

Dostoevsky had never dictated anything before. He'd have to transform his entire process, and the effects were impossible to anticipate—to *speak* the novel out to a listener, a stranger, rather than sit with it alone. He expressed his uncertainty. "But it may be worth trying . . ." A moment later he was resolute. "Yes, there is no other remedy," he said. "If this doesn't work, I'm done for."

But where could he get a stenographer? "Do you happen to know one?" he asked Milyukov.

. . .

Three days later, at 11:30 in the morning ("no earlier and no later," she was instructed), a young woman in a black dress, cloaked in a hood, called at apartment 13 of a forbidding building. Her instructor had given her the address on a folded slip of paper. This was her first job, and she had hardly slept the night before. She was thrilled to be independent, to begin earning a wage, to embark upon her career so auspiciously. She had purchased extra pencils earlier that morning along with a small portfolio that she hoped would make her seem more professional.

A middle-aged maid in a green shawl opened the door and asked her who she was. Her name was Anna Grigorievna Snitkina. "Your master is expecting me," she said. As she was removing her hood in the vestibule, a young man with dark, disheveled hair wearing house slippers and an unbuttoned shirt opened a side door, gasped, and quickly closed it. The maid led her to a small dining room. She noticed a chest of drawers and two large trunks covered with small rugs. Details from *Crime and Punishment* popped up—the way Dostoevsky's partitioned building resembled Raskolnikov's, how the maid's green worsted shawl appears on several of the Marmeladovs.

She had been reading Fyodor Dostoevsky's work for years. She wept while reading *Notes from a Dead House*. She wanted to help him somehow, to lighten the heavy load of his life in the prison camp. Reading *Dead House* was probably her father's suggestion. Dostoevsky had been her father's favorite author. She remembered how much he had loved *Poor Folk*, how upset he was that Dostoevsky was exiled to Siberia, and, years later, his astonishment when he discovered that Dostoevsky had returned to Petersburg and was about to start a magazine. "Thank the Lord he didn't disappear!" Sometimes her father fell asleep clutching an issue of *Vremya* (his health was already declining), and Anna would slip it out of his hands, hide somewhere in the garden, and read the new chapters of Dostoevsky's latest novel before her older sister could snatch the journal away.

She had imagined the writer so many different ways (tall and thin, fat and bald) that when Fyodor Dostoevsky greeted her in the dining room she was surprised by how familiar he looked after all. She must have seen his portrait somewhere. His face was pale and somewhat unhealthy, but he took care of his appearance. He wore a blue jacket that looked handsome against his gleaming white collar and cuffs. He kept good posture, and his hair was carefully styled and pomaded. There was, however, something wrong with his eyes. His right pupil was dilated—she couldn't see the iris.

He asked for her name and invited her into his study. He quickly excused himself, giving her time to scan the room. A shabby brown divan, a writing desk, a red cloth on a small table, an off-center mirror framed in black, and a green morocco couch. Aside from two large Chinese vases on the window-sills, it was the sort of furniture one would find serving a family of modest means. A woman's portrait hung in a walnut frame above the couch. Her black dress in the portrait made her look especially thin—"corpse-like," she thought. Anna Grigorievna wondered if Dostoevsky's children were being quiet and if the lady was preparing to greet her husband's stenographer.

But it was Dostoevsky who entered, apologizing for taking so long and wading into small talk. He asked her what her name was again.

"Have you been studying stenography a long time?"

"Only half a year."

He asked how many students were in the course. It began with 150, but only about 25 remained. Stenography is not an easy skill.

"That's always the way in our country with every new undertaking," he told her. "They start at fever heat, then cool off fast and drop it altogether. They see that you have to work—and who wants to work nowadays?"

It was a fusty thing to say, but he seemed younger as the conversation progressed. Was he thirty-five? The maid soon arrived with strong black tea and two rolls. Anna Grigorievna drank her cup despite feeling uncomfortably warm. She was unsure how to speak to her employer. She thought of literary people as singular creatures requiring special tones and forms of address. And what if he asked her to talk about his novels? She had forgotten some details, of course. But his mind seemed elsewhere. He was pacing around the room, smoking one cigarette after another. When he offered one to her, she declined.

"Perhaps you're refusing just to be polite?" It was a test. She assured him that she did not smoke, nor did she approve of women who did. He seemed satisfied with this, and yet he was surprisingly cautious, almost nervous. Their conversation was fragmented, but he was candid with her. He told her that he had epilepsy. He suffered a seizure just a few days before, in fact, which is how he had injured his eye: he hit something when he fell, and the doctor's medication dilated his pupil.

He was also candid about his doubts regarding this entire endeavor. "We'll give it a try . . . we'll find out whether it's possible . . ." Anna Grigorievna began to worry that her job would end before it could begin, so she encouraged him.

"Good, let's try it." If it's not working, she said, "you can tell me straight out. Please be assured that I won't hold it against you if the job doesn't come to anything."

He decided to dictate something from *The Russian Herald* as an experiment. She sat at the small table, opened her notebook, and readied her pencil, but he began reading exceedingly quickly. She stopped him. He should read at a normal, conversational rate—just the way he spoke. He started again, and she began filling her notebook pages with swerves and loops, jagged lines and stray marks. After he finished reading, she transcribed the warped script into Cyrillic. He began panicking at how long it was taking, and she tried calming him.

"But you see, I'll be transcribing your dictation at home, not here." She was just demonstrating how it works. He examined her work: she had missed a period, he said, and one of her letters was sloppy. He decided that they would press forward nonetheless, that he was ready to begin. And so was she. He began pacing again. She waited.

He asked her again what her name was. *Snitkina*—it's Ukrainian. He continued pacing, thinking, becoming unaware of her presence in the room while she sat motionless. And then he gave up. He couldn't dictate anything right now, he said. Could she return in the evening around eight o'clock?

S he was dejected when she left. "My dreams of independence were threatening to crumble into dust," she recalled thinking years later, and she minced no words about the famous writer. "I didn't like him: he made me feel depressed."

This is exactly how her instructor told her it would be—"gloomy and forbidding," he said. But when a friend asked him to recommend a capable stenographer who could handle a pressing task, he felt obliged to help: Anna Grigorievna was his best student. She had always excelled academically. She attended Russia's first secondary school for girls the year after it opened and graduated with prizes and a silver medal in 1864. When she began her higher education at the Pedagogical Institute for women, she was, like so many others, intrigued by the natural sciences and all they seemed to promise. But she soon found herself less interested in dissecting cats than in reading novels and attending lectures on literature.

Her studies began suffering as her father's illness became serious. In the summer of 1865, she withdrew from the institute to care for him full time. She would read Dickens to him for hours when he couldn't sleep. He regretted the fact that she had abandoned her studies, and when they came across an announcement for an evening stenography course, he encouraged her to enroll. The opportunity was exciting, but when the shorthand still seemed meaningless after the first few lectures, she planned to quit. Her father reproached her for her impatience and made her promise to continue. He was confident she would do well.

When her father died at the end of April 1866, Anna Grigorievna's grief was overwhelming. She stopped attending classes and spent entire days at her father's grave. Her mother was distraught and begged her to find work. The course was over by then, but when the teacher discovered why she had disappeared, he agreed to continue the lessons by correspondence through the summer. She practiced her speed by taking dictation from her brother for an hour almost every day. By early October, after fall classes resumed, the instructor knew she was the one. He approached her before class. Would she like a job? She would indeed, though she wasn't sure she was ready.

"Who is it who's offering the job?"

"It's the writer Dostoevsky." He's planning to dictate a new novel. She agreed immediately. But he had a warning for her: "I'm not sure how you will get along with him—he seemed to me such a surly, gloomy man."

When Anna Grigorievna returned at eight in the evening, Dostoevsky suggested she sit at the writing desk—*his* writing desk. He was cordial and more relaxed. He offered her ripe pears, some tea, a cigarette. What was her name again? Was she related to the young writer Snitkin who had recently died? She wasn't. He asked about her family, her education, how she had begun learning stenography. She kept her answers succinct, and she never smiled. She was formal—even stern. He liked her seriousness. He might have sensed what she knew quite well: that working in private homes meant being strictly professional and avoiding all familiarities in order to prevent anything untoward.

She was taking a risk by being here—at night, no less—and she was in mourning for her father. The circumstances made her seem both brave and vulnerable, and perhaps this is what encouraged Dostoevsky to begin talking openly about his past. He told her about the Petrashevsky Circle and his pre-dawn arrest, the monumental events she had heard about for years. He told her what it was like to stand on the platform in the middle of the Semenovsky Parade Ground, with the soldiers and crowds arrayed around them, to watch the three men ahead of him tied to the posts and blindfolded before the firing squad. "I knew that I had no more than five minutes left to live," he told her. "But those minutes seemed years—decades—so much time, it seemed, still lay ahead of me!" He thought of everything he could have accomplished, how he had wasted his young life. "I so longed to experience it all over again and live for a long, long time . . ." Then he heard the sound of the drums beating retreat and the pronouncement of his new sentence: four years of hard labor in Siberia. "That was the happiest day of my life," he told her.

His memories gave her goose bumps. She was amazed that someone so distinguished and withdrawn could be so forthright, that he could relive those life-altering moments right in front of her. "It seemed to me," she later recalled, "that I had known Dostoevsky for a long time."

It was long past time for them to begin again. She got her pencil and notebook. He began pacing the room, and each time he reached the furnace in the corner, he would rap it twice with his knuckles. He smoked constantly.

The story he was struggling to begin is about a group of vacationers in a German spa town. It is narrated by Alexei, a tutor for a Russian general's young children. Readers would hear Alexei's own account of how he careens from his passionate love for the general's stepdaughter to his hopeless addiction to roulette. The stepdaughter's name is Polina. She toys with Alexei while pursuing a marquis named des Grieux. The general, meanwhile, intends to marry a beautiful young Frenchwoman, named Mlle. Blanche, with ink-black hair. Alexei soon discovers he is entangled in a web of relations built upon debt and money-in-waiting. The general owes money to des Grieux—so much money, in fact, that he mortgaged all his property to him as collateral. And des Grieux needs money because he himself is in financial straits. Luckily, relief is on the horizon. The general will be able to repay des Grieux and marry Mlle. Blanche as soon as he gets his inheritance, and des Grieux will propose to Polina as soon as she gets hers.

The bequests would come from the general's wealthy aunt, affectionately called Grandma. Poor Grandma has been in declining health back in Moscow, and rumors of her demise are making their way to the spa town. But suddenly, instead of a telegram confirming her passing, Grandma herself unexpectedly arrives, vital and defiant, like the roulette wheel's improbable *zéro* personified. Everyone watches in dismay as multiple footmen carry her up the hotel steps in an armchair. The gray-haired, straight-backed grande dame gives sharp commands to the servants around her. Grandma is thoroughly alive, and she is rather curious about the casino.

The story would be called *The Gambler*. Dostoevsky managed to dictate the opening. It wasn't much, but it was already eleven o'clock at night, so he asked Anna Grigorievna to return at noon the next day with her Cyrillic transcription. She wanted to transcribe it perfectly (no missing punctuation, no sloppy characters), and her anxiety slowed her work down. Dostoevsky was distressed when she arrived thirty minutes late. He was convinced she wasn't coming back. He explained the urgency of his situation—his contract with Stellovsky, the awful deadline at the end of the month. He explained how this entire crisis was years in the making, how his brother's death left him with piles of debt, and how the contract for this gambling story saved him from debtors' prison but now threatened to take away nine years of future book royalties. He couldn't afford to lose a single evening's dictation or to start over with someone new. He didn't just need her to finish a story. He needed her to help him keep his future as a writer financially sustainable.

They signed a contract and quickly established a routine. Anna Grigorievna would take dictation and transcribe *The Gambler* for fifty rubles. From noon to 4:00 p.m. each day, Dostoevsky would dictate to her in half-hour bursts, and they would break for tea between sessions. He gave her ruled writing paper and precise instructions about the margin width she should leave for her transcriptions. She would transcribe at home—at night or in the morning—and he would revise the previous day's dictated text two or three times.

Dostoevsky found dictation difficult. It was like writing onstage, improvising before an audience of one, a young woman. He would speak and halt and think. He would ask her to reread what he had just dictated. Sometimes he would pull at his hair while he paced. But after a few days, he adapted. The sessions became more productive, the manuscript grew, and the tortured relationship between Alexei and Polina came into focus.

"I'd like to penetrate her secrets," Alexei confesses. "I'd like her to come to me and say: 'I love you,' and if not, if that madness is unthinkable, then . . . well, what should I wish for? Do I know what to wish for? I'm as if lost myself; all I need is to be near her, in her aura, in her radiance, forever, always, all my life."

As Anna Grigorievna recorded his words, it became clear that Dostoevsky was telling the story of a desperate love. Polina laughs at Alexei's feelings, ignores his questions, and treats him like a plaything. She commands him to insult a German baron and baroness ("I want to see the baron beat you with his stick"), and he does so gleefully. He is happy to humiliate himself for her amusement. "To be enslaved to you is a pleasure," Alexei tells Polina. There is pleasure in humiliation. "Devil knows, maybe there is in the knout, too, when the knout comes down on your back and tears your flesh to pieces . . . But maybe I want to try other pleasures as well." Alexei wants to be lower than her slave. He wants to throw himself off a mountain for her. He wants to "vanish into nothing before her"; he wants them both to vanish. He fantasizes about strangling her.

The relationship seemed so eccentric, so convoluted and relentless. At some point, Dostoevsky told Anna Grigorievna about the real Polina—Polina Suslova—and their tumultuous travels in Wiesbaden and Paris and Italy, how she cared only about a Spaniard named Salvador, and how rejection turned her indifference into despotic cruelty. Anna must have wondered how deep the parallels went. Perhaps the man who had so quickly divulged his past to her was always confessing his life in his work. Perhaps the gambling mania was his. Perhaps the slavishness was his. And what about the desire to be torn to pieces, to vanish into nothing? What about the malice? Alexei tells Polina, "Someday I'll kill you, do you know that? Not because I've fallen out of love or become jealous, but—just so, simply to kill you, because I sometimes long to eat you up."

Their chats over tea might have helped quell Dostoevsky's stage fright. He told her about the Peter and Paul Fortress prison, how the prisoners would tap on their cell walls to communicate. He told her about Siberia, about carrying bricks and grinding alabaster. He told her about the same convicts she had read about years earlier. He told her about his wife, Marya, looking on from her portrait on the wall, and how she succumbed to tuberculosis two years before. She was already so ill when the photograph was taken. He told her about his travels throughout Europe. She began comparing him with the other men she knew, admiring how much he had experienced.

On cloudy days, the study was dim and forbidding. The corpse-like woman's portrait looked on as they worked. One day, as she was sitting down at his desk, arranging her pencils and notebook, she noticed that one of the Chinese vases was gone.

"Surely the vase hasn't been broken?"

"No, not broken—taken to the pawnshop." He needed twenty-five rubles. The other vase was gone a few days later.

Another time, she noticed a wooden spoon on the dining room table's place setting. She made a joke about it—how wooden spoons are for buckwheat kasha—though that wasn't the reason.

"I sent the servant to pawn the silver spoons. But they offer a good deal less for an odd lot than for a full dozen—so I had to give up my own spoon as well."

It occurred to her that Dostoevsky was utterly alone. The table had just one place setting. She never saw any family members other than the dark-haired young man who appeared briefly in the doorway on her first day. It turned out to be his stepson, Pasha. He stopped her by the building's gate one day.

"You didn't recognize me?" He had an unhealthy complexion and tobacco-stained teeth.

"I don't like to go in when the two of you are working," he said, "but I'm curious to know—what is this 'stenography' all about? I'm going to start studying it myself one of these days. Allow me—" He took the notebook from her hands and examined her work.

"Odd thing, that." He gave it back.

Nothing about Dostoevsky's grim domestic circumstances seemed to daunt him or slow his mounting optimism. He kept asking Anna Grigorievna for updates on their progress. "And how many pages did we do yesterday? And how many do we have altogether? What do you think—will we finish in time?" Her reassurances always lifted his spirits, and so did her presence, her face. During their first week working together, he formed no memory of her appearance. He couldn't even recall the color of her hair, but an image began to come into focus. Her intelligent gray eyes, deep set and intense, her high forehead and full chin. She had Swedish ancestry. He noticed her bright smile, her full lips. The more he saw her, the more beautiful she was.

Once they began counting the pages together, it occurred to him that this young woman, a near stranger, was the only person who cared about his well-being. He found a lot to admire about her. At first it was her seriousness and efficiency. Then her taste and judiciousness (he noticed her disappointment when he once said something inapt), and then, most important, her warmth and empathy.

"Good Anna Grigorievna," he began calling her, now knowing her name. One day he called her *golubchik*—little dove. She was only twenty years old, rather young, and surely appealing to age-appropriate suitors.

As October progressed, the fortunes of Dostoevsky's characters in the German spa town began to decline. Grandma loses a large portion of her estate at the casino, and the two hopeful couples—Mlle. Blanche and the general, Polina and the Marquis des Grieux—predictably split apart. Polina becomes fruitlessly involved with a wealthy Englishman. Mlle. Blanche pursues a prince until she discovers that he's hoping to borrow money from *her*.

Alexei's fortunes take the sharpest turns. He wins 200,000 francs in a single evening, surely more money than the tutor has ever seen. Winning feels so powerful. The entire casino crowds around. The croupiers pile banknotes and gold in front of him. He bets recklessly and keeps winning. He stuffs the money in his pockets in ecstasy. Everything else pales against a feeling this intense—all other concerns, hopes, and memories. Even Polina becomes a faint memory shrinking down to nothingness.

Alexei's attentions turn to Mlle. Blanche. She adores his money, and he adores her "really delightful little foot, swarthy, small, not misshapen, like almost all those little feet that look so cute in shoes." He slides silk stockings up her leg and kisses her foot. She flicks him in the face with her toe. He follows her to Paris for champagne and fine clothing, "delirium and foolery." In three weeks, all his money is gone, and he returns to the casinos. No matter where he is, he feels caught up in an overwhelming whirlwind. Even if one day he could control himself, he says, "I will again break out of all order and sense of measure, and spin, spin, spin . . ." His final hope is to regain some control over his life by writing about it, but it's no use. He spends more than a year and a half at the casino in Homburg. "What am I now? *Zéro*. What may I be tomorrow? Tomorrow I may rise from the dead and begin to live anew!" In the end, Alexei learns that Polina has loved him all along, but it no longer matters because he will never leave. He is the casino's slave now.

Anna Grigorievna was engrossed in the story. She stopped attending her stenography lectures and rarely socialized. She eagerly awaited each midday, and when she left, she missed him. Everything else she did "seemed empty and futile," she later recalled. She developed strong opinions about the characters. She loved Grandma. She did not like Polina, and she told Dostoevsky exactly what she thought.

To her amazement, he took her thoughts seriously, considered them carefully. She was, after all, more than a stenographer. Maikov referred to her as Dostoevsky's "zealous collaborator," and while it might have been partly in jest, she really had become integral to his creative process. She was his first reader, an astute one. She *listened* to his story, and listening is a great creative power. He began listening to her as well. It was problematic that she had little sympathy for his protagonist, that she could neither understand nor forgive Alexei's weaknesses.

He defended Alexei. A person can be resolute and yet drawn irresistibly to roulette, he said. He himself had been in Alexei's position and had felt those feelings. He needed to make them clearer, to capture a gambler's distorted thoughts. He of course remembered his own gambling "system"—how riches would flow if he stayed calm and logical—but he knew that the thrill of roulette had nothing to do with either logic or riches. It's the thrill of power, and of being crushed by power. Dostoevsky captured this toward the end of *The Gambler*. Alexei thinks of gambling as a way to defy fate, to be exempt from the laws of probability, the laws that bind everyone else. Crucially, a gambler starts to believe that the only way to defy these laws is to be reckless, to stake too much money on the "wrong" number, to wager brazenly, to play long after you should walk away. "Yes," Alexei says,

> sometimes the wildest thought, the seemingly most impossible thought, gets so firmly settled in your head that you finally take it for something feasible . . . Moreover, if the idea is combined with a strong, passionate desire, you might one day take it, finally, for something fatal, inevitable, predestined, for something that can no longer not be and not happen!

This is the fantasy of the power of daring, that the very wildness of a gamble makes triumph inevitable. You can't lose if you dare brazenly enough. Alexei knows what Raskolnikov is just beginning to understand: this fantasy makes no sense. But it doesn't matter. Because the other thrill of gambling is whisking everything off to the devil.

Why is it, Fyodor Mikhailovich, that you remember only the unhappy times? Tell me instead about how you were happy."

"Happy? But I haven't had any happiness yet. At least, not the kind of happiness I always dreamed of. I am still waiting for it." She found it painful to hear that he was still searching after so many years.

He said he felt as if he were standing at a crossroads in his life, and he wanted to ask for her advice. He could exile himself somewhere exotic—Constantinople, Jerusalem—or return to the German casinos, or he could try settling down and starting a family.

Anna Grigorievna said he should find a wife.

"So you think I can marry again? That someone might consent to become my wife?"

She did think so.

"What kind of wife shall I choose then—an intelligent one or a kind one?"

"An intelligent one, of course."

He wasn't so sure. It might be good to have a kind wife, "so that she'll take pity on me and love me."

He asked her why she was not married herself, and she replied that she had two suitors, "both splendid people" whom she respected but did not love, and she wanted to marry for love.

"For love, without fail," he agreed. "Respect alone isn't enough for a happy marriage!"

Dostoevsky's work increased as the deadline drew near. He would continue writing after she left, and she'd stay up long into the night to transcribe everything and count the pages they had. Surely, they would meet the deadline, she would tell him, and then they would be finished.

"You know what I've been thinking, Anna Grigorievna?" She did not know. "You and I have been getting along so beautifully, we see one another every day in such a friendly way, we've grown so accustomed to our lively talks together—can it be true that all this will end when the novel is done? That would be a pity, truly! I shall miss you very much. And where will I ever see you again?"

"A mountain can't come to a mountain, as the saying goes, but people can meet without difficulty."

"But where, precisely?"

She didn't know how to answer.

"Well—in society . . . at the theatre, at concerts . . ."

That wasn't suitable. What kind of conversation could they have there? "Why don't you invite me to your house to meet your family?"

"Please do come," she said. Her family would be happy to meet him.

"Then when may I come?"

"We'll set a date after we finish our work."

Their final dictation session was October 29. In their twenty-six days together they completed 160 pages. Dostoevsky had never been so productive; working with her doubled his pace. They were proud of the story, and it proved to be among his most powerful shorter works. To celebrate, he planned a large dinner with several literary friends.

"Have you ever been to a restaurant?"

"No, never."

"But you will come to my dinner? I want to drink to the health of my dear collaborator!"

She pretended to seek her mother's permission, but the truth is that she was too shy to attend his celebration. She nevertheless returned the next day with the final pages of *The Gambler*. She walked in wearing a long lilac dress made of silk, and the sight made Dostoevsky flush. He had always seen her dressed in mourning. Today, however, was his birthday. Lilac suited her quite well, he said. She looked so tall and graceful.

He gathered himself together—they had business to attend to. He shook her hand firmly, gave her the fifty rubles she earned and thanked her warmly for collaborating with him.

She decided to leave after other birthday visitors arrived, and as Dostoevsky showed her out, he reminded her of her promise to meet her family. "When can I come, then? Tomorrow?" Tomorrow wouldn't work. Nor would the next day, nor the day after that.

"My Lord! All your time is taken up!"

"Come on November 3, on Thursday, at about seven in the evening."

"Not until Thursday? How far off that is! I shall miss you so much."

He told her that they should run off to Europe together.

Now it was clear. She wrote in her diary, "He loves me very much."

On November 1, his deadline, Dostoevsky went to Stellovsky's house to deliver the full manuscript, but the servant who answered the door informed him that Stellovsky was out of town, unfortunately, and it was unclear when he would return. Dostoevsky took the manuscript to the office of Stellovsky's publisher, but the manager refused to accept it. Stellovsky, he was obliged to say, hadn't authorized him to accept it.

Dostoevsky had expected that Stellovsky, scoundrel and pettifogger that he was, would do anything to prevent him from fulfilling his contractual obligation so he could seize his publication rights. He had told Anna Grigorievna as much, so she pursued legal advice. A lawyer recommended registering the manuscript with a notary or the police. After Dostoevsky had made his final revisions, he became anxious enough to pursue the matter himself. At

11:00 the night before, he called upon a justice of the peace for his advice. He told Dostoevsky the same thing.

By the time Stellovsky's manager turned him away, it was too late to find a notary, so Dostoevsky went to his local police station, where he received more bad news. The relevant officer for such matters wasn't there, and he wouldn't return until ten o'clock that night. Dostoevsky spent the evening fretting. What if the officer didn't report for duty? What if he was late? Why is it that he allowed nine years of future earnings to come down to this two-hour window?

When Dostoevsky returned to the police station that night, the relevant officer was there to receive the manuscript and sign a receipt that Dostoevsky drew up himself. The next day, *The Gambler* was delivered to Stellovsky by the police.

Twenty-Two

Tiny Diamond

The day after submitting *The Gambler*, Dostoevsky asked *The Russian Herald* for another five-hundred-ruble advance. Most of his income had been spent paying off interest on his debts and redeeming pawned possessions. He also asked for more time to work on the final section of *Crime and Punishment*, and he promised to work tirelessly. He planned to recapture the sensation he created when the novel's first installment appeared. He planned, in fact, to make it "much fuller and more sensational—incomparably so." The plot swerves. Nikolai is taken to jail after he bursts into Porfiry Petrovich's office and confesses to the murders, which is where the inspector's work should end. There is no evidence against Raskolnikov, and Nikolai willingly delivers himself to the authorities.

It isn't long before Porfiry walks silently up Raskolnikov's stairwell, insists he'll stay for just one cigarette, and expresses his regret for having made Raskolnikov suffer. "I feel an attachment to you."

Porfiry Petrovich was searching so fervently for real evidence—"some little trace!"—that he built a case upon hunches and accidents, rumors and suggestive details, like the way Raskolnikov fainted in the police station, and his bizarre outburst with the police clerk at the café, and his forced laughter when they first met, and the way that tradesman called him a murderer—"and you didn't dare ask him anything for the whole hundred steps!" But what did any of that matter? "A hundred rabbits will never make a horse, a hundred suspicions will never make a proof." He admitted he had "exactly nothing, and perhaps the final degree of nothing."

Then Nikolai burst into his office—"a thunderbolt!" He confessed eagerly under interrogation, though Porfiry believed none of it. Nikolai is simpleminded. He is also a Raskolnik—a Runner. He prayed ardently and studied the old religious texts, as Raskolniks are wont to do. But Petersburg corrupted him, and when he found a box containing earrings and some jewels that the murderer dropped, he pawned it for two rubles to get alcohol. The guilt of his wayward life made him crave punishment, as Raskolniks are wont to do. So Nikolai confessed to a crime he did not commit and begged for the tsar's punishment.

It was not such a curious thing. The matter at hand, Porfiry tells Raskolnikov, concerns a man with "bookish dreams, sir, a heart stirred up by theories." And what does such a man do? Something reckless. He took an impulsive, radical step, "as if he were throwing himself off a cliff or a bell tower," freeing himself to be pulled by gravity, and he killed two people "according to a theory." He stole a fraction of the pawnbroker's money because it's the punishment he really wants, Porfiry tells Raskolnikov. He craves punishment. And that's why he went back to her apartment. He wanted to hear that terrifying little doorbell ringing just as it did when he was inside, so he could feel, once again, "that spinal chill." No. Nikolai, Porfiry says, is not the murderer.

"Then . . . who did . . . kill them? . . ." Raskolnikov asks.

Porfiry recoils at the question. "What? Who killed them? . . ." He can't believe what he's hearing. He leans forward and whispers, "But *you* did, Rodion Romanych! You killed them, sir . . ."

Raskolnikov jumps up. Tiny spasms flit across his face. It feels like a revelation, as if he were just now grasping it. He sits back down and manages to whisper, "It wasn't me." He says it reflexively, like a child denying the obvious.

"No, it was you, Rodion Romanych, it was you, sir, there's no one else."

Porfiry makes him an offer: if he confesses, he'll do what he can to have his sentence reduced. He's going to give him a day or two to think about it. He knows Raskolnikov won't try to flee, but there is one thing that concerns him. If Raskolnikov should happen to do something drastic—"such as raising your hand against yourself"—he asks Raskolnikov to send him a note, "just two little lines" telling him where the loot is hidden. But he urges Raskolnikov to accept his punishment. In fact, Nikolai might be right about the need to suffer. "Suffering, Rodion Romanych, is a great thing."

D ostoevsky had imagined a drastic ending for a while. There's a heading at the back of his final *Crime and Punishment* notebook:

THE END OF THE NOVEL

Just beneath it he wrote, "Raskolnikov goes to shoot himself." It's a suitable ending for someone whose core desire is to whisk everything off to the devil. Surely, when things go wrong, the urge to wipe everything away would turn inward, compelling him to leap off a bell tower, perhaps. Dostoevsky outlined Raskolnikov's suicide repeatedly. In one version, the idea comes to Raskolnikov in a dream: "Better a bullet in the head." But in the sketch in the back of Dostoevsky's notebook, it is Svidrigailov who brings it up. "You'll shoot yourself," he tells Raskolnikov in the middle of the Haymarket, "with your character you won't stay alive."

There were two possible endings for Raskolnikov, two examples he could follow. Dostoevsky set them out in the final lines of his final notebook:

Svidrigailov is despair, the most cynical.
Sonya is hope, the most unrealizable.
He became passionately attached to both.

While the lure of suicide for Raskolnikov is clear, his unrealizable hope lies buried in the novel. Raskolnikov understands, dimly, that he has isolated himself in an egoism so complete that other people hardly exist. Sonya is his only possible escape from this isolation, not just because she might love him (his mother and sister love him, after all), but because what Raskolnikov craves is a family of his own. In one notebook sketch, he roams through the city "and dreams how he will be a good husband, father." In another sketch it comes to him as an epiphany. But Dostoevsky ultimately decided to keep this desire unspoken in the novel, so it becomes a ghost always trying to break into the young man's bookish dreams.

Raskolnikov wants to be a father all the more because his own father is dead. Even this goes almost entirely unmentioned throughout the novel. His mother mentions him occasionally (he wrote poetry and fiction, for example), but beyond that his father's only remaining trace is his silver watch—the "two-penny" keepsake that Raskolnikov pawns to the woman he will murder, the watch he keeps trying to retrieve, drawing him to Porfiry Petrovich. The departed father's watch is the real hidden treasure at the center of Dostoevsky's story. Raskolnikov wants to become a father because he wants to bring his own father back.

A nna Grigorievna dreaded Dostoevsky's visit, and it got worse as the minutes ticked away. He hadn't arrived by half past seven. By eight o'clock, he was an hour late, and she began to wonder if he had forgotten. She had bought a few things she knew he liked—some sweets, his favorite kind of pears. She compiled a mental list of entertaining conversation topics, but she was certain the evening would be a failure. Over the past month, they had a shared endeavor and a pressing deadline to keep conversations lively. Now he was likely to drift into boredom while sitting idly with her and her mother.

Their bell rang at half past eight. "So you managed to find me, Fyodor Mikhailovich?"

"I've been searching for you since seven o'clock, driving all around the neighborhood and asking everybody. They all know that a Kostromskaya Street exists—but how to reach it—that they couldn't tell me." He had to recruit a pedestrian to sit next to the cabdriver and guide them to his destination.

When her mother entered the dining room, Dostoevsky kissed her hand and emphasized how indebted he was to her daughter for her work. Her mother was coy at first, but he charmed her. By the time he finished retelling his misadventures submitting *The Gambler*, their conversation over tea felt as natural as it had always been, and Anna didn't need to pull anything from her mental list. At some point, the topic turned to work. He was about to begin the final section of *Crime and Punishment*, and he wanted her help.

"Working with you has been so easy," he said. "As a matter of fact, I would like to use dictation from now on, and I hope you won't refuse to be my collaborator."

"I'd do it gladly," she said, but her professor might have someone else in mind for him? Dostoevsky assured her that he was not interested in anyone else.

He stayed until eleven o'clock. She was thrilled with the evening until she discovered that someone had stolen a cushion from the sleigh waiting for Dostoevsky. He promised to repay the disconsolate driver. Anna Grigorievna was mortified. And didn't it confirm a larger problem? Dostoevsky's sister-in-law—Mikhail's widow—was curt with her, as if she, a barely trained amanuensis, were beneath them, as if she belonged in a neighborhood where even the cabdrivers were at the mercy of thieves.

Her own family was not supportive, either. She saw her sister the day after Dostoevsky's visit and began talking excitedly about her job as Dostoevsky's stenographer. Her sister listened carefully to the countless details of their daily meetings and waited until Anna was leaving to say it: "It's all for nothing," her sister told her, "your having such a crush on Dostoevsky." Anna was stunned. "Your dreams can't ever come about," she told Anna, "and thank goodness they can't—if he's that ill and overloaded with family and debts!" And, of course, there was the obvious problem of their age difference. She was twenty. He was forty-five.

Anna vehemently denied having any improper "dreams." She simply enjoyed working with such a talented man, a famous author who was so kind and intelligent and grateful to her. But now that the question was raised, she had to wonder if indeed this was what love was like. A relationship with him seemed so improbable—an "insane dream"—but could she prevent herself from having it? And if she was in love, what should she do? She couldn't quit. She needed the work, and he needed her help.

A couple days later, Dostoevsky arrived uninvited. She was playing the piano and didn't hear the bell. She turned around at the sound of his footsteps. "Do you know what I've done, Anna Grigorievna?" he asked her while shaking her hand. "All these days I've missed you so much, and all day today, ever since morning, I've been deliberating about it—should I come to see you or not?" Was it too soon? Would it be strange? What would her mother think?

He saw her just three days ago, after all. "I resolved not to come under any circumstances. And, as you see, here I am!"

She said she would always be happy to host him, but now that she was alone with him—and not taking dictation—she was too nervous to talk. The drawing room wasn't even heated. He noticed her gray silk dress and realized she was about to go somewhere. To her godmother's house, she said. Dostoevsky suggested that because her destination was on his way, they should share an open sleigh. She agreed. As the sleigh careened around a sharp turn, he tried putting his arm around her waist. She rebuffed him: "I won't fall out!"

He was embarrassed and slightly miffed. "How I wish you would fall out of the sleigh this minute!" She laughed. They both laughed.

S o you're here at last!" he said. She was thirty minutes late. He rushed out when he heard her and helped her out of her coat and hood. It was a cold and sunny day—sunny enough to brighten his study. She noticed something in his expression, something "fervid, almost ecstatic," as she later described it. He looked younger. Perhaps it was the excitement of working on the conclusion of *Crime and Punishment*. This was their first day working on it together.

She couldn't help remarking on his cheerfulness. "Has something pleasant happened to you?"

"Last night I had a marvelous dream," he said.

"Oh, is that all!" She chuckled.

"Please don't laugh. I attribute great meaning to dreams. My dreams are always prophetic." Bad dreams always portended calamity for him—his dead brother and father. Last night's dream was different.

"Do you see that big rosewood box? That is a gift from my Siberian friend Chokan Valikhanov, and I value it very much." Valikhanov, the promising Kazakh scholar, the friend whom Dostoevsky said he loved as much as his own brother, had died the previous year. He was only twenty-nine years old. Dostoevsky kept his important letters, keepsakes, and manuscripts in Valikhanov's box. In his dream he was rearranging some papers in the box when he noticed something sparkling, "some kind of bright little star." He couldn't quite see what it was—it would disappear, then reappear. He had to take out

all the papers until he found it. It was a diamond, "a tiny one, but very sparkling and brilliant."

"And what did you do with it?"

"That's the pity of it—I can't remember." The image dissolved into other
dreams and washed away. "But that was a good dream!"

"You know that dreams are usually explained as having the opposite
meaning," she said. Propitious signs are warnings, and vice versa. She immediately regretted saying it when she saw his expression.

"So you think no happiness will ever come to me? That all—all that is
only a vain hope?"

Surely not. She claimed no authority as a dream interpreter—he should
simply ignore her. But that's not what he would do.

"I've been thinking up a plot for a new novel," he said. "The thing is,
though, I can't seem to work out the ending." He needed her insight into the
psychology of a young woman.

"Who is the hero of your novel, then?"

"An artist, a man no longer young—well, in a word—a man about my
own age."

"Oh tell me, do tell me about it."

The story came flowing out, apparently inspired as never before—the
artist's harsh childhood, lonely nights in a school far from home, a mother
who died, a father meeting a tragic end. It could not have been long before
she saw through the simple costume. The artist is torn away from his art for
a full decade. He has an incurable disease—a paralyzed hand. He suffers
a tormented love, the loss of his wife and a beloved sister, debt and poverty.
His hero was "a man grown old before his time." He was gloomy and sensitive. He was difficult to get along with. Tempestuous, irritable, "incapable
of expressing his feelings," incapable of manifesting his artistic ideas completely.

"But why, Fyodor Mikhailovich, do you insult your hero so?"

"I see that you do not find him likeable."

"On the contrary, I find him very likeable." Despite so much misfortune,
his hero maintains his heart.

One day the artist meets a young woman—about her own age. He'd call
her Anya. She was "gentle, wise, kind, bubbling with life."

Anna wanted to know if his heroine was beautiful.

"She is very nice-looking. I love her face."

This seemed like high praise. "Can she really be all that?"

"She is just precisely 'all that!' I have studied her through and through!"

They see each other regularly in "art circles." He begins to dream of finding happiness with her and then reproaches himself for such dreams. "What could this elderly, sick, debt-ridden man give a young, alive, exuberant girl?" Even if she consented, she would come to regret it.

He wanted to know how the story should end. Might a young woman like Anya fall in love with the artist? Was it impossible?

"But why would it be impossible? For if, as you say, your Anya isn't merely an empty flirt and has a kind, responsive heart, why couldn't she fall in love with your artist?" Poverty and illness are unimportant. "If she really loves him she'll be happy, too." He wanted her to be certain.

"Put yourself in her place for a moment," he said. His voice was quavering. "Imagine that this artist is—me; that I have confessed my love to you and asked you to be my wife. Tell me, what would you answer?"

"I would answer that I love you and will love you all my life."

Anna Grigorievna recalled feeling "crushed by the immensity of my happiness" after Dostoevsky's proposal, unable to think or make decisions about the next steps. She was beaming at a large family dinner gathering that evening, shifting between laughter and reverie. Her mother was late to the dinner, and when she finally arrived, Anna ran to the vestibule, hugged her, and whispered into her ear, "Congratulate me—I'm engaged!" Her mother was stunned, but there was no time to talk, and the news was still apparently a secret. She would have to wait until they were home before her daughter could tell her she was marrying Fyodor Mikhailovich Dostoevsky.

It was unwelcome news. To marry a man so much older, her mother thought, a man with precarious income, a man with epilepsy, would lead to a difficult life. But she could see her daughter's irrepressible happiness, and she was wise enough to know that there would be no dissuading her, so she didn't try. Dostoevsky arrived the following day to ask Anna's mother for her blessing. "I give you my word that I shall do everything I can and more to make her happy. And to you I shall be the most devoted and loving son." His sincerity and full-heartedness washed away her misgivings, and she cried as she embraced him.

Dostoevsky would visit Anna nearly every evening. If he had an engagement, he would find a way to leave early. "I ran away like a schoolboy! We'll have half an hour together, anyway!" He would bring sweets from his favorite confectioner (a bridegroom must always bring gifts, he told her). She would serve tea and be sure to have his favorite pears, dried apricots, and a Russian dessert called *pastila*—a paste of apple and honey baked for two days. Each insisted the other had the sweet tooth. She would urge him to go home at ten o'clock lest he encounter any more criminal activity, though he insisted he could handle himself if any ruffians were to attack. She nevertheless told the yard keeper to follow his sleigh at a distance until he made it out of the neighborhood.

She remained in mourning in public, but at home she wore bright dresses—pink, cherry. She was buoyant, talkative, full of laughter. She asked him about all his family members. She asked him about the women he had loved. She asked him when exactly he fell in love with her. "I want to know everything there is to know about you," she would say, "to see your past clearly, to know you through and through!"

Dostoevsky loved the attention. Had anyone ever really wanted to know him? Through and through? And knowing him made her giddy. "What has become of that strict, strait-laced Anna Grigorievna who used to come to my house to take dictation?" he asked. A double must have replaced her. Anna. Anya. Anka. Anechka. Each day, when they finished working on *Crime and Punishment*, he'd beg her to stay ("ten minutes more, one little quarter of an hour more"). He added a postscript to what is possibly his first letter to her. "You are my future everything—hope, and faith, and happiness, and bliss—everything."

An organ grinder sometimes played underneath the window of Dostoevsky's study when they worked. It was always Verdi's aria "La donna è mobile"—"Woman is fickle." Dostoevsky would sing along, substituting the opening line for her name. A-nna Gri-*gori*evna. Then he'd toss the organ grinder a coin. She protested that she was not fickle at all, that she would love him forever. ("We shall see, we shall see!") Their union, she believed, was preordained. She might even have thought that her deceased father somehow brought them together. After all, he was the one who had introduced her to Dostoevsky's writing, the one who recommended she learn stenography and who urged her to continue when she wanted to quit. Perhaps their marriage was exactly what he would have wanted.

There were challenges, of course. They decided to keep their engagement a secret from his family until he was on firmer financial footing, but the secrecy might have made their plans seem precarious. She oscillated between confidence and insecurity. She worried that she wouldn't understand his ideas and he'd see how unintelligent she was. She worried that he would stop loving her or that his old feelings for Polina Suslova would reemerge. She worried that he never actually knew genuine love at all, that it was only a beautiful idea, something he had always imagined for himself. She worried that the way he sometimes shouted at servants and at Pasha augured badly for their future. He had never shouted at her, nor did he ever doubt her intelligence, but her youth stoked his paternalism toward her, prompting him to protect her from corrupting books, plays, and operas. Sometimes he found their age difference embarrassing. On this point, however, she swiftly reassured her fiancé: living with him was going to make her age rather quickly.

His family was openly hostile toward her. Pasha refused to greet her when she visited, though he made his presence felt by yelling at the maid and jostling things around in the dining room. He preferred Dostoevsky to focus on supporting him. His sister-in-law felt the same way, as did her children, as did Dostoevsky's brother Nikolai. At one point, the family decided to pawn Dostoevsky's winter coat, assuring him that he could get another advance from Katkov by the time winter set in. Dostoevsky arrived at Anna Grigorievna's house shivering one evening. When she saw his meager fall coat hanging up, she was incensed. "I lost all control over myself and talked like a madwoman," she recalled. He would get sick—and he *did* get sick, bedridden for two days. He would miss his deadlines. They had a wedding to prepare for. His relatives could take care of themselves; Pasha and Nikolai were adults, and his sister-in-law had two adult sons. She made him promise not to leave his house until he had the money to redeem his coat. Her outburst surprised him. He had pawned his coat so many times the previous winter that it hardly fazed him anymore, and his debt to his departed wife and brother felt bottomless.

Throughout the turmoil of their secret engagement, Anna Grigorievna was helping Dostoevsky create a fair copy of *Crime and Punishment*'s final chapters. He would dictate from the rough pages he wrote the night before, revising along the way, as she took it down in shorthand and transcribed it into clean, clear text for the journal. He was eating soup for dinner, revising until one in the morning, and losing sleep. He missed Anna's name-day party in December, partly because he was busy but mostly because he had suffered a seizure and felt weak.

By December, Dostoevsky was working on the novel's final study of entwined hope and despair. The narrative suddenly breaks away from Raskolnikov and follows Svidrigailov, as if pulled into a new orbit. Svidrigailov passes out of Raskolnikov's sight and has a rendezvous with his sister, Dunya. He's in a summery linen suit, and his thick blond hair and beard make him look too young for fifty. He has come to Petersburg for the women, the only thing he still enjoys—a thirteen-year-old he met at a dance hall, a servant from his deceased wife's estate. He's now engaged to the daughter of downtrodden parents. In just one month she will be sixteen, legally marriageable. A brothel madam arranged it.

But the woman he really wants is Dunya. Svidrigailov lures her to his apartment by promising to tell her a secret: her brother is a murderer. He overheard his confession to Sonya because one of her doors leads to his own neighboring apartment. The police are closing in on her brother, he says, but together they can save him. He'll get passports for all of them to flee the country together. "I love you infinitely," he begins raving. "Let me kiss the hem of your dress." Dunya runs to the door, but it's locked, and no one can hear them. The closest people are "five locked doors away," he reminds her. He'll use force if he has to, and he'll report Raskolnikov if she tells anyone, though it would be pointless for her to try. "No one will believe you: why on earth should a girl go alone to a single man's apartment?"

Dostoevsky initially imagined Raskolnikov bursting in to save his sister.

Instead, Dunya pulls out a revolver and cocks the hammer. Svidrigailov leaps up. "Aha! So that's how it is!" He has never seen her so beautiful. He steps forward, and she shoots. The bullet grazes his scalp. A trickle of blood slides down his right temple, and he wipes it away with a handkerchief. He tells her to shoot again, smiling, stepping closer. She pulls the trigger—the gun misfires. He grabs her by the waist, but she's adamant: "Let me go!" Her words somehow startle him, as if she has finally reached him.

"So you don't love me?"

Svidrigailov gives Dunya the key and she flees. That night, heavy clouds roll in and a thunderstorm brings torrential rains. The rain is so relentless it seems vengeful, as if the Almighty were starting over yet again, as if Petersburg would never be right. He checks into a ramshackle hotel around midnight, soaking wet, trembling and feverish. In bed, he begins slipping into dreams and hallucinations. A mouse darting under the pillow and skittering down his back. A country cottage filled with flowers. The coffin of the fourteen-year-old girl he defiled. There are no icons or candles around her. She can't have a religious burial because she drowned herself.

Svidrigailov hears cannon shots in the distance—the city's flood signal. The river is rising. It's near dawn, so he decides to check out. As he walks through the hotel's dark corridor, he sees something moving in a corner. He bends down with his candle and sees a five-year-old child in a raggedy dress. She's soaking wet, crying and shivering. He undresses her and wraps her in his blanket to keep her warm. Her color returns after she falls asleep, but it's unusually flush. Her lips become scarlet, and her eyelashes flutter. She begins to smile and breaks into disturbing laughter. He knows the look on her face. It's depravity. The face of a woman selling herself. The little girl stretches her arms out to him, and he's horrified.

"Nightmares all night long!" It's past dawn when Svidrigailov finally wakes up, and a thick fog covers the city. As he walks to the river, he decides he wants an "official witness." He heads toward a tall watchtower and approaches a man in a soldier's coat and a brass fireman's helmet.

"Good morning!"

The watchman says he's in the wrong place. Svidrigailov pulls out Dunya's revolver and cocks it.

"S-sir, s'not the place for joking!"

"Well, brother, never mind that. It's a nice place, and if someone asks you, tell them I've gone to America."

He puts the muzzle against his right temple.

"S-sir, not 'ere, s'not the place!"

He puts a bullet in his head.

Dostoevsky had always intended to tell the story of an egoism that devours itself after whisking everything away, an evil so profound and despairing that it can lead only to suicide. Svidrigailov takes the end that Dostoevsky originally imagined for Raskolnikov, and when he pulls the trigger, it is as if he frees Raskolnikov from a looming debt.

Raskolnikov also wanders through the city during the night of the thunderstorm. He walks up and down the Neva around sunrise and thinks about throwing himself in as the river floods, but he decides to do something else. He goes to his mother, tells her that he loves her, that he's about to go away—somewhere "very far"—and she can't go with him. He falls down and kisses her feet, and they both weep. After leaving his mother, he tells Dunya he's going to turn himself in. She embraces him, but when she says his suffering will begin to absolve him of the guilt of his crime, he bursts out, "Crime? What crime?" He's enraged. "I killed a vile, pernicious louse, a little old money-lending crone who was of no use to anyone." He killed a woman who fed off the poor—"is that a crime?"

"Brother, brother, what are you saying! You shed blood!"

"Which everyone sheds," he tells her, "which men spill like champagne, and for which they're crowned." He reverts to his old arguments, that he just wanted the means to become useful, that it wouldn't be a crime if he succeeded. He's never been more certain than now! He visits Sonya at dusk, and she gives him two crosses, one made of cypress ("for simple folk") and one of brass (Lizaveta's). She tells him to cross himself, and he does, but he still does not believe in God, nor does he know why he's confessing. When he realizes she's planning to follow him to the police station, he tells her to stay. "No need for a whole retinue!" He doesn't even say goodbye to her when he leaves.

He walks along a canal bank and suddenly, unthinkingly, turns toward the Haymarket. That's where he has to do it. The square had long been a public execution ground where thieves were flogged and branded. He squeezes through the crowd, past peddlers and drunks, to the middle of the square. An idea hits him. "It came to him suddenly in a sort of fit, caught fire in his soul from a single spark, and suddenly, like a flame, engulfed him." Tears stream down Raskolnikov's face, and he falls down on his knees. He bows down and kisses the dirt. He suddenly remembers that this was Sonya's idea. "Kiss the earth you've defiled," she said when he confessed to her, "then bow to the whole world, on all four sides, and say aloud to everyone: 'I have killed!'" In the distance, Raskolnikov can see her watching him behind a wooden stall. He stands up and does it again—bows down, kisses the ground.

"This one's plastered all right!" someone says, and people laugh.

He makes his way to the police station, opens the door, and sees listless scribes and officers. Lieutenant Gunpowder pops out. "Gr-r-reetings!" He's affable, chatty. Raskolnikov can hardly get a word in, and in the middle of his chatter the lieutenant mentions that a man named Svidrigailov committed suicide this morning. Raskolnikov turns pale and starts to flee until he sees Sonya standing near the entrance looking at him, wild-eyed and desperate.

He goes back upstairs to Lieutenant Gunpowder and declares, *It was I who killed the official's old widow and her sister Lizaveta with an axe and robbed them.* Lieutenant Gunpowder is stunned, his mouth open. Officers come running over. He repeats his confession for everyone to hear.

The entire sequence is unsettling. Why does Raskolnikov confess? The moments leading up to his decision on the stormy night are hazy—it is one of the only times the narrator leaves Raskolnikov. We know only what he tells Dunya, which is almost nothing because he has almost no memory of the night. Does he think his arrest is really imminent? Does his encounter with Svidrigailov give him a horrifying glimpse into his own unrestrained egoism? He experiences flashes of remorse with Dunya and Sonya, but they are fleeting. He gives some reasons—that he's proving he's strong enough to bear Siberia, that he's hoping for Porfiry's leniency—but even as he leaves Sonya's apartment, even as he walks up to the police station, he himself does not know why he is doing it. It just happens, the same way his feet take him to Haymarket on their own, the way he returns to the scene of the crime without thinking, the way he finds himself off in some obscure quarter of the city, or beyond the city gates, or beneath some bushes without knowing how he got there. For someone so invested in the power of his will, Raskolnikov is an automaton. The murders themselves seem to happen automatically. His most crucial actions are reflexive, like the twitching leg of a decapitated frog. When his confession finally happens, it's performative, drawn out, and empty. The same is true for the murders. Just before he picks up the ax, he feels pulled into the crime, "as if a piece of his clothing had been caught in the cogs of a machine and he were being dragged into it." And when he strikes the pawn-broker's head, he does it "without effort, almost mechanically."

But what's most unsettling is not that Raskolnikov's confession is unthink-ing. It's that his confession is unfeeling. He kisses the Haymarket ground, prostrates himself in public, and turns himself in without ever feeling any remorse for the women he killed. It's not just that he refers to Alyona Ivanovna as a "vile, pernicious louse" just before he confesses. It's that the other woman he killed—Lizaveta—isn't even worth mentioning. The omission is not ca-sual. At one point, Raskolnikov is dismayed by this persistent, eerie lapse: "Why is it that I almost never think of her, as if I hadn't killed her?" He keeps removing her from his accounts and recollections. Even when he confesses to Sonya, he keeps referring to having killed just "the old woman," "the old crone."

And he is not the only one who forgets Lizaveta. Razumikhin and his friend discuss the murder of "the old woman" while visiting Raskolnikov. His landlady's servant has to interject, "They killed Lizaveta, too!" The police clerk speaks to Raskolnikov as if only one murder took place in his precinct. Even Porfiry Petrovich, a stickler for detail, somehow overlooks her when he coaxes Raskolnikov into confessing. "It's good that you only killed a little old woman." It is as if everyone forgets the tall younger woman, the half sister in goatskin shoes who might be pregnant. Her unborn baby boy is unambiguous in Dostoevsky's notebooks, but he decided to obscure the pregnancy (or per-haps delete it) and to take away her daughter, Sassia, leaving her possibly childless and possibly easier to forget.

Even after Raskolnikov is exiled to Siberia, his victims remain unreal to him. We next see him in a fortress prison by the Irtysh River. It's more than a year after his crimes, and he's been sentenced to eight years in penal servitude. He still insists he did nothing wrong, "except perhaps a simple *blunder* that could have happened to anyone." His ideas and actions seem even less "stupid and hideous" to him than they did before. His confession, he thinks, was his only crime.

None of the other prisoners like Raskolnikov ("You don't believe in God!"), and he becomes withdrawn. Sonya follows him to Siberia, sees him at the prison gates on holidays, and meets him at the workshops during his work assignments. When he becomes seriously ill, she stands for hours in the hospital courtyard waiting for him to look out the window, but he avoids her.

His perspective finally begins to change early one summer morning. Raskolnikov has been assigned to grind alabaster. He sits down on a pile of logs outside the kiln shed and looks out at the wide river. The sky is clear, and from the river's high bank he can see far out across the Kazakh steppe. It seems so vast this morning, so open and empty. In the distance, he can see the Kazakhs' yurts, just tiny dots on the horizon. He can hear the faint sounds of singing, and he thinks, "Over there was freedom; over there lived people quite unlike the ones living here; over there time itself seemed to have stopped, as if the ages of Abraham and his flocks had not yet passed." And then his mind's babbling finally stops, if just for a moment. Out here at the edge of the empire, everything flattens into nothing.

For Raskolnikov, for Dostoevsky, the Kazakhs represent a world before prisons and promissory notes. It's nostalgia, of course, and it was so much easier for the nomadic herdsmen to become vessels for a Russian convict's fantasy in 1866, when the Russian Empire had largely taken the Kazakhs' independence, and when Valikhanov, the only Kazakh whom Dostoevsky really knew, was dead. Like every nostalgia, the distance supplies the beauty.

One surprise about *Crime and Punishment* is how little the punishment matters. What we expect to find in Siberia is an exiled criminal who has confessed out of genuine remorse, someone whose sentencing by the tsar has finally jolted him out of his egoism, materialism, and nihilism. We expect to find a convict who has had ample time to rid himself of his bookishness and lofty fantasies, a man in chains whose suffering helps him recover his humanity and turn to higher ideals, perhaps even to God. What we actually find is a character whose hollow contrition in the Haymarket crumbles into arid nostalgia on the Kazakh steppe, a character who stubbornly affirms all the principles of self-interest and egoism that Dostoevsky opposed. Raskolnikov ultimately admits that he confessed out of a "desire to live," which he ascribes to irrepressible instinct. He turns himself in when he sees the possibility of a new life with Sonya after eight years of suffering—exactly what a rational egoist would do. He finds a humbler version of a benevolent career guided by life alone, not by ideology or even by faith. Raskolnikov does not find God at the end of *Crime and Punishment*. Sonya's Bible lies under his pillow, but he has never opened it, and he does not open it now. The novel's final words gesture to Raskolnikov's future rebirth, a renewal that can only be told in another story, a story Dostoevsky will never write.

Twenty-Three

Buried in Furs

A steady stream of visitors came to Lacenaire's cell before his execution. Several tried to convert him back to his faith. Others offered gifts—sausages, wine, pâté. The inspector general of prisons asked for his observations about how the prisons were functioning. The chief of the Sûreté developed such a rapport with Lacenaire that he commissioned the criminal's portrait for his own collection. Lacenaire received letters from women all over France. They sent him food and fine chocolate. Some wrote him poetry. One grande dame requested his autograph to add to her collection. Another woman, convinced he was good luck, asked him for lottery numbers.

Newspapers and magazines printed anything he wrote—his poetry, his songs, a handful of letters, a vaudeville, a three-act play he composed in his school years. They ran the material even when the authorship was dubious. An old school friend, Jacques Arago, published extensive conversations he had with the condemned man in his prison cell. Lacenaire complained to Arago about the way the press ridiculed and slandered him. Every article, he said, contained "two true words, and the rest is a lie." After he dies, they'll say he killed fifty people and ate steaks made of little children. He spoke about his lost dreams for the stage, particularly vaudeville—he had thought of his best jokes during his crimes. He lamented the monotony of the average person's life, how people live only to suffer. He shared his thoughts about whether objects have souls or whether anyone exists at all. He considered himself more of a philosopher than an artist, and he gazed upon contemporary art with pity: "I don't like trifles."

Lacenaire continued to write poetry, including a swan song to the guillotine that celebrates the instrument of "sublime atonement," the machine that purifies the criminal "in the bosom of nothingness." Days of conversations left Arago with a singular impression: "This man is stronger than death."

T he guards came on January 8, 1836, to take Lacenaire to Bicêtre, where he would spend his final night. He had been longing for this moment since the day his father pointed to the infamous machine as the dreadful consequence of misbehavior. The blade severed his spine so many times in his dreams that he never imagined dying any other way. So when the jury had reached its verdict, at two in the morning, he was gratified to have brought it to pass. He basked in a certain pride even as the guards put him in a straitjacket. "I contemplate my strength, and I am whole within myself."

Less than two months had elapsed since his trial. François had been spared. Lacenaire and Avril were to be executed. He wrote roughly sixty thousand words of his memoirs, but neither this, nor his testimony, nor his interviews, nor the phrenological examinations would satisfy the public's desire to understand his motives.

A shared fate drew Avril and Lacenaire closer. Lacenaire wrote a drinking song to help them celebrate Christmas. He titled it "A mon ami Avril":

> Let's drink to the day that's coming
> To the oblivion of all our evils,
> To the oblivion of vengeance,
> The wicked and then the fools!

The murderers were locked in adjoining cells once they arrived in Bicêtre, and they joked about blood over their final meal together. They shared coffee, brandy, and a cigar. Canler and Allard visited and offered them extra time if they had more information to divulge, but Lacenaire had nothing more to tell them. "Gentlemen," he said, "I trust that I shall have the honor of seeing you tomorrow morning at the Barrière Saint Jacques?"

The guards could hear the prisoners talking through the walls after they were locked up for the night.

"Are you sleeping, Avril?" He wasn't. "Are you thinking about tomorrow?" Lacenaire remained calm, though every now and then he worried again about the possibility that the crowd would despise him. There could be nothing worse than the contempt of a crowd.

"I'm cold," he told Avril. "It froze today."

Avril was less inclined to talk. "Good night . . ."

"The ground will be very cold tomorrow . . ." Lacenaire said.

"Then ask to be buried in furs."

The priests came before dawn. The chaplain general of the prisons counseled Lacenaire, but he was unable to elicit any sense of remorse. "I am sorry for the trouble you have taken," Lacenaire told him, "your visit is useless."

Then the executioners came. Their assistants were instructed not to speak with the condemned as they prepared them for the guillotine, and the man they saw might not have been what they were expecting. Lacenaire's head had been shaved. He sat on a stool, and he was small and thin. The grooves on his scalp and the lines on his face seemed deeper in the light of the room's two candles.

"Would you be good enough to get my blue coat?" he asked. It was the same frock coat he'd worn at his trial. "I should like to wear it today."

Lacenaire was calm and smiling, his hands and feet loosely bound, when he emerged from the carriage at the Barrière Saint Jacques, Paris's southern gate. The scaffold had been erected quickly, by torchlight, just a few hours before. The ground was muddy, and the sky was pale. Lacenaire was displeased with the schedule. Executions were typically in the afternoon. The early hour was intended to reduce the crowd, but it turned out to be quite good.

Five to six hundred people had gathered. The onlookers were somewhat typical—workmen pausing on their way to jobs, neighborhood scamps, prostitutes, and an array of suspicious, disreputable people. Notices announcing the execution had been circulating. They recounted Lacenaire's crimes and reprinted one of his songs, though they got his name wrong ("Pierre-Joseph") and didn't mention the execution date. Yet despite the near-complete press silence regarding the execution date and the dark-of-night scaffold construction, word had gotten out to various quarters of the city. A dozen or so national guardsmen left their posts to watch, as did a fair number of actors and a group of ladies who had halted their carriage for the spectacle while on their way home from an official's ball.

The chaplain and the executioners—one for each prisoner—led the two condemned men past the cordon of municipal guards surrounding the guillotine. Lacenaire spotted Inspector Canler at the front of the crowd.

"There you are!" he said, bowing. "Good morning, Monsieur Canler. It is very kind of you to have come. Is M. Allard here?" Canler replied that he was, though he had apparently not made it close enough to bid the prisoners adieu. Lacenaire leaned toward the inspector and asked in a low voice, "Will you allow me to embrace you, M. Canler?"

Canler hesitated. "Well . . . no," he said quietly. "Yesterday evening, yes; it would have been with pleasure; but today, in front of all these people . . . frankly, I would not care to." He was worried that Lacenaire might try to bite his face.

Avril was the first to go. He and Lacenaire embraced before the executioners' men took him up the scaffold steps. As they were fastening him to the planks, he turned and shouted, "Goodbye, my old Lacenaire! Goodbye, courage! . . . I show you the way."

"Goodbye, goodbye!" Lacenaire shouted back.

The men hinged the plank horizontally and placed Avril's neck in the lunette, a wooden semicircle lined with copper. They lowered the top half down and locked it. When Lacenaire turned to watch, one of the men turned him back around. He looked again moments later. "I am not afraid," he said, "no, I am not afraid."

A small lever on the side of the red machine releases the blade, and a heavy weight above it speeds its path down the grooves in the vertical beams. Simplicity is the machine's great virtue. Lacenaire heard a moment of silence, then wood sliding on wood, a thump, and the crowd's reaction as Avril's head rolled on the planks.

It was Lacenaire's turn. The story that eventually appeared in the *Gazette des Tribunaux* was the story that officials wanted to report, the story that would demystify what Lacenaire had become for so many people. They wanted to announce that Lacenaire trembled before the guillotine, that he couldn't summon the strength to ascend the scaffold, that the executioner's men had to carry him. But that was not true.

Lacenaire walked steadily up the scaffold as he had always imagined he would, but it's impossible to imagine everything—pressing his neck against Avril's blood, the boot of the executioner's man standing beside him. Did he imagine feeling his head falling? Stories circulated about how guillotined people do not die immediately, about expressions changing on the severed heads, eyes shifting focus, making contact with a face, responding to a name. These were mostly just rumors, ghost stories, and perhaps, in a few cases, the unsettling effects of spasms in facial tissues.

And yet there is a small window of time—a second or two—when consciousness still clings, when the guillotined criminal might feel his head breaking free from his body, unencumbered, when the world spins until he feels the impact of the cold, wooden platform, and the last thing he hears is the first split second of the crowd's reaction. Lacenaire was facedown on the plank, waiting for an unusually long time before the executioner finally gave the signal and his man pulled the lever.

The blade got stuck—it was jammed halfway down. Maybe the damp weather had swollen the wood, narrowing one of the grooves just enough to block the fall. Maybe the machine was just old. Either way, seeing the blade suspended above the murderer was bone-chilling. They hoisted it up again. As the rope turned the squeaking wheel, Lacenaire contorted his torso enough to rotate his head upward in the lunette so that when the blade finally came he would be able to see it for himself. And it would be the most extraordinary view.

Twenty-Four

The Wedding

On December 27, Dostoevsky was lying awake in a cold sleeping car on an overnight train to Moscow. Charcoal fumes filled the damp air. He was suffering from what he described as a "pointless sadness" along with an intense toothache, but he was bringing with him the final pages of *Crime and Punishment*. He began thinking about all that had happened in the last few weeks, about how much had changed. He wrote to Anna soon after he arrived. "I kiss you countless times over," the letter read, though he confessed that he was afraid. "Pray about our union, my angel."

He had no money for the wedding, no money to establish a new household or even to pacify his creditors. He had warned her before departing that they'd have to postpone their marriage for a while, perhaps a year, unless Katkov was so satisfied with his work that he'd agree to extraordinary measures to keep him as a writer. Dostoevsky thought that submitting his conclusion to *Crime and Punishment* in person might maximize his leverage. When he found Katkov at the *Russian Herald* office, the editor was busy, as always, but he received his celebrated author warmly. Dostoevsky announced that he was planning to get married, and Katkov naturally offered his sincere congratulations and well wishes.

"In that case," Dostoevsky said, "I'll tell you straight out that my entire happiness depends on you. If you need me as a contributor—"

"Of course," Katkov jumped in, "for heaven's sake."

"—give me an advance of 2,000 rubles."

Because "advances like this aren't given," he told Katkov, "everything depends upon your good will."

Katkov needed to see if the journal had that much money available. Two days later, he agreed to give Dostoevsky one thousand rubles immediately and another thousand before his wedding. Dostoevsky wrote to Anna with the good news. "Thank God, thank God!" They could begin planning as soon as he returned. "With a wife like you and to be unhappy—is that really possible? Love me, Anya; I'll love you forever and ever." She read his letters repeatedly as she waited for his return.

Dostoevsky planned to tell his immediate family the news once his finances were settled, but the secret slipped out. He liked to chat with his cabdrivers, and coming home one evening, when he didn't have enough cash, he got money inside and sent the maid out with it. But there were three drivers at the gate. When she asked which one had just brought "the old gentleman," one of them responded, "You mean the bridegroom?"

The next morning, Pasha reproached his stepfather for not consulting him on the matter. He should be mindful of the fact that he is "already an old man"—unfit to begin a new life—and that he had other obligations. It took Pasha more than a week to congratulate Anna Grigorievna on the engagement.

Dostoevsky's relatives had their reasons to resent it. Katkov's first thousand rubles went largely to creditors, and the earnings on a book edition of *Crime and Punishment* had been designated for an old *Epoch* creditor long before the novel was even finished. Even with his most recent payment, Dostoevsky would still have three thousand rubles in unpaid promissory notes, and it wouldn't be long before creditors would threaten him with prison again. His relatives of course knew how he would solve this problem: he and his new wife would flee to Europe. Dostoevsky seemed to be choosing marriage and a new life over paying off the family's persistent debts.

The decision was not difficult. Anna was the first woman with whom he found a loving partnership and, at last, the prospect of a family—"that great and *only* human happiness." They scheduled the wedding for February 12, and when Katkov's second thousand rubles arrived on February 1, it felt like a godsend. He wrote to Katkov, "You have *saved* me (literally *saved* me) at the most critical moment of my life."

Dostoevsky notified guests at the last minute. The ceremony would take place Sunday evening—"if nothing too unusual happens," he wrote to one friend. Perhaps he sensed what was coming. Dostoevsky had a seizure a day or two before the wedding, and it left him weak and housebound. But there was little time remaining. Weddings are prohibited during Lent, which would begin the following week, so they had to reschedule it for Wednesday, three days later.

Anna Grigorievna woke up at dawn, attended Mass, and visited her father's grave site. She and her family gathered at her mother's house and waited nearly an hour. Dostoevsky's best man (one of his nephews) arrived just minutes before the ceremony was scheduled to begin. "Let's go! For goodness sake, let's start moving!" His uncle was surely panicking. Anna's mother embraced her, wrapped Anna in her fur coat, and sent her off to the cathedral. Neighbors were gathered on the stairs to kiss the bride, to offer blessings, and to sprinkle her with hops for prosperity.

The bride, accompanied by her sister and a footman, ascended the steps of the Trinity Cathedral, a large neoclassical edifice with grand Corinthian columns and bright blue domes adorned with gold six-pointed stars. It's dedicated to one of Russia's oldest Imperial Guard regiments, and the interior is filled with religious icons, paintings, relics, and battlefield trophies. Years later, Anna couldn't remember much about the ceremony beyond how pale Dostoevsky looked and the way he hurried her to the altar. She remembered that the cathedral was lit beautifully that night, that the choir's voices reverberated throughout the grand space, and that she wore a silk wedding dress with a long train as she stood beside the retired engineer-lieutenant, the litterateur, the criminal, the unfortunate, the gambler, the widow, the novelist Fyodor Mikhailovich Dostoevsky.

Something else happens at the end of *Crime and Punishment*, something other than Raskolnikov's nostalgia for a timeless way of life. As he looks out toward the horizon of the Kazakh steppe, Sonya sits down next to him. They hold hands while the guard's back is turned, and all that beautiful distance collapses. Raskolnikov suddenly flings himself down at her feet, embraces her knees, and begins weeping. They don't need to say anything. He loves her. "At last the moment had come . . ."

After the wedding ceremony's prayer of thanksgiving, Dostoevsky wrote their names in the church register, and a little boy dressed in a smart Russian suit—her stenography teacher's son—carried the icon and led the procession out to their carriage. He told everyone at the reception celebration how they kept kissing each other the whole way.

Anna described the days following the wedding as "merry chaos." They celebrated with friends and family over dinners capped with joyous toasts. She drank more champagne in those few days than she would ever drink again. And on their last indulgent night before Lent, Dostoevsky was telling a story to Anna's sister when he halted mid-sentence. He turned white and tried standing up from the couch, but he began falling toward Anna. She had never witnessed this before. His face contorted in pain, and he began shrieking. She described it as "inhuman"—a "howl." Her sister ran out of the room screaming, and her husband followed, leaving the newlywed couple alone.

Anna tried to ease him back down by his shoulders, but she couldn't keep his convulsing body from sliding farther. There was a chair with a lit lamp next to them. She shoved it aside, let him slip to the floor, and held his head in her lap as his body shuddered. When he touched back down to consciousness, he tried speaking, but only the wrong words came. He would try again, revise, but he could give her only a pile of little pieces. He moaned in pain. Then, an hour later, he felt it coming again.

Maybe she knew, as she held him, that his tremors may have been little more than the aftershocks of a great ecstasy—the seizure's aura. Maybe she knew that his body was just a meager channel for that brilliant experience when, for just one second, all doubts and fears, all ambiguity, all the barriers within himself and between himself and the world, all past and all future, melt away in a flash of salience and light worth an entire lifetime. Anna Grigorievna wondered if he would ever come back. His eyes stared wildly, and his face was like the face of a stranger's. She was beginning to know him through and through.

ACKNOWLEDGMENTS

A single book is the work of many people. I am grateful for my agent, Suzanne Gluck, for her guidance and advice over the years and for always believing in me and my work. I have been incredibly fortunate to have a brilliant and dedicated editor, Ginny Smith, who has been making me a better writer for more than a decade. Caroline Sydney provided invaluable edits and notes at every stage of my writing and helped shepherd this book through production. More people at Penguin Press helped put this book together than I can name, including copy editors, cold readers, and the production and sales teams. Stephanie Ross designed the striking, unforgettable jacket. Several agents at WME have been devoted to this project over the years, including Ashley Fox, Hilary Zaitz Michael, Caitlin Mahony, and Andrea Blatt.

Many people have contributed essential work and research to make this book better than anything I could have accomplished alone. I offer special thanks to River Adams for all their work translating Russian-language sources, for primary and secondary research, and for consultation on matters of Russian culture. Russia is far more vivid in this book because of them. Eric Idsvoog and Ludovic Trinquart provided crucial translation assistance from French sources and information about French culture, past and present, that has been indispensable. April White was brilliant, assiduous, and resourceful as she helped me dig up information about so many topics, from Wiesbaden gambling halls to nineteenth-century gold mining to prehistoric central Asian topography. During the pandemic Steven Cox, special collections curator at Pittsburg State University, generously provided scans of a rare nineteenth-century volume, when libraries across the country, and thus the interlibrary loan system, were shut down. James E. Duggan, director of Tulane Law Library, mailed me a copy of a much-needed book during that same shutdown, and I imagine he stretched library policy to do so. Greta Pane helped me acquire additional research material, and Sabrina Sadique alerted me to Cixous's interest in Dostoevsky. Dana Simmons provided help with French cultural background, and I have benefited from the expertise of Justine De Young and her excellent Fashion History Timeline: https://fashionhistory .fitnyc.edu/1830-1839.

Three excellent readers improved my drafts tremendously: Gabi Gage, Eric Idsvoog, and Sean Smith asked crucial questions, spotted key problems, and helped me see things from new perspectives. Their detailed notes sharpened my work on every page. Megan Marshall offered valuable advice and comments on a late revision, and I'm grateful for all her support. I have benefited from insightful discussions with Michael Gorra about the type of work that we do, and I understand it better now than I did before. More than a decade of lunches with Matthew Pearl have helped me stay motivated, focused, and entertained. I cherish his perspective, advice, and subtle charm. May there be many more lunches, despite distance and a pandemic. I wish the same for a fantastic group of nonfiction writers. Gabi Gage, Mo Moulton, Megan Kate Nelson, Tobey Pearl, and I discussed the joys and travails of the writing life over drinks when possible and over video chats when necessary, and their insights and experiences over the years have been restorative and inspiring. I offer my eternal thanks to my mother, Migdalia Birmingham; and to Julia Seol, for her fearless love and unending support and for bearing with me when I am difficult to bear. I am also grateful for our son, James, who listened to my revisions to the galleys just days after coming home from the hospital and who encouraged me even when he fell asleep.

This book was supported generously by the National Endowment for the Humanities Public Scholars program. Any views, findings, conclusions, or recommendations expressed in this book do not necessarily reflect those of the National Endowment for the Humanities. This book's acknowledgments will nevertheless be candid: scholarship in the humanities is produced largely by tenure-track professors at research universities where severely underpaid contingent faculty and graduate students do much of the work that keeps departments running so that a small fraction of the professoriate has more time, resources, and research assistance to publish. This arrangement is deliberate. The next time you pick up a biography, for example, or a book of literary criticism or cultural history, remember that the author relied upon the labor of countless unacknowledged scholars. I am indebted to them.

NOTES

ABBREVIATIONS

C&P = Fyodor Dostoevsky, *Crime and Punishment*, trans. Richard Pevear and Larissa Volokhonsky (New York: Vintage Classics, 1992).

Delo petrashevtsev I–III = Akademiya Nauk SSSR, Institut istorii, *Delo petrashevtsev*, 3 vols. (Moscow: Izdatel'stvo Akademii nauk SSSR, 1937–51).

DH = Fyodor Dostoevsky, *Notes from a Dead House*, trans. Richard Pevear and Larissa Volokhonsky (New York: Alfred A. Knopf, 2015).

DVS I–II = *F. M. Dostoevsky v vospominaniyakh sovremennikov*, ed. S. A. Makashin et al., 2 vols. (Moscow: Khudozhestvennaya literatura, 1990).

Frank I–V = Joseph Frank, *Dostoevsky*, 5 vols. (Princeton, N.J.: Princeton University Press, 1976–2002).

Yakubovich I, II = Irina Dmitrievna Yakubovich et al., *Letopis' zhizni i tvorchestva F. M. Dostoevskogo v trekh tomakh*, 3 vols. (St. Petersburg: Akademicheskii Proekt, 1993–95).

LI–V = Fyodor Mikhailovich Dostoevsky, *Complete Letters*, trans. and ed. David Lowe and Ronald Meyer, 5 vols. (Ann Arbor, Mich.: Ardis, 1988–91).

Lacenaire, ses crimes = Victor Cochinat and Pierre-François Lacenaire, *Lacenaire, ses crimes, son procés et sa mort* (Paris: Jules Laisné, 1857).

Mémoires et écrits = Pierre-François Lacenaire, *Mémoires et autres écrits*, ed. Jacques Simonelli (Paris: José Corti, 1991).

Memoirs = Pierre-François Lacenaire, *The Memoirs of Lacenaire*, trans. and ed. Philip John Stead (New York: Staples Press, 1952).

Notebooks = Fyodor Dostoevsky, *The Notebooks for "Crime and Punishment,"* trans. and ed. Edward Wasiolek (Chicago: University of Chicago Press, 1967).

Procès complet = Pierre-François Lacenaire, *Procès complet de Lacenaire et de ses complices imprimé sur les épreuves corrigées de sa main* (Paris: Bureau de l'Observateur des Tribunaux, 1836).

PSS = Fyodor Mikhailovich Dostoevsky, *Polnoe sobranie sochineniy v tridtsati tomakh*, 30 vols. (Leningrad: Nauka, 1972–90).

Reminiscences = Anna Dostoevsky, *Dostoevsky: Reminiscences*, trans. and ed. Beatrice Stillman (New York: Liveright, 1977).

A NOTE ON SOURCES

I rely upon available translations whenever possible, including the Pevear and Volokhonsky translations of *Crime and Punishment* and *Notes from a Dead House*. My use of alternate translations (such as Oliver Ready's translation of *Crime and Punishment*) as well as occasional alterations to published translations are always noted in the endnotes. All italics and ellipses in quotations are reproduced from original sources unless otherwise specified in the endnotes. Dates for all source material and events in Russia follow the Julian calendar, which, in the nineteenth century, was twelve days behind the Gregorian calendar used in the west. Letters sent between Russia and Europe indicate the date of composition in both locations (e.g.: "Aug. 10/22, 1865"). I have maintained standard anglicized transliterations of popular Russian names (Dostoevsky instead of Dostoevskii, for example). I narrate several scenes in Dostoevsky's works, weaving the fictional into the factual, with the hope of delving down to deeper truths of the story behind Dostoevsky's novel instead of settling for the "shallow sailing" of realists, as Dostoevsky put it, and of standard literary history.

In addition to the abbreviated sources listed above, several monographs have been particularly helpful: Andrew Gentes's body of research on Siberia, particularly *Exile, Murder, and Madness in Siberia, 1823–61* (New York: Palgrave Macmillan, 2010); Sergei Antonov's excellent study on virtually every aspect of nineteenth-century Russian debt, *Bankrupts and Usurers of Imperial Russia: Debt, Property, and the Law in the Age of Dostoevsky and Tolstoy* (Cambridge, Mass.: Harvard University Press, 2016); Claudia Verhoeven's detailed examination of Dmitri Karakozov's assassination attempt as well as the investigation, trial, and uproar surrounding it, *The Odd Man Karakozov: Imperial Russia, Modernity, and the Birth of Terrorism* (Ithaca, N.Y.: Cornell University Press, 2009); Abbott Gleason's *Young Russia: The Genesis of Russian Radicalism in the 1860s* (New York: Viking, 1980); and Franco Venturi's classic study, *Roots of Revolution: A History of the Populist and Socialist Movements in Nineteenth Century Russia* (New York: Knopf, 1960).

Dostoevsky's *Dead House* guides much of my narration of his prison years. Dostoevsky disguised names and altered enough details to present the work as fiction in order to appease the imperial censors, but the memories were so painful that he once became ill after reading excerpts. Official documents, independent accounts, Dostoevsky's friends, and modern scholars attest to the accuracy of his account. Biographers use it as their primary source for Dostoevsky's prison years, and historians use it to understand Siberian prisons. Andrew Gentes claims that *Dead House* contains "the most valuable descriptions of Siberian prison life under Nicholas I" that we have

(Gentes, *Exile, Murder, and Madness*, 200). Alexander Petrovich Milyukov claims to have heard stories directly from Dostoevsky and that the government's censors "did not sway Dostoevsky to deviate an iota from the truth" (see *DVS* I, 275).

A BLOODY ENIGMA

Quotations from Dostoevsky's *Crime and Punishment* notebooks are from *Notebooks*, 84, 67, 209, 103, 80, 79. Details and quotations regarding Dostoevsky writing in Wiesbaden are from *LII*, 167 (Aug. 10/22, 1865, to Suslova); *LII*, 169 (Aug. 12/24, 1865, to Suslova); *LII*, 165 (Aug. 3/15, 1865, to Turgenev); *LII*, 178 (Sept. 16/28, 1865, to Vrangel); *LII*, 177 (Sept. 16/28, 1865, to Vrangel). Quotations from Dostoevsky's proposal are from *LII*, 174–76 (Sept. 22–27, 1865, to Katkov).

For descriptions of Lacenaire, see, for example, *Mémoires et écrits*, "Actes d'Archive," 308–18; *Memoirs*, 21, 69–70. Details about the Chardon murders are from *Procès complet*, 10–11, 18–25, 35–38, 47–48, 90; *Lacenaire, ses crimes*, 137–43, 167, 201–4, 228–32, 245–50, 276–77; *Memoirs*, 16–17, 195–96; *Mémoires et écrits*, 145–46; Louis Canler, *Autobiography of a French Detective*, trans. Lascelles Wraxall (London: Ward and Lock, 1863), 33–34. For Fouquier's account of Lacenaire's crimes and trial, see Armand Fouquier, "Lacenaire, François et Avril," in *Causes célèbres de tous les peuples*, vol. 1, bk. 4 (Paris: H. Lebrun, 1858), 1–32.

Details of Lacenaire's trial and surrounding press commentary come from "Considérations générales a propos de l'execution de Lacenaire," *La France*, Jan. 3, 1835; *Gazette des Salons*, Jan. 1836, 62; *La France*, Jan. 14, 1835; *Times*, March 23, 1836; *La France*, Nov. 16, 1835; *Le National*, Nov. 13, 1835; *Vert-Vert*, Feb. 15, 1836; T. M., "Lacenaire," *La Mode*, Jan. 1836, 53–54; *La France*, Jan. 28, 1836; *Vert-Vert*, Nov. 25, 1835; *La Gazette du Bas-Languedoc*, July 10, 1836, 1; *La Presse*, March 8, 1837; *Vert-Vert*, Dec. 12, 1835; *Revue Critique des Livres Nouveaux*, April 4, 1837; *La France*, Nov. 23, 1835; *La France*, Dec. 12, 1835; *La Quotidienne*, Nov. 29, 1835; *Le Temps*, Nov. 18, 1835.

For discussions of Lacenaire's influence on Dostoevsky, see, for example, Frank III, 72–73, and IV, 66–67; Leonid Grossman, *Dostoevsky: A Biography*, trans. Mary Mackler (New York: Bobbs-Merrill, 1975), 344–45; Katharine Strelsky, "Lacenaire and Raskolnikov," *Times Literary Supplement*, Jan. 8, 1971, 47; Konstantine Klioutchkine, "The Rise of Crime and Punishment from the Air of the Media," *Slavic Review* 61, no. 1 (Spring 2002): 88–108. A sample of other works referencing the influence include Donald Fanger, *Dostoevsky and Romantic Realism: A Study of Dostoevsky in Relation to Balzac, Dickens, and Gogol* (Evanston, Ill.: Northwestern University Press, 1998), 186–87; Harriet Murav, *Holy Foolishness: Dostoevsky's Novels and the Poetics of Cultural Critique* (Stanford, Calif.: Stanford University Press, 1992), 52; Alex De Jonge, *Dostoevsky and the Age of Intensity* (London: Secker & Warburg, 1975), 88–89; Derek Offord, "Crime and Punishment and Contemporary Radical Thought," in *Fyodor Dostoevsky's "Crime and Punishment": A Casebook*, ed. Richard Peace (New York: Oxford University Press, 2006), 122; and Vadim Dmitrievich Rak, "Istochnik ocherkov o znamenitykh ugolovnykh protsessakh v zhurnalakh brat'ev Dostoevskikh," in *Dosto-evskii: Materialy i issledovaniya,* vol. 1 (Leningrad, 1974), 239–41. See also www.fedor dostoevsky.ru/works/lifetime/time/1861/Lacenaire.

Additional background comes from Eric Hobsbawm, *Age of Revolution, 1789–1848* (New York: Vintage Books, 1996); Jonathan Israel, *A Revolution of the Mind* (Princeton, N.J.: Princeton University Press, 2010), 231; *Journal des Débats,* Nov. 15, 1835; *Gazette de France,* Dec. 9, 1835; *Le Charivari,* Nov. 20, 1835; *La Gazette du Bas-Languedoc,* Nov. 22, 1835; Thomas Cragin, *Murder in Parisian Streets: Manufacturing Crime and Justice in the Popular Press, 1830–1900* (Lewisburg, Pa.: Bucknell University Press, 2006); Louise McReynolds, *The News Under Russia's Old Regime: The Development of a Mass Circulation Press* (Princeton, N.J.: Princeton University Press, 2014); A. and W. Galig-nani, *Galignani's New Paris Guide* (Paris: A. and W. Galignani, 1827); and Edward Planta, *A New Picture of Paris* (London: S. Leigh and Baldwin and Cradock, 1831).

2 **remain under surveillance until:** Frank V, 127.
3 **divided into "two hostile camps":** Fyodor Dostoevsky, "Mr. ——bov and the Question of Art," in *Occasional Writings,* trans. David Magarshack (Evanston, Ill.: Northwestern University Press), 89.
4 **"the artistic thinking of humankind":** Mikhail Bakhtin, *Problems of Dostoevsky's Poetics,* trans. Caryl Emerson (Minneapolis: University of Minnesota Press, 1984), 270, 3, 272.
5 **"from the depths of Asia":** *C&P,* 547.
6 **"each man thought that he":** Fyodor Dostoevsky, *Crime and Punishment,* trans. Oliver Ready (New York: Penguin, 2014), 654.
8 **"fixed idea to resist":** *Memoirs,* 195.
8 **state of undress:** Sources vary about how undressed Chardon was upon Lacenaire's arrival. See *Procès complet,* 10; *Memoirs,* 16; Fouquier, "Lacenaire, François et Avril," 9; *Journal des Débats Politiques et Littéraires,* Nov. 13, 1835.
10 **"Don Juan of Murder":** *Gazette des Théâtres,* Feb. 14, 1836, 320.
11 **"is a remarkable personality":** Dostoevsky quoted in Frank II, 72–73. Cf. *PSS* (Moscow, 1912), 18:90.
11 **devouring Victor Hugo's:** *LII,* 43, 43n (Jan. 2, 1863, to Milyukov); Orest Fyodorovich Miller and Nikolai Nikolaevich Strakhov, *Biografiya, pis'ma i zametki iz zapisnoy knizhki F. M. Dostoevskogo* (St. Petersburg: Tipografiya A. S. Suvorina, 1883), 244; Anna Grigorievna Dostoevsky, *Reminiscences,* 227; Anna Grigorievna Dostoevsky, *The Diary of Dostoyevsky's Wife,* trans. Madge Pemberton, ed. René Fülöp-Miller and F. Eckstein (New York: Macmillan, 1928), 303.
12 **"terrifying blankness," and:** Victor Hugo, *Les Misérables,* trans. Julie Rose (New York: Random House, 2008), 594, translation altered.
12 **"strange, deep, bitter":** Gustave Flaubert, *The Letters of Gustave Flaubert, 1830–1857,* trans. and ed. Francis Steegmuller (Cambridge, Mass.: Harvard University Press, 1980), 10–11.
12 **"Poverty is hell":** Hippolyte Bonnellier and Jacques Arago, *Lacenaire après sa condamnation, ses conversations intimes, ses poésies, sa correspondance, un drame en trois actes* (Paris: Marchant, 1836), 19.
12 **"Killing without remorse":** Bonnellier and Arago, *Lacenaire après sa condamnation,* 48–49.
13 **hailed him as "divine":** Maximilien Robespierre, "Dedication to Jean-Jacques Rousseau," quoted in Carol Blum, *Rousseau and the Republic of Virtue: The Language of Politics in the French Revolution* (Ithaca, N.Y.: Cornell University Press, 1986), 156.
13 **"The State, set on fire":** Jean-Jacques Rousseau, *The Social Contract; and, The Discourses,* rev. ed., trans. G.D.H. Cole (New York: A. A. Knopf, 1993), 217.
14 **"The social structure":** *Mémoires et écrits,* 113; cf. *Memoirs,* 152–53.
14 **"cultivate the seeds of discontent":** Bonnellier and Arago, *Lacenaire après sa condamnation,* 135–36.
14 **"Ah, sir! you believe":** Hippolyte Bonnellier, *Autopsie physiologique de Lacénaire, mort sur l'échafaud le 9 janvier 1836* (Paris: L. Mathias, 1836), 22, gallica.bnf.fr/ark:/12148/bpt6k56120181.

15 **"We are perfect"**: Max Stirner, *The Ego and His Own: The Case of the Individual Against Authority*, trans. Steven Byington, ed. James Martin (Mineola, N.Y.: Dover, 1973), 359.

15 **"A revolution never returns"**: Stirner, *Ego and His Own*, 242, punctuation altered.

15 **"the first of the gentleman criminals"**: Albert Camus, *The Rebel: An Essay on Man in Revolt*, trans. Anthony Bower (New York: Vintage, 1991), 52.

15 **"the paradise of the aesthetes"**: Michel Foucault, *Discipline and Punish: The Birth of the Prison*, trans. Alan Sheridan (New York: Vintage, 1995), 283–84.

16 **to "immediately construct paradise"**: *LII*, 193–94 (April 25, 1866, to Katkov).

17 **"about instincts and Lacenaire"**: Fyodor Dostoevsky, *Unpublished Dostoevsky: Diaries and Notebooks (1860–81)*, 3 vols., trans. T. S. Berczynski (Ann Arbor, Mich.: Ardis, 1973), 1:59.

18 **"the doctrine of nothingness"**: Lacenaire quoted in Bonnellier and Arago, *Lacenaire après sa condamnation*, 143.

18 **Dostoevsky hammered at the idea**: *Notebooks*, 55, 67, 71, 63.

19 **"What I love best"**: Hélène Cixous, "Without End, No, State of Drawingness, No, Rather: The Executioner's Taking Off," in *Stigmata: Escaping Texts* (New York: Routledge, 1998), 16.

ONE. THE DEAD LEAVES

Details and quotations from Dostoevsky's academy years are from the following letters: *LI*, 35 (Feb. 4, 1838, to Mikhail Andreevich Dostoevsky); *LI*, 17 (April–May 1834 to Maria Fyodorovna Dostoevskaya); *LI*, 71–72 (Feb. 27, 1841, to Mikhail Mikhailovich Dostoevsky—Dostoevsky's brother, hereinafter Mikhail); *LI*, 344 (May 17, 1858, to Zhdan-Pushkin); *LI*, 51 (May 5, 1839, to M. A. Dostoevsky); *LI*, 59–62 (Jan. 1, 1840, to M. A. Dostoevsky); *LI*, 37 (June 5, 1838, to M. A. Dostoevsky); *LI*, 42 (Oct. 30, 1838, to M. A. Dostoevsky); *LI*, 39–40 (Aug. 9, 1838, to Mikhail); *LI*, 44–45 (Oct. 31, 1838, to Mikhail); *LV*, 148–49 (Aug. 19/31, 1870, to Anna Dostoevskaya); *LI*, 49–53 (May 5–10, 1839, to M. A. Dostoevsky); *LI*, 55 (Aug. 16, 1839, to Mikhail); *LI*, 43 (Oct. 30, 1838, to M. A. Dostoevsky).

Additional information on the academy years is from Alexander Ivanovich Savel'ev, "Vospominaniya o F. M. Dostoevskom," in *DVS* I, 168, 163, 166; Konstantin Aleksandrovich Trutovskiy, "Vospominaniya o Fedore Mikhailoviche Dostoevskom," in *DVS* I, 172; Dmitri Vasil'evich Grigorovich, "Iz 'Literaturnykh vospominaniy,'" in *DVS* I, 200, 195–96, 193–94, 202; Alexander Egorovich Riesenkampf, "Vospominaniya o Fedore Mikhailoviche Dostoevskom," in *DVS* I, 176–91; Avdot'ya Yakovlevna Panaeva, "Iz 'Vospominaniy,'" in *DVS* I, 218; Andrei Mikhailovich Dostoevsky, "Iz 'Vospominaniy,'" in *DVS* I, 93–94, 118, 117–19; Frank I, 82, 19, 28–29, 80, 93, 17, 39–41, 83, 85–87; Miller and Strakhov, *Biografiya*, 42–43; Vera Stepanovna Nechaeva and Andrei Fyodorovich Dostoevsky, *Feodor Mikhailovich Dostoevsky v portretakh, illyustratsiyakh, dokumentakh* (Moscow: Izdatel'stvo Prosveshchenie, 1972), 70; Yakubovich I, 36, 28, 61.

Details of the post-academy years and Dostoevsky's quotations are from the following letters: *LI*, 89–91 (ca. Aug. 20, 1844, to P. A. Karepin); *LI*, 98–99 (Sept. 30, 1844, to Mikhail); *LI*, 92–93 (Sept. 7, 1844, to Karepin); *LI*, 95–97 (Sept. 19, 1844, to Karepin); *LI*, 98–99 (Sept. 30, 1844, to Mikhail); *LI*, 84–85 (March–April 1844 to Mikhail); *LI*, 86–87 (July–Aug. 1844 to Mikhail); *LI*, 54–55 (Aug. 16, 1839, to Mikhail); *LI*, 72 (Feb. 27, 1841, to Mikhail); *LI*, 74 (Dec. 22, 1841, to Mikhail); *LI*, 76–77 (Jan.–beginning of Feb. 1843 to Andrei Dostoevsky); *LI*, 75 (Dec. 1842 to Andrei Dostoevsky); *LI*, 90–91 (ca. Aug. 20, 1844, to Karepin); *LI*, 99–101 (Oct. 20, 1844, to Karepin); *LI*, 102–3 (Nov. 1844 to Mikhail). Additional information from Grigorovich, "Iz 'Literaturnykh vospominaniy,'" 207, 206; Alexander Egorovich Riesenkampf, "Vospominaniya o Fedore Mikhailoviche Dostoevskom," 180–81, 184, 186; Frank I, 115–16, 116n.

   Background information derives from Julie Buckler, *Mapping St. Petersburg: Imperial Text and Cityshape* (Princeton, N.J.: Princeton University Press, 2005), 143; Johann Georg Köhl, *Russia and the Russians in 1842: Petersburg* (London: Henry Colburn, 1842), 1:250–53; William Rae Wilson, *Travels in Russia, &c.* (London: Longman, Rees, Orme, Brown, and Green, 1828), 1:249–51; Dmitry Shvidkovsky and Yekaterina Shorban, *Russian Architecture and the West* (New Haven, Conn.: Yale University Press, 2007), 288–95; W. Bruce Lincoln, *In the Vanguard of Reform: Russia's Enlightened Bureaucrats, 1825–1861* (DeKalb: Northern Illinois University Press, 1988); Irina Reyfman, *How Russia Learned to Write: Literature and the Imperial Table of Ranks* (Madison: University of Wisconsin Press, 2016); Sergei Antonov, *Bankrupts and Usurers of Imperial Russia: Debt, Property, and the Law in the Age of Dostoevsky and Tolstoy* (Cambridge, Mass.: Harvard University Press, 2016).

24 **the wild berries:** Fyodor Dostoevsky, *Writer's Diary*, trans. Kenneth Lantz, 2 vols. (Evanston, Ill.: Northwestern University Press, 1999), 1:353.

27 **The two doctors:** Frank I, 85–87n; G. A. Fyodorov, "K biografii F. M. Dostoyevskogo: Domysly i logika faktov," *Literaturnaya Gazeta*, June 18, 1975, 7. After examining archival documents, Fyodorov concluded (supported by Frank) that Mikhail Andreevich Dostoevsky died of natural causes and that the Dostoevskys' neighbor spread false rumors of a murder in order to get the Dostoevskys' serfs exiled so that he could acquire their property more easily. The neighbors had been involved in a legal dispute about their land boundaries. Nechaeva rebuts Fyodorov's argument in *Rannii Dostoevsky, 1821–1849* (Moscow: Nauka, 1979), 89–94, and Yakubovich et al. find Nechaeva's argument credible. See Yakubovich I, 61.

27 **"apoplexy" could refer to:** George Tuthill, "Selections from the Lectures of Sir George L. Tuthill," in *The London Medical and Surgical Journal*, ed. Michael Ryan (London: Renshaw and Rush, 1833), 2:229; Alexander Tweedie and W. W. Gerhard, ed. and arr., *A System of Practical Medicine* (Philadelphia: Lea and Blanchard, 1840), 136–37.

28 **"Humanity is a mystery":** *LI*, 55 (Aug. 16, 1839, to Mikhail), translation altered. I've changed "Man" to "Humanity."

28 **"*I renounce my entire allotment*":** *LI*, 90 (ca. Aug. 20, 1844, to Karepin), my ellipsis.

29 **"it will be a long time":** Dostoevsky, *Writer's Diary*, 1:431.

TWO. THE DEVIL'S STREETLAMPS

Background information on Petersburg, its population, and its history is taken from Johann Georg Köhl, *Russia and the Russians in 1842*, vol. 1, *Petersburg* (London: Henry Colburn, 1842); W. Bruce Lincoln, *Sunlight at Midnight: St. Petersburg and the Rise of Modern Russia* (New York: Basic Books, 2002); Théophile Gautier, *Travels in Russia*, trans. and ed. F. C. de Sumichrast (Cambridge, Mass.: John Wilson & Son, 1902); Buckler, *Mapping St. Petersburg*; Robert Massie, *Peter the Great: His Life and World* (New York: Random House, 2012); George Munro, *The Most Intentional City: St. Petersburg in the Reign of Catherine the Great* (Madison, N.J.: Fairleigh Dickinson University

Press, 2008); Christopher Marsden, *Palmyra of the North: The First Days of St. Petersburg* (London: Faber and Faber, 1943); Vissarion Belinsky, "Petersburg and Moscow," Dmitri Vasil'evich Grigorovich, "The Petersburg Organ-Grinders," Nikolai Nekrasov, "Petersburg Corners," and Evgeny Grebenka, "The Petersburg Quarter," in *Petersburg: The Physiology of a City*, ed. Nikolai Nekrasov, trans. Thomas Gaiton Marullo (Evanston, Ill.: Northwestern University Press, 2009); Alexander Grigor'evich Tseytlin, *Stanovlenie realizma v russkoy literature (Russkiy fiziologicheskiy ocherk)* (Moscow: Nauka, 1965).

Information on Tsar Nicholas I's military, government, and reforms is taken from Frederick Kagan, *The Military Reforms of Nicholas I: The Origins of the Modern Russian Army* (Basingstoke, U.K.: Macmillan, 1999); Nicholas Riasanovsky, *Nicholas I and Official Nationality, 1825–1855* (Berkeley: University of California Press, 1959); Alexander Vasil'evich Viskovatov, *Istoricheskoe opisanie odezhdy i vooruzheniya rossiyskikh voysk*, 30 vols. (St. Petersburg: Pechatano v Voennaya Tipografiya, 1841–62), vol. 24; Irina Tarsis, "Laws and Lithographs: Seeing Imperial Russia Through Illustrations of Civil Uniforms in *Polnoe sobranie zakonov Rossiiskoi Imperii*," in *Slavic and East European Information Resources* 11, no. 2–3 (2010): 156–83; Rebecca Friedman, *Masculinity, Autocracy, and the Russian University, 1804–1863* (New York: Palgrave Macmillan, 2014); David Saunders, *Russia in the Age of Reaction and Reform, 1801–1881* (New York: Longman, 1992); Lincoln, *In the Vanguard of Reform*; W. Bruce Lincoln, "The Daily Life of St. Petersburg Officials in the Mid-nineteenth Century," *Oxford Slavonic Papers* 8 (1975): 82–100; Walter M. Pintner, "The Social Characteristics of the Early Nineteenth-Century Russian Bureaucracy," *Slavic Review* 29, no. 3 (Sept. 1970): 429–43; Elise Kimerling Wirtschafter, *Social Identity in Imperial Russia* (DeKalb: Northern Illinois University Press, 2015).

Details on the mid-nineteenth-century Russian literary scene come from Jeffrey Brooks, *When Russia Learned to Read: Literacy and Popular Literature, 1861–1917* (Evanston, Ill.: Northwestern University Press, 2003); William Mills Todd III, "Periodicals in the Literary Life of the Early Nineteenth Century," in *Literary Journals in Imperial Russia*, ed. Deborah Martinsen (Cambridge, U.K.: Cambridge University Press, 2010); William Mills Todd III, "Dostoevskii as a Professional Writer," in *The Cambridge Companion to Dostoevskii*, ed. W. J. Leatherbarrow (Cambridge, U.K.: Cambridge University Press, 2002); Riasanovsky, *Nicholas I and Official Nationality*; Charles Ruud, *Fighting Words: Imperial Censorship and the Russian Press, 1804–1906* (Toronto: University of Toronto Press, 1982); Edward Morton, *Travels in Russia* (London: Longman, Rees, Orme, Brown, and Green, 1830); Herbert Bowman, *Vissarion Belinski, 1811–1848: A Study in the Origins of Social Criticism in Russia* (Cambridge, Mass.: Harvard University Press, 1954); Thomas Gaiton Marullo, "Editor's Introduction," in *Petersburg: The Physiology of a City*; Vissarion Belinsky, "The Literature of Petersburg," in *Petersburg: The Physiology of a City*; Belinsky's "Thoughts and Notes on Russian Literature" as well as "Survey of Russian Literature in 1847: Part Two," in *Belinsky, Chernyshevsky, and Dobrolyubov: Selected Criticism*, ed. Ralph E. Matlaw (New York: Dutton, 1962); Aleksandr V. Nikitenko, *Diary of a Russian Censor* (Amherst: University of Massachusetts

Press, 1975); Robert Belknap, "Survey of Russian Journals, 1840–1880," in Martinsen, *Literary Journals in Imperial Russia*; Saunders, *Russia in the Age of Reaction and Reform*; Richard Peace, "The Nineteenth Century: The Natural School and Its Aftermath, 1840–55," in *The Cambridge History of Russian Literature*, ed. Charles Moser (Cambridge, U.K.: Cambridge University Press, 1992); Reyfman, *How Russia Learned to Write*; McReynolds, *News Under Russia's Old Regime*; Miranda Beaven Remnek, "The Expansion of Russian Reading Audiences, 1828–1848" (PhD diss., UC Berkeley, 1999); P. V. Annenkov, *The Extraordinary Decade: Literary Memoirs*, trans. Arthur P. Mendel (Ann Arbor: University of Michigan Press, 1968).

Information about Belinsky and his writings comes from Bowman, *Vissarion Belinski*; Victor Terras, "Belinsky the Journalist and Russian Literature," in Martinsen, *Literary Journals in Imperial Russia*; Andrzej Walicki, *A History of Russian Thought from the Enlightenment to Marxism*, trans. Hilda Andrews-Rusiecka (Stanford, Calif.: Stanford University Press, 1979); Ralph Eugene Matlaw, introduction to *Belinsky, Chernyshevsky, and Dobrolyubov*; Annenkov, *Extraordinary Decade*; Turgenev, *Literary Reminiscences and Autobiographical Fragments*, trans. and ed. David Magarshak (New York: Grove Press, 1959), 117–24, 143–51; Frank I, 119–26, 177–92.

Background on Chaadaev is from Dale E. Peterson, "Civilizing the Race: Chaadaev and the Paradox of Eurocentric Nationalism," *Russian Review* 56, no. 4 (Oct. 1997): 550–63; Richard Tempest, "Madman or Criminal: Government Attitudes to Petr Chaadaev in 1836," *Slavic Review* 43, no. 2 (Summer 1984): 281–87; Yuri Glazov, "Chaadaev and Russia's Destiny," *Studies in Soviet Thought* 32, no. 4 (Nov. 1986): 281–301; Mary-Barbara Zeldin, introduction to *Peter Yakovlevich Chaadayev: Philosophical Letters and Apology of a Madman*, trans. Mary-Barbara Zeldin (Knoxville: University of Tennessee Press, 1969), 4–13; Walicki, *History of Russian Thought from the Enlightenment to Marxism*, 81–87; Janusz Dobieszewski, "Pëtr Chaadaev and the Rise of Russian Philosophy," *Studies in East European Thought* 54, no. 1–2 (2002): 25–46. All quotations from Chaadaev's "First Philosophical Letter" are from Zeldin, *Peter Yakovlevich Chaadayev*, 34–41.

Unless otherwise specified, Hegel quotations are from *Reason in History*, trans. Robert S. Hartman (Indianapolis: Bobbs-Merrill, 1953), 11, 43, 29. My discussion also draws upon Hegel's *Philosophy of History*, trans. John Sibree (New York: Dover, 1956). I am indebted to Dennis O'Brien, *Hegel on Reason and History: A Contemporary Interpretation* (Chicago: University of Chicago Press, 1975), and Peter Singer, *Hegel* (New York: Oxford University Press, 1983).

31 **Dostoevsky described the capital:** Dostoevsky, *Occasional Writings*, 17–30.
31 **"the most abstract and premeditated":** Dostoevsky, *Notes from Underground, and The Gambler*, trans. Jane Kentish (New York: Oxford University Press, 1991), 10. Translation altered: I've changed "on the face of the earth" to "on earth."
33 **shadows are bigger:** See the National Research Council Canada website for information on shadow length factors for various latitudes and locations at summer and winter solstices: www.nrc-cnrc.gc.ca/eng/services/sunrise/advanced.html.

33 **"Everything is deception"**: Gogol, "Nevsky Prospect," in *Collected Tales of Nikolai Gogol*, trans. Richard Pevear and Larissa Volokhonsky (New York: Vintage, 1998), 277–78, translation altered.

34 **"there is order"**: Nicholas I quoted in Riasanovsky, *Nicholas I and Official Nationality*, 1.

38 **literacy rate was low**: Official literacy records were not kept until the late nineteenth century. Kahan cites the mid-nineteenth-century rural literacy rate at 11.85 percent (16.6 percent for men and 7.1 percent for women). See Arcadius Kahan, *Russian Economic History: The Nineteenth Century* (Chicago: University of Chicago Press, 1989), 186. Todd offers a substantially lower estimate: "In Dostoevskii's youth the figure was probably between 5 and 10%, but this would have included many people with minimal functional literacy." See Todd, "Dostoevskii as a Professional Writer," 68. Broadberry and O'Rourke estimate that Russian literacy didn't reach 15 percent until 1870. See Stephen Broadberry and Kevin O'Rourke, *The Cambridge Economic History of Modern Europe*, vol. 1, *1700–1870* (Cambridge, U.K.: Cambridge University Press, 2010), cited in "Our World in Data": ourworldindata.org/literacy.

39 **"It's an oligarchy"**: *LI*, 105–6 (March 24, 1845, to Mikhail).

39 **"Scribblers in frieze coats"**: Belinsky, "Thoughts and Notes on Russian Literature," 22.

40 **"I feel sorrow"**: *LIII*, 324 (Dec. 1847 to Botkin), quoted in Bowman, *Vissarion Belinski*, 200.

40 **"Thinking and feeling"**: Belinsky quoted in Bowman, *Vissarion Belinski*, 39. Bowman's source is Belinsky's letter to Botkin, March 1, 1841.

40 **"Reality—that is the motto"**: Belinsky quoted in Bowman, *Vissarion Belinski*, 163.

41 **as "living statistics"**: Belinsky quoted in Peace, "Natural School," 206.

41 **insects smeared on the walls**: Nekrasov, "Petersburg Corners," 134.

41 **"in the dark corners"**: Faddei Bulgarin quoted in Marullo, "Editor's Introduction," xlvi–xlvii.

41 **"in all its nudity"**: Belinsky, "On the Russian Story and the Stories of Gogol," quoted in Bowman, *Vissarion Belinski*, 72.

41 **"*Here is the Russian spirit*"**: Belinsky quoted in Bowman, *Vissarion Belinski*, 160.

42 **"There are no rules"**: Chaadaev, "First Philosophical Letter," 34, translation altered, my ellipsis.

42 **"direct attack on the past"**: Uvarov quoted in Tempest, "Madman or Criminal," 282.

42 **"jumble of insolent absurdities"**: Nicholas I quoted in Peterson, "Civilizing the Race," 556. The subsequent lifetime publication ban for Chaadaev was later revoked.

43 **some simply do not**: See, for example, Hegel, *Philosophy of History*, 173. See also O'Brien, *Hegel on Reason and History*, 150.

44 **Hegel considered Napoleon**: See, for example, Hegel, *Philosophy of History*, 31. See also O'Brien, *Hegel on Reason and History*, 124.

44 **"What good is it"**: Belinsky to Botkin, March 1841, quoted in Walicki, *History of Russian Thought from the Enlightenment to Marxism*, 124. For commentary on Belinsky's flip from conservative to liberal Hegelianism, see Bowman, *Vissarion Belinski*, 90–114, 132–36, 147–48. For Belinsky's concerns about Russia producing a world-historical literature, see Belinsky, "Thoughts and Notes on Russian Literature."

THREE. SHARP CLAWS

Details of Grigorovich and Nekrasov reading *Poor Folk* and Dostoevsky's meeting with Belinsky are taken from Dostoevsky, *Writer's Diary*, 2:840–42; Ivan Ivanovich Panaev, "Iz 'Vospominaniya o Belinskom,'" in *DVS* I, 217; Grigorovich, "Iz 'Literaturnykh vospominaniy,'" in *DVS* I, 207; Riesenkampf, "Vospominaniya o Fedore Mikhailoviche Dostoevskom," 184–86; *LI*, 108 (May 4, 1845, to Mikhail); *LI*, 113 (Oct. 8, 1845, to Mikhail); Annenkov, *Extraordinary Decade*, 102, 149. Details and quotations from Turgenev are found in *Literary Reminiscences*, 120–23, 144–57; Frank I, 137, 173; Bowman, *Vissarion Belinski*, 45–47, 92, 171. *Poor Folk* passage accessed online: www.gutenberg.org/files/2302/2302-h/2302-h.htm.

Background on *Die Freien* and Max Stirner comes from Ronald W. K. Paterson, *The Nihilistic Egoist: Max Stirner* (New York: Oxford University Press, 1971), 3–11, 36–41; David McLellan, *The Young Hegelians and Karl Marx* (London: Macmillan, 1969), 118. Stirner quotations come from Max Stirner, *The Ego and His Own: The Case of the Individual Against Authority*, trans. Steven Byington, ed. James Martin (Mineola, N.Y.: Dover, 1973), 185, 174, 13–14, 217, 139, 190, 5.

For Dostoevsky's responses to Stirner, see Nadine Natov, "Dostoevsky Versus Max Stirner," *Dostoevsky Studies*, n.s., 6 (2002): 28–38; John Carroll, *Break-Out from the Crystal Palace: The Anarcho-psychological Critique: Stirner, Nietzsche, Dostoevsky* (Boston: Routledge, 1974); N. Otverzhennyi and A. Borovoi, *Shtirner i Dostoevskii* (Moscow: Golos Truda, 1925); Frank I, 187–89, 197–98, 233.

Dostoevsky offers his own account of his turbulent introduction to literary society in letters to Mikhail: *LI*, 113–14 (Oct. 8, 1845); *LI*, 117–19 (Nov. 16, 1845); *LI*, 121 (Feb. 1, 1846); *LI*, 124 (April 1, 1846). For Dostoevsky's recollections of Belinsky, including his socialism and atheism, see *Writer's Diary*, 1:126–29, 362, 285–86. For more details and background, see Avdot'ya Yakovlevna Panaeva, *Vospominaniya, 1824–1870*, rev. ed., ed. K. Chukovsky (Leningrad: "Academia," 1927), 110–11, az.lib.ru/p/panae wa_a_j/text_0010.shtml; Frank I, 9–10, 38, 41, 162–97, and II, 237; Ivan Panaev, "Literaturnyye kumiry, diletanty i proch," in *PSS*, 5:1–11; Kornei Ivanovich Chukovsky, "Dostoevsky i pleyada Belinskogo," in *Nekrasov: Stat'i i materialy* (Leningrad: Izdatel'stvo "KUBUCH," 1926), 326–49; Leonard Schapiro, *Turgenev: His Life and Times* (Cambridge, Mass.: Harvard University Press, 1982), 139.

Quotations regarding Dostoevsky's falling-out with Belinsky as well as Dostoevsky's health and money problems come from *LI*, 123 (Feb. 1, 1846, to Mikhail); *LI*, 124–25 (April 1, 1846, to Mikhail); *LI*, 135 (Oct. 7, 1846, to Mikhail); *LI*, 142 (Nov. 26, 1846, to Mikhail); *LI*, 152 (April 1847 to Mikhail); *LI*, 130 (May 16, 1846, to Mikhail). Additional information and details come from *LI*, 127 (April 26, 1846, to Mikhail); *LI*, 149 (Jan.–Feb. 1847 to Mikhail); *LI*, 251 (March 24, 1856, to Totleben); *LI*, 158 (May 14, 1848, to Yevgenia Maikova); Yakubovich I, 99; James Rice, *Dostoevsky and the Healing Art: An Essay in Literary and Medical History* (Ann Arbor, Mich.: Ardis, 1985); and Jacques Catteau, *Dostoevsky and the Process of Literary Creation*, trans. Audrey Littlewood (Cambridge, U.K.: Cambridge University Press, 1989).

Additional detail and background information can be found in Ruud, *Fighting Words*; McReynolds, *News Under Russia's Old Regime*; Reyfman, *How Russia Learned to Write*; Belinsky, "Survey of Russian Literature in 1847: Part Two"; Bowman, *Vissarion Belinski*; Riesenkampf, "Vospominaniya o Fedore Mikhailoviche Dostoevskom"; Stepan Dmitrievich Yanovskiy, "Vospominaniya o Dostoevskom," in *DVS* I, 230–51; Annenkov, *Extraordinary Decade*; Nikolai Vasilievich Gogol, *Selected Passages from Correspondence with Friends*, trans. Jesse Zeldin (Nashville: Vanderbilt University Press, 1969); Wirtschafter, *Social Identity in Imperial Russia*; Saunders, *Russia in the Age of Reaction and Reform*.

48 "To you, an artist, the truth": Dostoevsky, *Writer's Diary*, 2:842.

48 "I sincerely wish him the worst": Belinsky to Botkin, July 7/19, 1847, in *Selected Philosophical Works* (Moscow: Foreign Languages Publishing House, 1956), 529–30.

49 "We haven't yet decided": Belinsky quoted in Turgenev, *Literary Reminiscences*, 123.

49 "There will come a time": Belinsky quoted in Frank I, 123, my ellipses.

51 "governs the whole living world": Belinsky quoted in Annenkov, *Extraordinary Decade*, 212–14.

51 "Who is this Dostoevsky?": Kraevsky quoted in *LI*, 117 (Nov. 16, 1845, to Mikhail).

52 "I am now almost drunk": Dostoevsky quoted in Frank I, 160. Cf. *LI*, 118 (Nov. 16, 1845, to Mikhail).

52 "a lot of wordiness": Gogol quoted in Kenneth A. Lantz, *The Dostoevsky Encyclopedia* (Westport, Conn.: Greenwood Press, 2014), 162.

52 "Dostoevsky is not an artist": Konstantin Aksakov quoted in Frank III, 104.

53 offer his cheek: *LII*, 257 (Aug. 16/28, 1867, to Apollon Maikov).

53 his liminal status: Wirtschafter, *Social Identity in Imperial Russia*, 47; Saunders, *Russia in the Age of Reaction and Reform*, 128. Dostoevsky's father became a collegiate assessor for his civil service in 1828. Nicholas I's June 11, 1845, manifesto raised the hereditary nobility threshold for civil servants from the eighth rank (collegiate assessor) to the fifth rank (state councillor). The changes were partly in response to the rapid growth of the noble ranks.

53 "I have a terrible defect": Dostoevsky quoted in Frank I, 169, my ellipsis. Cf. *LI*, 125 (April 1, 1846, to Mikhail).

54 "every single passage": Belinsky quoted in Bowman, *Vissarion Belinski*, 96.

54 "The fantastic can have a place": Belinsky quoted in Frank I, 177.

54 top hat from Zimmerman's: Yanovskiy, "Vospominaniya o Dostoevskom," 231.

54 "Dostoevsky's simply lost his mind!": Panaeva, "Iz 'Vospominaniy,'" 201.

55 "What terrible rubbish!": Belinsky quoted in Frank I, 181.

55 a "vicious" condition: Riesenkampf, 183.

56 "What have I accomplished?": Belinsky quoted in Annenkov, *Extraordinary Decade*, 210.

56 "sent directly from Heaven": Gogol, *Selected Passages from Correspondence with Friends*, 43.

56 "They who were born": Gogol, *Selected Passages from Correspondence with Friends*, 137–38.

56 "One cannot keep silent": Belinsky, "Letter to N. V. Gogol," in *Belinsky, Chernyshevsky, and Dobrolyubov*, 83–85, 90.

57 "Belinsky is dead!": Rice, *Dostoevsky and the Healing Art*, 11–12. See also Frank I, 181.

FOUR. *NÉMÉSIS*

Details are principally from *Memoirs* and *Mémoires et écrits*. All quotations are from *Memoirs* unless otherwise specified. Additional information is from Fouquier, "Lacenaire, François et Avril"; Bonnellier and Arago, *Lacenaire après sa condamnation;* James Morton, *The First Detective: The Life and Revolutionary Times of Eugène-François Vidocq* (New York: Overlook Press, 2011); Pamela Pilbeam, *The 1830 Revolution in France* (London: Macmillan, 1994); François-Vincent Raspail, *Réforme pénitentiaire: Lettres sur les prisons de Paris* (Paris: Tamisey et Champion, 1839), 2:356–61; Patricia O'Brien, *The Promise of Punishment: Prisons in Nineteenth-Century France* (Princeton, N.J.: Princeton University Press, 2014); Maxime Du Camp, *Paris, ses organes, ses fonctions et sa vie dans la seconde moitié du XIX siècle* (Paris: Hachette, 1875), 3:10; *Galignani's New Paris Guide* (1827); Ulysse Tencé, ed., *Annuaire historique universel pour 1836* (Paris: Thoisnier-Desplaces, 1837), 213; Victor Alexis Désiré Dalloz, *Jurisprudence générale du Royaume* (Paris: Au Bureau de la Jurisprudence Générale ou Journal des Audiences, 1839), 211.

59 **"Because I do not know how to obey"**: Bonnellier and Arago, *Lacenaire après sa condamnation*, 53.

61 **"M. Arthemise urges"**: *Le Constitutionnel*, June 13, 1829, 4. The theft took place on the prior Tuesday, June 9.

62 **"A thief who doesn't know the slang"**: Lacenaire, "Sur les prisons et le système pénitentiaire en France," in *Mémoires et écrits*, 263–65.

62 **"the science of crime"**: *Procès complet*, 141.

62 **surrounded by scum**: Lacenaire to Vigouroux (end of July 1834), in *Mémoires et écrits*, 276.

62 **"Vierge immortelle, attends-moi"**: "La sylphide," in *Mémoires et écrits*, 191–92.

64 **"It's too stupid"**: Du Camp, *Paris*, 3:10. See also *Mémoires et écrits*, 340.

65 **"Ce qui vient"**: "La flûte et le tambour," in *Mémoires et écrits*, 186.

66 ***I have received the manuscript***: *Mémoires et écrits*, 138. Cf. *Memoirs*, 186–87.

66 **"Be persuaded, sir"**: Lacenaire to Vigouroux (end of July 1834), in *Mémoires et écrits*, 276.

66 **"My friends and I"**: *Memoirs*, 188, translation altered. Cf. *Mémoires et écrits*, 139.

66 **"incorrigible rogues, wasps"**: Lacenaire, "Sur les prisons et le système pénitentiaire en France," quoted in *Memoirs*, 145. See also *Mémoires et écrits*, 263–65, 369.

FIVE. THE PETRASHEVSKY CIRCLE

Details of the 1848 revolutions derive from John Baughman, "The French Banquet Campaign of 1847–48," *Journal of Modern History* 31, no. 1 (1959): 1–15; William Fortescue, *France in 1848: The End of Monarchy* (New York: Routledge, 2004); Mike Rapport, *1848: Year of Revolution* (New York: Basic Books, 2010); Hobsbawm, *Age of Revolution*; Jonathan Sperber, *The European Revolutions, 1848–51*, 2nd ed. (Cambridge, U.K.: Cambridge University Press, 2005); Roger Price, ed., *Documents of the French Revolution of 1848* (London: Macmillan, 1996); Daniel Stern, *Histoire de la Révolution de 1848* (Paris: Balland, 1985); Alain Pauquet, "Les représentations de la barricade dans l'iconographie de 1830 à 1848," in *La barricade*, ed. Alain Corbin and Jean-Marie Mayeur (Paris: Publications de la Sorbonne, 1997), 97–112; Patricia O'Brien, "The Revolutionary Police of 1848," in *Revolution and Reaction: 1848 and the Second French Republic*, ed. Roger Price (New York: Barnes and Noble Books, 2005); Norbert Truquin, "Memoirs and Adventures of a Proletarian in Times of Revolution," in *The French Worker: Autobiographies from the Early Industrial Era*, trans. and ed. Mark Traugott (Berkeley: University of California Press, 1993); Manfred Gailus, "Food Riots in Germany in the Late 1840s," *Past and Present* 145 (Nov. 1994): 157–93.

For Russian reactions to 1848 (including Dostoevsky's), see David Saunders, "A Pyrrhic Victory: The Russian Empire in 1848," in *The Revolutions in Europe, 1848–1849: From Reform to Reaction* (New York: Oxford University Press, 2002); Fyodor Dostoevsky, *Dostoevsky as Reformer: The Petrashevsky Case*, trans. and ed. Liza Knapp (Ann Arbor, Mich.: Ardis, 1987); J. H. Seddon, *The Petrashevtsy: A Study of the Russian Revolutionaries of 1848* (Dover, N.H.: Manchester University Press, 1985); Isaiah Berlin, "Russia and 1848," *Slavonic and East European Review* (April 1948): 341–60; Friedman, *Masculinity, Autocracy, and the Russian University*; Riasanovsky, *Nicholas I and Official Nationality*, 218–19; Ruud, *Fighting Words*; Annenkov, *Extraordinary Decade*; Charles Ruud and Sergei Stepanov, *Fontanka 16: The Tsar's Secret Police* (Montreal: McGill–Queen's University Press, 1999); Sidney Monas, *The Third Section: Police and Society Under Nicholas I* (Cambridge, Mass.: Harvard University Press, 1961).

Details regarding Petrashevsky and the Petrashevsky Circle come from *Dostoevsky as Reformer*; Nikolai Fyodorovich Bel'chikov, *Dostoevskii v protsesse petrashevtsev* (Moscow: Nauka, 1971); Frank I, 44, 240–67, 282–90, and II, 9–11, 90–91, 270, 274; Seddon, *Petrashevtsy*; *Delo petrashevtsev*, vols. 1 and 3; John Evans, *The Petraševskij Circle, 1845–1849* (The Hague: Mouton, 1974); Liudmila Ivanovna Saraskina, *Nikolai Speshnev: Nesbyvshaiasia Sud'ba* (Moscow: Nash Dom–L'Age d'Homme, 2000).

The details of Dostoevsky's arrest are derived from Alexander Petrovich Milyukov, "Fyodor Mikhailovich Dostoevsky," in *DVS* I, 270–71. See also *Dostoevsky as Reformer*, 97–98. Milyukov's source is Dostoevsky's own account in O. A. Milyukova's album, dated May 24, 1860. Additional arrest details are from Andrei Mikhailovich Dostoevsky, "Iz 'Vospominaniy,'" in *DVS* I (1990), 142–47; *LII*, 35 (June 6, 1862, to Andrei Dostoevsky); *LI*, 242 (March 23, 1856, to Vrangel); *Dostoevsky as Reformer*, 98, and Frank II, 9–11.

Additional background information comes from Charles Halperin, "Did Ivan IV's Oprichniki Carry Dogs' Heads on Their Horses?," *Canadian-American Slavic Studies* 46, no. 1 (2012): 40–67; Arcadius Kahan, "Natural Calamities and Their Effect upon the Food Supply in Russia," in *Jahrbücher für Geschichte Osteuropas Neue Folge* 16, no. 3 (Sept. 1968): 353–77; Kahan, *Russian Economic History*; Charles Halperin, *Russia and the Golden Horde: The Mongol Impact on Medieval Russia* (Bloomington: Indiana University Press, 1993); Walicki, *History of Russian Thought*, 153–60; Charles Fourier, "The Phalanstery," in *Selections from the Works of Fourier*, trans. Charles Gide (London: Swan Sonnerschein, 1901), 137–54; John Bushnell, "Did Serf Owners Control Serf Marriage? Orlov Serfs and Their Neighbors, 1773–1861," *Slavic Review* 52, no. 3 (1993): 419–45; Jerome Blum, *Lord and Peasant in Russia: From the Ninth to the Nineteenth Century* (Princeton, N.J.: Princeton University Press, 1961); Antonov, *Bankrupts and Usurers of Imperial Russia*; William Blackwell, *The Beginnings of Russian Industrialization, 1800–1860* (Princeton, N.J.: Princeton University Press, 1968); Peter Gatrell, *The Tsarist Economy, 1850–1917* (London: B. T. Batsford, 1986); Kagan, *Military Reforms of Nicholas I*.

70 **"Suddenly, like an electric spark"**: Saltykov-Schedrin quoted in Seddon, *Petrashevtsy*, 198.
70 **"The age-old order"**: "Dostoevsky's Statement," in *Dostoevsky as Reformer*, 33.
70 **"After invoking the help"**: Nicholas I quoted in Riasanovsky, *Nicholas I and Official Nationality*, 5. See also Saunders, "Pyrrhic Victory," 137.
71 **"organ of the government"**: Ruud, *Fighting Words*, 87.
71 **"Gentlemen! I have no police"**: Riasanovsky, *Nicholas I and Official Nationality*, 209.
72 **"feared and respected"**: Benckendorff quoted in Monas, *Third Section*, 230.
73 **"slaves of the tsar"**: Marshall Poe, "What Did Russians Mean When They Called Themselves 'Slaves of the Tsar'?," *Slavic Review* 57, no. 3 (Autumn 1998): 585–608.
73 **"What is your idea"**: "Dostoevsky's Testimony," in *Dostoevsky as Reformer*, 46.
76 **"*monastic-industrial* discipline"**: Fourier, "Phalanstery," 138.
77 **"so essentially robbers of fruit"**: Fourier, "Phalanstery," 153.
77 **"Expensive editions were piled"**: Kropotov quoted in Seddon, *Petrashevtsy*, 64.
78 **"Our trouble, gentlemen"**: "Dostoevsky's Testimony," in *Dostoevsky as Reformer*, 65–66, *Delo petrashevtsev* III, 458.
78 **"our system of propaganda"**: Antonelli's Report," in *Dostoevsky as Reformer*, 79.

78 **"Emperor Nikolai is not a man":** *Delo petrashevtsev* I, 280. Translation from Seddon, *Petrashevtsy*, 141.

79 **"Wouldn't it be a good thing":** *Delo petrashevtsev* III, 409; Seddon, *Petrashevtsy*, 205. Seddon's translation.

79 **"The author only has":** *Delo petrashevtsev* III, 412, 441–42; *Dostoevsky as Reformer*, 38, 80; Seddon, *Petrashevtsy*, 173–74; Frank I, 250.

79 **a calf was worth more:** Andrew A. Gentes, *Exile, Murder, and Madness in Siberia, 1823–61* (New York: Palgrave Macmillan, 2010), 121–22.

80 **demanding loved ones:** Frank argues for the connection between Dostoevsky's anti-serfdom and his father's death. See Frank I, 48, 88, 257.

80 **his first trip to St. Petersburg:** Dostoevsky, *Writer's Diary*, 1:326–27. Cf. *Notebooks*, 139, 153, 64n.

80 **"No! The most crying":** Golovinsky quoted in Seddon, *Petrashevtsy*, 219–20. See also *Dostoevsky as Reformer*, 49–51, 79–80, and *Delo petrashevtsev* III, 425–27.

81 **"Then let there be a revolt!":** Dostoevsky quoted in Frank I, 270, translation altered. See also *Dostoevsky as Reformer*, 12, and Miller and Strakhov, *Biografiya*, 85.

81 **one hundred rubles "*immediately*":** *LI*, 161–64 (Feb. 1, 1849, to Kraevsky).

81 **"I need fifteen now":** *LI*, 170 (first half of April 1849 to Kraevsky), my ellipsis. See also *LI*, 166 (March 25–26, 1849, to Kraevsky).

82 **"believes in nothing":** Speshnev quoted in Seddon, *Petrashevtsy*, 79.

82 **Speshnev enjoyed Stirner's:** Seddon, *Petrashevtsy*, 81, 99–100.

82 **"Every State is a *despotism*":** Stirner, *Ego and His Own*, 196. Succeeding quotations are from ibid., 216, 161–62, 359, 200.

82 **"*individuality* and *egoism*":** "Dostoevsky's Statement," in *Dostoevsky as Reformer*, 38.

82 **"Speak out boldly":** Filippov quoted in Seddon, *Petrashevtsy*, 222.

83 **"What she needs":** Belinsky, "Letter to N. V. Gogol," in *Belinsky, Chernyshevsky, and Dobrolyubov*, 84–86.

83 **"That's it!":** *Delo petrashevtsev* III, 433–35. See also Frank I, 287. Seddon, *Petrashevtsy*, 220.

84 **"The whole company":** *Delo petrashevtsev* III, 436; translation in Seddon, *Petrashevtsy*, 220.

84 **"the retired engineer-lieutenant":** Arrest Orders, in *Dostoevsky as Reformer*, 76.

SIX. THE EXECUTION

Details regarding the Petrashevists' imprisonment, interrogation, and execution are principally from *Dostoevsky as Reformer*; *Delo petrashevtsev* III; Seddon, *Petrashevtsy*; Andrei Dostoevsky, "Iz 'Vospominaniy,'" in *DVS* I, 147–52; Bel'chikov, *Dostoevskii v protsesse petrashevtsev*; Dmitri Dmitrievich Akhsharumov, "Iz knigi 'Iz moikh vospominaniy (1849–51),'" in *DVS* I, 312–24; Frank I, 263–83, and II, 6–7, 12–24, 47–62; Ivan L'vovich Jastrzembsky, "Memuary I. L. Yastrzhembskogo," in *Petrashevtsy v vospominaniyakh sovremennikov; sbornik materialov*, ed. P. S. Shchyogolev, 3 vols. (Moscow-Leningrad: Gosudarstvennoe izdatel'stvo, 1926–28), 1:147–67; Alexei Nikolayevich Pleshcheev, "Vospominaniya," and Ivan Vasil'evich Vuich, "Dnevnik," in *F. M. Dostoevskii v zabytykh i neizvestnykh vospominaniyakh sovremennikov*, ed. Sergei Belov (St. Petersburg: Andreev i Synov'ya, 1993); Miller and Strakhov, *Biografiya*. Quotations from Antonelli's reports are taken from *Delo petrashevtsev* III, 397–437. Quotations from Dostoevsky's written responses to interrogators are from "Dostoevsky's Statement," in *Dostoevsky as Reformer*, 31–37, 41–43, 53, 56, 63–65.

Quotations from Dostoevsky regarding his imprisonment come from *LI*, 172–73 (July 18, 1849, to Mikhail); *LI*, 174–75 (Aug. 27, 1849, to Mikhail); *LI*, 172 (July 18, 1849, to Mikhail); *LI*, 177 (Sept. 14, 1849, to Mikhail), and *LI*, 178–81 (Dec. 22, 1849, to Mikhail). Additional details about the prison and execution are from the following letters: *LI*, 171 (June 20, 1849, to Andrei); *LI*, 175n; and *LI*, 178 (Dec. 22, 1849, to Mikhail). Background information is from Annenkov, *Extraordinary Decade*, and Lincoln, *Sunlight at Midnight*. For Akhsharumov's sketches of the Semenovsky Parade Ground, see Nechaeva and A. F. Dostoevsky, *Feodor Mikhailovich Dostoevsky v portretakh, illyustratsiyakh, dokumentakh*, 141.

87 **"What is your name"**: "Dostoevsky's Formal Interrogation," in *Dostoevsky as Reformer*, 44.

88 **"did not play cards"**: Quoted in Frank I, 249, translation altered. See also *Dostoevsky as Reformer*, 8.

89 **"read Belinsky's letter in answer"**: "Records of Persons Attending Petrashevsky's Friday Meetings from March 11 of This Year," in *Dostoevsky as Reformer*, 77.

89 **"One can say"**: Seddon, *Petrashevtsy*, 64.

89 **"retired engineer-litterateur"**: *Dostoevsky as Reformer*, 77.

89 **"His Majesty the Emperor orders"**: Jastrzembsky, "Memuary I. L. Yastrzhembskogo," in *DVS* I, 163.

90 ***"like a freethinker"***: "Dostoevsky's Statement," in *Dostoevsky as Reformer*, 31.

90 **"Do you have *another* brother?"**: Andrei Dostoevsky, "Iz 'Vospominaniy,'" 154, my emphasis.

90 **"I cannot believe"**: Frank II, 17, translating Miller and Strakhov, *Biografiya*, 106–7.

93 **"all-embracing plan"**: Liprandi quoted in Monas, *Third Section*, 258.

93 **"conspiracy of ideas"**: Seddon, *Petrashevtsy*, 15–16.

93 **"Even if it is all just a lot"**: Nicholas I to Orlov quoted in *Dostoevsky as Reformer*, 7, translation altered. See also Frank II, 7.

93 **"nerves and fantasy"**: *LI*, 148 (Jan.–Feb. 1847 to Mikhail).

94 **"What are you living on?"**: *LI*, 172 (July 18, 1849, to Mikhail). Question mark supplied.

94 **"Why was I educated"**: "Dostoevsky's Statement," in *Dostoevsky as Reformer*, 33.

96 **"you and I are poets"**: Maikov quoted in *Dostoevsky as Reformer*, 99–100, my emphasis. See also Frank I, 267.

96 **"Since we are left with nothing"**: Speshnev quoted in Victoria Frede, *Doubt, Atheism, and the Nineteenth-Century Russian Intelligentsia* (Madison: University of Wisconsin Press, 2011), 111. See also Saraskina, *Nikolai Speshnev*, 161; Frank I, 263–64.

97 **"from now on I have"**: Yanovskiy, "Vospominaniya o Dostoevskom," 248–49, Frank's translation. See Frank I, 269–70. See also Saraskina, *Nikolai Speshnev*, 13, 13n.

98 **"Who's there?"** Nabokov: Nabokov quoted in *Dostoevsky as Reformer*, 104, trans. Knapp. Maikov told his story to A. A. Golenshchev-Kutuzov.

98 **"I never acted"**: Dostoevsky quoted in *Dostoevsky as Reformer*, 75, translation altered. I'm using Frank's "almost accidentally." See Frank II, 48.

99 **"Today you will hear"**: Akhsharumov, "Iz knigi 'Iz moikh vospominaniy (1849–51),'" 317–19.

99 **"involved in conspiracy"**: "Decision of the High Military Court," in *Dostoevsky as Reformer*, 93.

99 **"The Military Court finds"**: "Decision of the High Military Court," in *Dostoevsky as Reformer*, 91, translation altered, my ellipses. See also Frank II, 53–54.

100 **"It's not possible"**: Dostoevsky quoted in Frank II, 54.

100 **"Brothers! Before death"**: Akhsharumov, "Iz knigi 'Iz moikh vospominaniy (1849–51),'" 320.

100 **"Nous serons avec le Christ"**: F. N. L'vov, "Zapiska o Dele Petrashevtsev," quoted in Frank II, 57–58.

101 **"Load weapons!"**: Vuich, *"Dnevnik,"* 40.

101 **"Long live His Majesty"**: Vuich, *"Dnevnik,"* 40. See also L'vov, "Zapiska o Dele Petrashevtsev," 188.

101 **"It would be better"**: Hippolyte Debu quoted in Akhsharumov, "Iz knigi 'Iz moikh vospominaniy (1849–51),'" 323.

101 **"When I look back"**: Frank II, 62, Frank's translation. See also *LI*, 181 (Dec. 22, 1849, to Mikhail).

102 **"filled with impertinent freethinking"**: "The Case of the Retired Engineer-Lieutenant Dostoevsky," in *Dostoevsky as Reformer*, 85.

102 **"Can it be that I will never"**: Frank II, 60, Frank's translations. See also *LI*, 180 (Dec. 22, 1849, to Mikhail).

SEVEN. EXILE

Details of Dostoevsky's journey to Omsk come from *LI*, 183–93 (Jan. 30–Feb. 22, 1854, to Mikhail); Frank II, 72–77; Alexei Ivanovich Markevich, "K vospominaniyam o F. M. Dostoevskom," in *Dostoevskii v zabytykh i neizvestnykh vospominanyakh sovremennikov*, 50–51; Alexander Egorovich Vrangel', *vospominaniyakh o F. M. Dostoevskom v Siberii, 1854–56* (St. Petersburg: A. S. Suvorin, 1912), 108–15; Maria Dmitrievna Frantseva, "Vospominaniya," in *Istoricheskiy Vestnik* 32 (June 1888): 610–40; Pyotr Kuz'mich Mart'yanov, "V perelome veka," in *DVS I*, 333–44; Miller and Strakhov, *Biografiya*; Viktor Solomonovich Vaynerman, *Dostoevskii i Omsk* (Omsk: Omskoe Knizhnoe Iz-datel'stvo, 1991).

Some travelogues consulted include George Kennan, *Siberia and the Exile System*, 2 vols. (1891; New York: Praeger, 1970); S. S. Hill, *Travels in Siberia* (1854; New York: Arno Press, 1970); Giulio Adamoli, "Adamoli's Notes on a Journey from Perm to Tashkend," *Calcutta Review* 76 (1869; Calcutta: Thomas S. Smith, 1883); Georg Adolf Erman, *Travels in Siberia*, trans. William D. Cooley (London: Longman, Brown, Green, and Longmans, 1848); and Charles Cottrell, *Recollections of Siberia, in the Years 1840 and 1841* (London: J. W. Parker, 1842).

Background information on Siberia, Omsk, the Siberian exile system, and Ka-zakhs derives principally from Gentes, *Exile, Murder, and Madness in Siberia*; Andrew Gentes, "Katorga: Penal Labor and Tsarist Siberia," in *The Siberian Saga: A History of Russia's Wild East*, ed. Eva-Maria Stolberg (Frankfurt: Peter Lang, 2005); Daniel Beer, *The House of the Dead: Siberian Exile Under the Tsars* (New York: Vintage, 2017); Alan Wood, *Russia's Frozen Frontier: A History of Siberia and the Russian Far East, 1581–1991* (New York: Bloomsbury, 2011); Alan Wood, "The Use and Abuse of Ad-ministrative Exile to Siberia," *Irish Slavonic Studies* 6 (1985): 65–81; Alan Wood, "Sex and Violence in Siberia: Aspects of the Tsarist Exile System," in Massey Stewart and Alan Wood, *Siberia: Two Historical Perspectives* (London: Great Britain–USSR Asso-ciation and the School of Slavonic and East European Studies, 1984); Alan Wood, "Crime and Punishment in the House of the Dead," in *Civil Rights in Imperial Russia*, eds. Olga Crisp and Linda Edmondson (New York: Oxford University Press, 1989), 215–34; W. Bruce Lincoln, *The Conquest of a Continent: Siberia and the Russians* (New York: Random House, 1994); Janet Hartley, *Siberia: A History of the People* (New Haven, Conn.: Yale University Press, 2014); Igor V. Naumov, *The History of Siberia*, ed. David Collins (New York: Routledge, 2006); John J. Stephan, *The Russian Far East: A History* (Stanford, Calif.: Stanford University Press, 1994); Yuri Semyonov, *The Conquest of Siberia: An Epic of Human Passions*, trans. E. W. Dickes (London: George Routledge and Sons, 1944); Sergey Vasil'evich Maksimov, *Sibir' i Katorga*, 3rd ed. (St. Petersburg: Izdatel'stvo V. I. Gubinskago, 1900).

Additional details are from P. Hersteinsson and D. W. Macdonald, "Diet of Arctic Foxes (*Alopex lagopus*) in Iceland," *Journal of Zoology* 240, no. 3 (1996): 457–74; Alina Iakovleva, "Palynological Reconstruction of the Eocene Marine Palaeoenviron-ments in South of Western Siberia," *Acta Palaeobotanica* 51, no. 2 (2011): 229–48; V. F.

Molchanov, "The Gospel in F. M. Dostoevsky's Life and Work (Optical-Electronic Reconstruction of Marginalia in Dostoevsky's Copy of the New Testament)," in *The New Russian Dostoevsky: Readings for the Twenty-first Century*, ed. Carol Apollonio (Bloomington, Ind.: Slavica, 2010), 37–42; Shane O'Rourke, *The Cossacks* (Manchester, U.K.: Manchester University Press, 2007); Abby M. Schrader, *Languages of the Lash: Corporal Punishment and Identity in Imperial Russia* (DeKalb: Northern Illinois University Press, 2002); Kermit E. McKenzie, "Chokan Valikhanov: Kazakh Princeling and Scholar," *Central Asian Survey* 8, no. 3 (1989): 1–30; Steven Sabol, "Kazak Resistance to Russian Colonization: Interpreting the Kenesary Kasymov Revolt, 1837–1847," *Central Asian Survey* 22, no. 2/3 (June/Sept. 2003): 231–52; Walter Ratliff, *Pilgrims on the Silk Road: A Muslim-Christian Encounter in Khiva* (Eugene, Ore.: Wipf and Stock, 2010); David Sneath, *The Headless State: Aristocratic Orders, Kinship Society, and Misrepresentations of Nomadic Inner Asia* (New York: Columbia University Press, 2007); "Vysochayshe utverzhdyonnyy ustav o sibirskikh kirgizakh," in *Polnoye sobraniye zakonov Rossiyskoy imperii* 38, no. 29.127 (1822–23), especially chap. 4; Nikolai Mikhailovich Yadrintsev, "Statisticheskie materialy k istorii ssylki v Sibir'," in *Zapiski*, 9: 312–95 (full publishing information is not available, but further details are available at www.worldcat.org/search?q=no%3A83657288); W. P. Morrell, *The Gold Rushes* (New York: Macmillan, 1941); Ian Blanchard, *Russia's "Age of Silver": Precious-Metal Production and Economic Growth in the Eighteenth Century* (New York: Routledge, 1989).

Details about life in the fortress prison are drawn principally from *DH*; *LI*, 183–93 (Jan. 30–Feb. 22, 1854, to Mikhail); *LI*, 219 (Oct. 18, 1855, to Praskovya Yegorovna Annenkova); *LI*, 201 (Nov. 6, 1854, to Andrei Dostoevsky); Frank II, 69–149; Sergei Vladimirovich Belov, "Katorzhniki omskogo ostroga, 1852–1853," *Dostoevskii i mirovaya kul'tura*, 14–15 (2000–2001): 258–63; Simon Tokarzewski, "In Siberian Prisons, 1846–1857," trans. *Sarmatian* staff in *Sarmatian Review* 25, no. 2 (2005), www.ruf.rice.edu/~sarmatia/405/254tokar.html; Nikolai Mikhailovich Yadrintsev, "Dostoevskii v Sibiri," in *F. M. Dostoevskii v zabytykh i neizvestnykh vospominaniiakh sovremennikov*, 67–71; Irina Dmitrievna Yakubovich, notes to F. M. Dostoevsky, *Sobraniye sochineniy v pyatnadtsati tomakh*, ed. G. Fridlender and T. Ornatskaya ("Nauka," Leningradskoye Otdelenie, 1988–1996), vol. 3, accessed online: rvb.ru/dostoevski/02comm/19.htm; Nina Perlina, "Dostoevsky and His Polish Fellow Prisoners from the House of the Dead," in *Polish Encounters, Russian Identity*, ed. D. Ransel and B. Shallcross (Bloomington: Indiana University Press, 2005), 100–109; Peter Sekirin, trans. and ed., *The Dostoevsky Archive: Firsthand Accounts of the Novelist from Contemporaries' Memoirs and Rare Periodicals* (Jefferson, N.C.: McFarland, 2013).

109 **"In shackles?":** Jastrzembsky quoted in Miller and Strakhov, *Biografiya*, 125–26.
110 **he was "exceptionally calm":** Markevich, "K vospominaniyam o F. M. Dostoevskom," 50–51
110 **"a petty barbarian":** *LI*, 186 (Jan. 30–Feb. 22, 1854, to Mikhail).
111 **"We paced back and forth":** Frantseva, "Vospominaniya," 47–48.
111 **"prisoners in the full sense":** Quoted in Frank II, 75.

112 **"Omsk is a vile little town":** *LI*, 188 (Jan. 30–Feb. 22, 1854, to Mikhail).
112 **"the key and the gate":** Peter the Great quoted in Sabol, "Kazak Resistance to Russian Coloniza-tion," 234.
112 **two hundred Russians were enslaved:** Ratliff, *Pilgrims on the Silk Road*, 4.
113 **"leeches sucking the blood":** Kenisari quoted in Sabol, "Kazak Resistance to Russian Colonization," 242.
114 **"drunk as a cobbler":** *LI*, 186 (Jan. 30–Feb. 22, 1854, to Mikhail).
114 **"like a malicious spider":** *DH*, 273–74, translation and punctuation altered.
115 **"Who is that?":** Tokarzewski, "In Siberian Prisons."
115 **"Wha-a-at?! Insolence? That's insolence!":** *DH*, 269–70.
115 **"I'll show you!":** Tokarzewski, "In Siberian Prisons."
115 **"Age: 28":** K. Nikolaevskiy, "Tovarishchi F. M. Dostoevskogo po katorge," *Istoricheskiy vestnik* (Jan.–March 1898): 219–24.
115 **"These belong to the category":** Sekirin, *Dostoevsky Archive*, 108, Sekirin translation of "The Book of Arrivals and Departures," Archives, CGVIA, file 312/2, no. 1280, 2.
117 **"Sleep on your right side":** *DH*, 31; *LI*, 186 (Jan. 30–Feb. 22, 1854, to Mikhail). See also Tokarzewski, "In Siberian Prisons"; Frank II, 81n.
117 **"You're going to see":** *DH*, 36.
117 **"You nobles, iron beaks":** *LI*, 186–87 (Jan. 30–Feb. 22, 1854, to Mikhail), translation altered.
119 **"I came here":** *DH*, 44–46, translation altered; Gentes, *Exile, Murder, and Madness in Siberia*, 212; Frank II, 139.
120 **"the most excellent of spirits":** *DH*, 16–17, 249. Dostoevsky later discovered Ilinsky's exoneration, and he became a model for Dmitri in *The Brothers Karamazov*.
120 **"I can say positively":** *DH*, 54–57. For more on Orlov, see Vrangel' *Vospominaniya o F. M. Dostoevskom v Siberii, 1854–56*, 108–9, 119–20, and Frank II, 148–49.
121 **"You Moldavian plague!":** *DH*, 27, translation altered.
121 **"Am I bothering you?":** *DH*, 101–2. Dostoevsky named Andrei Shalomentsev "Petrov" in *Dead House*.
122 **"the most fearless":** *DH*, 102. For background on Shalomentsev, see Yakubovich I, 540.
123 **"We're a beaten folk":** *DH*, 17.
123 **"Lord Jesus Christ":** *DH*, 163–64.

EIGHT. THE SOCIAL CONTRACT

Details of Lacenaire's various bank robbery attempts, as well as the attempted murder of Genevay, are principally from *Mémoires et écrits*; *Memoirs*; *Procès complet*; *Lacenaire, ses crimes*; Fouquier, "Lacenaire, François et Avril"; and Canler, *Autobiography of a French Detective*.

126 **"You go like that":** Fouquier, "Lacenaire, François et Avril," 7.
126 **"too young for me":** *Memoirs*, 190.
127 **to have Lacenaire arrested:** *Memoirs*, 195. After seeing Lacenaire "writing" (apparently producing forgeries), a mutual associate told Lacenaire that Chardon "would have me arrested when he next saw me." The threat is notably oblique; the reason for the arrest is not specified. Lacenaire never discussed his sexuality in print, so its relation to his crimes can only be conjecture.
127 **"I know you":** *Memoirs*, 196.

NINE. THE DEAD MAN

Details from Dostoevsky's prison life derive primarily from *DH*; Fyodor Mikhailovich Dostoevsky, *Moya tetradka katorzhnaya (Sibirskaya tetrad')*, eds. V. P. Vladimirtsev and T. Ornatskaya (Krasnoyarsk: Krasnoyarskoe knizhnoe izdatel'stvo, 1985); *LI*, 183–93 (Jan. 30–Feb. 22, 1854, to Mikhail); Frank II, 80–102; Tokarzewski, "Iz knigi

'Katorzhane,'" in *DVS* I, 325–26; Nikolaevskiy, "Tovarishchi F. M. Dostoevskogo po katorge," *Istoricheskiy vestnik* (Jan.–March 1898): 219–24; Belov, "Katorzhniki omskogo ostroga, 1852–1853"; A. P. Milyukov, "Fyodor Mikhailovich Dostoevsky," 259–90; A. K. Rozhnovsky, "Iz vospominaniy o F. M. Dostoevskom," in *F. M. Dostoevskii v zabytykh i neizvestnykh vospominaniiakh sovremennikov*, 62.

Background information is from Gentes, *Exile, Murder, and Madness in Siberia*; Schrader, *Languages of the Lash*; Wood, *Russia's Frozen Frontier*; Wood, "Crime and Punishment in the House of the Dead"; Semyonov, *Conquest of Siberia*; Georg Bernhard Michels, *At War with the Church: Religious Dissent in Seventeenth-Century Russia* (Stanford, Calif.: Stanford University Press, 1999); Robert O. Crummey, *Old Believers and the World of the Antichrist: The Vyg Community and the Russian State, 1694–1855* (Madison: University of Wisconsin Press, 1970); Lincoln, *Conquest of a Continent*; Basil Dmytryshyn, *Medieval Russia: A Source Book, 850–1700* (Gulf Breeze, Fla.: Academic International Press, 2000); Joseph Staples, *A Few Practical Observations on the Art of Cupping* (London: Longman, Rees, 1835); John S. Haller, *American Medicine in Transition, 1840–1910* (Chicago: University of Illinois Press, 1981); Stanley Finger, *Origins of Neuroscience: A History of Explorations into Brain Function* (New York: Oxford University Press, 1994); John Cooke, *A Treatise on Nervous Diseases* (Boston: Wells and Lilly, 1824); Thomas Mapleson, *A Treatise on the Art of Cupping* (London: John Wilson, 1830); Edward Henry Sieveking, *On Epilepsy and Epileptiform Seizures: Their Causes, Pathology, and Treatment*, 2nd rev. ed. (London: John Churchill, 1861). For details regarding Dostoevsky's Bible in Siberia and a detailed spectrophotometric examination of its pages, see Konstantin Abrekovich Barsht, B. S. Raykhel', and T. S. Sokolova, "O metode tsifrovoy spektrofotometrii v izuchenii rukopisi pisatelya (na primere 'Sibirskoy tetradi' F. M. Dostoyevskogo)," *Izvestiya Rossiyskoy Akademii Nauk* 71, no. 4 (2012): 20–43.

Detailed description of a temporal lobe primary seizure followed by a secondary complex generalized tonic-clonic seizure derives from several sources: R. K. Wong, R. D. Traub, and R. Miles, "Cellular Basis of Neuronal Synchrony in Epilepsy," *Advances in Neurology* 44 (1986): 583–92, europepmc.org/article/med/3706021; Elliot H. Smith et al., "The Ictal Wavefront Is the Spatiotemporal Source of Discharges During Spontaneous Human Seizures," *Nature Communications*, March 29, 2016, 11098, doi .org/10.1038/ncomms11098; Andrew J. Trevelyan et al., "The Source of Afterdischarge Activity in Neocortical Tonic-Clonic Epilepsy," *Journal of Neuroscience* 27, no. 49 (Dec. 5, 2007): 13513–19; W. Truccolo et al., "Single-Neuron Dynamics in Human Focal Epilepsy," *Nature Neuroscience*, March 27, 2011, 635–41; L. Martinet et al., "Human Seizures Couple Across Spatial Scales Through Travelling Wave Dynamics," *Nature Communications* 8 (2017): 14896, doi.org/10.1038/ncomms14896. For discussion of Dostoevsky's epilepsy, see, for example, Rice, *Dostoevsky and the Healing Art*. The event described is the type of temporal lobe seizure most likely associated with pre-ictal ecstatic auras, which Dostoevsky reported experiencing. Additional sources regarding Dostoevsky's specific diagnosis are listed in the notes for chapter 20.

130 "Not enough gray cloth": *DH*, 12.

130 "Here, 'unfortunate,' take a little kopeck": *DH*, 20.

131 "to annihilate a man": *DH*, 22.

131 "Be a father to me!": *DH*, 188–90, translation altered. Cf. Dostoevsky, *Memoirs from the House of the Dead*, trans. Jessie Coulson (New York: Oxford University Press, 1965), 228.

132 "It burns, it scorches like fire": *DH*, 196.

132 five thousand strokes: *DH*, 185–87; Belov, "Katorzhniki omskogo ostroga, 1852–1853," 262.

133 "Zhokhovsky! I offended you": *DH*, 278.

134 "changing their fate": *DH*, 70, 78.

134 "There is not a country": Speransky quoted in Gentes, *Exile, Murder, and Madness in Siberia*, 4.

134 "for all of us": See Michels, *At War with the Church*, 83. See also Paul Meyendorff, *Russia, Ritual, and Reform: The Liturgical Reforms of Nikon in the Seventeenth Century* (Crestwood, N.Y.: St. Vladimir's Press, 1991).

134 as the *Skoptsy*: See Laura Engelstein, *Castration and the Heavenly Kingdom: A Russian Folktale* (Ithaca, N.Y.: Cornell University Press, 1999), 12–18, 34, 95–96, 174.

135 "At the end of the world": Dostoevsky, *Moya tetradka katorzhnaya*, 6, entry 14. For commentary, see *Moya tetradka katorzhnaya*, 63.

135 "Money is minted freedom": *DH*, 19.

136 "throw it away like wood chips": *DH*, 78–79. For Dostoevsky on binges, see *DH*, 39–43.

137 "Suddenly something in him": *DH*, 107.

137 "Where's the rioter?": Milyukov, "Fyodor Mikhailovich Dostoevsky," 276–78.

137 "revel in the most boundless": *DH*, 107–8.

138 "It's convulsions": *DH*, 79–80.

138 "I never acted with malice": Dostoevsky quoted in Frank II, 48. Cf. *Dostoevsky as Reformer*, 75.

138 scraps of paper: Barsht, Raykhel', and Sokolova, "O metode tsifrovoy spektrofotometrii v izuchenii rukopisi pisatelya," 41. The date of the notebook's creation has been disputed for decades, but Barsht, Raykhel', and Sokolova have analyzed the notebook's paper and ink using digital spectrophotometry. They conclude that notebook entries 1–268 were written at the same time. A comparison with Dostoevsky's dated letters places the composition in the summer of 1855. See ibid., 35, 40–41. The authors also contend that Dostoevsky was recopying these entries from scraps (ibid., 41).

138 "The iron beaks have pecked": Notebook quotations are from Dostoevsky, *Moya tetradka katorzhnaya*, 5–12, entries 59, 129, 88, 2, 103, 67, 1, 62, 45.

139 of Charles Dickens: See Tom Hubbard, "Heart and Soul: Dickens and Dostoevsky," *Slavonica* 25, no. 2 (2020): 89–105.

140 "I have not written": Mart'yanov "V perelome veka," 342–44. Mart'yanov claims the notes were stored in the hospital by "one of the hospital's chief medics."

140 a whole hour: *DH*, 210.

140 "I look, I see a man": Notebook quotations taken from Dostoevsky, *Moya tetradka katorzhnaya*, 6–8, entries 21, 29, 69, 38.

141 would "turn cold": *LI*, 233–34 (Jan. 18, 1856, to Apollon Maikov).

143 "I sense that I am losing": *LI*, 275–76 (Nov. 9, 1856, to Mikhail).

143 "am now literally not in my right mind": *LI*, 337 (Feb. 8, 1858, to Yakushkin).

143 "Hi! You're still alive!?": Dostoevsky, *Moya tetradka katorzhnaya*, 5, entry 10.

143 "the Dead Man": Rozhnovsky, "Iz Vospominanii o F. M. Dostoevskom," 60. Cf. Vaynerman, *Dostoevskii i Omsk*, 113–18.

144 "What are you doing": *DH*, 255–65.

144 "but how can you": Dostoevsky, *Memoirs from the House of the Dead*, trans. Coulson, 322. Cf. Frank II, 102.

144 "are separated from common people": *DH*, 254, translation altered.

145 "For the first time": *DH*, 155. For the entire prison theater scene, see *DH*, 151–63.

147 "such riches, feeling, heart": *DH*, 252–53.

147 "profound, strong, marvelous": *LI*, 190 (Jan. 30–Feb. 22, 1854, to Mikhail).

148 Kazakh nomads: *DH*, 227–28. The term Dostoevsky uses in this passage and throughout his letters is "Kirghiz," which at the time was the imperial Russian name for the Kazakhs.

148 **"I will no longer write trifles":** Dostoevsky quoted and trans. in Frank II, 167. Cf. *LI*, 189 (Jan. 30–Feb. 22, 1854, to Mikhail).

TEN. AUNT RAZOR

Details of the Chardon crime scene, Canler's investigation, and Lacenaire's capture and emerging celebrity are taken primarily from *Mémoires et écrits*; *Memoirs*; *Procès complet*; *Lacenaire, ses crimes*; Fouquier, "Lacenaire, François et Avril"; and Canler, *Autobiography of a French Detective*. Background information is from Michael Stephen Smith, *The Emergence of Modern Business Enterprise in France, 1800–1930* (Cambridge, Mass.: Harvard University Press, 2006).

153 **his capital *M*:** Capital *M*s can be found in Simonelli's reproductions from Lacenaire's letters and manuscripts. See *Mémoires et écrits*, plates 17–20. Reproductions of a few manuscript pages from Lacenaire's memoirs are available online: www.pba-auctions.com/lot/18549/3906346?npp=10000&.

158 **"How is it that your intelligence":** *Lacenaire, ses crimes*, 191, quoted and trans. in Morton, *First Detective*.

158 **"This man is immortal":** Léon Gozlan, "A Propos de Lacenaire," *Revue de Paris* 25 (1836): 252–68.

159 **an "exceptional death":** Bonnellier and Arago, *Lacenaire après sa condamnation*, 146.

159 **"Do you think they will":** *Lacenaire, ses crimes*, 194, Cochinat's emphasis. See also *Procès complet*, 150.

ELEVEN. THE RESURRECTION

Information on Dostoevsky's Siberian army years and marriage to Marya Dmitrievna is taken from *LI*, 189–306; Frank II, 175–216. Background information about Petersburg and Russia in the 1860s is from Blackwell, *Beginnings of Russian Industrialization*; Lincoln, *Sunlight at Midnight*; Buckler, *Mapping St. Petersburg*; Riasanovsky, *Nicholas I and Official Nationality*; Gregory Freeze, "Reform and Counter-reform, 1855–1890," in *Russia: A History*, ed. Gregory Freeze (New York: Oxford University Press, 2002), 199–233; Vrangel', *Vospominaniya o F. M. Dostoevskom v Sibiri*; Kennan, *Siberia and the Exile System*. For background on Valikhanov, see McKenzie, "Chokan Valikhanov"; and Michael Futrell, "Dostoyevsky and Islam (and Chokan Valikhanov)," *Slavonic and East European Review* 57, no. 1 (Jan. 1979): 16–31.

Quotations regarding Dostoevsky's literary ambitions and frustrations in Siberia are from *LI*, 224–25 (Jan. 13–18, 1856, to Mikhail); *LI*, 190 (Jan. 30–Feb. 22, 1854, to Mikhail); *LI*, 256–57 (April 13, 1856, to Vrangel); *LI*, 351 (Sept. 13, 1858, to Mikhail); *LI*, 383 (Oct. 4, 1859, to Totleben); *LI*, 205–6 (April 15, 1855, to Yevgeny Yakushkin); *LI*, 234 (Jan. 18, 1856, to Apollon Maikov); *LI*, 196 (end of Jan.–third week of Feb. 1854 to Fonvizina); *LI*, 190 (Jan. 30–Feb. 22, 1854, to Mikhail); *LI*, 368 (July 1, 1859, to Mikhail). For Dostoevsky's plans for *The Double*, *Notes from a Dead House*, *Notes from Underground*, and other ideas, see *LI*, 380 (Oct. 1, 1859, to Mikhail); *LI*, 390–93 (Oct. 9, 1859, to Mikhail). For quotations regarding plans for a new journal, see *LI*, 351 (Sept. 13, 1858, to Mikhail); *LII*, 69 (Sept. 18/30, 1863, to Strakhov); *LI*, 363 (May 9, 1859, to Mikhail); *LI*, 419–20 (Nov. 12, 1859, to Mikhail).

Background information on the 1860s literary scene, *Vremya* and its beginnings, Chernyshevsky, and Katkov is from Ruud, *Fighting Words*; McReynolds, *News Under*

Russia's Old Regime; V. S. Nechaeva, *Zhurnal M. M. i F. M. Dostoevskikh, "Vremya," 1861–1863* (Moscow: Nauka, 1962); Todd, "Dostoevsky as a Professional Writer"; Belknap, "Survey of Russian Journals"; Gregory Guroff and S. Frederick Starr, "A Note on Urban Literacy in Russia, 1890–1914," *Jahrbücher für Geschichte Osteuropas* 19, no. 4 (1971): 520–31; Irina Paperno, *Chernyshevsky and the Age of Realism: A Study in the Semiotics of Behavior* (Stanford, Calif.: Stanford University Press, 1988); Frank III, 32–35, 48–57; Miller and Strakhov, *Biografiya*; Franco Venturi, *Roots of Revolution: A History of the Populist and Socialist Movements in Nineteenth Century Russia* (New York: Knopf, 1960); James Scanlan, "Nicholas Chernyshevsky and Philosophical Materialism in Russia," *Journal of the History of Philosophy* 8, no. 1 (Jan. 1970): 65–86; Walter Moss, *Russia in the Age of Alexander II, Tolstoy, and Dostoevsky* (London: Anthem Press, 2002); Seddon, *Petrashevtsy*; Walicki, *History of Russian Thought*; Freeborn, "Age of Realism"; Nikolai Gavrilovich Chernyshevsky, "The Anthropological Principle in Philosophy," in *Selected Philosophical Essays* (Moscow: Foreign Languages Publishing House, 1953); Elise Kimmerling Wirtschafter, *Structures of Society: Imperial Russia's "People of Various Ranks"* (DeKalb: Northern Illinois University Press, 1994); Susanne Fusso, *Editing Turgenev, Dostoevsky, and Tolstoy: Mikhail Katkov and the Great Russian Novel* (DeKalb: Northern Illinois University Press, 2017); Karel Durman, *The Time of the Thunderer: Mikhail Katkov, Russian National Extremism, and the Failure of the Bismarckian System* (Boulder, Colo.: East European Monographs, 1988); Martin Katz, *Mikhail Katkov: A Political Biography, 1818–1887* (The Hague: Mouton, 1966).

Details about Russia's 1860s reforms, serf emancipation, and emerging radicalism derive from Saunders, *Russia in the Age of Reaction and Reform*; Abbott Gleason, *Young Russia: The Genesis of Russian Radicalism in the 1860s* (New York: Viking, 1980); Gatrell, *Tsarist Economy*; Alexander Gerschenkron, "Economic Backwardness in Historical Perspective," "Social Attitudes, Entrepreneurship, and Economic Development," and "Russia: Patterns and Problems of Economic Development, 1861–1958," in *Economic Backwardness in Historical Perspective: A Book of Essays* (Cambridge, Mass.: Harvard University Press, 1962); Kahan, *Russian Economic History*; Geroid Tanquary Robinson, *Rural Russia Under the Old Regime* (New York: Macmillan, 1967); Richard Pipes, *Russia Under the Old Regime* (New York: Scribner, 1974); Blum, *Lord and Peasant in Russia*; Steven Hoch, "The Banking Crisis, Peasant Reform, and Economic Development in Russia, 1857–1861," *American Historical Review* 96, no. 3 (1991): 795–820; Antoine Horn, "A History of Banking in the Russian Empire," in *A History of Banking in All the Leading Nations* (New York: Journal of Commerce and Commercial Bulletin, 1896), 2: 341–69; Artur Attman, "The Russian Market in World Trade, 1500–1860," *Scandinavian Economic History* Review 29, no. 3 (1981): 177–202; David Goldstein, *Dostoevsky and the Jews* (Austin: University of Texas Press, 1981).

Details about utilitarianism, physiology, and materialism come from Jeremy Bentham, *An Introduction to the Principles of Morals and Legislation*, www.earlymoderntexts.com/assets/pdfs/bentham1780.pdf; Carroll, *Break-Out from the Crystal Palace*;

Frederick Gregory, *Scientific Materialism in Nineteenth-Century Germany* (Boston: D. Reidel, 1977); Ludwig Büchner, *Force and Matter: Empirico-philosophical Studies, Intelligibly Rendered*, trans. J. Frederick Collingwood (London: Trübner, 1870); Ivan Sechenov, *Reflexes of the Brain* (Cambridge, Mass.: MIT Press, 1965); Maya Koretzky, "Sensation(al) Science: Ivan Sechenov's *Reflexes of the Brain* and Revolutionary Physiology, Literature, and Politics of the Russian 1860s," *Ezra's Archives* (2013): 75–91; Christine Frances Donaldson, "Russian Nihilism of the 1860's: A Science-Based Social Movement" (PhD diss., Ohio State University, 1979); Victoria Thorstensson, "The Dialog with Nihilism in Russian Polemical Novels of the 1860s–1870s" (PhD diss., University of Wisconsin–Madison, 2013).

161 **"It is better to begin abolishing":** Alexander II quoted in Freeze, "Reform and Counter-reform," 173.
161 **"our Angel-Tsar":** *LI*, 271 (Nov. 9, 1856, to Vrangel).
161 **"I adore him":** *LI*, 256 (April 13, 1856, to Vrangel).
161 **"a woman's heart":** *LI*, 209 (June 4, 1855, to Marya Isaeva).
162 **"I'll either go mad":** *LI*, 237–38 (March 23, 1856, to Vrangel).
162 **"I am ready to go to jail":** Quoted in Frank II, 209–10. Cf. *LI*, 260 (May 23, 1856, to Vrangel).
162 **"I have *genuine falling sickness*":** *LI*, 305–6 (March 9, 1857, to Mikhail).
162 **"a man with no future":** Pyotr Semyonov, "My Meeting with Dostoevsky in Siberia," in Sekirin, *Dostoevsky Archive*, 117.
162 **"Tell me please":** Quotations in this paragraph are from *LI*, 183 (Jan. 30–Feb. 22, 1854, to Mikhail); *LI*, 347 (May 31, 1858, to Mikhail); *LI*, 349 (July 19, 1858, to Mikhail), my ellipsis; *LI*, 374–75 (Sept. 19, 1859, to Mikhail).
163 **"You write me that you love me":** *LI*, 276–79 (Dec. 14, 1856, to Valikhanov), translation altered. I've changed the imperial Russian term "Kirghiz" to the endonym "Kazakh."
164 **"All my former life":** *DH*, 294–95.
164 **"all the *behind-the-scenes secrets*":** *LI*, 283 (Dec. 21, 1856, to Vrangel), translation altered.
164 **about Olga N.:** This is the pseudonym of the Russian writer and translator Sof'ia Vladimirovna Engel'gardt.
164 **twenty-eight pieces of paper:** Barsht, Raykhel', and Sokolova, "O metode tsifrovoy spektrofotometrii v izuchenii rukopisi pisatelya," 22, 26, 33.
165 **"With feelings of reverence":** *LI*, 435 (Oct. 10–18, 1859, to Tsar Alexander II).
165 **"Poor fellow!" We killed:** Translation in Frank II, 237. I. I. Panaev, "Literary Idols, Dilettantes," in Panaev, *PSS*, 5:7.
165 **"Dostoevsky is finished":** Frank II, 264.
167 **"We live in an epoch":** Statement translated in Frank III, 35.
167 **"its talent for universal reconciliation":** Dostoevsky, "Introduction" in *Occasional Writings*, 61–62, translation altered.
167 **subscriptions were "so-so":** *LII*, 29 (July 31, 1861, to Yakov Polonsky).
167 **"I understand what":** *LII*, 14–15 (May 3, 1860, to Alexandra Shubert).
168 **"It revived my literary reputation":** *LII*, 151 (March 31–April 14, 1865, to Vrangel).
168 **"Get hold of *Notes from a Dead House*":** Tolstoy to Countess A. A. Tolstaya, Feb. 22, 1862, in *Tolstoy's Letters*, 2 vols., trans. and ed. R. F. Christian (New York: Scribner, 1978), 1: 155, translation altered.
168 **"I don't know":** Tolstoy to N. N. Strakhov, Sept. 26, 1880, in *Tolstoy's Letters*, 2: 338.
168 **fracturing into "two hostile camps":** "Mr. ——bov and the Question of Art," *Occasional Writings*, 89.
168 **a "second Savior":** Quoted in Paperno, *Chernyshevsky and the Age of Realism*, 40.
168 **"we still need an iron dictatorship":** Chernyshevsky quoted in Venturi, *Roots of Revolution*, 157.
168 **"The sooner it collapses":** Chernyshevsky quoted in Venturi, *Roots of Revolution*, 139.
168 **the "eternal struggle":** Chernyshevsky quoted in Venturi, *Roots of Revolution*, 134, 152.

169 called "trashy weakness": Chernyshevsky, "The Russian at the *Rendez-vous*," in *Belinsky, Cherny-shevsky, and Dobrolyubov*, 113–15.
169 They are "literary Robespierres": Turgenev quoted in Venturi, *Roots of Revolution*, 157.
169 a "stinking cockroach": Translation in Frank II, 246.
169 "unpleasant, reedy little voice": Tolstoy quoted in Moss, *Russia in the Age of Alexander II*, 24. See Tolstoy to Nekrasov, July 2, 1856.
169 "liberating the Russian mind": Katkov quoted in Durman, *Time of the Thunderer*, 16.
169 "predestined for something great": Katkov quoted in Fusso, *Editing Turgenev, Dostoevsky, and Tolstoy*, 8.
170 "universal reconciliation": Dostoevsky, "Introduction," in *Occasional Writings*, 61–63.
170 the "golden mediocrities": Dostoevsky, "Introduction," in *Occasional Writings*, 71–72.
170 "a fop perfumed with patchouli": Katkov quoted in Fusso, *Editing Turgenev, Dostoevsky, and Tolstoy*, 122.
170 "incontinent and quick-tempered": Dostoevsky quoted in Fusso, *Editing Turgenev, Dostoevsky, and Tolstoy*, 122.
170 "You need to lash out": *LIII*, 136 (Feb. 26/March 10, 1869, to Strakhov).
171 "Beauty is useful": "Mr. ——bov and the Question of Art," in *Occasional Writings*, 136.
173 "Our task is to create": Translated in Fusso, *Editing Turgenev, Dostoevsky, and Tolstoy*, 100.
174 His anti-Semitism: See Goldstein, *Dostoevsky and the Jews*.
174 "All people are egoists": Chernyshevsky, "Anthropological Principle in Philosophy," 124, 120.
174 humans make no choices: Chernyshevsky, "Anthropological Principle in Philosophy," 94, 99, 124.
175 "sum up the values": Bentham, *Principles of Morals and Legislation*, 22–25.
175 "instability of views": Chernyshevsky, "Anthropological Principle in Philosophy," 86–87.
175 "the Bible of Materialism": Gregory, *Scientific Materialism in Nineteenth-Century Germany*, 105.
176 "can be reduced": Sechenov, *Reflexes of the Brain*, 2–3.
177 "exact scientific analysis": Chernyshevsky, "Anthropological Principle in Philosophy," 102–3.
177 "Reality is infinitely diverse": *DH*, 252, translation altered.

TWELVE. FEROCIOUS MATERIALISM

Fouquier's commentary on Lacenaire and coverage of Lacenaire's trial can be found in Fouquier, "Lacenaire, François et Avril." *Vremya*'s version of Fouquier's article was translated and reprinted in *Vremya* 1, no. 2 (Feb. 1861): 1–50. Vadim Dmitrievich Rak notes that two editions would have been available to Dostoevsky. Both contain the same illustrations. See Vadim Dmitrievich Rak, "Istochnik ocherkov o znamenitykh ugolovnykh protsessakh v zhurnalakh brat'ev Dostoevskikh," in *Dostoevskii: Materialy i issledovaniia* (1974), 1: 239–41. See Viktor Viktorovich Dudkin in notes to F. M. Dostoevsky, *Polnoe sobranie sochineniy v chetyryokh tomakh. Izdanie v avtorskoy or-fografii i punktuatsii: kanonicheskie teksty* (Petrozavodsk: Izdatel'stvo Petrozavodskogo universiteta, 2000), 4: 938–55 for discussion of Dostoevsky's active role in the transla-tion of Fouquier's article as well as Lacenaire's influence on *Crime and Punishment*.

Details and all quotations from testimony during Lacenaire's trial can be found in *Procès complet*, 18–120; Cochinat, *Lacenaire, ses crimes*, 195–310. For homosexuality in nineteenth-century France, see William Peniston, *Pederasts and Others: Urban Cul-ture and Sexual Identity in Nineteenth-Century Paris* (New York: Routledge, 2012); O'Brien, *Promise of Punishment*, 91–98; and Michael Sibalis, "The Palais-Royal and the Homosexual Subculture of Nineteenth-Century Paris," *Journal of Homosexuality* 41, no. 3–4 (2002): 117–29.

180 **"egoism and materialism":** See, for example, *La Quotidienne*, Nov. 29, 1835.
180 **"transmitted with the exactness":** *PSS*, 18: 90. See also Strelsky, "Lacenaire and Raskolnikov," and Frank III, 72.
189 **"more exciting than all possible novels":** Dostoevsky quoted in Frank III, 72. For original, see *PSS*, 18: 90. See also www.fedordostoevsky.ru/pdf/Lacenaire.pdf.

THIRTEEN. THE BIRTH OF NIHILISM

Details about the rise of nihilism in the 1860s, student protests, and government re-actions are principally from Gleason, *Young Russia*; Venturi, *Roots of Revolution*; Frank III, 134–77, 210–12; Ruud and Stepanov, *Fontanka 16*; Dmitri Pisarev, *Selected Philosophical, Social, and Political Essays* (Moscow: Foreign Languages Publishing House, 1958); Peter Pozefsky, *The Nihilist Imagination: Dmitrii Pisarev and the Cultural Origins of Russian Radicalism (1860–1868)* (New York: Peter Lang, 2003); Frede, *Doubt, Atheism, and the Nineteenth-Century Russian Intelligentsia*; Edward J. Brown, "Pisarev and the Transformation of Two Russian Novels," in *Literature and Society in Imperial Russia, 1800–1914*, ed. William Mills Todd III (Stanford, Calif.: Stanford University Press, 1978), 151–72; Donaldson, "Russian Nihilism of the 1860's."

Quotations from "To the Young Generation" are found in Venturi, *Roots of Revolution*, 246–51, and Gleason, *Young Russia*, 161. "Young Russia" quotations are found in Venturi, *Roots of Revolution*, 292–96, and Gleason, *Young Russia*, 171–72. Quotations from Pisarev's review of Turgenev are from *Fathers and Children*, 2nd ed., trans. and ed. Michael Katz (New York: W. W. Norton, 2009), 193–215. Katkov's nationalist and anti-nihilist quotations are from Katz, *Mikhail Katkov*, 111, 123, 69, 75–76, 128. For Dostoevsky's reaction to the Petersburg fires and his meeting with Chernyshevsky, see Dostoevsky, *Writer's Diary*, 1: 148–49, and N. G. Chernyshevsky, "Moi Svidaniya c F. M. Dostoevskim," in *DVS* II, 5–7.

See also Kagan, *Military Reforms of Nicholas I;* Blackwell, *Beginnings of Russian Industrialization*; Boris Mironov, "Wages and Prices in Imperial Russia, 1703–1913," *Russian Review* 69 (Jan. 2010): 56 (table 5) and 57 (fig. 2); Victoria Thorstensson, "Nihilist Fashion in 1860s–1870s Russia: The Aesthetic Relations of Blue Spectacles to Reality," *Clothing Cultures* 3, no. 3 (2016): 265–81; Cathy Frierson, *All Russia Is Burning!* (Seattle: University of Washington Press, 2012); Lincoln, *Sunlight at Midnight*. For Chernyshevsky's novel, see Nikolai Chernyshevsky, *What Is to Be Done?*, trans. Michael Katz (Ithaca, N.Y.: Cornell University Press, 1989), esp. 375–78. For Dostoevsky on *Vremya*'s ban, his own and his wife's illness, and Mikhail's hardships, see *LII*, 48–50 (June 17, 1863, to Turgenev); *LII*, 51 (June 19, 1863, to Turgenev); *LIII*, 316–17 (Feb. 10/22, 1871, to Strakhov).

190 **"stupid and ignorant":** "Great Russia" quoted in Venturi, *Roots of Revolution*, 237.
191 **"If to achieve our ends":** "To the Young Generation," quoted in Venturi, *Roots of Revolution*, 249, translation altered.
192 **"We act on the basis":** Turgenev, *Fathers and Children*, 40, 42, 19
193 **"grim, wild, huge":** Turgenev to K. K. Sluchevsky, April 14/26, 1862, *Turgenev's Letters*, 183.
193 **"gaunt, green, with roving eyes":** Chernyshevsky quoted in Lidiya Yakovlevna Ginzburg, *O litera-turnom geroye* (Leningrad: Sovetskiy Pisatel', Leningradskoe Otdelenie, 1979), 52–53.

194 **"make discoveries or commit crimes"**: Pisarev quoted in Frank III, 175.
194 **"the philosophers, the poets"**: Pisarev, "Progress in the Animal and Vegetable Worlds," in *Selected Philosophical, Social, and Political Essays*, 305.
194 **"In this very frog"**: Pisarev quoted in Pozefsky, *Nihilist Imagination*, 33, translation altered.
194 **"I know only what I see"**: Pisarev, "Nineteenth-Century Scholasticism," in *Selected Philosophical, Social, and Political Essays*, 104.
195 **"I began to construct for myself"**: Pisarev quoted in Pozefsky, *Nihilist Imagination*, 74–75.
195 **"not only read his works"**: Unnamed official quoted in Frank IV, 78n, my emphasis.
195 **"Here is the ultimatum"**: Pisarev, "Nineteenth-Century Scholasticism," quoted and trans. in Pozefsky, *Nihilist Imagination*, 37. See also Frank III, 173–74.
195 **its own Max Stirner**: Few scholars connect Pisarev and Stirner. Joseph Frank notes the resemblance between Max Stirner and Bazarov (and therefore, by extension, Pisarev), and he claims that Pisarev's depiction of Bazarov likely led Dostoevsky to think of Raskolnikov penning his own article, "On Crime." See Frank III, 170, 175, and IV, 76.
195 **"Now Pisarev has gone"**: Dostoevsky quoted in Frank III, 173–74.
196 **"Only the peasants' axes"**: Quoted in Venturi, *Roots of Revolution*, 159.
196 **"it would be better not to be born"**: Chernyshevsky quoted in Venturi, *Roots of Revolution*, 136.
196 **Per capita income**: Blanchard, *Russia's "Age of Silver,"* 293–94, 354 (table A2.17). Similarly, national income was 40 percent lower in 1860 than it was in 1810.
198 **"Like an immense snake"**: Peter Kropotkin, *Memoirs of a Revolutionist* (Boston: Houghton Mifflin, 1899), 157–61, quoted in Gleason, *Young Russia*, 166–68.
199 **"Look at what your nihilists"**: Turgenev, "Apropos of Fathers and Children," quoted and trans. in Frank III, 163.
200 **"cannot distinguish hydrogen"**: Mikhail Nikiforovich Katkov, "O nashem nigilizme. Po povodu romana Turgeneva," *Russkiy Vestnik*, July 1862, 407, quoted and trans. in Pozefsky, *Nihilist Imagination*, 25.
200 **"terrifying, omnipotent force"**: Tolstoy quoted in Todd, "Dostoevsky as a Professional Writer," 84.
201 **"What is dead and rotten"**: Pisarev, "Shedo-Ferroti's Pamphlet," quoted and trans. in Pozefsky, *Nihilist Imagination*, 6. See also Pisarev, *Selected Philosophical, Social, and Political Essays*, 146–47.
202 **"as though he had somehow just arrived"**: Quoted in Pozefsky, *Nihilist Imagination*, 6–7.
202 **"a perfidious design"**: Quoted and trans. in Fusso, *Editing Turgenev, Dostoevsky, and Tolstoy*, 131–32.

FOURTEEN. A GAMBLING SYSTEM

Dostoevsky's descriptions of gambling in Wiesbaden are quoted from *LII*, 57–59 (Aug. 20/Sept. 1, 1863, to Varvara Konstant); *LII*, 63 (Sept. 8/20, 1863, to Mikhail), and *LII*, 56 (Aug. 16/28, 1863, to Pavel Isaev, hereinafter Pasha). Additional details regarding Dostoevsky's gambling habits as well as his 1862 European travels are taken from the following letters: *LII*, 232 (May 6/18, 1867, to Anna Grigorievna Dostoevskaya); *LII*, 52 (July 20, 1860, to Kovalevsky); *LII*, 165 (Aug. 3/15, 1865, to Turgenev); *LII*, 306 (Jan. 16, 1862, contract with Alexander Bazunov); *LII*, 38–39 (June 26/July 8, 1862, to Strakhov); *LII*, 256 (Aug. 16/28, 1867, to Apollon Maikov); *LII*, 71–72 (Sept. 18/30, 1863, to Strakhov); *LII*, 157 (April 19, 1865, to Nadezhda Suslova); *LII*, 66 (Sept. 8/20, 1863, to Varvara Konstant); *LII*, 67 (Sept. 18/30, 1863, to Pasha).

Dostoevsky's observations on his European travels are taken from *Winter Notes on Summer Impressions*, trans. David Patterson (Evanston, Ill.: Northwestern University Press, 1988), 36, 37, 44, 35, 57, 48, 52. Dostoevsky's descriptions of his early draft of *The Gambler* are from *LII*, 70–72 (Sept. 18/30, 1863, to Strakhov). Additional details are from *LII*, 62–63 (Sept. 8/20, 1863, to Mikhail); *LII*, 118–19 (April 14, 1864, to Pyotr Boborykin), and *LII*, 116 (April 13–14, 1864, to Mikhail). Quotations from Dostoevsky's letters during Marya Dmitrievna's illness and death are from *LII*, 75 (Nov. 19, 1863, to Varvara Konstant); *LII*, 120 (April 15, 1864, to Mikhail); *LII*, 92, 90 (Feb. 29, 1864, to Pasha); *LII*, 87 (Jan. 31, 1864, to Pasha); *LII*, 86 (Jan. 28, 1864, to Pasha); *LII*, 112 (April 10, 1864, to Pasha); *LII*, 100–101 (March 26, 1864, to Mikhail); *LIV*, 269 (Jan. 7, 1876, to Pasha); *LII*, 151 (March 31–April 14, 1865, to Vrangel). Additional details are from the following letters: *LII*, 85 (Jan. 10, 1864, to Varvara Konstant); *LIII*, 50 (March 3/ 15, 1868, to Katkov); *LII*, 97–98 (March 20, 1864, to Pasha); *LII*, 100 (March 26, 1864, to Mikhail); *LII*, 117 (April 13–14, 1864, to Mikhail).

Quotations from Dostoevsky's letters regarding *Epoch* and writing *Notes from Underground* are from *LII*, 107, 111, 110 (April 9, 1864, to Mikhail); *LII*, 104, 102 (April 2, 1864, to Mikhail); *LII*, 88 (Feb. 9, 1864, to Mikhail); *LII*, 114 (April 13–14, 1864, to Mikhail). Additional detail is from *LII*, 127 (July 29, 1864, to Andrei Dostoevsky); *LII*, 76 (Nov. 19, 1863, to Mikhail Dostoevsky); *LII*, 134–35 (Sept. 20, 1864, to Turgenev). Dostoevsky's quotations about his own poor health are from *LII*, 88 (Feb. 9, 1864, to Mikhail); *LII*, 93–94 (March 5, 1864, to Mikhail); *LII*, 92 (Feb. 29, 1864, to Pasha). See also *LII*, 95 (March 20, 1864, to Mikhail) and 101 (March 26, 1864, to Mikhail).

Quotations and details from Suslova's diary are from Fyodor Dostoevsky and Apollinaria Suslova, *The Gambler, with Polina Suslova's Diary*, trans. Victor Terras, ed. Edward Wasiolek (Chicago: University of Chicago Press, 1972), 202–8, 214–24, 237, 364–65.

Joseph Frank's coverage of this chapter's events can be found in Frank III, 252–64, 271–84, 291–300, 348–49. Details and background on gambling at Wiesbaden's casino are from Charles Rossel, *Wiesbaden and Its Environs: A Guidebook for Strangers*, trans. St. Bede Syll (Wiesbaden: C. W. Kreidel, 1864); Everett John Carter, "The Green Table: Gambling Casinos, Capitalist Culture, and Modernity in Nineteenth-Century Germany" (PhD diss., University of Illinois at Urbana-Champaign, 2002); Thomas Gemmell, *Trip to the Rhine and Paris* (London: Hamilton, Adams, 1859), 114–18; "Holyday Makers," *Times* (London), Aug. 22 and 23, 1865, 7, 10; "Gambling Sketches," *London Society: An Illustrated Magazine of Light and Amusing Literature*, June 1866, 491–500; "Legalized Gambling at Wiesbaden," *Evansville Daily Journal*, Aug. 1, 1867, 2. Additional details and impressions of Dostoevsky's experience of gambling are taken from *The Gambler* in Dostoevsky, *The Double and The Gambler*, trans. Richard Pevear and Larissa Volokhonsky (New York: Vintage Classics, 2005).

For details regarding the Crystal Palace, see Jan Piggott, *Palace of the People: The Crystal Palace at Sydenham, 1854–1936* (Madison: University of Wisconsin Press, 2004); Samuel Phillips, *Guide to the Crystal Palace and Its Park and Gardens* (London: Bradbury and Evans, 1858), esp. 144–46; Crystal Palace Company, *The Crystal Palace Penny Guide* (Sydenham, U.K.: R. K. Burt, 1858).

206 **high-level French civil servant:** Christian Morrisson and Wayne Snyder, "The Income Inequality of France in Historical Perspective," *European Review of Economic History* 4, no. 1 (2000): 59–83, 73, table 7.
206 **"the air of a conqueror":** Dostoevsky, *Gambler*, 293–94.

209 **"I like Paris this time":** *LII*, 54 (Aug. 16/28, 1863, to Nikolai Dostoevsky).
211 **"like sliding down a snowy hill":** Dostoevsky, *Gambler*, 278.
211 **"how could I fail":** *LII*, 63 (Sept. 8/20, 1863, to Mikhail). Question mark supplied.
213 **"sick egoist":** *LII*, 157 (April 19, 1865, to Nadezhda Suslova). See also Frank IV, 27.
213 **"Let me know immediately":** *LII*, 56 (Aug. 16/28, 1863, to Pasha).
216 **"The fact that I'm not with you":** *LII*, 96 (March 20, 1864, to Mikhail), translation altered.
217 **"not finished but transitional":** Dostoevsky quoted in Frank III, 300, translation altered.
217 **pouring nothing into nothingness:** Cf. Dostoevsky, *Notes from Underground*, trans. Jane Kentish (New York: Oxford University Press, 1991), 20.
218 **"My brother is dying":** *LII*, 124 (July 8–9, 1864, to Pasha).
218 **"That man loved me":** *LII*, 126–27 (July 29, 1864, to Andrei Dostoevsky).

FIFTEEN. AN EVIL SPIRIT

Details and quotations regarding Dostoevsky's writing progress and his struggles with *Epoch* come from *LII*, 151–55 (March 31–April 14, 1865, to Vrangel); *LII*, 82–83 (Dec. 23, 1863, to Turgenev); *LII*, 148 (Feb. 13, 1865, to Turgenev); *LI*, 207 (May 14, 1855, to Mikhail); *LI*, 403 (Oct. 20, 1859, to Mikhail); *LII*, 125–28 (July 29, 1864, to Andrei Dostoevsky); *LIII*, 116 (Dec. 11/23, 1868, to Maikov); *LIII*, 83–85 (June 22/July 4, 1868, to Maikov); *LII*, 161 (May 30, 1865, to Pasha). Additional information derives from *LII*, 99 (March 26, 1864, to Mikhail); *LII*, 162 (June 6, 1865, to Kovalevsky); *LIII*, 22 (Feb. 1/13, 1868, to Vera, Sofya, and Maria Ivanova); *LIII*, 356 (May 8/20, 1871, to Vasily Gubin); *LII*, 273 (Sept. 28/Oct. 10, 1867, to Stepan Yanovskiy); *LII*, 281 (Oct. 10/22, 1867, to Pasha); *LII*, 350 (April 21/May 3, 1871, to Maikov). Quotations and details from *The Drunkards* are from *Notebooks*, 81, 84.

For details and quotations regarding Bocharov, Stellovsky, and Stellovsky's contract, see *LIII*, 356–57 (May 8/20, 1871, to Vasily Gubin); *LII*, 164 (June 8, 1865, to Kraevsky); *LIII*, 200–202 (Oct. 27/Nov. 8, 1869, to Maikov); *LIII*, 292 (Dec. 30, 1870/ Jan. 11, 1871, to Maikov); *LIII*, 311–14 (Jan. 26/Feb. 7, 1871, to Maikov); *LII*, 281 (Oct. 10/ 22, 1867, to Pasha); *LIII*, 92 (Aug. 9/21, 1868, to Emilia Dostoevskaya); *LII*, 161–62 (June 6, 1865, to Kovalevsky); *LII*, 200 (June 17, 1866, to Anna Korvin-Krukovskaya); *LII*, 330 (March 19/31, 1871, to Maikov); *LII*, 165 (Aug. 3/15, 1865, to Turgenev).

Further details are in Frank III, 350–51, 369, and IV, 30–41; Yakubovich II, 23, 25, 29–34; and Boris Nikolaevich Tikhomirov, *"Lazar'! Gryadi von": Roman F. M. Dostoevskogo "Prestuplenie i nakazanie" v sovremennom prochtenii* (St. Petersburg: Serebryanyy Vek, 2006), 129–30, 137–40; Lantz, *Dostoevsky Encyclopedia*, 411–12. For promissory note reform and debt prison details, see Antonov, *Bankrupts and Usurers of Imperial Russia*.

For gambling and Dostoevsky's time in Wiesbaden, see *LII*, 57–58 (Aug. 20/Sept. 1, 1863, to Varvara Konstant); *LII*, 232 (May 6/18, 1867, to Anna Dostoevsky); *LII*, 165–66 (Aug. 3/15, 1865, to Turgenev); *LII*, 171 (Aug. 24/Sept. 5, 1865, to Vrangel); *LII*, 166–67 (Aug. 10/22, 1865, to Suslova); *LII*, 169–70 (Aug. 12/24, 1865, to Suslova). Additional gambling and Wiesbaden details from *LII*, 166 (Aug. 8/20, 1865, to Turgenev), and *LII*, 173 (Sept. 10/22, 1865, to Vrangel). Additional information is in Frank IV, 32–44, and Rossel, *Wiesbaden and Its Environs*.

For the Chistov murders and Dostoevsky's interest in the story, see *Golos*, no. 247–49 (Sept. 7/19, 1865); Anastasiya Nikolaevna Pershkina, "Kakiye prestupleniya vdokhnovili Dostoyevskogo," *Arzamas*, May 2, 2017, arzamas.academy/mag/425-crimes; Klioutch-kine, "Rise of Crime and Punishment from the Air of the Media," 97–98.

For physical details regarding Dostoevsky's notebooks, see Wasiolek's discussion in *Notebooks*, 3, 92, 155, 177; Fyodor Dostoevsky and Ivan Ivanovich Glivenko, *Iz arkhiva F. M. Dostoevskogo. Prestuplenie i nakazanie: Neizdannye materialy*, ed. Ivan I. Glivenko (Moscow: Gosudarstvennoe izdatel'stvo khudozhestvennoy litera-tury, 1931); V. Milyukov and K. A. Barsht, *Risunki Fyodora Dostoevskogo* (Moscow: Voskresen'e, 1998). The chronological order of Dostoevsky's three notebooks does not match their numbered designations. Drafting began with "Notebook 2," which dates from September to October 1865 and covers his work in Wiesbaden. "Notebook 1" follows and "Notebook 3" was the last. Dostoevsky did not always write consecutively in his notebook pages; that is, the top of the first page was not necessarily his first entry in a given notebook.

For Dostoevsky's accounts in letters on writing the first passages of *Crime and Punishment* and early proposal rejections, see *LIII*, 67 (March 23/April 4, 1868, to Anna Suslova); *LII*, 173 (Sept. 10/22, 1865, to Vrangel); *LII*, 177 (Sept. 16/28, 1865, to Vrangel); Milyukov, "Fyodor Mikhailovich Dostoevsky." Early notebook details and quotations can be found in *Notebooks*, 78, 84, 102, 107, 114, 93–94, 56. Additional material is from *Notebooks*, 160–61, 110, 115, 169, 105. For Dostoevsky's draft of the attack on Raskolnikov's landlady, see *Notebooks*, 139–40. For Dostoevsky's *Crime and Punishment* proposal to Katkov, see *LII*, 174–76 (Sept. 10/22–15/27, 1865, to Mikhail Katkov). See also Frank IV, 39–41.

Post-proposal drafting details and quotations come from *Notebooks*, 84, 122, 126, 131–32, 102–4, 122, 126, 131–32, 102–4, 80, 82–85, 54, 165, 48, 88–89. Further details come from *Notebooks*, 108, 123–25, 154, 142, 163–64, 106, 159, 91, 151, 64, 96. For Dostoevsky's departure for Petersburg, Suslova proposal, and seizures, see *LII*, 189 (Feb. 18, 1866, to Vrangel); *Suslova Diary*, 301–2, 257; *LII*, 157 (April 19, 1865, to Nadezhda Suslova); *LII*, 179–90 (Nov. 8/20, 1865, to Vrangel); *LII*, 181 (Nov. 22, 1865, to Yanyshev); *LII*, 182 (Dec. 15, 1865, to Nikolai). For Dostoevsky's revisions to *Crime and Punishment*, see *Notebooks*, 79, 239, 24, 55, 52, 24.

Additional background is from Fusso, *Editing Turgenev, Dostoevsky, and Tolstoy*; Klioutchkine, "Rise of Crime and Punishment from the Air of the Media"; Köhl, *Russia and the Russians in 1842*; and Sergei Vladimirovich Belov, "The History of the Writing of the Novel," in *Crime and Punishment*, trans. Jessie Coulson, ed. George Gibian, 3rd ed. (New York: W. W. Norton, 1989), 488–93.

220 **"He is the unhappiest of mortals":** Nikolai Dostoevsky quoted in Frank III, 350–51.
221 **to cease publishing *Epoch*:** The announcement of the journal's end was circulated on June 9, 1865. See Yakubovich II, 32.
222 **"Everything would be fine":** Gavrilov quoted in Yakubovich II, 29.
224 **"I even feel sorry":** Arthur Benni quoted in Frank IV, 29–30; Yakubovich II, 30.

224 **"otherwise the inventory will be conducted"**: Yakubovich II, 30–31. See also Leonid Grossman, *Dostoevsky: A Biography*, trans. Mary Mackler (New York: Bobbs-Merrill, 1975), 347.

225 **"undertook business for him"**: *LIII*, 357 (May 8/20, 1871, to Vasily Gubin).

225 **"under the lash"**: Quoted in Frank III, 369. Cf. *LII*, 155 (March 31–April 14, 1865, to Vrangel).

225 **Kraevsky rejected it anyway**: *LII*, 163 (June 8, 1865, to Kraevsky); Frank IV, 30–32.

227 **"ever stronger and stronger"**: *Gambler*, 296.

227 **"The moment I hear"**: *Gambler*, 321.

227 **young Russian physician**: *The Gambler, with Polina Suslova's Diary*, 231, 283.

228 **"more a shade of gray"**: Dostoevsky, *Winter Notes on Summer Impressions*, 31–33.

232 **"could have beaten"**: Altered from Wasiolek's "could have beat" in *Notebooks*, 40.

233 **"I guarantee its originality"**: Quoted in Frank IV, 38. See Milyukov, "Fyodor Mikhailovich Dostoevsky," 281–82.

238 **"*instinctive* joy of"**: *Notebooks*, 119, my emphasis.

238 **"Can it be that"**: *Notebooks*, 102, question mark supplied.

244 **"At the end of November"**: *LII*, 188 (Feb. 18, 1866, to Vrangel). Belov believes that Dostoevsky actually did burn the novella version. See Belov, "History of the Writing of the Novel," 489. Joseph Frank is more skeptical. See Frank IV, 93.

SIXTEEN. AN AX

Murder scene details and quotations are from *C&P*, 4–8, 63–86, unless otherwise specified. See also *Crime and Punishment*, trans. Oliver Ready, 92–106. Quotations regarding publication uncertainty are from *LII*, 183–85 (Dec. 1865 to Katkov). Glimpses of violence in drafts are from *Notebooks*, 176, 53. Excerpts of murder scene are from *C&P*, 74–80. Passages about despotism and power in Dostoevsky's drafts are from *Notebooks*, 57–58, 188, 141, 58, 219, 189. Quotations relevant to the development of the novel's motive mystery are from *Notebooks*, 153, 58. Sonya's character development and drafted confrontation with Raskolnikov are from *Notebooks*, 49, 87, 93, 140, 208, 89, 240, 87, 66–67, 63, 56, 71, 188, 228.

255 **"must trample down many"**: Hegel, *Reason in History*, 43. Cf. Hegel, *Philosophy of History*, 32.

SEVENTEEN. HEADSMEN AND VICTIMS

For Lacenaire's address to the public, see *Memoirs*, 55–56. Quotations regarding Lacenaire's social protest, self-education, and ideological leanings are from *Memoirs*, 155–57, 75, 152–54, 174, 69, 147, 111. Lacenaire's conviction that egoism rules the world is from *Memoirs*, 84, 125, 173–74. Additional details are from *Memoirs*, 74, 86–92, 101, 113–14, 121, 128–29, 196, 205–6, 158. Further details and background information come from Bonnellier and Arago, *Lacenaire après sa condamnation*, 89, 57–58; Canler, *Autobiography of a French Detective*, 48–49; "Détails donnés par le docteur Fossati," in *Procès complet*, 166–68; George Combe, *Elements of Phrenology*, 3rd ed. (Edinburgh: John Anderson, 1828); Eugène Pottet, *Histoire de la Conciergerie du Palais de Paris depuis les origines jusqu'à nos jours, 1031–1898* (Paris: L.-Henry May, 1898). For images of Lacenaire's manuscript, see Pierre Bergé et Associés website: www.pba-auctions.com /lot/18549/3906346?npp=10000&.

262 **organ of benevolence:** Bonnellier, *Autopsie physiologique de Lacenaire*, 9–15; *Vert-Vert*, Jan. 22 and March 13, 1836; *Bulletin Médicale Belge* 3, no. 2 (1836), 248; *Le Mercure de France* 2, no. 1 (1836): 40. Free-will impairment is from *Bulletin Médicale Belge*. Bonnellier quotes Dumoutier.

262 **"restricted his free will":** *Bulletin Médicale Belge* 3, no. 2 (1836), 248.

262 **"The truth." And there wasn't:** Lacenaire quoted in Bonnellier and Arago, *Lacenaire après sa con-damnation*, 18.

262 **"certainly many women:** *Vert-Vert*, May 24, 1836.

263 **"wallowed in evil readings":** Father Rendu, *Le Réparateur* (Lyons), Dec. 31, 1835, quoted in *Mémoires et écrits*, 329–30.

265 **Anne Marie Yvon Chardon:** *Mémoires et écrits*, 348. Simonelli cites Poissy prison registers for Jean-François Chardon. Some press accounts omit her name even when giving her son's full name. See, for example, the November 13, 1835, editions of *La France* and *Le Courrier*.

EIGHTEEN. DISEASED IMAGINATION

Dostoevsky's concerns about the publication of *Crime and Punishment* are from *LII*, 189–90 (Feb. 18, 1866, to Vrangel). Reviews and reactions to the novel are from Nikolai N. Strakhov, "F. M. Dostoevsky. *Prestuplenie i nakazanie*," in *Kritika 60-kh godov XIX veka (Biblioteka russkoĭ kritiki)*, ed. L. Sobolev (Moscow: Izdatel'stvo Astrel', 2003), 372–407. "Literaturnye zametki," *Nedelia*, April 10, 1866, 72, 73, quoted in Fusso, *Editing Turgenev, Dostoevsky, and Tolstoy*, 148; "O romane 'Prestuplenie i nakazanie,'" *Glasnyy Sud*, March 16, 1867; Grigoriy Zakharovich Eliseev, "Zhurnalistika," *Sovremennik* 113, no. 2 (1866): 32–79; Ivan Turgenev, *Turgenev's Letters*, trans. Antony Knowles (New York: Scribner, 1983), 128. For Pisarev's review, see Dmitri Ivanovich Pisarev, "Bor'ba za zhizn' ('Prestuplenie i nakazanie' F. M. Dostoevskogo. Dve chasti, 1867 g.)," in *F. M. Dostoevskiĭ v russkoy kritike: Sbornik statey*, ed. Abram Aleksandrovich Belkin (Moscow: Izdatel'stvo khudozhestvennoy literatury, 1966), 162–228; Leo Tolstoy, "Why Do Men Stupefy Themselves?," in *Crime and Punishment*, Norton Critical 3rd ed., 487–88.

Additional information taken from Frank IV, 45–46, 100; Todd, "Dostoevsky as a Professional Writer"; Evgeny Lampert, *Sons Against Fathers: Studies in Russian Radicalism and Revolution* (Oxford: Clarendon Press, 1965); Pozefsky, *Nihilist Imagination*.

For the Danilov murder and Dostoevsky's comments on the resemblance, see Sergei Mikhailovich Kazantsev, *Sud prisyazhnykh v Rossii: Gromkiye ugolovnyye protsessy, 1864–1917 gg.* (Leningrad: Lenizdat, 1991), 94–116; *Moskovskie Vedomosti*, Jan. 21, 1866; and *LIII*, 114 (Dec. 11/23, 1868, to Maikov).

For dialogue about Raskolnikov's debt, see *C&P*, 98–103. For Razumikhin's talk about speculators as "sharks," see *Notebooks*, 155. For Dostoevsky's continued writing and loneliness, see *LII*, 186–87 (Feb. 13, 1866, to Domnika Dostoevskaya); *LII*, 226 (April 13, 1867, to Alonkin); *LII*, 190 (Feb. 18, 1866, to Vrangel). Descriptions of Raskolnikov's room are in *C&P*, 27–28, 118, 3, 40, 142–43, 231, 417. For Dostoevsky on his continuing seizures and illness, see *LII*, 188–89 (Feb. 18, 1866, to Vrangel), and *LII*, 186 (Feb. 13, 1866, to Domnika Dostoevskaya). For debt and prison fears, see *LII*, 186 (Feb. 13, 1866, to Domnika Dostoevskaya); *LII*, 189–90 (Feb. 18, 1866, to Vrangel); *LII*, 350 (April 21/May 3, 1871, to Maikov).

Background on Russian pawnbrokers, debt prison, and debt reforms derives from Antonov, *Bankrupts and Usurers of Imperial Russia*. See also Jason J. Kilborn, "Treating the New European Disease of Consumer Debt in a Post-Communist State: The Groundbreaking New Russian Personal Insolvency Law," *Brooklyn Journal of International Law* 41, no. 2 (2016): 656–719. For women's economic power, see Antonov, *Bankrupts and Usurers of Imperial Russia*; Michelle Lamarche Marrese, *A Woman's Kingdom: Noblewomen and the Control of Property in Russia, 1700–1861* (Ithaca, N.Y.: Cornell University Press, 2002); and Galina Ulianova, *Female Entrepreneurs in Nineteenth-Century Russia* (London: Routledge, 2009).

For details and quotations regarding Dmitri Karakozov and his assassination attempt, see Claudia Verhoeven, *The Odd Man Karakozov: Imperial Russia, Modernity, and the Birth of Terrorism* (Ithaca, N.Y.: Cornell University Press, 2009), esp. 109–12, 130–45. See also Gleason, *Young Russia*, 324–29, and Venturi, *Roots of Revolution*, 345–47. For the crime's aftermath, including rumors and the White Terror, see Verhoeven, *Odd Man Karakozov*, 16–17, 43–44, 47, 117, 132, 176–77. For Dostoevsky's reaction, see Frank IV, 47–49. For nihilist arrest records, see Donaldson, "Russian Nihilism of the 1860s," table 11, app. B. Additional detail and background is from Alexander Ivanovich Volodin, "Raskolnikov i Karakozov: K tvorchestkoy istorii D. Pisareva 'Bor'ba za zhizn,'" *Novyy Mir* 11 (1969): 212–31; Vladislav Evgen'evich Evgen'ev-Maksimov, "Delo Karakozova i redaktsiia Sovremennika," *Zavety*, no. 6 (1914): 95–96; Gleason, *Young Russia*; Pozefsky, *Nihilist Imagination*; Thorstensson, "Nihilist Fashion in 1860–1870s Russia"; Ruud, *Fighting Words*. For details surrounding the Komisarov myth, see Verhoeven, *Odd Man Karakozov*, 67–78. For Karakozov's attempt as an act of terrorism, see Verhoeven, *Odd Man Karakozov*, 3–6, 148–49, 174–75. For Katkov benefiting from nationalism, see Katz, *Mikhail Katkov*, 136–38, 170. For Katkov's censorship advocacy in print, see Katkov quoted in Verhoeven, *Odd Man Karakozov*, 46. For Dostoevsky's response to Katkov, see *LII*, 193–94 (April 25, 1866, to Katkov).

266 **"this novel may be a superb thing":** *LII*, 189 (Feb. 18, 1866, to Vrangel), translation altered.

266–67 **"with a truthfulness that shakes the soul":** Strakhov, "F. M. Dostoevsky. *Prestuplenie i nakazanie.*" See also Strakhov, "The Nihilists and Raskolnikov's New Idea," in *Crime and Punishment*, Norton Critical 2nd ed., 485–86.

267 **"What is this thing":** Review in *Glasnyy Sud*.

268 **"educated and highly developed":** Pisarev, "Bor'ba za zhizn'." English translations of a few phrases are taken from Edward J. Brown, "Pisarev and the Transformation of Two Russian Novels," in *Literature and Society in Imperial Russia*, 151, 172, 167, 170, and Fusso, *Editing Turgenev, Dostoevsky, and Tolstoy*, 153. Brown notes that Pisarev's paragraph about "morbid mental states" is often omitted in reprints, possibly because it introduced the second installment of his review, and the second introduction was not necessary when reprinting both installments. Pisarev's review is online here: ru.wikisource.org/wiki/Борьба_за_жизнь_(Писарев).

270 **a "handsome dandy":** See "O romane 'Prestuplenie i nakazanie,'" *Glasnyy Sud*.

270 **illegal—interest rates:** Antonov, *Bankrupts and Usurers of Imperial Russia*, 37, 42. Russian law capped interest at 6 percent.

272 **"There are, brother, such sharks":** *Notebooks*, 155, translation altered.

276 **"bring good to the people," he said:** Karakozov, "To My Worker Friends," quoted in Gleason, *Young Russia*, 327–29.

277 the **"gentry parasites"**: Karakozov, "To My Worker Friends."
278 **"The Tsar has been shot"**: Frank IV, 47–48, my exclamation and emphasis.
282 **pronouncements: "That which can be smashed"**: Pisarev, "Nineteenth-Century Scholasticism," quoted and trans. in Pozefsky, *Nihilist Imagination*, 37.

NINETEEN. THE INVESTIGATOR

For Dostoevsky's difficulty writing, see *LII*, 192 (April 25, 1866, to Katkov). For details of Raskolnikov's meeting with Porfiry Petrovich and all quotations, see *C&P*, 248–67. Quotations from Dostoevsky's interrogation scene drafts are from *Notebooks*, 69, 229, 178, 203, 172. Additional details are from *Notebooks*, 62–63, 67–69, 89, 167, 220. Raskolnikov's encounter with the tradesman as well as his subsequent ruminations and nightmare are from *C&P*, 271–78.

TWENTY. DOUBLE-EDGED EVIDENCE

For *Crime and Punishment*'s success and Dostoevsky's debts and legal proceedings, see *LII*, 197 (May 9, 1866, to Vrangel); *LII*, 195–96 (April 29, 1866, to Yanyshev); *LII*, 186 (Feb. 13, 1866, to Domnika Dostoevskaya); *LII*, 228 (April 23/May 15, 1867, to Suslova); *LII*, 248 (May 19/31, 1867, to Pasha Dostoevsky), and Yakubovich II, 65. For Dostoevsky's work despite seizures, see *LII*, 228–29 (April 23/May 15, 1867, to Suslova); *LII*, 197 (May 9, 1866, to Vrangel); *LII*, 195–96 (April 29, 1866, to Yanyshev). For Dostoevsky's drafts of Svidrigailov, see *Notebooks*, 64, 194–98, 237. For Svidrigailov details in the finished novel, see *C&P*, 244, 278, 285, 290, 470.

For details about the Karakozov investigation, trial, and execution as well as the Ishutin Circle, see Verhoeven, *Odd Man Karakozov*. See also Gleason, *Young Russia*, 299–330, 324–29; Venturi, *Roots of Revolution*, 331–50; Ivan Aleksandrovich Khudyakov, *Zapiski karakozovtsa* (Moscow: Molodaya Gvardiya, 1930), microfilm. For Karakozov as the inspiration for Pisarev's review of *Crime and Punishment*, see Volodin, "Raskolnikov i Karakozov," esp. 223–30.

For Dostoevsky warning of an impending seizure, see N. N. Fon-Fokht, "K biografii F. M. Dostoevskogo," in *DVS* II, 50–52. For Dostoevsky's seizure while visiting Milyukov, see Milyukov, "Fyodor Mikhailovich Dostoevsky," 289–90.

For details and discussion of Dostoevsky's temporal lobe seizures, see Norman Geschwind, "Dostoievsky's Epilepsy," in *Psychiatric Aspects of Epilepsy*, ed. Dietrich Blumer (Washington, D.C.: American Psychiatric Press, 1984), 325–34; P. H. Voskuil, "The Epilepsy of Fyodor Mikhailovitch Dostoevsky (1821–1881)," *Epilepsia* 24 (1983): 658–67. See also Christian Baumann et al., "Did Fyodor Mikhailovich Dostoevsky Suffer from Mesial Temporal Lobe Epilepsy?" *Seizure* 14 (2005): 324–30. Dostoevsky's accounts of his postictal symptoms are from *LIV*, 46 (June 14, 1872, to Anna Dostoevskaya); *LV*, 174 (Dec. 27, 1879, to Viktor Lorents); *LIV*, 96 (Aug. 13, 1873, to Anna Dostoevskaya); *LIV*, 152 (June 28/July 10, 1874, to Anna Dostoevskaya); *LIV*, 96 (Aug. 13, 1873, to Anna Dostoevskaya); *LII*, 252 (Aug. 16/28, 1867, to Apollon Maikov).

My description of the long-term effects of temporal lobe epilepsy follows descriptions of Geschwind (or Gastaut-Geschwind) syndrome and draws upon the following sources: Stephen G. Waxman and Norman Geschwind, "The Interictal Behavior Syndrome of Temporal Lobe Epilepsy," *Archives of General Psychiatry* 32, no. 12 (Dec. 1975): 1580–86; David Bear and Paul Fedio, "Quantitative Analysis of Interictal Behavior in Temporal Lobe Epilepsy," *Archives of Neurology* 34, no. 8 (1977): 454–67; Dietrich Blumer, "Evidence Supporting the Temporal Lobe Epilepsy Personality Syndrome," *Neurology* 53, no. 5, supplement 2 (1999): S9–S12; John R. Hughes, "The Idiosyncratic Aspects of the Epilepsy of Fyodor Dostoevsky," *Epilepsy and Behavior* 7, no. 3 (Nov. 2005): 531–38. For temporal lobe epilepsy and gambling behavior, see Dalma Tényi et al., "The Possible Role of the Insula in the Epilepsy and the Gambling Disorder of Fyodor Mikhailovich Dostoyevsky," *Journal of Behavioral Addictions* 5, no. 3 (2016): 542–47; Fabienne Picard, "State of Belief, Subjective Certainty, and Bliss as a Product of Cortical Dysfunction," *Cortex* 49, no. 9 (Oct. 2013): 2494–500; Hughes, "Idiosyncratic Aspects of the Epilepsy of Fyodor Dostoevsky"; Andrea E. Cavanna et al., "Clinical Correlates of Pathological Gambling Symptoms in Patients with Epilepsy," *Epilepsia* 49, no. 8 (2008): 1460–64; Kirsten Labudda et al., "Decision Making in Patients with Temporal Lobe Epilepsy," *Neuropsychologia* 47, no. 1 (2009): 50–58.

For Dostoevsky's log of his seizures, see Rice, *Dostoevsky and the Healing Art*, 89–90, 287–98. For Dostoevsky's descriptions of postictal depression, see *LIV*, 379 (July 7, 1877, to Anna Dostoevskaya); *LIII*, 325 (March 18/30, 1871, to Strakhov), and Rice, *Dostoevsky and the Healing Art*, 293. For Dostoevsky's descriptions of ecstatic auras, see Miller and Strakhov, *Biografiya*, 214, quoted in Frank II, 96. See also Rice, *Dostoevsky and the Healing Art*, 37, 83–86, and Catteau, *Dostoevsky and the Process of Literary Creation*, 114–15. For his description of auras in *The Idiot*, see Dostoevsky, *The Idiot*, trans. Richard Pevear and Larissa Volokhonsky (New York: Vintage, 2003), 225–27. While medical descriptions of ecstatic auras predate Dostoevsky, his case was instrumental in its modern identification and development. See Fabienne Picard and A. D. Craig, "Ecstatic Epileptic Seizures: A Potential Window on the Neural Basis for Human Self-Awareness," *Epilepsy and Behavior* 16 (2009): 539–46, and Rice, *Dostoevsky and the Healing Art*, 9–10.

Discussion of the anterior insular cortex and ecstatic auras draws from the following research: A. D. Craig, "How Do You Feel—Now? The Anterior Insula and Human Awareness," *Nature Reviews Neuroscience* 10, no. 1 (Jan. 2009): 59–70; Markus Gschwind and Fabienne Picard, "Ecstatic Epileptic Seizures: A Glimpse into the Multiple Roles of the Insula," *Frontiers in Behavioral Neuroscience* 10 (Feb. 2016), article 21; Picard and Craig, "Ecstatic Epileptic Seizures," and Fabrice Bartolomei et al., "The Role of the Dorsal Anterior Insula in Ecstatic Sensation Revealed by Direct Electrical Brain Stimulation," *Brain Stimulation* 12, no. 5 (Oct.–Nov. 2019): 1121–26; Fabienne Picard and Florian Kurth, "Ictal Alterations of Consciousness During Ecstatic Seizures," *Epilepsy and Behavior* 30 (Jan. 2014): 58–61; Michael Trimble and Anthony Freeman, "An Investigation of Religiosity and the Gastaut-Geschwind Syndrome in Patients with Temporal Lobe Epilepsy," *Epilepsy and Behavior* 9, no. 3 (2006): 407–14.

For Dostoevsky's summer in Lyublino and plan for the Stellovsky submission, see *LII*, 201 (June 22, 1866, to Pasha); *LII*, 206–8 (July 10–15, 1866, to Milyukov), and *LII*, 200–201 (June 17, 1866, to Korvin-Krukovskaya); M. A. Ivanova, "Vospominaniya," in *DVS* II, 41–45; Fon-Fokht, "K biografii F. M. Dostoevsky," 53–55. Dostoevsky's worries about writing with epilepsy are from *LII*, 289 (Nov. 1–2/13–14, 1867, to Yanovskiy); *LIV*, 96 (Aug. 13, 1873, to Anna Dostoevskaya); *LIV*, 154 (June 28/July 10, 1874, to Anna Dostoevskaya); *LIV*, 383 (July 11, 1877, to Anna Dostoevskaya); *LV*, 174 (Dec. 27, 1879, to Viktor Lorents); *LIII*, 74 (April 9/21, 1868, to Maikov).

Background on the Russian police and detectives as well as details about Russian law and legal reforms are from John P. LeDonne, "Criminal Investigations Before the Great Reforms," *Russian History* 1, no. 2 (Jan. 1974): 101–18; William Burnham, "The Legal Context and Contributions of Dostoevsky's 'Crime and Punishment,'" *Michigan Law Review* 100, no. 6 (2002): 1227–48; Claire Whitehead, "Shkliarevskii and Russian Detective Fiction: The Influence of Dostoevskii," in *Dostoevsky's Overcoat: Influence, Comparison, and Transposition*, ed. Joe Andrew and Robert Reid (New York: Brill, 2013); W. Bruce Lincoln, *The Great Reforms: Autocracy, Bureaucracy, and the Politics of Change in Imperial Russia* (DeKalb: Northern Illinois University Press, 1990); Antonov, *Bankrupts and Usurers of Imperial Russia*; Richard Wortman, *Russian Monarchy: Representation and Rule* (Boston: Academic Studies Press, 2013).

Raskolnikov confronts Porfiry in his office in *C&P*, 331–51. For trends in European criminology, see Piers Beirne, "Adolphe Quetelet and the Origins of Positivist Criminology," *American Journal of Sociology* 92, no. 5 (1987): 1140–69; Oscar Boris Sheynin, "A. Quetelet as a Statistician," *Archive for History of Exact Sciences* 36, no. 4 (1986): 281–325; Adolphe Quetelet, *A Treatise on Man and the Development of His Faculties* (Edinburgh: William and Robert Chambers, 1842). For Porfiry's rejection of "the general case," see *C&P*, 339. For Raskolnikov returning to the scene of the crime, see *C&P*, 170–74. For Dostoevsky's drafts of Raskolnikov's confession, see *Notebooks*, 52, 66, 68, 70–71, 214, 216, 220–21. For the published version of his confession, see *C&P*, 410–19.

291 **"The more money you repay":** *LII*, 228 (April 23/May 15, 1867, to Suslova), translation altered.
293 **Details about Karakozov:** See Verhoeven, *Odd Man Karakozov*. Verhoeven's excellent study of Karakozov goes further than anyone to detail correspondences between Karakozov and Raskolnikov. Joseph Frank also notes that Karakozov's failure to pay tuition resembles Raskolnikov. See Frank IV, 47.
294 **the "moral depravity":** Muraviev report quoted in Verhoeven, *Odd Man Karakozov*, 23.
295 **"feel hatred for hatred":** Ishutin quoted in Venturi, *Roots of Revolution*, 336.
297 **"coming unhinged":** *LII*, 252 (Aug. 16/28, 1867, to Apollon Maikov). Dostoevsky is referring to 1866 and, more specifically, the reasons that led him to leave Russia for Europe in early 1867.
302 **A series of judicial statutes:** The November 1864 law was implemented in Petersburg on April 17, 1866. See Burnham, "Legal Context and Contributions of Dostoevsky's 'Crime and Punishment,'" 1244n.
303 **"Evidence, my dear, is mostly double-edged":** *C&P*, 338, translation altered. Here and throughout, I opt for Oliver Ready's translation "double-edged," rather than Pevear and Volokhonsky's "double-ended." See *Crime and Punishment*, trans. Ready, 406.

304 **"I wasn't delirious!":** *Crime and Punishment*, trans. Ready, 414.
306 **"the Pelasgian race":** Quetelet, *Treatise on Man and the Development of His Faculties*, 88–89.
307 **believed "official secrecy":** *LII*, 194 (April 25, 1866, to Katkov).
309 **Karakozov answered, "Nothing":** See D. M. Karakozov et al., *Pokushenie Karakozova* (Moscow: Izdatel'stvo Tsentrarkhiva RSFSR, 1928), 1: 263, microfilm. Verhoeven favors this account of their exchange over other exchanges rumored at the time, partly because it was an official part of Karakozov's defense at trial and partly because no eyewitnesses present at the trial contested it. See Verhoeven, *Odd Man Karakozov*, 178.
309 **"A circle of young people":** Verdict quoted in Verhoeven, *Odd Man Karakozov*, 29–30, 53.

TWENTY-ONE. LITTLE DOVE

315 **"evidence of *nihilism*":** *LII*, 207 (July 10–15, 1866, to Milyukov).
326 **"sometimes the wildest thought":** *Gambler*, 292.
328 **"He loves me very much":** Anna Grigorievna Dostoevskaya, *Dnevnik 1867 g*, ed. S. V. Zhitomirskaya (Moscow: Nauka, 1993), 365.

TWENTY-TWO. TINY DIAMOND

Details of Dostoevsky's discussion with Milyukov are from Milyukov, "Fyodor Mikhailovich Dostoevsky," 283–85. Additional detail from Fon-Fokht, "K biografii F. M. Dostoevsky," and *LII*, 227 (April 23/May 5, 1867, to Suslova), and *LII*, 210 (Nov. 2, 1866, to Lyubimov). All details and quotations regarding Anna Grigorievna and her meetings with Dostoevsky, unless otherwise specified, derive from *Reminiscences*, esp. 12–63. Additional information from *LII*, 227 (April 23/May 15, 1867, to Suslova); *LII*, 211 (Nov. 2, 1866, to Lyubimov); Anna Grigorievna Dostoevskaya, *Vospominaniya, 1846–1917*, ed. I. S. Andrianova and B. N. Tikhomirov (Moscow: Boslen, 2015); Frank IV, 58, 153–60.

Quoted passages regarding Alexei's relationship with Polina are from *The Gambler*, 260, 208, 203, 216, 205, 309–10, 306, 277, 322. Details surrounding the Stellovsky submission are from *Reminiscences*, 34–38; *LIII*, 358 (May 8/20, 1871, to Vasily Gubin); Frank IV, 162–63; and Yakubovich II, 81.

330 **five-hundred-ruble advance:** *LII*, 210–12 (Nov. 2, 1866, to Lyubimov). After he was granted this further advance, Dostoevsky was eleven hundred rubles in debt to the journal.
330 **"much fuller and more sensational":** *LII*, 212 (Nov. 3, 1866, to Lyubimov).
331 **"bookish dreams, sir":** *Crime and Punishment*, trans. Ready, 547–48.
335 **died the previous year:** McKenzie, "Chokan Valikhanov," 21.
338 **"You are my future":** *LII*, 215–16 (Dec. 9, 1866, to Anna Snitkina).
339 **their engagement a secret:** *LII*, 218 (Dec. 29, 1866, to Anna Snitkina).
339 **never actually knew genuine love:** Anna Dostoevsky, *The Diary of Dostoevsky's Wife*, trans. Madge Pemberton, ed. René Fülöp-Miller and F. Eckstein (New York: Macmillan, 1928), 303, 156.
341 **"S-sir, s'not the place for joking!":** *Crime and Punishment*, trans. Ready, 613. Cf. *C&P*, 511.
342 **originally imagined for Raskolnikov:** *Notebooks*, 209.
345 **"Over there was freedom":** *Crime and Punishment*, trans. Ready, 656. Cf. *C&P*, 548–49.
346 **"desire to live":** *C&P*, 544–45.
346 **does not open it now:** *C&P*, 550.

TWENTY-THREE. BURIED IN FURS

For Lacenaire's visitors and press attention, as well as conversations with his old school friend Arago, see Bonnellier and Arago, *Lacenaire après sa condamnation*. Additional details are from T. M., "Lacenaire," *La Mode*, Jan. 1836, 54. Details and quotations of Lacenaire's final night and execution are taken from *Memoirs*; *Mémoires et écrits*; *Lacenaire, ses crimes*; and Canler, *Autobiography of a French Detective*. Additional details are from Paul Friedland, *Seeing Justice Done: The Age of Spectacular Capital Punishment in France* (Oxford: Oxford University Press, 2012); Harold Hillman, "An Unnatural Way to Die," *New Scientist*, Oct. 27, 1983, 276–78; Arthur Isak Applbaum, "Professional Detachment: The Executioner of Paris," *Harvard Law Review* 109, no. 2 (1995): 458–86.

348 **"in the bosom of nothingness":** "Le dernier chant," in *Mémoires et écrits*, 193–94.
348 **in a straitjacket:** *La France*, Nov. 19, 1835. See also *Lacenaire, ses crimes*, 310, 326.
348 **"Let's drink to the day":** Lacenaire, "A mon ami Avril," in *Lacenaire, ses crimes*, 320–22.
349 **head had been shaved:** Lacenaire's head was already shaved when Dumoutier prepared him for his phrenological mold. For an image, see *Mémoires et écrits*, fig. 14, n.p.
349 **"Would you be good enough":** *Memoirs*, 228.

TWENTY-FOUR. THE WEDDING

Final engagement days and wedding details are taken from *Reminiscences*, 51–76. Dostoevsky's quotations are from *LII*, 217 (Dec. 29, 1866, to Anna Snitkina); *LII*, 220–22 (Jan. 2, 1867, to Anna Snitkina); *LII*, 190 (Feb. 18, 1866, to Vrangel); *LII*, 223 (Feb. 1, 1867, to Katkov); *LII*, 223 (Feb. 9, 1867, to Strakhov). Additional details are from *LII*, 252 (Aug. 16/28, 1867, to Maikov); *LII*, 287–88 (Nov. 1–2/13–14, 1867, to Yanovskiy); *LII*, 281 (Oct. 10/22, 1867, to Pasha); *LII*, 224 (Feb. 11, 1867, to Strakhov). See also Yakubovich II, 86, and Frank IV, 167–68, 184–85, 195. For Dostoevsky's honeymoon seizures, see *Reminiscences*, 79–81.

353 **creditors would threaten him:** *LII*, 252 (Aug. 16/28, 1867, to Maikov). Dostoevsky would indeed decide to leave for Europe in late March. The couple departed on April 14, 1867. See Yakubovich II, 97, 104. Dostoevsky wrote that "at the time I left," two creditors (Latkin and Pechatkin) initiated proceedings against him for their money.
355 **"At last the moment had come":** *C&P*, 549.

ILLUSTRATION CREDITS

Insert page 1, top: Mock execution illustration from Alamy Stock Photos.

Insert page 1, bottom: Photograph of Siberian convict with branded face is from J. Young Simpson, *Side-Lights on Siberia* (1898), courtesy of Cambridge University Library.

Insert page 2: Fritz Eichenberg's "Man Whipped by Soldiers" and "Prisoners Washing" are courtesy of Harvard Art Museums/Fogg Museum, Gift of the Fritz Eichenberg Trust. Copyright: © 2021 Estate of Fritz Eichenberg / Licensed by VAGA at Artists Rights Society (ARS), NY.

Insert page 3, top: Dostoevsky and Valikhanov (1859) from Alamy Stock Photos.

Insert page 3, bottom: Portrait of Marya Dmitrievna from Heritage Images.

Insert page 4, top: Dostoevsky lithograph courtesy of Harvard University Library.

Insert page 4, bottom: Portrait of Mikhail Dostoevsky from Alamy Stock Photos.

Insert page 5, top: Lacenaire illustration from *Causes célèbres de tous les peoples* from Alamy Stock Photos.

Insert page 5, bottom: Lacenaire on trial from Alamy Stock Photos.

Insert page 6: Images from Dostoevsky's notebooks from the Scientific Research Department of Manuscripts of the Russian State Library (NIOR RGB) and the Russian State Archive of Literary Art (RGALI) in Moscow.

Insert pages 7, top, and 8, top: Images of Anna Grigorievna Dostoevskaya from Harvard University Library.

Insert page 7, bottom: Photograph of Dmitri Karakozov from Alamy Stock Photos.

Insert page 8, bottom: Late photographic portrait of Dostoevsky from Getty Images.

INDEX